AF787987

COMPUTERS and WRITING

State of the Art

COMPUTERS and WRITING

State of the Art

Edited by

Patrik O'Brian Holt
Heriot-Watt University

Noel Williams
Sheffield City Polytechnic

intellect
Oxford, England

SPRINGER-SCIENCE+BUSINESS MEDIA, B.V.

Copyright © 1992 Science+Business Media Dordrecht
Originally published by Kluwer Academic Publishers in 1992
Softcover reprint of the hardcover 1st edition 1992

All rights reserved. No part of this publication may be reproduced, stored in a retrieval system, or transmitted, in any form or by any means, electronic, mechanical, photocopying, recording, or otherwise, without written permission.

Consulting editor: Masoud Yazdani
Copy editor: Richard Palmer
Cover Design: Mark Lewis

British Library Cataloguing in Publication Data available

Library of Congress Cataloging-in-Publication Data available

ISBN 978-94-010-5267-2 ISBN 978-94-011-2854-4 (eBook)
DOI 10.1007/978-94-011-2854-4

Contents

	Preface *Patrik O'Brian Holt*	vii
1.	**New Technology. New Writing. New Problems?** *Noel Williams*	1
2.	**Three Modes of Collaborative Authoring** *Julian Newman and Rhona Newman*	20
3.	**Is There a Reader in this Labyrinth? Notes on Reading Afternoon** *J. Yellowlees Douglas*	29
4.	**Narrative Computer Systems: The Dialectics of Emotion and Formalism** *Peter Bøgh Andersen and Berit Holmqvist*	40
5.	**A Language-Sensitive Text Editor for Dutch** *Gerard Kempen and Theo Vosse*	68
6.	**Boxweb: A Structured Outline Program for Writers** *Peter Wayner*	78
7.	**An Author's Cross-referencer** *Harold Thimbleby*	90
8.	**Text to Hypertext and Back Again** *Claude Ghaoui, Steven M. George, Roy Rada, Martin Beer and Janus Getta*	109
9.	**Word Frequency Based Indexing and Authoring** *Mahmoud Mhashi, Roy Rada, Hafedh Mili, Geeng-Neng You, Akmal Zeb and Antonis Michailidis*	131
10.	**Text Indexing: The Problem of Significance** *C. Korycinski and A.F. Newell*	149
11.	**Factors Affecting Organisational Acceptance of an Automated Writing Aid** *A.E. Winterbauer*	172
12.	**Supporting Writing with an Undo Mechanism** *Yiya Yang*	187

13. **Internationalisation: The Programmer, the User and the Writer** 197
Lindsay F. Marshall

14. **Controlled English (CE): From COGRAM to ALCOGRAM** 206
Dirk Schreurs and Geert Adriaens

15. **Action Centred Manuals or Minimalist Instruction? Alternative Theories for Carroll's Minimal Manuals** 222
Stephen W. Draper and Keith Oatley

16. **A Dictionary View of Technical Writing** 244
Agnes Kukulska-Hulme

17. **Textbase Technology: Writing with Reusable Text** 254
Richard A. Buchanan

18. **A Hypertext-Based Support Aid for Writing Software Documentation** 266
Gary Born

19. **An Automated Grammar and Style Checker for Writers of Simplified English** 278
James E. Hoard, Richard Wojcik and Katherina Holzhauser

20. **Ruskin to McRuskin - Degrees of Interaction** 297
Steve McGowan

21. **Representing Writing: External Representations and the Writing Process** 319
Mike Sharples and Lyn Pemberton

22. **The CONST-Project: Computer Instructed Writing Techniques** 337
J. Beeken, G. Geerts and W. van Belle

23. **"IV Storybase": Using Interactive Video to Develop Creative Writing Skills** 355
Rosetta McLeod

24. **Story Building with Computers: Effects on Reading Comprehension, Vocabulary, Attitude and Writing** 375
Deborah Little

Preface

Patrik O'Brian Holt
Heriot-Watt University

After speech, writing is the most common form of human communication and represents the cornerstone of our ability to preserve and record information. Writing, by its very definition, requires artifacts in the form of tools to write with and a medium to write on. Through history these artifacts have ranged from sticks and clay tablets, feather and leather, crude pens and paper, sophisticated pens and paper, typewriters and paper; and electronic devices with or without paper. The development of writing tools has straightforward objectives, to make writing easier and more effective and assist in distributing written communication fast and efficiently.

Both the crudest and most sophisticated forms of writing tools act as mediators of human written communication for the purpose of producing, distributing and conserving written language. In the modern world the computer is arguably the most sophisticated form of mediation, the implications of which are not yet fully understood.

The use of computers (a writing artifact which mediates communication) for the production and editing of text is almost as old as computers themselves. Early computers involved the use of crude text editors and a writer had to insert commands resembling a programming language to format and print a document. For example to underline a word the writer had to do the following,

```
This is an example of how to
.ul
underline
a single word.
```

in order to produce:

> This is an example of how to <u>underline</u> a single word.

All formatting, e.g. line spacing or right justification, involved the use of similar commands. Graphics, e.g. simple line drawings, had to be constructed in a similar way through the use of a series of commands which resembled programming. The writer had to be knowledgeable about the commands needed and various potentially complex operations of the computer. Document production with such systems is also time consuming and requires imagination by the writer since the final look of a document has to reside in the imagination of the writer as the final version of the document can not be seen until the commands embedded in the text are executed.

Old fashioned approaches like the one mentioned above are still used but today writers have available text editors and word processors which support the writing process in a much more natural and powerful way. With modern systems the writer does not have to embed commands in the text for later execution, rather, formatting is done through simply choosing commands from a menu. So to underline a word the writer simply selects the words and then chooses the underline command from a menu which offers a selection of formatting commands. Almost all formatting requirements can be done in this manner, i.e. selecting text and then choosing an appropriate command which is executed instantly. Graphics do not have to be specified with commands; rather a graphic is produced using software specifically designed to allow diagrams to be drawn in a manner similar to drawing on paper with a pencil. The graphic is then relatively painlessly inserted into the document being produced.

WYSIWYG (What You See Is What You Get) displays which allow the writer to see the text on screen in exactly the format it will be printed are an important development for writers. However, modern word processors offer a range of additional facilities which support the writing process and the production of documents. These include functions such as undo, cutting and pasting text and graphics, finding and changing text automatically throughout the document, spelling checkers, automatic generation of content pages and subject indices, to name but a few. Very modern word processors also support proof-reading, e.g. the detection of double words (the the) and offer advice on various grammatical aspects of written style, e.g. the detection of split infinitives.

Designing and developing computer based support for writing is clearly an important area of concern in modern technological society. As mentioned above, 'sophisticated' support for writing is now available. We must however bear in mind that 'sophisticated' is a relative concept and as with all high technology, today's sophistication is history tomorrow. The use of computers to support writing is in its infancy, both in terms of the technology and our understanding of how writers write. This is really the central issue in studying computers and writing, i.e. the relationship between our understanding of the writing process and the technology which claims to support it.

The study of computers, writers and the writing process offers enormous potential for our understanding of human written communication and for technological development. We must not however forget the implications that such understanding and development may have on our society and on inter-cultural communication.

It is impossible to classify the study of computers and writing as falling neatly within one particular academic area. Firstly, the study of writing is of interest to many academic disciplines, e.g. psychology, linguistics, sociology, cognitive science, artificial intelligence, education, computer science etc. Secondly, there are many groups, in addition to researchers, which have a fundamental interest both in the study of writing and writing tools, e.g. creative writers, technical writers, journalists etc. The result is that the study of computers and writing really covers anyone who writes with or without computers. The reason for including those who write by putting pen to paper is that the study of computers and writing increases our understanding of the writing process generally and this knowledge may impinge on all writers.

The study of computers and writing has grown substantially over the past ten years, but in particular the last five years or so. There now exist several strong research laboratories and numerous serious application sites, particularly in education, ranging from primary schools to universities. The topics under study and corresponding application areas vary enormously, a good reflection of the diverse interests in writing.

This book represents state-of-the-art work in the area of computers and writing as reflected by the following list:

- Software for technical writing (e.g. managing software documentation; production and maintenance of aircraft manuals; support for technical writers whose first language is not English).
- Teaching children composition, using computers.
- Training adult writers.
- Organisational issues in introducing computer based writing tools.
- Alternative structures for computer manuals.
- Cognitive models of the writing process.
- Automatic story generation.
- Software support for the creation of multi-media (the combined use of text, graphics, video and sound) narrative.
- Outlining.
- Human Computer Interaction, i.e. the design of highly interactive writing tools.
- Automatic style checking.
- Teaching machines to understand written style.
- Technological implications for writing and writers.
- Collaborative authoring.
- Hypertext (the authoring and reading of non-linear documents).
- Interactive fiction (the use of hypertext in creative writing).
- Indexing and cross referencing.
- The construction and use of computer based dictionaries.

These diverse topics represent the interests of three main groups, researchers (academic and industrial), education (teachers and trainers) and writers (technical writers and creative writers). There is of course considerable and inevitable overlap between each of the categories.

Communication and dissemination of information between the groups interested in computers and writing takes several forms. Workshops are organised periodically by various interest groups to discuss topics of interest, e.g. collaborative authoring, and computers in the teaching of writing. For the past four years an annual international conference on computers and writing has been organised alternately at Sussex University, Sheffield City Polytechnic and Heriot-Watt University in Edinburgh.

The conferences have brought together diverse groups interested in all aspects of computers and writing and have resulted in the breaking down of many of the traditional boundaries between the people attending. These gatherings have also resulted in other activities. At the 1989 conference The Computers and Writing Newsletter(published quarterly) was established and in 1990 the Computers and Writing Association was formed in Edinburgh. The Association aims to promote the interests of all groups interested in computers and writing by enabling communication through conferences, workshops and publications. The Newsletter is currently the only publication in the UK solely devoted to computers and writing while during 1992 a new journal covering all aspects of computers and writing will be launched.

As an area of concern the study of computers and writing is still defining its own boundaries in terms of issues worthy of investigation. The conferences during the past four years have not attempted to force through any definitions of the area or issues, except indirectly through the papers submitted and the ensuing discussions. Further conferences, the activities of the Association and publications will undoubtedly clarify many of the uncertainties.

It seems clear however that in order to produce computer based tools to support writers and the writing process we must increase our knowledge of how writers conduct their craft. An increased understanding of writers' requirements and the tasks involved in writing will form the basis of the next generation of writing tools. Many researchers are therefore turning their attention to acquiring a more fundamental and detailed knowledge of the writing process.

The use of hypertext and hypermedia in writing and collaborative writing are currently receiving considerable attention and will continue to do so. Hypertexts are non-linear texts organised in terms of related concepts or pieces of information. Many believe that the importance of this form of writing lies in the notion that the human mind organises information in an analogous fashion. Hypertexts certainly offer increased flexibility in writing and reading but there are inherent problems such as navigation, i.e the reader tends to get lost in non-linear text. Hypermedia is a form of hypertext which incorporates other media such as graphics, video and sound. The potential of such systems for writing is fairly obvious but the design of software tools and subsequent use needs further investigation. Collaborative writing (a subset of computer assisted collaborative work) investigates how writers work when more than one writer authors a document, a phenomena which is certainly common in many professions. Investigations centre both on collaborative writing in general and on the design and testing of software tools which support collaborative authoring.

With the advent of the common European market there will be increased communication between the commercial and industrial sectors of many countries. Here computer based tools will play an increasingly important role both in terms of assisting with translation and with the production of language, e.g. supporting technical and other writers who write in English as a second (or third!) language. Several projects of this kind were reported at the third computers and writing conference and these were the first indications of important future trends. These developments demonstrate an important point. The effect of using computer based tools is not confined to individuals or even small groups but is likely to have far reaching implications in breaking down traditional language barriers between cultures.

Patrik O'Brian Holt, 1992

1

New Technology. New Writing. New Problems?

Noel Williams
Sheffield City Polytechnic

Abstract

The proliferation of new technologies for writing, both hardware and software, undoubtedly serves many needs of many writers. At the same time, two other effects of new writing technology can be observed:

- New forms of writing result from new media.
- Writers are faced with new problems.

Whilst the medium is seldom the message, the medium necessarily constrains or facilitates particular messages. Constraints imposed (e.g. by style checker or text editor) may limit writers and lead them to new conventions (e.g. emoticons in email). Openness, e.g. in networks or hypermedia (or the two combined) may offer too much freedom. Writers may transfer habits acquired in one medium to another, with weakened effect. Increasing the number of available media and the functionality of existing media may also increase the problems facing the writer. The writer may face more complex decisions over how to communicate, and a more problematic process of writing effectively.

1. Introduction

The proliferation of new technologies for writing, both hardware and software, undoubtedly serves many needs of many writers. But the attraction of this effect tends to disguise two other profound effects of new writing technology:

- New forms of writing result from the new computerised media.
- Writers are faced with new problems.

The first of these I do not intend to deal with here, except for a few peripheral remarks. Instead I aim to catalogue some of the difficulties technology brings to writers which we might also begin to look to technology to reduce. Most of the problems of writing with computers which have been well discussed are not really specific to writing or writers. Such problems include:

- Hardware and software failure.
- User anxiety.
- The length of analyses provided by software.
- Understanding complex terminology.
- The failure of software to meet user expectations.
- Poor documentation.
- Inadequacy of explanations.

I have examined some of these elsewhere, and suggested ways that we might begin to deal with them by machine (Williams 1990; Williams forthcoming).

But for some writers it is the very writing tools themselves, the functions they offer and the actions they permit which create the problems. Their complexity, their novelty, the very freedom they permit, as well as the constraints they impose may alter writers' behaviour and create new difficulties for them to overcome.

Six areas in particular, which are increasingly interconnecting, give writers new tools that bring them new difficulties. These are:

- Portable computing.
- Desktop publishing.
- Hypertext and hypermedia.
- Networked writing (e.g. email, bulletin boards).
- Collaborative writing technologies (with or without networks).
- Interactive writing, e.g. interactive fiction.

Most of these are topics of other papers in this volume, so I do not wish to consider any one of them at great length. Instead I want to make the general point that for the writer interested in writing, rather than in using technological tools; or for the user to whom writing is only a means to some other end and the computer is the means to that means, the growth of additional functionality and flexibility may make the task harder, not easier.

I want to suggest that this efflorescence of functionality and flexibility creates three sets of problems, namely:

- Coping with generic difficulties of the technology
- Working with constraints imposed by writing technology
- Waking sense of the new functionality.

2. Coping with generic difficulties

2.1. Learning: playground tussles

> "The basic functions of the generation of knowledge by exploration is a reduction of complexity or elimination of possibilities by actively manipulating an unknown field of action."(Greif 1988.)

> "the profound truth contained in the simple advice of one pithy piece of computer documentation: 'This is one of those computer gizmos that's easier to use than it is to explain. Just play with Up and Down: you'll get the idea.'The event of a new sense of reality calls forth the primary human learning response: play. Play belongs intrinsically to ontological discovery, to the defining of realities emergent from chaos, to the finesse of free discovery contained within the limiting constraints of our world". (Heim 1987, quoting the User's Guide for CED:DOS Command Editor, a public

domain program, copyrighted by Christopher J. Dunford).

Seigfried Greif and Michael Heim here suggest in language rather more elevated than the concept, what most of us who spend much time with computers know, the best way to learn a computer application is to play with the system. One of the payoffs of word processors for children and the potential richness of media like Hypermedia (but also, for some users, desktop publishing and networking) is the ease of risk-free hacking. Writers can enjoy the freedom to play; to explore and experiment in an environment where no text is permanent and any writer's whim can be indulged. Of course, this brings its own dangers, as with any other unstructured experience, but the sample generation of text, almost randomly 'brain dumping', as some refer to it, can be very important for getting inroads into a writing task: its function is an exploratory one –to find out what a writer knows.

Similarly play and hacking are basic functions of using computer systems. All of us find out about computers by finding out about computers.

> "I suppose it might be my system, although to be fair to it I'm one of those people who learn by doing rather than by reading manuals, although it's an awful manual." Tom Sharpe (quoted in Hammond 1984).

We do not sit down with the manual, or the tutorial, and work through from page 1 to page 501 before pressing a key for our own purposes. We first see what we can do, and only fall back on authority when, like Humpty Dumpty, we feel shattered.

But such play is not possible under conditions of anxiety. We cannot be worried about what we are doing, or we will not do it. The writing environment must be both comforting and challenging. We must want to get to grips with it but feel comfortable doing so. The experience of writing by computer should be like that of reading escapist fiction: you can go to the edge of the universe, tamper with heart strings, indulge in dastardly murder and not feel threatened. Writing is the same kind of vicarious exploration – the challenge of new star systems, new dark strangers and new ravelled mysteries must be there, but they must not be *really* there.

If we add exploration of the computer system to exploration of the writing task we must ask: will using a computer system, especially a novel one (that is, one seldom used, the probable status of many writing support tools) increase anxiety? Will the worry outweigh the wonder? Is computerising the writing task making learning too hard? Does it shift the emphasis from exploring the novel writing task to exploring the computer environment?

Where anxiety already exists, it seems more than likely that the anxiety of one may increase the anxiety of the other. In other words, the use of computers as writing aids may well be counterproductive for writers with problems, especially if they are not already adept with machines or with the software or its interface. If a user has to learn about how to learn, and is worried about using the writing tool as well as worried about the writing task the user may well learn nothing and accomplish no task.

Research must therefore address the extent to which writers actually *write* with computers, as opposed to using computers to place words onto paper. If the struggle of learning the computer and using the system outweighs the importance of wrestling with language, we will find many frustrated writers and many poor documents.

2.2. Interfaces, integration and interaction

Lacking familiarity with a computer writing system, familiarity with the interface may stand in its place. The user wants to address the writing task, not the task of learning the system. The user wants the minimum amount of learning, the maximal correspondence between applications s/he is already familiar with and that of the new writing system. For the novice writer the Macintosh desktop or the word processor with cut and paste (rather than insert and delete) *may* seem that much more familiar and so that much easier to learn, simpler to use. But it is the nature of computer systems not to be desks and not to be usable like scissors and glue. The metaphors of use remain metaphors and, whilst they may help understand the system task, they may not help understand the system. The interface may disguise the real complexity of the system, so users can interact with it, but that complexity is still there and the task of using it efficiently may still remain a complex one.

This may be why some writers simply resist using the new writing media.

> "All I really managed to do with word processing was to increase my workload. I spent more time thinking about my word processor than the words I was writing. Writers who are frightened of it are right to be so." Tom Sharpe (quoted in Hammond 1984).

> "I don't go near a word processor, or even a typewriter. I can't imagine how thinking can take place on those awkward machines. There is no substitute for ink." Iris Murdoch (quoted in Chandler 1990).

> "I've never had a word processor, nor have I any intention of having one." Frederick Forsyth (quoted in Chandler 1990).

The author of fiction has the luxury of determining which writing tools to use. The typical office user has not. Writing tools are made available at the urge of management, persuaded by purchasing departments (which may include technophiles) who in turn are influenced by software marketing, whose message is a biased gloss over the limitations of software and hardware development. In this complex wrapping of meanings and purposes in messages and purchases, the office writer has little say and less influence, and is compelled to use or ignore the systems in the office, an increasing number of multi-functional systems.

One might expect, for example, that advanced office systems would make the task of writing in the office easier. That, presumably, is one of their objectives. Certainly, as everyone knows, certain writing tasks are simplified by (for example) using word processors, desktop publishing and laser printers. But advanced office systems may also cause:

- Increases in the information available.
- Qualitative changes in the information available.
- Alteration of access to information.
- Needs for new information.
- Changes of presentation needs (e.g. in handling new protocols and media).
- Changes to effective channels of communication.
- Increases in external demands for quantity and quality of information.
- Changes to expectations and standards.

All of these, resulting from technology in the office for the writer, make the writer's task harder. By integrating a wide range of disparate information handling functions, and placing them under the hands of one individual at one desktop, information flow is concentrated more intensely in the decision making of some individuals. The task of writing, turning information of one kind into another, can become intensely complicated for these people.

Increasing the number of available media and the functionality of existing media may also increase the problems facing the writer, who may face more complex decisions over how to communicate, and a more problematic process of writing effectively. No longer are writing decisions simply a matter of balancing the constraints of audience, purpose, content and style; now each of these variables may itself require or be constrained by particular technologies. Is it more efficient to send a message by memo (typed? hand-written? word processed?) or by wire (fax? email? bulletin board?); if by fax, should it be typed; if email, can I use my word processor or must I put up with the mainframe line editor; if I use the word processor, do I need a special file format; do I bother with a spelling checker/style checker just for a memo; should I make sure it is formatted attractively, given the audience; didn't I have a memo format stored somewhere on one of these disks?

2.3. Ergonomics and design

A related issue concerns the ergonomics of the physical system. Why, we might ask, does the much vaunted paperless office not yet exist, whilst some people contribute endlessly to email conferences and bulletin boards networks, but never put pen to paper? What is the relationship between these people and their writing technology? Do the ergonomics of their actual technology affect their enthusiasm?

Some writers like the feel of pen and paper. Some are clearly attracted by the computer device itself. Douglas Adams has eight computers, using them for computer music, games and desktop publishing as well his writing. He enjoys using the technology. A writer will not enjoy his or her writing tools if the physical process of use is not satisfactory. If the user does not like using it, no engagement with those writing tools may take place. Some writers may treat the medium obsessionally, but it is perhaps true that all writers have preferred physical equipment, a favoured pen, a specially configured keyboard. Hartley and Knapper quote academic writers; popular writers express similar views; students and colleagues of mine often claim that a particular screen, computer, keyboard, mouse, desk, pen, chair or position is better (or worse) for their work:

> "I ... get obsessed by stationary and pens. I keep changing from pencils to Pentels to fountain pens and so on." Hartley and Knapper (1984).

> "I need lots of desk space so I can spread out papers etc....God help anyone who touches one precious scrap of paper!" Hartley and Knapper (1984).

> "Pencils must be round. A hexagonal pencil cuts my fingers after a long day." John Steinbeck.

> "I use the world's most efficient keyboard, the Dvorak Simplified." Piers Anthony (Anthony 1984).

> "I should imagine that many professional writers are becoming disenchanted even with their industry word processors and are more than willing to get back to the Olivetti or Olympia. The VDU is making it too easy to write badly. There is a lack of blacksmith muscle in the tapping of the console. If you make an error it's too easy to correct it." Anthony Burgess (quoted in Dorner 1990).

Writers prefer certain ways of doing things. They like the feel of certain apparatus for their actions – the quality of paper, the feel of the tools, the sensation of the keyboard, the glare of the VDU, the hammering of the printer, the rattle of the mouse against coffee cups – all of these minutiae of the ergonomics of the workplace must be satisfactory for the writer to feel comfortable with the writing process. It is not sufficient for the tool to be, by some mechanical definition, more efficient or more productive than previous tools, it must be a tool writers want to use, or it will be less efficient and less productive, for, lacking desire, they will avoid using it. And where they are constrained to use it, despite their misgivings, as, for example, unconsulted office users, they will seek opportunities to avoid the work, to stick with older technologies, to interrupt work on the computer for trivial reasons – in short, any advantages of putative efficiency and productivity will be lost.

When we consider the last remark quoted, that by Anthony Burgess, we can see that the task of the designer of writing tools may be an impossible one, if the aim is to satisfy the needs of all writers, for here we have a writer complaining with a paradox that the reason he dislikes word processing is the very feature it was designed for, ease of error correction. If a writer sees writing as necessarily a task of struggle, of engagement with ideas, of wrestling with words, then the writer does not want to be given a machine gun for simplifying that struggle: only in hand to hand combat can the words (and the author) be tested. Burgess, in fact, reinforces my first category of generic problem: that writers find the computer disengages them from the real task of writing. Possibly such attitudes are relics of an earlier age, a rationalisation of writers' psychology, justifying the fear of new writing systems by appeal to a mystical theory of writing. If so, they still need dealing with. If writers adhere to a mystical belief that certain tools create better writing (as Fay Weldon says: *I choose to believe that there is some kind of mystic connection between the brain and the act of writing in longhand.* Quoted in Chandler 1990), then that mysticism may have to be supported by new writing tools. We may have to see mice in the shape of round pencils linked by infrared to paper-thin handwriting recognition systems before such writers' needs are satisfied.

2.4. Interference by computers in the writing process

If I change tack now from writing support systems to writing tutoring, here computers may also be seen as 'interfering' in the 'natural' processes of writing with potentially harmful effects, particularly in areas such as English teaching or 'creative' approaches to writing. For example, J. R. Martin lists the following areas of possible worry for writing teachers using computers in the writing class:

> "Text is private property, not to be tampered with, but computers open it up both to public analysis and to public dissemination."
>
> "Writing is creative expression, so computer-based critiquing can crush the learner as poet. Originality is not favoured in computer-based critiques."
>
> "Writing teaching can destroy individuality. Instead it encourages adherence to a set of mechanistic rules, conformity to the least common denominator in bland writing, (e.g. by conformity to readability formulae)." (Martin 1986.)

Using a computer to aid writing may provide the most substantial form of interference. Practising writers want relevant feedback when they want it (i.e. when they have a problem) not when others think it desirable. So to be dependent on the provision of computer feedback only when the computer thinks (or rather, when those who designed the computer system think) it is desirable, means that the writing task is being structured not by the writer but by some external agency. The natural writing process is replaced by an external model of what that process might, or should, be. Such advisory structuring can be helpful when it is sensitive to particular situations and needs, but when it forces writers to conform to some generalised model of writing, an abstraction of real processes, it will more often be a source of harm and frustration.

2.5. The generic problem

All of the above, learning problems, interface and complexity issues, ergonomics and interference effects are objects of research, though all are probably under-researched. All are sources of frustration, and that is the generic problem for users of computer systems. Yesterday I sat in a computer laboratory for an hour and counted seven separate sets of unquotable expletives from expert users as they tried to make the machine do what they, not it, wished. For novice users, writing technology, far from liberating communication may trap by its complexity.

3. Constraints, imposed and removed

They may also be trapped by the constraints machines impose. Whilst the medium is seldom the message, the medium necessarily constrains or facilitates particular messages. Constraints imposed by computer may limit writers, restricting them in ways that paper would not. Hardware constraints are, generally, obvious and their effects capable of physical remedy. For the user they sit squarely alongside ergonomic dissatisfaction:

> "At times I work very quickly and I haven't found that possible with the screen. It has something to do with the size of the screen. It's become something of a habit with me to use quarto-size paper and I haven't got a quarto screen on my word processor, of course. The screen is very peculiar and I don't think it is easy to read." Tom Sharpe (quoted in Hammond 1984).

Software constraints may be less palpable, and thus less easy to deal with. For example, the advice of style checkers is seldom either as specific as an individual context requires, nor as flexible as a human tutor might offer. Writers therefore find themselves advised in generic terms, using approximate rules which may simply not apply to their situation. For example, anyone relying on the defaults in the (now venerable) Writer's Workbench (Cherry 1981, 1982; MacDonald *et al.* 1982) will find themselves applying the standards of Bell Labs technical memoranda to their work.

Other constraints may affect writers, almost arbitrarily. My favourite example is Douglas Adams abbreviating sentences to fit on the page in his desktop published text. Here the software dictates the content, surely the ultimate influence of writing technology on writing.

Conversely constraints may lead writers to new conventions as they strive against those limitations. As an example, consider the advent of emoticons in email. Emoticons are little iconic faces, created through combinations of punctuation symbols, to indicate the state of mind, the tone, that governs a particular sentence. These are a genuine attempt to add to flat email discourse some equivalents for non-verbal signals in face to face conversation or for intonation in phone conversation. email discourse feels, to many participants, as informal as such conversation, as transcripts of such discourse shows (frequent use of informal address notations, many contractions, choice of colloquial expressions and synonyms, casual punctuation expressive of breath groups rather than sentence structure and so on), but does not carry all the meaning of well-established conversational media. It is conversational writing, so new writing conventions are needed to attempt to convey those lost meanings. The limitations of character-based display are transcended by a resignifying of particular character combinations, groups of symbols becoming no longer verbal but iconic, graphic – which is a rather inflated way of saying that the punctuation code is reinterpreted. (It should be said, however, that emoticons seldom seem to be used seriously, that is, with the literal significance the emoticon was ostensibly designed for. Rather they are used in a joking or ironic fashion, which at once indicates the user's feeling that they are inadequate for the purpose yet are a system of signifying which can be used in complex constructs.)

Potentially more problematic than the imposition of constraints, however, is the release of those constraints, most notably the opening up of communication through networks and hypermedia (or the two combined). Do they offer too much freedom?

At one level there are significant problems of security, access, copyright and ownership associated with the information made available in such ways. For example, writer B adds a note (perhaps a paragraph in length) to writer A's entry in a developing hyper-document. Writer C then adds a comment to that note, making a link which stands for 'refutation'. Now, the refutation note can not stand without the note it is a refutation of, so the user will always have to read the original note in its entirety to understand the refutation. Therefore the refutation is effectively 'quoting' B's entire 'document'. Quoting an entire publication is breach of copyright. On the other hand, if we take the view that the entire document is really the complete hyper-document (the stack, let us say, in Hypercard) then writer A owns both B's and C's contributions even though writer A did not write them (nor, effectively, edit or publish them).

At a more interesting level, the whole notion of authorship begins to break down, as the above example shows. No-one is the authority in such a document, it rests with a communal voice, which includes (in this example) dissent and contradiction. Suddenly notions of 'good' and 'bad' writing, of 'correct' and 'incorrect' views, of 'effective' and 'ineffective' writing fly out of the pop-up window, for the same document may contain all these, and different chunks of that document will be found at different poles of these dichotomies by different readers. Writing becomes anonymous and polyvocal.

Research on hypermedia seems to show that only by imposing constraints (structure, maps, conventions, expectations) will users be able to make sense of the open text. (Reading large amounts of networked conferencing material has similar problems – only through a convener or moderator can the 'delegate' at such a conference make sense of the whole discourse.) Therefore we may begin to look to writing software not to lift constraints from writing but to impose them, by helping the writer to formulate or explicate the constraints that apply, by helping the writer to work within a set of constraints, by guiding through a way of working within a set of conflicting constraints or, most radically, by forcing constraints on otherwise unstructured, fragmentary discourse.

Thus software might offer templates for structural constraints, can facilitate information retrieval and reduce resource constraints, e.g. by abstracting a text using keywords, can ensure cotextual constraints are met by making sure a limit across the text is followed accurately, such as a spelling convention or a presentational feature (indentation) or by forcing users to label maps of hyper-documents.

We may find that the new media must recreate the old media in order to make sense of themselves.

4. Making sense of the new functionality

Writers are not alone in having to cope with the influx of new devices (mainly software devices) full of functions. But these functions may well come from some source other than writerly needs specification. Sharples and Pemberton note:

> "Computer systems to support the writing process will be of most help if they fit the writer's perception of the task and assist whichever strategy the writer chooses to adopt." (Sharples and Pemberton 1989.)

It is rare to find software that has paid much attention to the writer's perception of the task. Rather it pays attention to the designer's perception of the writer's task. The designer, of course, may be neither writer nor writing teacher. We do not have to look for sinister or cynical motives for this (though they may well be there), software may not address writers' task perceptions simply because there are so many writers, tasks and perceptions.

The Writer's Assistant of Sharples *et al*, following their precepts, aims to circumvent this problem by offering a set of tools which the user can take or leave, choosing strategies for using those tools according to the particular perception and particular need (Sharples *et al.* 1989). We must all applaud this rare sensitivity in writing tool design. However, the problem with such an approach is that to choose a strategy the writer needs to know what strategies are available. This in turn entails all sorts of other knowledge, such as:

- What are the media available to me?
- What do they do? what can they offer me? what are their values?
- How do I decide which is most appropriate for my needs?
- What do I need in the way of skills to carry it out?

In other words, the systems themselves affect the tasks, or at least sub-tasks, and the functions they offer and the constraints they impose will not be separable from the task itself. If I want to produce a leaflet to publicise a new course, one of the first things I will look at are the ways it might be done; i.e. the different versions of the task I might construct. I do not decide precisely what I want to achieve and then look for the ideal way to do it; real writing does not take place that way. Seldom does a writer decide on a task and a form of information to handle that task without knowledge of the tools that can be used and their possibilities. You would need to know the Writer's Assistant in order to decide whether to use the Writer's Assistant.

Yes, writing is (in the words of Flower and Hayes, 1980) juggling constraints, and one of the constraints is the overlapping of media and available techniques. Offering new functions to the writer can only help if the writer recognises those functions; if, to return to my earlier point, those functions are already familiar to the writer, or can quickly become known through play.

4.1. New functions affecting writing

I would like to conclude this paper by enumerating some of the new characteristics of writing which the technology promotes, but which compound the complexity of the writer's task. Whilst not all of them are *problems* as such, potentially they make new demands on writers, requiring them to acquire new skills and knowledge.

Important amongst the new functions offered to writers, in terms of their effects and potential effects are:

- Document design.
- Reusable writing.
- Visual writing.
- Multiply structured documents.
- Reader-oriented writing.
- Managing and editing multiperson communication.
- Writing as talking (email).
- Ephemeral writing.

Document design

Writers traditionally did not need to be overly concerned with the appearance of their documents. With the placing of desktop publishing tools in writers' hands, and the removal of the editor, publisher and printer from document publication (e.g. in networked communication and in some forms of electronic publishing), the writer has new tools and a new responsibility: and must now construct a complete document, not merely the content of that document.

Writers who have espoused the technology seem, by and large, happy to take on the extra task of preparing their materials for publication, but how many have a good understanding of the task, or the design skills necessary to carry it out? Yet how many writers use DTP, or sophisticated word processors with DTP-like control (such as Word 4) to present their text? How many of the papers in this volume were hand-written? How many were presented fully formatted, for the volume editors to undo and redo?

Reusable writing

Reusable writing has been a well-known boon of word processors since their inception. Both working writers and writing teachers find the permanent malleability of electronic text a significant attraction offering, for example:

- Increased productivity.
- The ability to use the same text in different contexts without retyping.
- Flexibility for experiment.
- Ease of quotation and abstraction.
- Ease of multiple drafts.

(See, for many examples, Daiute 1985.)

Yet this very ease brings potential penalties. First is the bugbear of copyright and ownership. If the copyright of text is made over to someone other than the author, then the author must seek permission to reuse that text in a different context. But if the reused text is merely the starting point of the new document, and the author adapts it during that reuse, at what point does it become 'new' text, whose copyright rests with the author? To put it as a writer's problem: how much work do I have to do on this text to make it mine again?

A second worry follows from the laziness that reusable writing encourages. If a writer already has some text which can be reused, which 'more or less fits the bill', why bother creating new text from scratch? Habitual reuse of text may increase productivity, in terms of the number of documents that result, but those documents may all have very similar content. Typically revision of text addresses style and possibly structure, but content is generally left alone. 'Reused text' is often merely 're-edited text', so the documents that result from reusable text may well simply reiterate old ideas and discourage the writer from the struggle of new creation.

Less problematic, perhaps, but still a problem that results from reusing text, is the likelihood of uncoordinated documents. If a given document is a patchwork of text already on disk, stitched together from different sources, it may well look and feel to the reader like such a patchwork. Naturally, for some applications this is not a problem (e.g. collections of writings, list-like texts and some hypertext applications). However, for producing conventional, monological, univocal text, in which the reader expects to find a single voice, a single style, a coherent structure and a unified set of messages, the writer must exercise a new set of editing skills, needing to be much more reader- oriented than previously.

Visual writing

The phenomenon of fontitis is well known, whereby new users of DTP indulge in a riot of visual confusion by mixing multiple fonts upon the page. Why does this happen? Partly, it is the enthusiasm of the user, experimenting, playing as we would wish them to do. Partly it is lack of guidance. No DTP system supports the user in good use of visual material. Such systems offer the physical tools but not the conceptual tools. Help facilities explain the functions, but not their value.

The same lack is evident wherever writers are moving into visual communication. The areas of multimedia, hypermedia, animation, paint tools, graphic imports to word processing and image scanning all begin to offer to writers visual resources they previously had no access to and, by and large, no interest in. Now the visual medium is available and convenient, so writers are drawn to choose between word and image, choose between different images, decide on sizing, spacing and quality of image and generally do so without knowledge or support.

It is perhaps becoming likely that electronic communication generally will also become more visual. Emoticons are twee. Icons and micons are currently only available to the hackers amongst writers. But, with the increasing domination of graphical interfaces, it seems inevitable that visual communication tools will be offered to the writer. Icons, for pasting into documents (both paper and electronic) will make certain areas of communication much more efficient; at least, in terms of time. For example, one of the weakness of hypertext is the lack of visual semanticity in links. It seems clear to me that the pasting of iconic buttons, which signify graphically conceptual or 'textual' connections between chunks of text, will be among the next developments for providing such semanticity. Here, then writers will decide (as they already may in Hypercard) the proper 'semantic image' for connecting their texts.

Multiply structured documents

Rarely does an author consider that a document has more than one structure within it. Most authors struggle with the task of achieving that single coherent structure in their texts. They may consider multiple audiences, though this is less common than one might wish, but seldom would the separate audiences merit multiple structures within a single document. So working with hypermedia adds a new task to the burden, the task of assessing, assigning and assimilating structures within the hyper document appropriate for each readership.

We know, of course, that an attraction of hypermedia is reader control, that the reader can select material to meet his or her own needs, in effect the reader can create his or her own structure within the hyper document. But the reader's structure is a subset of those made available by the author. The possible structures have been predetermined by authors and the reader selects from within them. An author who is not clear about audience needs, or inexplicit about the structures and coherence relationships within his or her hypertext is likely to suffer from what Patricia Wright has called 'linkitis'(analogous to 'fontitis'), the making of every and any link that comes to mind at any and every opportunity within the text (Wright and Lickorish 1989). Such links will be made on the grounds that 'the reader might want to go this way', but as all the research on both navigation problems and browsing strategies shows, readers benefit from the guidance of implicit or explicit structures, and flounder in unstructured hypertext.

Changes in the reader-writer relationship

Traditional documents are built with the notion of writer-oriented reading.

The reader is guided by the writer; the reader discovers what the writer intended; the reader consumes what the writer has provided. Whilst the writer has, necessarily, taken account of the readership, it has been a relatively passive reader who has been looked to, a reader who receives the writer's offering and accepts or rejects it, but who otherwise does not interact with the text or the author. Typically the author's decisions are 'does my reader need this information?', 'where can I put this so it fits most logically for the reader?'and 'how can I put this so my reader will understand?'.

Electronic media shift the emphasis towards reader-oriented writing. Not only must the hypermedia writer consider multiple structures for multiple audiences but also must select styles, content, tone and approaches which match many different audience needs. The email/bulletin board writer is competing with a huge corpus of similar ephemera. If the writer wants to be read, the reader must be hit exactly, must either target precisely the right audience, or provide an item of such wit, ingenuity, perspicacity or aptness that readers pick it from their bulging email-bags, and conference moderators select it from the megabytes of similar messages.

In both contexts the reader may interact more directly, more immediately and more extensively with the text than in any conventional document. Ownership of electronic documents is often unclear, so copying, extracting and modifying are at once both physically easier through the electronic media and psychologically more acceptable.

Readers may respond instantly by email, may circulate amended versions of someone's emailing or hyper document, may alter an interactive fiction so it becomes a completely different text, may extract, amend and reply in ways the author simply had not anticipated. And, with a large readership, a document could rapidly go out of control. I know of no instances of this, as yet, within the electronic field, but one has only to consider the parallells of folk culture (its most contemporary manifestation being, perhaps, the promulgation of 'xeroxlore'), of software piracy and of viruses to see how a text which fits the needs of some readership somewhere might rapidly assume a life, development and dissemination well beyond that intended by the author.

Of course, we have always had countercultures, such as the culture which appropriates and distributes music tapes or photocopies books. Electronic media simply place one further set of technologies in the hands of such countercultures, which many of us might applaud. The author on the other hand must decide whether the text is in some sense to be privileged, hence protected and thus restricted to a narrow audience, more or less in the author's control; or whether simply to disseminate it, allowing receivers to make of it, literally, whatever they will.

If the latter, the author may forget about responsibility for the readership entirely, regard the text simply as self-expression and simply throw it upon the ether and see if it blows anywhere. Clearly one of the reasons why so many people do communicate electronically is that they like the sound of their own keyboard. But if the author has a purpose, a desire to be fulfilled through that text (more than merely the desire for self-expression), then multiple audiences must be addressed.

Managing and editing multiperson communication
A more defined problem, but perhaps an extension of the reader-writer relationship problem, is the new task of collaboration. Again we have new tools to facilitate collaborative writing. Such tools, however, do not manage themselves. To use them effectively in collaboration, writers must establish and employ new conventions. These conventions in turn will constrain and facilitate different forms of collaboration.

In an electronic collaboration the distinction between editor and writer may become less clear than through traditional media, with attendant penalties and benefits. All contributing writers may become editors of each others texts, almost certainly improving the proof-reading and the editorial quality of each contribution, but also increasing the amount of interaction about the nature of the text rather than its content.

It is interesting to see, for example, that the Computers and Composition Digest (a moderated version of an email conference, to which most contributors are writing teachers) spends most of its time not discussing writing, or even computers and writing, but the process of communicating by email. Here the medium is certainly the message, in a very literal sense.

Writing as talking
Colette Daiute suggested some years ago that 'talky writing' was one increasing effect of electronic writing (Daiute 1985). Certainly one fault of student word processing is, in composing at the keyboard, that their writing veers to the natural fluidity of their speech, by incorporating their speech characteristics. Sentences tend to be heavily rightward branching, for example (by which I mean that, as students type, new modifications and new thoughts occur and are simply tagged on as modifications to the current sentence). Rather than capturing a thought entire in a single sentence, then placing that sentence on the page, the thought emerges during the process of typing and modifications are made as the sentence or paragraph goes along. It can sometimes then be difficult to go back through such a paragraph and tease out the separate thoughts, excising the superfluous asides. And in real-time networking, of course, such a task is impossible.

Talky writing is also evident, to some extent, in hypertext. Where hypertext is used as a conferencing medium, or where the intended audience is some notional 'general' reader, the language of hypertext tends towards the informality and relative simplicity of speech. Here, if the decision is deliberate and the effect controlled, talky writing may be no bad thing. The modern trend in information-rich documents is to simplify, to make the language as familiar to the reader as possible, in the name of readability, and hypertext information may simply reinforce that Plain English trend.

But talky writing is most evident in email communication. And here we have writing that is as talky as it can get. The errors of rapid and immediate communication (Chomsky's performance errors) are rampant, including spelling, punctuation and simple grammatical errors as well as more sophisticated problems of incomplete utterances and disjunct clauses within single sentences. Punctuation is used very creatively and emphatically, with all sorts of different pausing conventions used to map the breath group of speech and the intonation contours of informality, in the way that letters to friends often are.

This perhaps does not seem strange, except when we remember the relative status and familiarity of some of these contributors. They may never meet, be unaware of each other's gender, age, disability, race, politics, background, experience and expertise. Consequently many of the power relations exercised in face to face communication (for example) may be dispensed with, or muted, in electronic communication.

Ephemeral writing

Electronic writing creates new kinds of ephemera, which are perhaps more ephemeral than any earlier form of written communication. For example, email text and bulletin board messages may live in a system for a very short period before being removed, never seeing form as paper. email messages may be so prolific, and the information overload of receivers so great, that many may never be read. Who would know? Similarly, readers may find routes through hypertext systems which bypass large chunks of information, remaining unread. Like the unheard sound of the falling tree in the forest, are those messages really there?

We may need an educational shift around notions of effective writing. If electronic communication (and overload of information from other sources) continues to increase; if the media also become more widespread, as they are likely to do (e.g. with the advent of domestic interactive media), then the traditional emphasis on effective writing as the construction of long, considered, well-structured documents for an audience with the leisure to peruse (the three volume novel and the academic thesis being archetypes) will be increasingly inappropriate. Writers will need the skills of summary, the skills of the minute taker; the skills of brevity and immediacy, taking the reader by the throat in the first line and saying all that need be said in the time it takes to find the next entry on the system, the skills of the writer of advertising copy; the skills of abbreviating and stitching together fragments of text from different sources (into a hyper document, into an email conference, into a collaborative text, into a single document fashioned of reusable writing), the skills of the magazine editor. Cruder writing, talky writing, writing with a higher error content may become the norm because both the writer and reader expect rapid consumption of throwaway text.

5. Implications of new writing tools

If any of the above suggestions have real substance (and I suspect most do) then the computers and writing community needs to explore a long list of implications. I will attempt to produce that entire list here, but I think implications in three areas at least should be reviewed:

- Needs for additional writing tools.
- Evaluation.
- The philosophy of writing.

I will conclude with just a few words on each of these.

5.1. Needs for additional writing tools

All of the above problems and effects of computerised writing tools suggests that new aids to using those tools may be necessary. If the new technologies of writing offer new problems for writers, then solutions are needed to those problems which, presumably, we could look to the technology to provide. Such tools need to address the new needs, answering needs such as:

For hypermedia:

- Selecting hypermedia and structures.
- Building hypermedia structures.
- Constructing effective cards/nodes.
- Giving the reader appropriate links.
- Determining reader needs and interactivity.

For desktop publishing:

- Understanding the terminology of print and typesetting.
- Designing documents.
- Presenting effectively.
- Understanding relationships between different DTP tools (e.g. different ways of altering spacing).

For networked communication:

- Writing ephemera.
- Attracting the reader.
- Writing elegant, effective and brief messages.
- Conveying attitudes, beliefs and tone verbally.

5.2. Evaluation

The evaluation of writing tools is, in any case, a problem area, as with much other user-centred software evaluation. It is made doubly difficult by the impossibility of measuring benefits against costs, for the comparison is often between unlike variables. For example, if a system facilitates reusable writing, then it may well increase writer productivity. More documents will flow more rapidly from the printer. But will it reduce quality? Will it stultify the creativity of the writer?

Take another example: a post-writing system focuses a student on the mechanics of writing (spelling, grammar, punctuation) and these aspects of her writing improve. Will this result in the student also paying more attention to the other aspects of her writing (because she is now more critical) or will it distract her from more content-oriented, organisational or presentational issues (because all her attention is concentrated on the mechanical errors)? This question may be answerable, but which of the possible answers will lead us to conclude that such post-writing software is less problematic than traditional writing behaviour?

5.3. Philosophy of writing

As I have briefly suggested above, the new writing technologies argue for a new set of writing skills. In particular, there seems an increasing case for replacing the skills of the report writer and essay writer with those of the minute taker, advertising copy writer and magazine editor. The falling costs of DTP, multimedia and graphical communication argue for writers with graphical, design and production skills (and, we might argue, skills associated with aural channels also). The new electronic writer may perhaps be a writer of small, discrete texts, using televisual writing codes, rather than purely textual codes, who works as one of a team whose membership s/he may not know, and contributes to a multi-authored, constantly changing work.

A philosophy of writing which treats the long, unified text as its paradigm, written by a single author and read by a homogeneous audience may well lead to writing research, the creation of models of writing and the development of writing support tools which are totally inappropriate for the actual writing tasks computer-based writers perform and the actual needs they have.

6. References

Anthony, P. (1984) *Bearing an Hourglass,* Granada Publishing, London.

Chandler, D. (1990) Do the write thing?, *Electric Word,* Jan/Feb.

Cherry, L. L. (1981) Computer Aids for Writers, *ACM SIGPLAN Notices* 16:6, June.

Cherry, L. L. (1982) Writing tools, *IEEE Trans actions on Communications,* 30 Jan. Special issue on communications in the automated office.

Daiute, C. (1985) *Computers and Writing,* Addison Wesley, Reading, MA.

Dorner, J. (1990) Writers right now, *Electric Word,* July/Aug.

Flower, L. and Hayes, J. R. (1980) The dynamics of composing: making plans and juggling constraints. In L. W. Gregg and E. R. Steinberg (Eds) *Cognitive Processes in Writing: An Interdisciplinary Approach.* Lawrence Erlbaum, Hillsdale, NJ.

Greif, S. (1988) Genetic growing systems and self controlled training, paper delivered to Swedish-German Workshop in Stockholm, Dec 12th-15th 1988.

Hartley, J. and Knapper, C. K. (1984) Academics and their writing, *Studies in Higher Education,* 9, 2.

Hammond, R. (1984) *The Writer and the Word Processor*, Coronet Books, London.

Heim, M. (1987) *Electric Language: a Philosophical Study of Word Processing*, Yale University Press, New Haven and London.\par

MacDonald, N. H., Frase, L. T., Gingrich, P. S. and Keenan, S. A. (1982) The Writer's Workbench -computer aids for text analysis, *IEEE Transactions on Communications*, COM-30, 1, Jan.

Martin, J. R. (1986) Intervening in the process of writing development, *ALAA, Occasional Papers* 9.

Sharples, M., and Pemberton, L. (1989) Representing writing: an account of the writing process with regard to the writer's external representations, unpublished ms, School of Cognitive Sciences, University of Sussex.

Sharples, M., Goodlet, J. and Pemberton, L. (1989) Developing a writer's assistant. In Williams, N. and Holt, P. (Eds), *Computers and Writing: Models and Tools.* Blackwell, Oxford.

Williams, N. (1990) Writers' problems and computer solutions, *CALL: Special Issue on Computers and Composition*, 1, 2, June.

Williams, N. (forthcoming) *The Computer, the Writer and the Learner*, Springer Verlag, New York.

Wright, P. and Lickorish, A. (1989) The influence of discourse structure on display and navigation in hypertexts In Williams, N. and Holt, P. (Eds), *Computers and Writing: Models and Tools.* Blackwell, Oxford.

2

Three Modes of Collaborative Authoring

Julian Newman
Glasgow Polytechnic

Rhona Newman
University of Ulster at Jordanstown

Abstract

While computer aids to writing are increasingly embraced by individual authors, remote on-line collaborative authoring remains very much the exception and is generally motivated by enthusiasm for exploring new media, rather than by intrinsic benefits. This paper reviews the development of on-line collaboration systems, analyses the process of co-operative writing, identifies three different modes of collaborative authorship and draws some conclusions for collaboration systems.

1. Introduction

Attempts to provide computer and communications support for authors collaborating over a substantial distance may be traced back more than 20 years: for example, LS/AUGMENT provided split-screen and voice conferencing features as part of a "knowledge workstation" (Engelbart 1975, Engelbart *et al.* 1973); yet while such computer aids to writing as outliners and style analysers are increasingly embraced by individual authors, remote on-line collaborative authoring remains very much the exception and is generally motivated by enthusiasm for exploring new media, rather than by the intrinsic benefits of the system used.

2. The development of on-line collaboration systems

Unlike most early computer conferencing systems, which were essentially message switching software with very limited facilities for text manipulation, LS/Augment (developed at Stanford Research Institute) aimed to support a "knowledge worker" in individual or collaborative on-line creation, manipulation and retrieval of text and graphics, access to specialised computing resources through a consistent interface, management of organisational and personal information and participation in a distributed community (Engelbart 1975, 1979, Engelbart *et al.* 1973). The LS "knowledge workstation" could provide a pair of authors with a limited windowing facility together with the combination of voice and text communications, thus supporting authors working on a joint document. LS however found limited acceptance, which has commonly been attributed to poor human factors and to the difficulty of cost-justification. In the early 1980s, the BLEND project aimed to support all the activities involved in the publication of an academic journal, through the medium of a computer-based message system (Shackel 1982 1985; Shackel *et al.* 1986; Pullinger 1984; Pullinger *et al.* 1985). Activities supported by BLEND included submission, refereeing, editorial decision-making, electronic publication and on-line browsing. BLEND supported text communication only.

Most authors who published electronically in the BLEND journal prepared their text using their local word processing facilities and then uploaded a finished text to the BLEND host; but one paper, published in printed form, was written entirely "over the network" (Wilson *et al.* 1984) and the group process of writing this paper is analysed by Maude *et al.* (1985: see below). The experience of group communication via BLEND also provided an impetus to the COSMOS project, and the funding proposal for the Cosmos project (which involved staff at five different sites) was drafted using an on-line bulletin-board system (Wilbur *et al.* 1986)

More recently the HICOM system (Pullinger 1988 Wilson 1989) was established to support communication amongst the Human-Computer Interaction community in the UK; HICOM also hosts other interest groups in Languages and in Computer-Supported Co-operative Work. At least one paper, by a group of three "distributed" authors, has been written via HICOM and is currently "in submission". Individual authors have also used HICOM to solicit comments upon drafts and to seek relevant references for work in hand. HICOM also publishes electronic book-reviews. These reviews are usually by single authors, but the conferencing system readily allows the attachment of comments by other readers (thus building up a multiple review, but not a true jointly-authored document).

The study of joint authoring in BLEND by Maude *et al.* (op. cit.), draws conclusions concerning the pattern of development, the functioning of normative pressure and the type of activities that were well or badly supported by the particular system used (NOTEPAD).

The group activities, according to Maude *et al*, followed a pattern of development similar to that identified by Bales (1958) for face-to-face group working, i.e. a 3-stage process of collecting information, evaluating the information and finally pressing for consensus. The writing was actively led by a group member who took on the role of project organiser, divided work amongst the group members and intervened where he thought necessary to encourage members to "stick to the point". There appeared to be effective normative pressure on those who did login "to contribute some message, no matter how trivial ... to maintain a presence"; yet "mechanisms for eliciting contributions from reluctant members appear to be much weaker than those available in fact-to-face groups". Of 12 members of the original group, four finally ended up as named authors of the published paper. The system was "particularly suited to ensuring that participants ... focus on predetermined goals", but summarising and massaging of information and ideas was poorly supported.

Wilbur *et al.* (1986) describe problems in using a bulletin-board system to get a draft document agreed amongst members of a geographically distributed research team. One member of the team used a bulletin board and sought proposed amendments before a meeting at which the document was to be approved. Although the message received before the meeting indicated at least qualified approval of the document, at the face-to-face meeting the document provoked fierce argument, "dominated by those who had contributed least to the CBMS-based discussion", and no decision was reached concerning the document.

3. Joint authorship

The appearance of a particular name as one of the "authors" of a published document may be the outcome of several different processes: for example, an author may be a person who disposes of the resources that have been used in the research, as a head of department or manager of a research group: such an author may have taken minimal or no part in the writing of the paper, but may be credited as an author for reasons of power or prestige.

An author may also be someone who contributed a crucial idea in discussion, without which the paper would never have been written, but who took no part in the actual drafting, or who perhaps confined his or her subsequent activity to criticising and commenting on the draft written by another. Or an author maybe a sort of commissioning editor, who plans the outline of the document, divides the work amongst other writers, and then pulls their contributions together and gives them a final polish. But often collaborative authorship involves the gradual emergence of a jointly-authored text out of discussions between the authors concerning fragments written by different members of the team, or concerning some other joint activity which they wish to report or analyse: such discussions will often take place over a period of time, in a variety of situations, sometimes arising spontaneously and sometimes planned so as to have access to visual aids or other resources, or to provide isolation from the distraction of other tasks or demands.

The meaning of "authorship" varies, then, according to formal and informal role structures, and according to the processes whereby group work is organised. It also varies according to the nature of the text that is to be produced, and the relation of that text to the functions of information-delivery and knowledge-creation. Information we would define, in conformity with traditional information theory, as that which reduces uncertainty. Information is the answer to a question. Knowledge, on the other hand, is the framework within which questions can be posed. Some texts, even by academic authors, treat knowledge as relatively unproblematic: these texts we would define as principally concerned to communicate information. Other texts work towards a reconceptualisation or redefinition of knowledge. A similar distinction as that between Communication and Conversation or between Formal and Cultural language[1] .

However, "cultural language", in Robinson's (1989) usage, appears to refer to the metalinguistic practices whereby collaborators discuss their joint task: in the development of a text that purports to create or advance knowledge, the product of the task may be an attempt to describe a definition of reality, but may equally be a critique or comment on previous definitions of reality. Robinson argues (op. cit.) for the need to support "Double Level Language", that is, for those who are collaborating in writing, bargaining or whatever to be able to communicate not only through a formalised medium (e.g. a multi-user shared outliner, a spreadsheet, etc.), but also through another channel (e.g. voice) to converse or meta communicate about their communications in the first channel.

4. Activities in authoring

Several researchers have published analyses of authorship which identify a number of stages, strategies or activities. For example O'Malley and Sharples (1986, building on Flower and Hayes 1981 and Sharples 1985) identify five different "writing strategies": Thought dumping, Thread Following, Dialectic, Draft-redraft, and Plant-draft-revise. Outliners such as "Brainstorm" provide computer support for moving from thought dumping to plan generation, following which it is implicitly assumed that the writer will follow a plan-draft-revise strategy. The Writer's Assistant (O'Malley and Sharples op. cit., Sharples *et al.* 1989) aims to help a writer to move naturally amongst all these strategies.

Another classification of authoring activities, oriented towards hypermedia rather than text publication, has been presented by Hahn *et al.* (1989), who aim to provide software support for different stages in the co-authorship of a hypermedia project. They see hypermedia document authoring as involving idea. processing, document design and document generation. Where a hypermedia document is co-authored by a group, they identify the activities the system must support as: generation of content issues, document outlines and hypertext fragments, critical annotation by other group members, and the final configuration of ideas, design decisions and hypertext into a coherent object. Tools to support this will include electronic conferencing devices and multi-access information retrieval facilities.

Smart (1989) analyses the assemblage of descriptive technical documentation by a technical editor:

> "Large technical documents are rarely produced by just one person. They are created by teams of authors, whose work is brought together and standardised by an editor, working for a documentation manager".

1 "Communication is a process of transmission of information between and among group members. Conversation... implies a process of concept sharing and development of agreement of the interpretation of meaning of events." Grantham and Carasik (quoted in Robinson 1989.)

Smart describes a system, SIMPR, designed to help such an editor to index, validate and store the information in such a way that a reader can search the information base produced, to find the answer to a query.

Valuable as these various contributions are, they do not fully address the joint authorship of text. The O'Malley-Sharples model of writing is capable of embracing writing activities oriented to knowledge-production, but does not cover collaborative authorship. The models used by Hahn (op. cit.) and Smart (op. cit.) are oriented to joint authorship but not to knowledge-production. Thus, we would argue, the models that deal with collaboration are confined to the solution of a structured problem, generally under some form of central co-ordination. As the account by Maude *et al.* makes clear (see above), the on-line joint authorship of the paper by Wilson *et al.* (1984) was also handled as the solution of a problem which the team, or at least the co-ordinator, already knew how to decompose.

As we have indicated in our introduction, we recognise such a paradigm as a legitimate mode of authorship; but would argue that however successful a computer conferencing system may have been in supporting this mode of joint authorship, papers that attempt to reconceptualise knowledge may require considerably richer communications channels.

The problems of normative regulation and consensus-generation have concerned several psychological researchers into computer-based communications. Kiesler *et al.* (1984) identify the following as differentiating computer-based text-communication from other media (including face-to-face communication and telephony): absence of regulating feedback (e.g. resolution of such co-ordinating problems as telling another person you already have knowledge of something he or she is explaining); dramaturgical weakness; few status and position cues; depersonalisation; and the need to develop new norms appropriate to the new medium.

> "Using traditional communication, norms, social standards and inferences about individuals are made salient by observable social structural artefacts ... and by communication itself, including non-verbal involvement ... [Computer-Mediated Communications] do not efficiently communicate nuances of meaning and frame of mind, organisational loyalties, symbolic procedural variations and, especially, individuating details about people that might be embodied in their dress, location, demeanour and expressiveness ..." (op. cit.)

These factors, they suggest, may lead to overall weakening of normative regulation. They report experiments which suggest that group members communicating by computer participate more equally, are more uninhibited in their verbal behaviour and take longer to arrive at consensus, than groups who meet face-to-face; and that this cannot be accounted for by time taken up in typing. Computer-mediated groups were also more liable to take "extreme" decisions.

Hiltz *et al.* (1981) compared the ability of groups to reach consensus using computerised conferencing with face-to-face communication. They concluded that the effectiveness of computer conferencing depended on the nature of the task: "Fairly well-structured tasks that involve some data or knowledge are more easily handled in computer-mediated communication, as compared to fairly amorphous tasks based on the exchange of highly subjectivised opinions." They also found that consensus in the computerised medium required either the explicit structuring of a human leadership role, or the provision of a computer analysis and feedback of data on the group's preferences.

In preparation of technical documents, or of instructional materials (whether text, hypertext or multimedia) there will be a relatively structured problem to solve. In collaborative authorship of academic papers, the degree of prior structure may vary: suppose the paper aims mainly to report some completed empirical investigation, then the authors have a similar task to those preparing instructional materials: they have to give an adequate account of the work that was undertaken, within certain constraints –for example acceptable length for the intended journal etc.. Often such constraints may make it necessary to fragment the reporting of a single piece of work between several journals ... then it is necessary to adopt a suitable modularisation strategy. While this can lead to strong disagreements and problems of judgement, the issues on which the authors will disagree will be largely "at the margin" e.g. the relative risks of excessive succinctness Vs verbosity.

These types of disagreement may be contrasted with the joint authorship of a position paper or critical subject review: here discussion may turn on the negotiation of reality not of the institutions of publishing or the cognitive capacities of the intended readership, but of the substantive subject area with which the paper is concerned .... unlike the team members "bidding" to produce segments of a multimedia training package, who know they have a project, joint authors working on a critical paper may well have to put together two partial (possibly conflicting) views of reality ... thus the performance of joint authorship may not only require that the collaborators maintain individual credibility in one anothers' eyes as competent colleagues, but moreover that they maintain the mutual credibility of their joint project. Time management of such a joint effort is also particularly difficult, inasmuch as the overall structure of ideas to be expressed, the structure of the paper, the amount of redrafting that will be required, etc. etc. are all dependent on a possibly changing negotiated reality.

One area in which it is often hoped that computer-based message systems will aid research is collaboration between specialists in different specialisms, by breaking down the physical distance between groups of specialists. Here, we would argue, the problems of jointly negotiating a definition of reality, may be particularly acute. Collaboration at a distance can exacerbate problems in interdisciplinary communication. We interviewed a group of industrial mathematicians who were collaborating with remotely-sited groups of researchers in fire-engineering. Their communications were by electronic mail, by telephone and by face-to-face research visits. The mathematicians were much concerned about the problems of technical language: the meaning of the same technical terms could differ widely between mathematicians and engineers. The engineer, for example, would use the word "mapping" in accordance with an intuitive notion; however a mapping to a mathematician is a mathematical entity. The employment of the word by non-mathematicians was seen as "abusage". Similarly the word "function" has changed its meaning in mathematics since the early 60s from embracing many-valued to single-valued relations. Differences between mathematicians and engineers in the understanding of "set" and "collection" were seen to cause difficulties in discussions which involved reasoning about probability. Richer media than electronic mail were felt to be essential to prevent the growth of misunderstandings. This exemplifies Robinson's point that "In a real conversation, utterances are often integral parts of other utterances. They take their meaning from their immediate context. They are temporary place markers in a fluid whole." (op. cit.)

5. Three modes of collaborative authorship

To bring some order to this field, we propose that three main modes of collaborative authorship may be identified, in terms of the type of text produced and the relationship between that text and the negotiated construction of reality: these modes we refer to as Literature, Documentation and Critical Discourse.

In "Literature", the authors negotiate a common definition of reality: this definition is then an "input" to the production of a text which attempts to describe it. The actual production of the text may be shared, or may be undertaken by one individual author. In their understanding of reality, the authors have reached "closure", such that there is a clear understanding of the joint project and little need for normative pressure or imperative co-ordination. Existing computer conferencing or electronic mail systems could readily support the writing-up process for Literature: how far they could support the initial negotiation of reality is more open to doubt.

In "Documentation", the definition of reality (which may well be embodied in a product or other artefact) is decided before the writing begins, and the writers have little role in its negotiation. On the basis of this predefined view of reality, an editor or co-ordinator divides the detail-work of writing between a number of authors, each of whom produces an allocated text segment which the co-ordinator then combines into the final text, in accordance with the predefined plan.

In "Critical Discourse" the authors begin, as in "Literature", by negotiating a definition of reality and producing a text that purports to describe that reality: but they then engage in negotiation about the reality of the text, constructing a definition of reality which we may call "metatext", and in the light of this they produce a revised text. Revisions in Critical Discourse differ from those in Literature of Documentation, in that they are not minor polishing, rearrangements or adjustments, but may involve total reconceptualisations, on the part of one or more of the authors, of the definition of reality which the text attempts to describe.

In all these modes of collaborative authorship, problems of group co-ordination and the negotiation of consensus arise. But the issues are likely to be quite different: for example, in Documentation the problems of co-ordination are likely to focus on such issues as accuracy, productivity, conformity to conventions, satisfaction of constraints and appropriate decomposition, whereas in Critical Discourse they are more likely to focus on ill-defined issues such as competence and ontology.

6. Design of collaboration systems

The most basic level at which computer-based communication systems might support remote collaborative authorship is that of resource sharing, be it the transfer of raw data, the provision of information available to one author but not to the others, access to skills and packages that are available at one site but not at another, or the "shipping" of text segments for comment, editing or final make-up. How useful CBMS may be for such purposes depends to a considerable extent on how well they are integrated into the author's normal working environment. This immediately suggests a potential conflict between these low-level uses, and systems to support higher-level negotiation-oriented writing, since as we have seen the latter are likely to require a rich variety of communication channels. In principle it might be argued that desktop conferencing systems should provide the capability of multimedia communication between pairs or amongst groups of authors: but the problems of compatibility, the communications costs and the difficulties of cost-justification are likely to be considerably greater than for a well-integrated low-level system. We would argue, therefore, that the role of computer-based message systems in collaborative authorship should be approached with realism and caution: it should be recognised that the major advantage of using the computer is the help it gives with lower-level tasks, and it should not be expected to substitute for face-to-face communication in the more complex areas of the advancement of knowledge.

7. Acknowledgements

Thanks are due to members of the Mathematics Department at the University of Ulster.

8. References

Bales, R. F. (1955) How people interact in conferences *Scientific American,* 192,.3.

Borelli, C., Copelli, S. and Paolini, P. (1989) A Set of Software Tools for a Document Workstation *ESPRIT Office and Business Systems: Results and Progress of ESPRIT Projects in 1989* Brussels: Commission of the EC, Directorate General XIII.

Engelbart, D (1975) LS teleconferencing features *SRI-ARC33076*, Menlo Park, CA

Engelbart, D. (1979) Consistency in LS. Workshop on man-computer communication, *EIFIP*, Le Bischenberg, Strasbourg, France, February 1979.

Engelbart, D, Watson, R and Norton, J (1973) The augmented knowledge workshop national computer conference, *New York, AFIPS Conference Proceedings*, 42, Montvale, AFIPS Press, NJ.

Hahn, U., Jarke, M., Eherer, S., Kreplin, K. Farusi, M and Pimpinelli, F. (1989) COAUTHOR; A hypermedia group authoring environment *ESPRIT Office and Business Systems: Results and Progress of ESPRIT Projects in 1989.* Brussels: Commission of the EC, Directorate General XIII.

Hiltz, S.R., Turoff M. and Johnson, K. (1981) The effect of structure, task and individual attributes on consensus in computerised conferences. In R. Uhlig (Ed) *Computer Message Systems.* North-Holland, Amsterdam.

Kiesler, S., Siegel, J. and McGuire, T. (1984) Social-psychological aspects of computer-mediated communications *American Psychologist*, 39.

Maude, T. I., Heaton, N. O., Gilbert, G. N., Wilson, P. A. and Marshall, C. J. (1985) An experiment in group working on mailbox systems. In B. Shackel, (Ed) *Human-Computer Interaction: INTERACT '84.* North-Holland, Amsterdam.

O'Malley, C. and Sharples, M. (1986) Tools for management and support of multiple constraints in a writer's assistant. In M. D. Harrison and A. F. Monk (Eds) *People and Computers: Designing for Usability.* Cambridge University Press, Cambridge.

Pullinger, D. (Ed) (1988) Human-computer interaction and electronic communication: Special feature. *Behaviour and Information Technology*, 7.2 (Whole Issue).

Robinson, M. (1989) Double level languages and co-operative working COSMOS *Information Exchange Network*, 6, Nov 1989

Sharples, M. (1985) *Cognition, Computers and Creative Writing.* Ellis Horwood Chichester.

Smart (1989) SIMPR Structured information management processing and retrieval ESPRIT office and business systems: *Results and Progress of ESPRIT Projects in 1989.* Brussels: Commission of the EC, Directorate General XIII.

Wilbur, S., Rubin, T. and Lee, S. (1986) A study of group interaction over a computer-based message system. In M. D. Harrison and A. F. Monk (Eds) *People and Computers: Designing for Usability.* Cambridge University Press, Cambridge.

Wilson, P. A. (1989) Some notes on a European network or collaboratory for research and development *European Workshop on Computer Supported Collaborative Work in Research Laboratories, ISPRA*, Italy, 4-5 December 1989.

Wilson, P. A., Maude, T. I., Marshall, C. J. and Heaton, N. O. (1984) The active mailbox:Your online secretary. In H. T. Smith (Ed) *Computer Based Message Services.* North-Holland, Amsterdam.

3

Is There a Reader in this Labyrinth? Notes on Reading *Afternoon*

J. Yellowlees Douglas

Abstract

Interactive fiction is a novel way of writing and reading which depends on hypermedia software. The novelty inherent in such systems may cause several problems both for readers and writers and clearly this new technology raises a number of questions relating to creative writing. The paper explores the characteristics and problems associated with hypermedia fiction through the author 's reading of Joyce's interactive fiction *Afternoon*.

1. Introduction

In a study conducted in 1900, Mercedes-Benz estimated that the world-wide demand for cars would not exceed one million. Why a million? Because of the limitation of chauffeurs available to drive them. In 1908, Henry Ford invented the assembly line and democratised the automobile; by 1920, there were 8 million Model T's in America alone.

There appear to be two assumptions underlying this imagined requirement for chauffeurs: namely, that only people who could afford chauffeurs could afford automobiles because early automobiles were hand-built, scarce and expensive and, more importantly, that driving a motor car would require considerable more expertise than driving a horse and carriage.

We can find this anecdote humorous because we can see, with the aid of 20/20 hindsight, that Mercedes-Benz was relying on what Marshall McLuhan called "rear-view mirror" thinking, that they were guilty of projecting onto the new technology a set of expectations based upon their knowledge of a prior technology. But we might also claim that the company erred by not adequately grasping or gauging conditions that already existed. The Industrial Revolution which introduced mass production also gave a rising middle class some disposable income; the eye-hand co-ordination and perceptual skills already used for driving carts and carriages alike provided the basis for acumen needed behind the wheel; and the interface between driver and motorised vehicle would be simple enough to permit the man on the street to pilot automobiles.

Today, the difficulties we face are of a slightly different character: we are dealing with Model T's –in terms of the shape of existing technology - and cruising through the future in Lotus Esprits. Or, at any rate, the concepts and systems some of us dream of implementing involve technology not yet developed. At the moment, the technology seems to enable us at the same time it confines us – which has been the story of tools ever since their inception. We see ourselves reined in by the limitations of our technologies and speak of shaping systems according to what systems can deliver and what we would like them to deliver. But somewhere in the throes of all our planning and dreaming, we need to take into account not simply what narratives might look like when freed of print constraints, but what capabilities and restrictions the living, breathing reader brings to the text, to any text.

What happens when readers encounter a text? How do we read stories? Why do we read fiction? What underlying assumptions enable us to understand Plato's *Phaedrus*, *The Naked Lunch* or *The Wasteland*? Understanding the limits of a reader's willingness to suspend disbelief or boredom or outright confusion will guide us in designing future hypermedia writing tools as well as in writing present and future interactive fictions. After all, technologies do not necessarily media make. New media forms tend to arise when older media forms have become saturated and new technologies –which have insinuated themselves into a niche –become readily available. Since niches can be said to be made up mostly of user's desires, needs, capabilities and limitations, a new medium can either sink or swim according to how accurately the features it offers match the abilities and needs of its audience of users. Although Bell's conviction that his newly invented telephone was best suited for carrying symphonic music over the wires turned out to be a mere hiccup in the widespread implementation of telephone systems, some of his most innovative creations have languished on the shelf for lack of a niche suited to contemporary users' needs ... and Mercedes-Benz lost out on the sale of a few million cars.

Nowadays, when many of us think of a book, we think of its limitations: it is static; it is linear; it is monolithic. As Plato noted, no matter how many times we return to it, it just keeps saying the same thing. The human mind has adapted to this cognitively cumbersome, severely limited and often awkward means of representing the world around us to the extent that it has become transparent, one of our environments. What we seldom question is whether or how this same system is admirably adapted to certain cognitive and perceptual faculties most of us possess, certain ways of perceiving the world which might likewise form the bedrock of narratives in other media and of our transactions with the world around us. Put more simply (without the hand-waving), we might ask what virtual glue holds a narrative together after we unstick the pages, shuffle and re-shuffle their order and strike the folios from them: what guides do readers rely on to move from one passage to the next? How do they keep reading? We might even ask, do they keep reading – and what happens to their overall perception of the narrative?

2. Interactive fiction and hypermedia

To begin to address these questions, I turned to a hypertext application, StorySpace, which offered separate reading and writing interfaces, a set of boxes for containing text called "places", links between places called "paths", and the means for graphically generating a cognitive map of an entire narrative. Then I selected an interactive narrative called "Afternoon: a Story". Originally written by one of the designers of StorySpace as a "test" file, this particular narrative can be described broadly as a cross between Borges'(1979) *Book of Sand* and a fluid form of Julio Cortazar's *Hopscotch.* Where Borges' Book *of Sand* was infinite and no page ever yielded the same contents twice, Cortazar's *Hopscotch* is written –Cortazar notes in a preface –to be read as "many" books, but is confined, by virtue of its binding and the numbering system he employs, to existing as merely two. Joyce's *Afternoon* presumably has a restricted number of possible configurations, although to wander down all the same paths twice in *Afternoon,* recreating the same virtual narrative twice, one would need either a map of an earlier reading or a hefty chunk of time in which to run through all the possible permutations and combinations of places within it.

There are 538 places in *Afternoon* with an average length running to about half a page of text. These are passages, as opposed to paragraphs, which carry titles and are linked by named paths, via a set of conditions stipulated by the author of the hypertext, or whoever has elected to map and script the narrative. These conditions –or guard fields –enable the author/ scriptor to restrict how the reader may assemble the text –something simultaneously enabling and disabling. Few readers would be either willing or able to piece together a narrative from so many often extremely disparate pieces; at the same time, readers' choices in how they will construct their own texts are governed by conditions, interpretations and intentions manipulated by the author .

In *Afternoon,* readers may travel from one place to another by selecting words from the text that they find intriguing, which match with words that the author has selected as guard fields, or they may travel a certain path by virtue of the previous places visited or paths travelled, or a combination of the two. A third possibility for movement –accessible only through selecting the print button whilst holding down the option key –exists in a display revealing a full list of path names and their destination places which branch out from each place, enabling readers to select paths and use a "Follow"option to enter any of the paths listed. What makes *Afternoon* a problematic text to read in basic, physical terms is the difficulty readers have in ascertaining just how they managed to move from one place to another, since words that yield are not flagged in the text, and the default option – where readers simply press a carriage return to continue along a path –works in conjunction with the sequence of places already visited.

As Joyce puts it during one place in *Afternoon*:

> ".... A word which doesn't yield the first time you read a section may take you elsewhere if you choose it when you encounter the section again; and sometimes what seems a loop, like memory, heads off again in another direction".

This means that one place may crop up in multiple contexts, and virtually insures that no two readings of *Afternoon* will be the same. Why readers might want to know whether they moved through the text according to their own choices or via choices made by the scriptor mapping out the text is an issue we'll tackle shortly.

Read by default from first to a last, "terminal"place that obstinately refuses to default, *Afternoon* involves an un-named narrator's frenetic search for his estranged wife and son, and his attempts to verify whether the bodies of a woman and child at the scene of an accident –glimpsed briefly on his way to work –signify the death of his child and former wife. With straight carriage returns as a response to the end of each place, this version of *Afternoon* visits 36 of the text's 538 places and takes approximately 45 minutes to read. If, during a second encounter with the text, the reader changes a single yield, an entirely new sequence takes shape, along with a new set of places. Counter-intuitively, in the end the most interesting feature about the narrative is not its ability to offer up new passages from a seemingly inexhaustible supply; it is the passages which one encounters over and over again – because they are encountered in multiple and often radically different contexts, yielding up fresh significance with each reading, until the experience of reading *Afternoon* begins to resemble an archaeological excavation of sorts, where fresh layers reveal the disparate uses which different surroundings or contexts have made of the same tools or circumstances. The following passage, for example, appears in a number of contexts:

> He asks slowly, savouring the question, dragging it out devilishly, meeting my eyes.
>
> <How... would you feel if I slept with your ex-wife? >
>
> It is foolish. She detests young men.

Seen in the context of the narrator's frenetic search for his ex-wife, and a lunch-time meeting between he and Wert, the query – given a modifying clause in the passage which follows it, where the narrator describes Wert as "thinking of what to say"–seems an effort to distract the narrator from his anxiety, an interpretation buttressed seven places later, when Wert saucily bombards their waitress with sexual innuendo because, the narrator says, "he means in this fashion to cheer me".

When I encounter the passage again in a second session (where I read the text until it refused to default), I have learned in the meantime that Wert employs the narrator, Peter, and, because the passage which follows details their lunch, I assume the conversation takes place during a business lunch. Since no hint of any anxieties, not to mention an accident, either precede it or immediately follow it this time around, the "thinking of what to say" seems merely a natural pause falling between two businessmen who lunch too frequently together. I subsequently discover that the narrator is involved with a woman also working for Wert, for whom Peter believes Wert feels a form of skewed Freudian possessiveness, as she, Nausicaa, was analysed by Wert's wife, Lolly. On a third reading, I encounter the passage again, framed this time by my knowledge that the narrator, has unknowingly involved himself in a triangle: through Nausicaa's voice, I discover that she is sleeping with both Wert and Peter, making Wert's query either a means of gauging Peter's probable response to a discovery of the triangle, or –less likely – part of the odd sort of Freudian connection which surfaced during my second reading.

Before I stumble across this passage again during a fourth reading, I am shocked to discover a passage related by Lolly describing how Peter loses concentration at the wheel after being distracted or stunned by the sight of his ex-wife riding in Wert's truck. Subsequent places seem to imply that Peter has caused the accident which had triggered the anxieties detailed in the first version of "Afternoon,"making the text a sort of Borgesian Möbius strip, and also making Wert's "what if I were sleeping with your ex-wife?"a very real question.

The often artful design of *Afternoon* aside, there are a number of assumptions or structures which enabled me to arrive at my readings and interpretations of the text. First: the actual language of the text in that particular place did not change. Its context, however, changed radically, bringing to mind an experiment conducted quite accidentally by cinema theorist V.I. Pudovkin. A shortage of film stock in the Soviet Union shortly after the Revolution obliged Russian film makers to create films and sequences out of existing footage. In this instance, a single close-up of an actor's neutral expression was inter-cut with three images: a child playing, a dressed out corpse and a steaming bowl of food. When the sequence was shown to viewers, the audience exclaimed at the actor's ability to subtly portray the emotions of joy, grief and hunger.

Apocryphal or not, results similar to Pudovkin's "experiment" were noted in a relatively obscure monograph by Baron Michotte, who animated a trio of neutral physical shapes in a film sequence and discovered that his viewers overwhelmingly described their spatial arrangement and movements in causal terms: objects were seen to be "dragging"one another, or "deflecting"each other, rather than seen to be moving discretely. These are "primitive perceptions", he noted, "and they are quite irresistible: we see cause." (Bruner 1986). A spate of related studies have yielded similar results in even the surprised expressions of infants, whose changes in expression, heart rate and blood pressure revealed surprise when time-space arrangements which had been seen by adults to be "caused"were interspersed with non-causal presentations –suggesting that this perceptual proclivity is innate in human beings (Bruner 1986). Critic Frank Kermode put it somewhat differently:

> "First we look for the story, events sequentially related (possessing ... a minimum of 'connexity') ... and sequence goes nowhere without his doppelgänger or shadow, causality."(Kermode 1981).

What we take for granted is the connection of one place with another: I do not assume that the conversation between Wert and Peter is removed from the events surrounding it, or that the question "what if I were sleeping with your ex-wife?"is the same question each time I encounter it. I believe, instead, that Wert's question arises directly from the circumstances surrounding it: from a desire to comfort a distressed employee, to fill an awkwardly lengthy pause during lunch time conversation, to gauge a reaction to his affair with Peter's lover, to begin to reveal his relationship with Peter's ex-wife or simply to play cat's paw with the unsuspecting Peter. As I read *Afternoon* or a Borges story or watch any film from "Workers Leaving a Factory"to "Persona" I continually perceive events or things which are proximate to each other as causally related and, as such, part of a sequence. This is, after all, also the component integral to cinema as a medium: we see time and events existing across shots and even the grammar of the familiar shot-reaction-shot sequence is based upon this particular way of perceiving the world.

If we change the language of the conversation between Peter and Wert and modify Wert's query along the lines of "Wert asked hypothetically, seeking to distract Peter from his anxieties about the whereabouts of Lisa and Andy", the likelihood that I will read and interpret this passage radically differently in the four separate contexts is reduced considerably. The language throughout *Afternoon* seems remarkably inexplicit, but, on examination, this is due merely to the relative brevity of passages compared to print chapters or stories, and their isolation from immediate contexts –unlike print narratives, where the jumble of pronoun "she""he"and "its"would be seen as clearly referring to textual precedents and antecedents. These places where the text ceases to be explicit, where I am forced to draw my own conclusions based on my wider knowledge of the text as a whole, or of other texts, or, failing that, my own experience in the world –as theorists from Sartre to Barthes have noted – is where interpretation begins: "Texts have indeterminacies about them that make them readable and enable meaning, in that they draw the reader into the text: language and texts, because they aren't real things, lack the determinacy of real objects," Iser wrote in *The Act of Reading* ". It is the elements of indeterminacy that enable the text to 'communicate' with the reader ... they induce him to participate both in the production and the comprehension of the work's intention."(Iser 1978)

For years structuralists have argued that the very slipperiness of language –or the slippage which constantly occurs between words as signifiers and the physical world they ostensibly represent – makes texts into traps, riddled with holes which oblige readers to construe or to construct their own virtual texts, fleshed out by their own experiences of other texts, genres and contact with the physical world. Texts that have too much flesh on them –typically, the genre escapades: the Mills & Boon romances, the worlds perpetuated by Marples and Poirots, the pulpy sci-fi fantasies, and the tidy realms of Middle Earth-type sagas –are guilty of over-inventing their worlds, of violating the classical edict, "to suggest is to create; to name is to destroy". As the eponymous narrator of the great ur-hypertext, *The Life and Opinions of Tristram Shandy* suggests:

"No author who understands the just boundaries of decorum and good breeding would presume to think all: the truest respect which you can pay to a reader's understanding is to halve this matter amicably, and leave him something to imagine, in his turn, as well as yourself". (Sterne 1966).

Great literature, Jerome Bruner argues, occurs where the narrative and fabula succeeded in touching timeless and universal nerves, where the story and the manner in which it was told evoke concerns and emotions in a manner inexplicitly but sufficiently suggestive to play across cultural and chronological continua. In *Afternoon* we can see that these same indeterminacies possess a further function, enabling texts to be not simply re-read but wholly re-played and re-invented with each fresh encounter.

But what happens in other hypertexts? Or how do readers react when the writer/scriptor has given birth to a bad version of Last Year at Marienbad? The answer is, at least at the moment, readers can more easily be befuddled than stimulated by existing hyperfiction. Like the extremely modestly-scaled maze at Hampton Court, sometimes you can get so lost amid the false beginnings and loops and intricate passages, you wonder what persuaded you to cough up the price of admission in the first place. Bombard readers with too much esoterica or require them forge too many links themselves and it becomes highly likely they will stop reading. But, in a hypertext where a sizeable number of connections work while others seem obscure or simply incomprehensible, readers are likely in continue to make their own inroads into the narrative.

In his controversial *Is There a Text in This Class?* Stanley Fish, a reformed formalist and leading light of the American school of pragmatism, argues that "interpretation is not the art of construing but the art of constructing. Interpreters do not decode poems; they make them". (Fish 1980).

Fish has painstakingly chronicled the process by which a classroom of students schooled in interpreting religious poetry construct a religious poem from a list of names of prominent linguists left over on the classroom blackboard from an earlier linguistics course. It is a particular type of scrutiny that turns pedestrian things into aesthetic objects, Fish claims. The act of recognising a poem or narrative is triggered not by the presence of qualities in the object itself but by an act of attention normally trained on things with the expectation of seeing those qualities. In other words, I see *Afternoon* as a constellation of coherent narratives because I know that I am approaching a piece of fiction, albeit one in an alien environment which falls outside the margins of contemporary genres and conventions.

Fish's contentions have been buttressed by similar findings involving case studies in communication. Where most of a sequence is comprehensible to listeners, for example, the insertion of noise into a part of the sequence is perceived by listeners as an intelligible part of the signal. Richard Warren asked listeners to respond to a tape of spoken sentences where phonemes had been erased and replaced by the sound of a cough and discovered that all of his listeners heard the missing sounds as clearly as if they had been physically present. When the undoctored tape was played back to them, none of the participants were able to distinguish the sounds they imagined from those actually heard, nor were they able to locate the cough in its correct place in the sentences. Because the cough lacked meaning, it seemed to float free in time. When a brief silence replaced the missing phoneme –similar to those which would punctuate a normal conversation – listeners invariably fixed its exact position. (Campbell 1989). When the ratio of signal to noise is sufficiently high to enable us to discern significance and sequence, we are able either to background it or to actually perceive it as part of the signal. Whether we are discussing Fish's "interpretive communities"or Joseph Campbell's "mythologically constructed community", as human beings we display an overriding tendency to perceive things in a way that makes sense, or, failing that, to impose sense upon them where none may actually exist because they believe that the intention underlying all communication is to convey something intelligible.

Regardless of the particular type of transaction we engage in, whether it is a face-to-face conversation or reading the likes of *Afternoon*, our first instinct –our default mode, if you will – is to perceive something as signal and to see something as noise only when the degree of noise seems to displace the signal entirely. When I stumbled across a passage involving tigers and a golden radio early in my first reading of *Afternoon*, I incorporated these images into the narrative by assigning them a hallucinogenic value, relegating them to the realm of the unreal, dream-territory, by connecting them with the intense heat of summer described in the narrative and making them part of the narrator's method of exploring the worlds around him, both real and imagined. In another reading, however, I discovered the same passage in the context of a narrative strand involving Nausicaa's stint in an Indian brothel, a sequence which jarred me into a bit of retrospection on passages in another reading of *Afternoon* where Nausicaa is given voice in some first-person reflections on both Wert and Peter, in terms that imply a prostitute's eye toward how each may be sexually manipulated. At the time I read those passages, I had gleaned nothing from the details concerning Nausicaa's background and character to suggest, however remotely, a career of prostitution, nor did the details jive with the sensitivity her character seemed to display or with the tone of her speech. Although I was confused by these odd references to "tricks", I did not discard these passages or exclude them from my endeavours to interpret the intricate web of relationships and deceit; instead, I foregrounded what seemed intelligible and relegated the rest to background. We possess the ability not only to suspend disbelief willingly , to use Coleridge's expression, but to forge links between seemingly disparate, discrete events, given our knowledge that they exist in the context of a text, written to be not only understood but to be interpreted. To open a text is an invitation to see connections and to deal with signifiers and, more importantly, significance – whether the text exists in static, monolithic, linear form or as a fluid assembly of places, paths and words that can, and sometimes do, yield.

The difference between hypertext and print narratives in this respect is that it is more difficult to drift through the narrative without beginning to draw explicit conclusions about some of its elements. Although the act of translating abstract, written language into something representing, commenting upon or standing in for the real world can hardly be called passive, one can physically progress through a text without making any active decisions about it. In other words, in order physically to read *Jane Eyre,* I am not required to decide whether Mr Rochester has unjustly imprisoned his wife Bertha for violating Victorian conventions or whether Jane should revile him for having actively deceived her. I can simply keep reading. Likewise, if I lose the thread of the narrative at some point in the midst of, say, Mrs Dalloway, I can persevere and perhaps struggle onto more secure ground, narratively speaking, in a few pages. But to read *Afternoon,* readers have to be actively engaged in the narrative: they must make choices at the end of each passage, deciding whether the present narrative is worth pursuing, what they are after during a particular read, and when they should stop. Sometimes, if the narrative strand is particularly interesting, they may want to ferret out which links seem most likely to follow that narrative as it develops and which possible versions they may be neglecting by their choices. At others, however, when the path seems to have wandered away from the text's more central concerns, or when the places encountered seem to contain too much esoterica - which can seem the case with certain segments of *Afternoon* – readers are cast back on the horns of the proverbial Minotaur of literary theory: intentionality.

There are a number of places in *Afternoon* which do not default, effectively tripping readers in full stride because they do not seem to be intrinsically tied to the structure of the particular narrative sequences in which they occur. The issue of intentionality rears its ugly snout here and in moments when readers attempt to choose words that yield, only to discover that their choices have not matched with the yields intended by the writer/scriptor and that they have moved forward by default –presumably following the writer's primary intention. Since they are the express creation of the writer/scriptor and do not invite any collaborative decision from the reader, defaults acquire a certain priority over links created by words that yield. When the default path halts abruptly, or when readers' concepts of words "with texture"(as Joyce calls the words that yield in his metatextual preamble to *Afternoon*) do not seem to coincide with those selected by Joyce, readers become overtly aware of the text as a structure created with the intention to communicate something. And, in order to proceed through the text, they must in some way either anticipate or discover what those intentions may have been and their bearing upon the structure of the text, the links between places and the contents of the places themselves. They begin to suffer from the something of the same dilemma decried by Socrates in Plato's *Phaedrus*:

> "And once a thing is put in writing, the composition, whatever it may be, drifts all over the place...And it when it is ill-treated and unfairly abused, it always needs its parent to come to its aid, being unable to defend or help

itself".

The advent of reader-response criticism marked the beginning of a gradual interest in the much-neglected role of the reader in the transaction between text, author, and reader. Much of the writing of theorists from Roland Barthes to the reception aesthetics of Jauss, Ingarden and Iser effectively sketched out theories of reading and the construction of meaning which seem to anticipate hypertext environments and called for greater understanding of the creative powers and autonomy of the reader. But the hypertext environment which seems, on the face of it, to require greater interaction and to provide more autonomy from readers, may actually place them more fully in the author's thrall, transforming the author from the *deus ex machina* of the print world, whose trace must be heeded but whose absence can be ignored, to the opponent in a sophisticated game of "Mastermind", whose strategies must be discovered to insure the player's survival.

3. Conclusion

In the end, we need to remember that intentionality is not quite the bugbear twentieth century critics have decried, that it has fallen from grace as an interpretive strategy largely because it is a spectacularly irrelevant tool when used in a medium where authors are either generally not only remote but sometimes positively dead. No matter how painstakingly we trace the author's history, regardless of how assiduously we research the background to his writing, we can no more verify an apparently valid approximation of what Dickens intended in Bleak House than we can one sketching out what passed through the mind of Lee Harvey Oswald in the seconds after he recognised Jack Ruby across the crowded Dallas police station.

Used in day-to-day conversation or in contexts –like this one –where the writer or speaker is accessible, intentionality becomes a tool guiding understanding and interpretation. In *Is There a Text in This Class?* Stanley Fish begins interpreting the mutual misunderstanding between the student asking the essay's famous question and the instructor construing it –aided completely and utterly by his knowledge of that student's original intention behind the query. When impediments exist to our immediate understanding, we attempt to discern the intention behind the sentence or sequence that has eluded our comprehension.

But in an environment where the writer who has scripted our encounter is conspicuously absent, readers are left with the added burden of having to make assumptions about the text in order to physically move through enough of it to enable them to begin interpreting it. This is not to condemn hypertexts or to claim that interactive narratives hobble readers where they should enable them. Armed with an awareness of how readers engage texts, we should be able to construct environments for interactive narratives which allow readers to roam as freely through hyperspace as they do corporeal space.

4. References

Barthes, R. (1979) *The Barthes Reader.* Hill and Wang, New York. (Translated by Howard, R. Edited by Sontag, S).

Borges, J.L. (1979) *The Book of Sand.* Penguin, Harmondsworth.

Brand, S. (1987) *The Media Lab: Inventing the Future at MIT.* Viking, New York.

Bruner, J. (1986) *Actual Minds, Possible Worlds.* Harvard University Press, Cambridge MA.

Campbell, J. (1989) *Winston Churchill's Afternoon Nap.* Paladin, London.

Fish, S. (1980) *Is there a Text in this Class?* Harvard University Press, Cambridge MA.

Iser, W. (1978) *The Reader in the Text: a Theory of Aesthetic Response.* Johns Hopkins University Press, Baltimore.

Joyce, M. *Afternoon: a Story.* Unpublished software.

Mitchell. W.J.T. (Ed) (1981) *On Narrative.* University of Chicago Press, Chicago.

Sterne, L. (1966) *The Life and Opinions of Tristram Shandy.* Pocket, New York.

4

Narrative Computer Systems: The Dialectics of Emotion and Formalism

Peter Bøgh Andersen
Berit Holmqvist
University of Aarhus

Abstract

This paper describes work done partly under the Venus project and partly within a research programme on Computer Support of Co-operative Design and Communication. The Venus research programme is primarily a pedagogical project motivated by a fundamental conviction that adult education can be more imaginative and creative than is traditionally the case. The aim of the project is to develop an educational approach which emphasises creative and imaginative involvement in the learning process. The project seeks to develop pedagogical tools which will provide the students with images and contexts rather than just words, concepts and fragments.

1. Introduction. The media perspective

One fundamental part of the education at our institute, the Department of Information and Media Science, University of Aarhus, is to look upon computer systems as media (Andersen 1986, Holmqvist 1989, Holmqvist and Andersen 1991). The system designers create a symbolic representation of the world; they can be looked upon as senders of messages and the users as receivers and interpreters of the messages. The media perspective is a fruitful analytical tool to evaluate and design user interfaces. So far we have been occupied with computers as media in this metaphorical way to evaluate administrative systems. Now we want to be more serious about the media perspective and also use it in a constructive way as a real medium like film, television, theatre.

Although there is a great resemblance between other arts and systems design, there is also one fundamental difference; interaction plays an important part in the computer medium whereas it is absent in other arts.

To make our intention clear we have started on a project where we use the computer to create serious interactive fiction. As opposed to other system types e.g. graphical systems, filing systems, or process control systems, we want to define a new class of systems that we call *narrative systems*. The characteristic feature of these systems is that their main purpose is communication, so their functionality is almost the same as the interface. Examples are teaching systems, databases, mail systems, and video games. Our purpose is to find out:

- What kind of techniques are useful for telling a story where interaction is a fundamental part?

- What kind of methods for systems development is optimal?
- And at the same time discover more general narrative techniques that can be used in non-fiction applications like e.g. data bases and teaching systems.

There is no tradition for creating fiction with computers other than the one developed around computer games. However, it is not a computer game we want to create, it is something more like a short story. The attraction of the story should not be based upon the win/loose paradigm of games, but rely on traditional literary techniques for creating excitement and tension.

We are both linguists by profession, but are different in other respects. Much of Beirut's professional life has been concerned with communication in organisations, while Peter has some programming experience. In private, we are an amateur novelist and painter, so we made a division of labour: Berit was to act as a script writer and photographer, while Peter should take care of the artwork and the programming.

Theoretically, we base our work on the European semiotic tradition (Greimas 1966, Bremond 1986, 1970, 1973). We use it not only as a general theoretical background, but also as a practical basis for programming. A detailed account of how this tradition can be adapted to be useful for designing computer systems can be found in a forthcoming book by Andersen.

On the technical side, we had access to a Mac II computer with a colour screen, plus a scanner, and used two main tools: Hypercard, a programming environment (which was later replaced by Supercard), and VideoWorks, a system for making and running cartoon movies. The basic code is written in the Hypertalk (Supertalk) language from where the cartoon system, running on top of Hypercard can be controlled. We hope to exchange or supplement the cartoons with real video.

The work reported in the following falls into two phases: sections 2-7 cover work from January to August 1989. In this period we built the first parts of the story. We concentrated on the visual aspects of the computer, and interaction was not the principal aesthetic ingredient. This phase went very smoothly since we could rely on existing traditions from film and picture aesthetics.

However, when in August we began work on the last part where interaction was the most important means of expression, we simply got stuck. We discovered that this part of the project contained far more practical and theoretical difficulties than we had ever dreamt about, and it took half a year (from August to January 1990) before we had sorted things out so much that we could get going again. Sections 8-9 report work from this period, and mainly address the problems of interaction aesthetics. Section 10 summarises the preceding sections.

2. Idea generating

When you want to explore the computer in a new field like this you need a topic that fascinates you enough not to be boring, and that is difficult enough to be a real challenge. We agreed that eroticism must be it. We knew from the results in other media, where many attempts have been made, that it is very difficult to create something interesting in the field. Either it gets too pornographic to create anything but disgust or too sophisticated to create anything but boredom. We were not convinced that we would be able to create a fascinating computer-based erotic novel, but we were convinced that the subject is a real challenge and also the right challenge within the specific media.

To use a computer for this purpose almost sounds absurd –computers are inhuman and controlled by strict formalism while eroticism is an utterly human phenomenon governed by senses and feelings.

It is true that formalisation often connotes standardisation and inhumanity, but as a matter of fact it can also be taken just to mean *to give form.* That is what we did, because it is what you do in all serious arts like poetry, theatre, film, etc. We want to show that *good formalisms are a prerequisite for creating good computer-based novels,* just as poetry needs good rhythmic patterns, and dance good choreography.

The problem with our subject is that it deals more with inner experiences than outer impressions, is more about what you feel than about what you see. The only real erotic experience you have is your own. It might be interesting for yourself, but how do you visualise it and make it exciting to others? We have to find some general abstract ingredients that can be varied when made concrete. Something general and something specific. At the one hand something that the reader can recognise and on the other hand something that is unknown and surprising.

Well, there is at least one domain that most people have in common. Dreams. You very seldom remember details in your dreams, what you remember is feelings (of fear, joy, stress, happiness, distortion etc.) Here we have our general themes. Another typical ingredient is that the scenario and the actors are taken from bits and pieces of your daily life mixed with more fictive or surrealistic surroundings, like a collage. A typical ingredient in dreams is also that you can to some degree control them yourself. Dreams are for example often interrupted when it is getting to exciting, dangerous or boring. It is as if unconsciously your cultural self interacts with your unknown self. So computer systems and dreams have one important thing in common: the user/dreamer can interact with the program/dream.

First we needed a script.

After having confronted herself with the generality of her own sexual dreams and having it (the generality) confirmed by others, Berit sorted out three themes that should be the base for the story:

- Romance.
- Aggressiveness.
- Everyday life.

She very soon found out that it was no good to start telling the story by verbal means only.

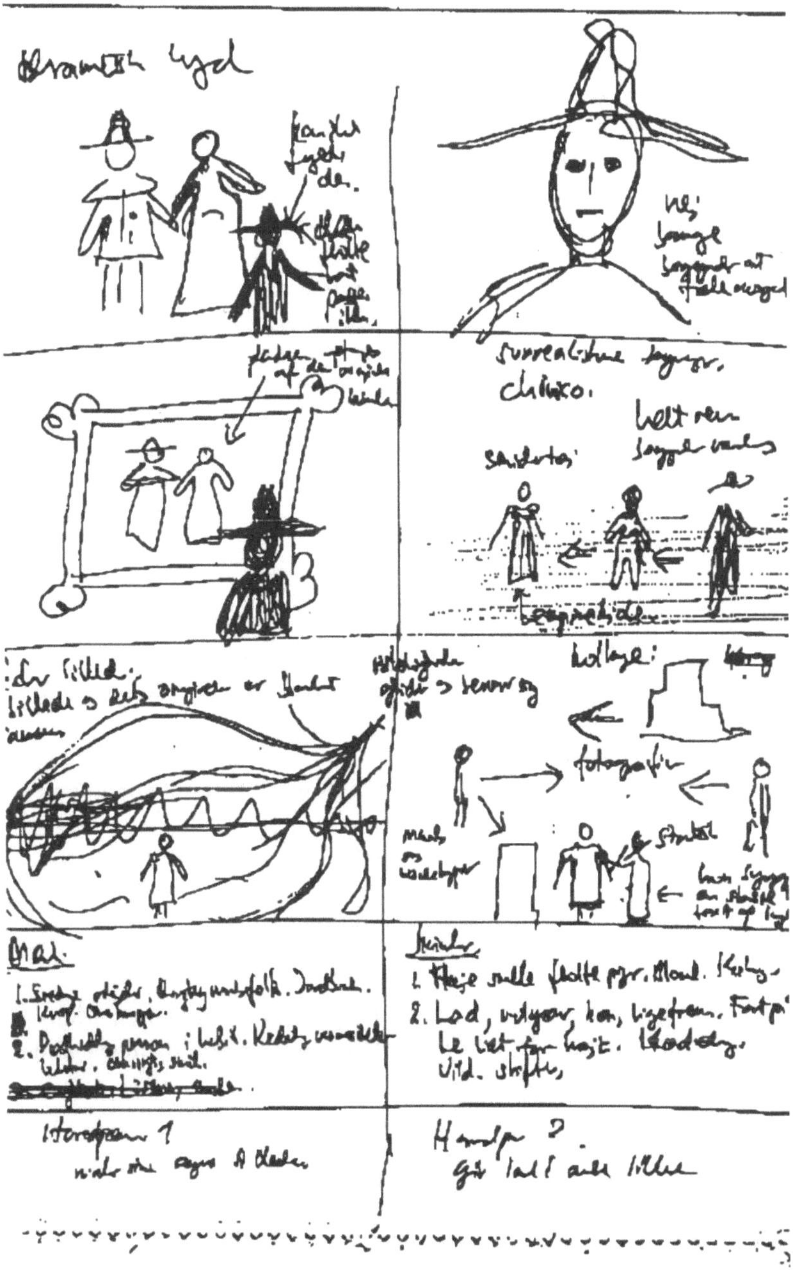

Figure 1. Early sketches.

This partly has to do with the problem of verbalising dreams. Dreams are very seldom verbal, they are pictorial. To describe a dream is as difficult as describing one of Picasso's paintings without looking at it. But it is also due to the fact that the computer is an unexplored medium.

Instead of writing a full script she made short notes that she explained to Peter. It became a close interactive process where Berit talked and Peter made drawings at the same time. It turned out that *verbal and visual epics together created a constructive process.*

Figure 1 shows some of the early sketches many of which were never used. It seems as if the waste in building narrative systems is just as great as in other art forms. The reason is probably that narrative systems must talk to the senses, and sensuous experiences are hard to plan or predict. They must be tried out. The result of this idea generating phase was hundreds of sketches and crazy ideas. Many of them we are not going to use, but it helped us to find out what was workable or not. After many late evenings we had our first script. A story in three acts or themes: romance, aggressiveness and daily life combined with three different surroundings: at the lake, in the bar, and at home in the suburb.

Epic Script

Woman passive	**Woman Active**
She arrives at the lake	She arrives at the lake
She lays down and falls asleep	She lays down but does not fall asleep
The man arrives at the lake	The man arrives at the lake
He stands still close to the woman	He throws his towel and undresses
He undresses	
	He walks out in the water
	He swims and walks ashore
	The woman takes his towel
	They stand still and look at each other for a long time
	They move towards each other
He bends down and kisses the woman on the thigh	The woman takes the towel and dries him
The woman draws up her legs but continues to sleep	
She spreads her legs	With mild force she makes him sit down
He "takes" her	She "takes" him
He dresses and leaves alone	They leave together

Figure 2. Early epic script. The script consists of two possible independent stories.

In short, the story is about a woman who breaks out of her current dismal conditions and starts a journey to find a new life. She seeks a new context. On her travels, she passes through different settings, meets different persons and becomes involved in events she cannot control herself. She wanders around in a world of deceit and stubbornly seeks "true" happiness.

At this time we started to implement small ideas from the first scene. We found out that we had spent a lot of time to tell parallel stories and realised that we were ending up with a slide show with very few interactive possibilities. See Figure 2.

However, our purpose was to make an interactive story, not a slide-show. Our epic script was too boring from an interactive perspective, and giving it a more exciting interaction can not be just a question of allowing the users to choose one or the other fixed sequence of events – they should be able to influence the sequence of events themselves. This means that the canned narrative syntagmas must be much smaller than that above and their possibilities of combination much richer. The events must interact with each other so that a choice in an earlier event has consequences for later events.

We also soon found out that direct manipulation was tricky. In some video games the user identifies with the hero. The user acts in the first person (Hutchins *et al.* 1986, Laurel 1986) and manipulates the other persons in the game as objects. In an erotic narrative this borders on bad taste; to escape the problem, we invented a helping prop that could carry the role of an interactive sign. We decided to use the towel in the script, and our epic script was turned into an interactive script that looked like Figure 3.

The two scripts show two point of interest: the first one is that *scripting and programming should be done in cycles* so that they can influence each other, not in separate phases. The process cannot be broken down into two phases in which the contents are determined in the first one, and the form added on in the second one. Form and content are interdependent, a new form giving rise to new contents. The second point concerns the notion of a "text". A computer-based novel should neither be seen as a single text, nor as a collection of single texts. Rather, its *main message lies between the texts.* A computer-based novel is not a textual but an inter-textual object. The individual runs of the program should give rise to parallelisms and contrasts.

The two scripts exhibits many cohering segments that are related by rhetorical figures. There are parallelism *(She arrives at the lake)*, antithesis *(she is awake* Vs *she sleeps)* and partial chasms *(she makes him sit down* Vs *he kisses her, she "takes" him* Vs *he "takes" her)*. The latter figures are related to the general theme of the scene: active Vs passive.

But –as said before –we got stuck, and concentrated our efforts about the visual aspects.

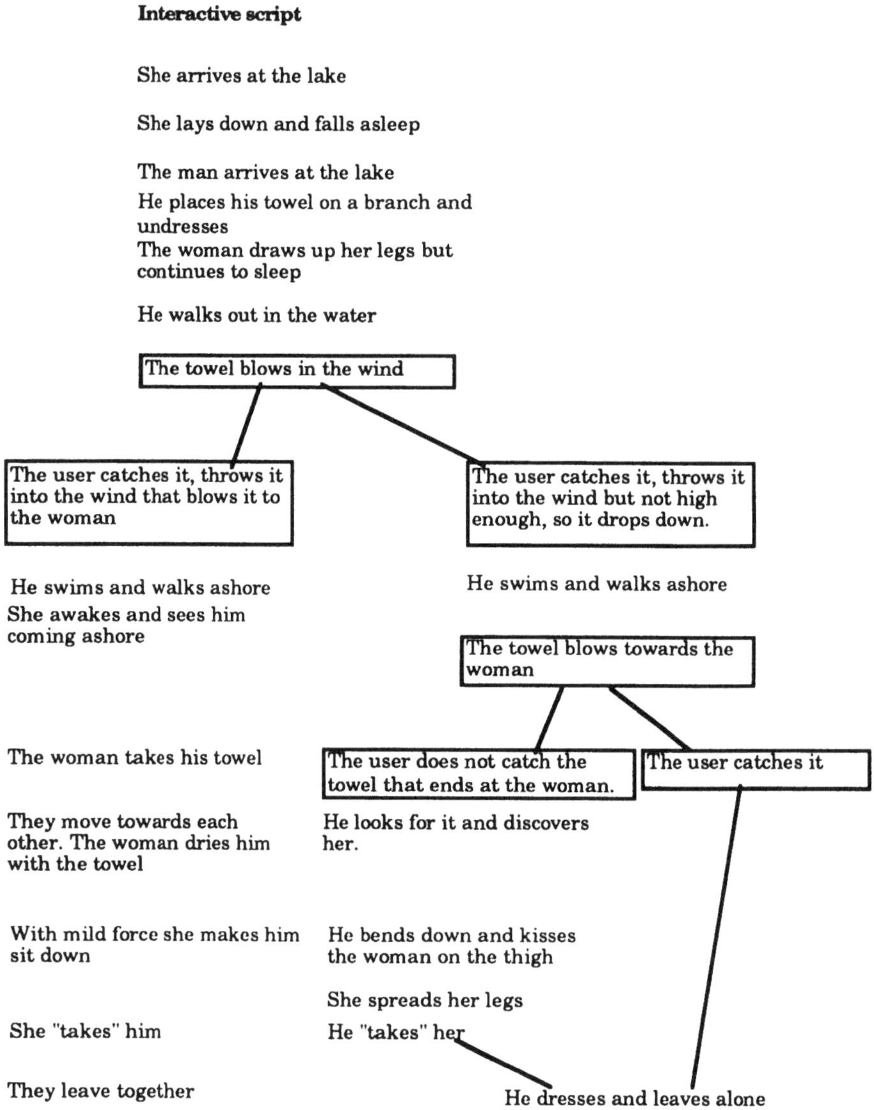

Figure 3. Early interactive script. The script has three main outcomes that depend upon the reader's actions.

3. Pictures

The story should be based on drawings because verbal interaction would create a distance we wanted to avoid.

First we found out that it was no good to draw directly on the screen. Peter started to make series of paper drawings that were subsequently scanned into the system. The drawings had to be very simple. And they demanded reparation on the screen anyway, because the lines became to thick. Figure 4 shows the scanned-in raw version together with the corrected version. It is no coincidence that the original drawing is naked and the final one dressed. Clothes are too irregular with too many shadows and delicate lines to give a good picture when scanned. The details are merged into one black morass, and you completely loose the feeling of a body. Naked bodies are simpler and more regular, and can later be dressed while still keeping the feeling of the body intact.

Just drawings were not enough. By mixing photos with drawings we got an interesting contrast of texture: the simple and clean drawings Vs the irregular photos. We started to use photos as background for the drawings. The contrast creates a desired distance, because pure naturalism does not suite the medium. The medium can never achieve the quality of a film or a photograph, and trying to get it only emphasises the shortcomings of the medium in this respect, and gives slightly ridiculous results.

As we already had made up our minds about the scenes, we had to search for suitable backgrounds in real life, and when we could not find our motives, we constructed them by manipulating photos.

We needed for example a tree and a bush, but could not find any with the right distance between them. Therefore, the picture shown in Figure 5 is constructed from two separate pictures of tree and bush.

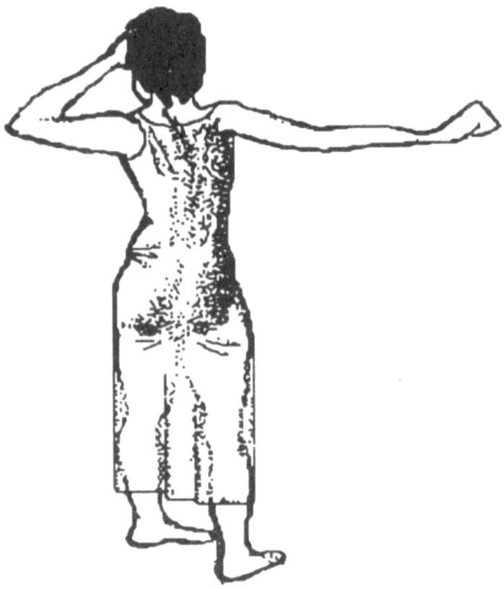

Figure 4. Lines drawings. The upper figure is the scanned-in raw version, the bottom figure a 'patched-up version.'

Figure 5. Screen picture produced by manipulating two separate photos.

The picture shown in Figure 6 is from the same scene as the script and shows the effect of having drawn persons and photographs as background. The background is a photo and its irregular texture is clearly perceived when contrasted to the towel on the branch, and woman in the foreground.

The nice effects produced by these simple experiments gave us the idea that the computer should be seen as a *collage medium*. One the one hand, a scanned-in version of drawings or photos can never compete with the originals, since resolution and control of colours are insufficient. But on the other hand, we have got the opportunity to put all kinds of pictures into one medium where they are represented in exactly the same way, namely as pixels on a screen, and exploit the *contrast between them* as an aesthetic effect.

Figure 6. Collage of photos and line drawings.

We looked for other graphical possibilities, and began to add paintings from art books (see Figure 7) and experimenting with variations of the drawing/photo opposition. What would happen if we reversed the situation, so that the background is a drawing while the persons are photos?

The Apple Scanner we used offered some variations of scanning mode. Figure 8 is done with "halftones", while Figure 9 use "line art". The latter mode can sometimes produce very nice effects that resembles photo graphics, as the next picture shows.

We conclude this section with a real *tour-de-force* of collage technique. Figure 10, which is a sketch of a background, consists of five layers of pictures. At the bottom is a mediaeval castle in halftone. To create a hazy impression we placed a transparent light grey graphic on top of it. In the left corner at the bottom is then added a picture of dancers, but since they are not the main characters they are "backgrounded" with a grey filter. On the very top of the layers are then placed the main characters: two halftone photos and one piece of chalk painting in line art!

Figure 7. The beginning of the story. The protagonist is imprisoned in the frame of a painting, which itself is enclosed in a computer window.

4. Scenes

The scene of the computer medium is the screen, and nowadays a computer-based scene is often built of *windows*. In "normal" programs, windows are used for the following purposes:

- One *window* displays one object, two windows different objects. A word processor can for example display two texts in two different windows.
- Windows can contain different *panes*, each showing different parts of the same object. If a window shows a text, its panes can display different parts of the text.

- Windows can also be used to show the same object from different perspectives. Then they are said to convey different *views*. Microsoft Word, which we use to write this paper, can present the same text in an *outline view* where only headings are shown, in a *page view* where the page is displayed in natural size, in a *print preview*, where one or two pages are shown in small size, and the normal view used during writing.

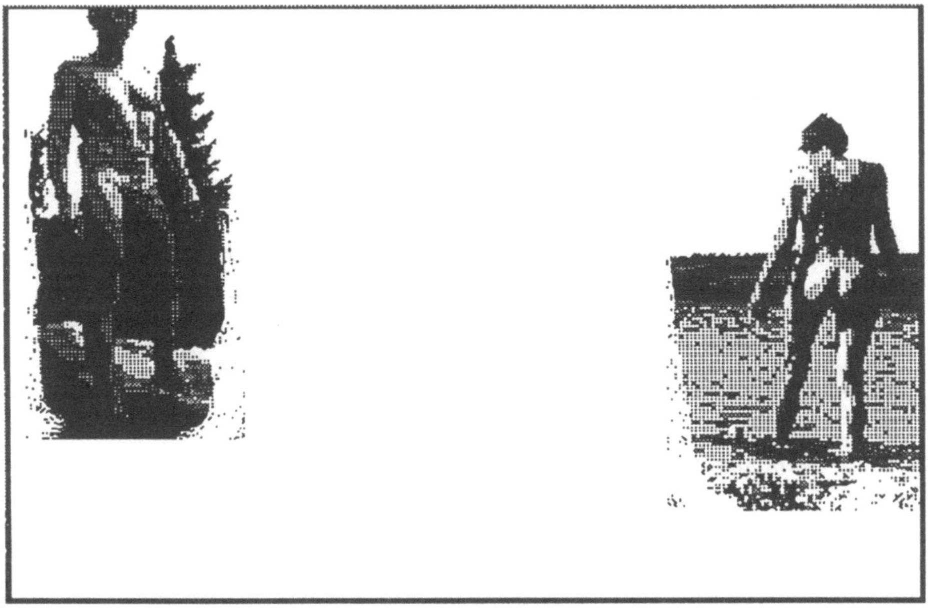

Figure 8. Half-tone photos.

In our story we experiment both with panes and views. The protagonist moves through a landscape, from a wood to a beach. We cannot show this walk naturalistically, so we start by having the wood in one pane, the protagonist moves out of the pane, and appears in the next pane that displays the beach (Figure 11). It gives the reader the illusion that he watches a larger landscape through the panes of the screen.

Multiple windows must be used with care in order not to confuse the reader. We have to show where the main action takes place, so that the reader can focus his attention. In the theatre this is done by means of light, and we have also used that method in our story. Those panes whose action is over are covered by a grey transparent mask, while the action panes are white. Supercard offers good facilities for this.

The mask is merely a graphical object whose pattern is grey and whose ink is "or". Figure 11 shows the effect. The action in the wood is over, and the wood-window is therefore darkened by a grey mask.

Figure 9. "Line art" photos. Notice the similarity to photo graphics.

Figure 11 also shows another use of light, namely as a means to create a specific tone or atmosphere. The tone of the beach-window is intended to be dream-like and poetic, and we have tried to achieve this by placing a light grey mask with a "Xor" ink over the background.

Panes can also be used to present simultaneous actions. The next example, shown in Figure 12, presents two parts of the same scene, one in which the male character is drying himself after a swim, and another in which the female character is looking for at place to sleep.

In the last part we plan to work with two different views, expressed in different windows that narrate exactly the same course of events, but seen from two different perspectives.

Love poems (and our story is about love) often uses metaphors. The loved one is compared with everything from a red rose to the daily nutritious bread. But such metaphors only work if we simultaneously think of the real meaning, so that a tension between the two descriptions arise. On the screen this can be done by having the metaphor (e.g. the rose) in one view, while the real person acts in the other, and defining a mapping between events in the two windows. The traditional arsenal of similes has mappings like "a dew drop on the rose -> a tear in a woman's eye", "the rose withers -> the woman pines away", etc., etc.

Figure 10. Collage picture. Sketch to decoration composed of mediaeval pictures, chalk paintings, and photos. The scanning modes are line-art and halftone, and two transparent rasters are used to background pictorial elements.

All this is about the contents we express *in* the windows. However, we have also sometimes attributed meaning to the very form of the window. In the beginning, the protagonist is placed as a part of Degas' painting "Absinth" (see. Figure 7). She wishes to get out of the melancholic picture, to break its confining framework (see Figure 13). And she does move out of the painting, but in order to emphasise her quest for freedom, we remove the borders around the computer window! This makes a strong effect on experienced Macintosh users who are used to windows with frames and do not expect them to go away.

5. Movement

Our system is mainly a picture story, and we use static as well as animated pictures. Animation is important: the actor must be able to raise her hands in joy, to fall on her knees or to bend her head in sorrow – and all other postures that are used by actors on the stage. Therefore it must be possible to define different postures of the actor.

If the actor is small and the movement simple, real animation like a cartoon can be achieved. In our story, we use a butterfly as a narrator that advances the plot, and it was animated as a conventional cartoon. We used seven pictures which gave a charming impression of a flittering butterfly.

Figure 11. Two panes show different parts of the same landscape and thereby creates the illusion of a space larger than the limited area of the screen. The action in the wood to the right is over, and we should only be reminded of it while the main action occurs on the beech. Therefore the wood is covered with a grey mask.

The nicest result we got by running VideoWorks on top of Supercard (see Figure 14) but this technique has its limitations. When the graphics become larger, the differences between the postures grow, and the effect is a jerky kind of movement known from video-games. In addition, the screen begins to blink disagreeably, which is a disaster if you want to create a poetic atmosphere. In addition, this technique is very time-consuming: if more complicated movements than a flittering butterfly are required, a lot of drawings must be made. To make the figures in Figure 8 bend down in a realistic manner, would require several days' work.

So we looked around for other and easier ways of doing it. Inspired by Will Eisner's excellent book on cartoon drawing (Eisner 1986) we found that often only a few distinctive postures are necessary to tell a complicated story. If you want to say that a person sits down, it is enough to draw him standing and then sitting –that is, provided the drawings are skillfully done.

In Supercard it is easy to make that kind of pseudo-animation (Figure 15). The postures are represented as graphics on a card. At any time, only one graphic is visible, the others are hidden. Animation can be done by hiding and showing different graphics. Spasmodic movements and blinking can be avoided by using two identical cards, of which one is invisible. When the actor is to assume a new posture, the new posture is first made visible on the invisible card, which is then shown employing the visual effect "dissolve".

Figure 12. Two panes showing concurrent actions. The male character comes up from a swim, while the female character lies down to sleep.

The result is a poetic, dreamlike "fading" from one posture to another giving a tone we wanted in our story.

Although the reader may think that this is really unnecessary details, it is not. If you work seriously with communication and aesthetics, it is important to be able to find the right expression for the contents you want to convey.

6. The global narrative structure: the actant role of the reader

An important part in systems development is to write a general "logical" system description that describes the general structure of the system without going into details. For "normal" systems development, description techniques like data flows and system models exist (DeMarco 1978, Jackson 1983), but they are not suitable for narrative systems, since the system structure of a narrative system is identical to its global narrative structure; a system description for narrative systems should capture the general structure of the narrative. During the last decades, semi-formal models of narratives have been developed within semiotics and literary analysis (Propp 1958, Greimas 1966), and these models seem to be good candidates for system description tools for narrative systems.

In Figure 16 we show how to use the classical actant model of Propp and Greimas.

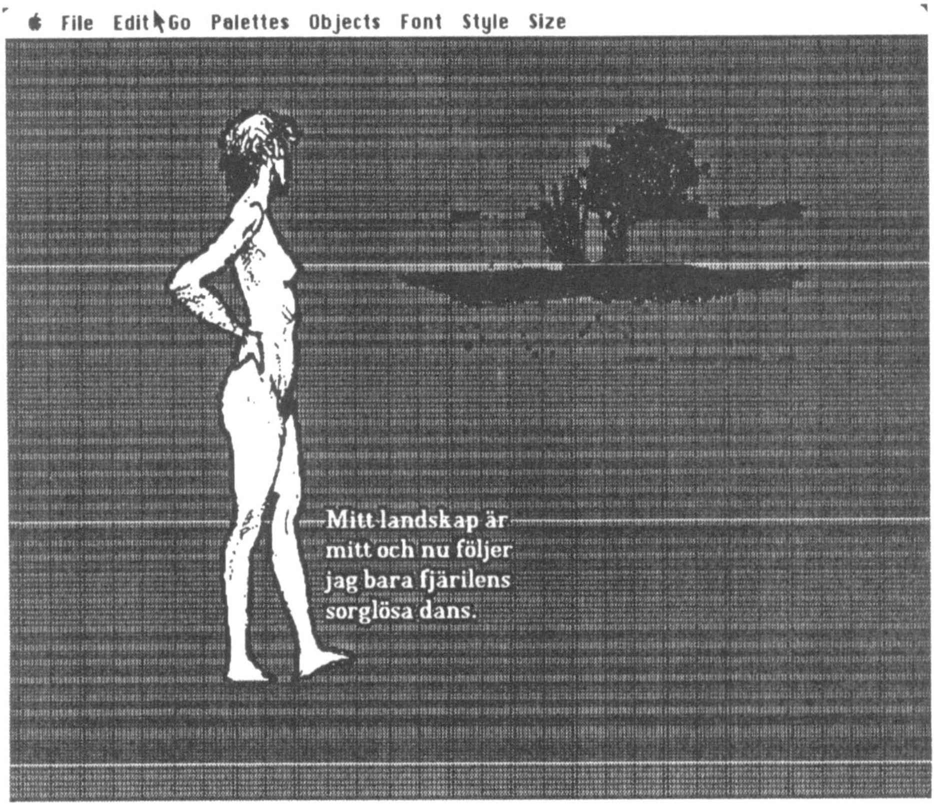

Figure. 13. Aesthetic usage of the window frame. The protagonist has literally "broken the frame" of the window. The intended content is freedom, but also lack of belonging.

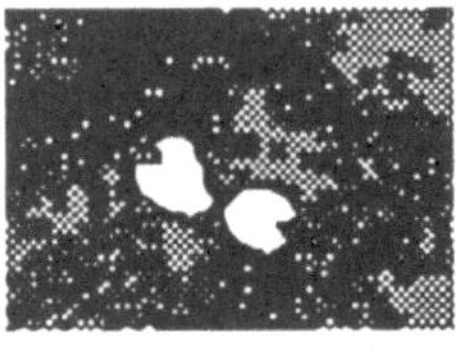

Figure 14. Video Works movie run on top of Supercard. Pictures of this size can produce nice animation.

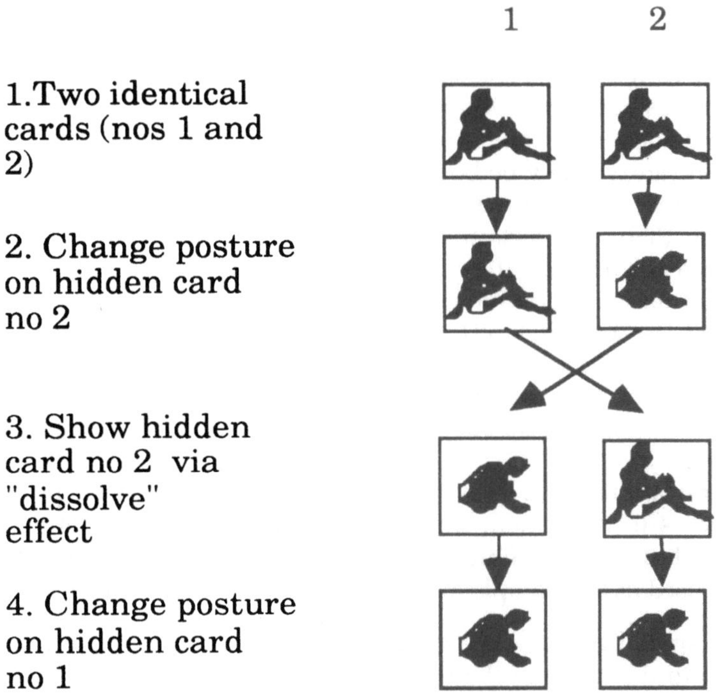

Figure 15. "Soft" fading animation of large graphical objects. Two identical cards are used, of which only one is visible. 1: Start. We see only card 1. 2: Hide old posture and show new one on hidden card (2). 3: Show hidden card 2 with dissolve effect. 4: Hide old posture and show new one on hidden card 1.

In the diagram below, we have six actants: the subject (the hero) that desires something (the object, e.g. the princess), which someone (the giver, e.g. the king) can give him. He meets animals that test and later help him (helpers) in his fight against the evil troll (antagonist) that tries to prevent him from rescuing the princess. This model serves as a very abstract description of a fairy tale.

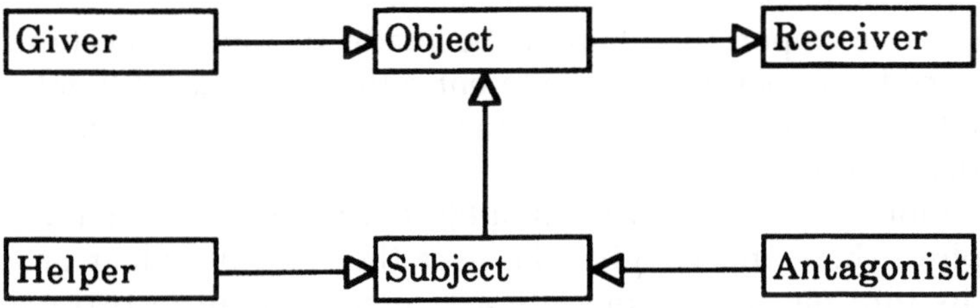

Figure 16. The actant model.

However, much has to be specified before we reach the level of detail of the actual text. We have to specify which actual actors fill the actant roles in the narrative, e.g. that the giver actant is filled with the "king" and the helper actant with a bird, a snake, and a pig.

Each actant slot can be filled by several actors (both bird, snake and pig are Helpers), and conversely, one actor can fill more than one actant slot (e.g. the youngest son can typically be both subject (the actor that desires the princess) and receiver (the actor that marries the princess).

Although there is a certain correspondence between the actants and the actual grammatical roles they play in the text (the subject becomes the grammatical subject in certain types of sentences, e.g. *The youngest son (subject) slays the troll, the king (subject) gives his daughter (object) to the youngest son (receiver),* the actants can fill other grammatical roles than those naturally associated to them; thus, although the princess fills the object actant, she can certainly be the grammatical subject of many sentences *(The princess eats the poisoned apple).*

There are various ways to use the actant model as a basis for programming. One method is to implement the actants as object classes, defined by their action possibilities. The definition of the action sphere of the helper in Propp 1958 can be used as an example of what such possibilities will look like.

- The spatial transference of the hero (e.g. a flying horse can bring the hero to the castle of the troll).
- Liquidation of misfortune or lack .
- Rescue from pursuit (e.g. a bird can divert the attention of the witch pursuing the hero and the princess).
- The solution of difficult tasks.
- Transfiguration of the hero.

The actors, e.g. the actual manifestations of the actants, can then be implemented as object instances.

Another way, which we employ, is to implement the six actants as global variables. The particular events (like *a bird can divert the attention of the witch pursuing the hero and the princess*) are characterised by sets of event-specific roles, e.g. pursuer, pursued, and diverter. The rules that fill these specific roles refer to the global actants. For example, there may be a rule saying that the antagonist fills the role of the pursuer, the subject and object the role of the pursued, and the helper the role of the diverter.

There is one important point to be made in this connection. In non-interactive media, it makes no sense to enter the reader directly into the actant schema, but since our narrative is interactive, we have to assign an actant role to the reader as well.

As mentioned before, the role of subject will not do, since this will create pornography. Therefore, we give the user the roles of helper or antagonist, which in its turn means that the interactive actions fall in two main classes: *helping* somebody to do something or *preventing* it.

7. Interactive narrative segments

There is a long way from the actant structure to the actual text. One decision that has to be taken concerns the structure of the narrative segments. A narrative segment can be defined as the smallest segment with a clear beginning and ending and a separate narrative function. Bremond (1966, 1970, 1973) investigated French folk tales and suggested the following schema as a possible narrative segment (Figure 17):

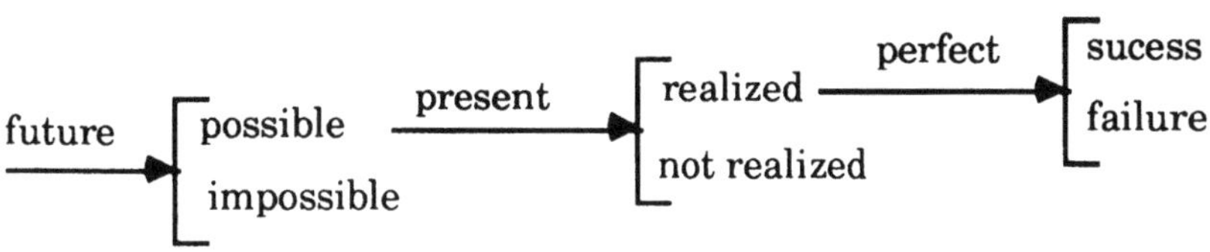

Figure 17. Basic narrative segment.

First the event is presented in the future, as possible or impossible (a theft planned, a quest is made possible). If it is possible, then it can either be realised or not realised (the thief starts his evil actions or the hero embarks on the quest), and if realised, it can either succeed or fail (the goods are stolen, the destination of the quest is reached).

In our interpretation, all these sub-segments must be manifested, viz. they are parts of actual texts or pictures. The possible misfortune must be signalled by phrases like Snoopy's "It was a dark and stormy night" or by pictures creating a ominous atmosphere.

Also they are not bound to the textual medium, but can be found in film (in American jargon, the future segments are called *set-up's* and the perfect segments *pay-off's)*.

Since our aim is to create interactive narrative segments, it is very convenient that Bremond formulated his segments in terms of *choices*. The reader can then decide whether the future possibility should turn into present reality, and he/she can influence the success of the failure of the action. The difference between ordinary texts and interactive stories is that these choices are latent in texts, but actual possibilities in interactive stories.

8. A machine for generating interpretations

This is so far we got in the first phase of our project. In the next phase we wanted to promote interaction to become the primary ingredient of the story, and we had some general ideas of how it could be done within our framework, cf. the preceding section on Bremond's work. But when we began to do concrete work it turned out to be all wrong.

One problem mentioned in section 2 was that "paper contaminates". It is very difficult to write an inherently interactive story on a piece of paper that is inherently non-interactive. We needed a tool that enabled us to work directly with interaction in the authoring process, and began to construct a story editor called "The Director's Workbench". The descriptions in the following sections are taken from this tool.

Another problem was that we were stuck with an interface whose value as a general story aesthetics is doubtful. The basic concepts in the Macintosh interface is the *hand* (cursor) that can take *tools* (palettes, menus) and apply these tools to work *material* (the main window representing text or drawing paper). But it is really difficult to tell a love story by means of a hand, a set of tools, and some working material!

The solution of the problem consists in recognising that behind a particular interface type (e.g. a direct manipulation interface) lies a specific perspective on the roles of user/reader and designer/author and their relation to the interface. The first and most important choice to make is the choice of perspective, each perspective giving rise to particular type of interaction. We chose to use three different perspectives on interaction in the story, each motivated by narration:

- *The tool perspective* displays interaction as consisting of the user's hand, some tools, and some working material. The user acts *on* the story, not *in* it.
- *The dialogue perspective* displays interaction as a conversation or other social event, in which the user takes part. The user now acts *in* the story, not *on* it.
- *The mass media perspective* compares the computer to a film or video. The user has very few interaction possibilities (just starting and stopping the film), and his role is that of a *viewer*.

These roles are related to the composition of the story in the following way.

The interactive story itself is seen as a "machine for generating interpretations"[1] —a story machine. The reader's motivation for running the machine at all[2] is to get exciting or moving stories out of it. However, he does not get this for free. He is required to involve himself in the story in a particular manner. For example, if he is courageous and inventive, the machine may accelerate into third gear and will produce exciting stories, whereas if he acts too cowardly, the machine will slow down into first gear. Or maybe the opposite will happen –there are rich opportunities for the traditional hide-and-seek play between author and reader.

In this way we keep the motivation of the video-games – only the reader is not rewarded by accumulating scores but by partaking in exciting stories. The

[1] The phrase is borrowed from Umberto Eco who used it about books

[2] Motivation can be quite a problem in interactive stories. In the first serious hypertext fiction, Afternoon, by Michael Joyce, the individual pieces are very well written, but I, and others, have difficulty with the lack of coherence between the pieces. One misses the motivation created by authors in normal text and for this reason stop reading after a short while.

purpose of the reader is not longer to reach a certain final "winning" state, but rather to keep the story engine running.

In the story we are currently creating, there are 3 'gears', each corresponding to a particular perspective.

1. The *editor* gear is based on the tool perspective and the interaction style is normal Macintosh interaction with a few finesses. The role of the reader is somewhat like an author composing the story. The material he works on is not fictive persons, but pieces of paper displaying persons he can move around on the scene and whose postures he can change. These activities are surveyed by a battery of *connectors* (often called *demons* in the literature), program modules that all the time check for a particular state, and perform some action when it is fulfilled. If the "editor" succeeds in composing a scene with meaningful groups of actors in meaningful postures, the machine goes into second gear. For example, a man and a woman are placed at some distance with their bodies turned away from each other. If the editor moves the woman to the man, and makes them face each other, a connector notices this and starts an episode.

2. The *participant* gear is based on the dialogue perspective. The reader is a part of the fiction, and his action possibilities are equal to those of the other actors. He no longer interacts with cardboard drawings, but with (fictive) persons. The user's role is that of a *co-actor.*

   The interaction is controlled by pre-programmed events, e.g. a group of people dancing on the screen and the female protagonist trying to get into the dance. Conceptually, this gear differs fundamentally from normal Macintosh interaction. There is no hand, no tools and no materials on the screen. Instead, there are actors that are attracted and repulsed by each other. Formally, this is done by defining *vectors* between them. A vector goes from a source to a destination, has a certain direction (positive, negative), force, and range. If the destination is within the range, the source is moved a certain distance to or from the destination, depending upon the direction and force of the vector. The reader himself is just another actor, and can only influence the event indirectly, through the way the other actors are attracted to or repelled from him, that is: through the network of vectors he is a part of. We shall say a little more about this type of interaction in the next section.

   There are also connectors on the lookout in second gear; one type of connector will simply start another second gear event, if the current one is ended. For example, we can have a pursuit (programmed very simply by means of a positive vector from pursuer to pursued, and a negative vector from pursued to pursuer) that results in the pursued being caught. A connector notices this, and may start a rape event.

   Other connectors may slow the story engine down to first gear, and still others may bring it into third gear.

3. The *Spectator* gear is based on the mass media perspective. The user can in principle only view the event. Technically, the spectator gear is realised by a "slide show" of pictures shown after each other, or by means of a real time video clip being played on the screen. Aesthetically, the spectator gear symbolises the "point of no return", the climax, the literary consequences of the choices made previously by the reader. We plan to use it for the emotional and dramatic parts of the story, because they seem easier to do on real video than by means of graphics on the computer screen.

The power of reader and author are inversely related and change in the three gears. In the editor gear, the reader can do many things, and the author's influence is small, whereas in the third gear the author has full control over the video clips and the reader is reduced to spectator. In the middle gear there is a balance of power: the reader still has a set of action possibilities but they are constrained within the fictive universe, and the author exercises some power by designing the vector structure. However, if the structure is just a little complicated, it is difficult for the author to predict all causes of events.

9. Second gear: interaction in a space of vectors

To us the second gear interaction is the most interesting because it represent a break with conventional interaction styles.

The screen consists of actors, props, and vectors between them. Figure 18 shows a situation where the woman is repelled by the man in the black sweater who is attracted to the woman. The length of the arrows symbolises the force of the vector, and the circles the range of them. Thus, the negative vector from the woman towards the black man is not active at the moment, since the man is outside its range, while the man's attraction towards the lady is operative, because she is inside the range of the vector. The system works by moving the persons stepwise according to the vectors that influence them, so the man will slowly move towards the woman, while the woman will not do anything. However, when the man comes inside the small circle, the woman's negative vector begins to work ("she discovers him"), and she backs away while he follows.

The reason why we chose this method of interaction is simply that many good stories are about emotional relations between people, so the system should provide good means of expression for representing this. Ambiguous feelings are a particularly good basis for interesting stories, for example a woman being attracted and repelled by the same man.

There are two different ways of visualising the vectors. The system can display the sum of the vectors, or it can move a person along all active vectors, showing each influence separately. The latter is useful for displaying contradictory feelings. For example, if the woman is attracted and repelled by the same force, displaying the vector sum will not result in any movement on the screen, and thus communicate nothing to the reader, while displaying the woman walking to and from the man will visualise her conflicting feelings.

The system is programmed in object-oriented style and uses message-passing as the main control mechanism. Figure 19 shows a simplified diagram of the second gear. There is a controlling event that activates the actors of the scene. Each activation makes the actor send messages to the scene object requesting it to record the changes the actor must undergo due to the vectors working on it. A change consists of a change of location and/or of posture. Note that the (invisible) cursor is also an actor, and can influence actors via vectors; thus, actors can be attracted or repelled by the cursor[3]. When all actors have had their say, the scene object begins to display the accumulated changes. It first displays the first change of all actors, then the next, etc., and stops when there are no more changes to display. By queuing changes in this way, the system can display concurrent movements of many actors.

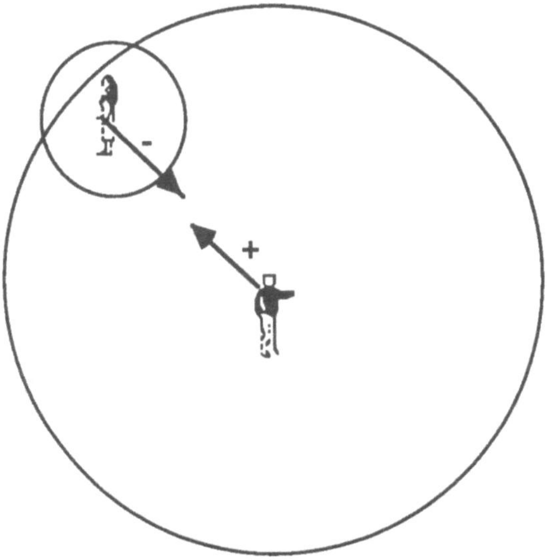

Figure 18. Vector based interaction.

As shown in the diagram, an actor can also send messages to another actor, requesting a particular position or posture of the other. For example, a fight can be implemented by having the combatants sending kick-messages to each other. The receiver of the kick-message will then decide if he was in fact hit, and if

[3] In fact, ordinary Macintosh interaction can be described as a special instance of vector interaction. For example, the cursor is an actor with a strong positive vector towards the mouse, and dragging can be described in this way: when the mouse is clicked, the cursor object receives a *mousedown* message, and creates a strong positive vector from icon to cursor. The range of the vector is the contour of the icon. so dragging only occurs when the cursor is inside the icon.

this is the case, will request the scene to display him in prostrate posture.

It is possible to build a structure with a controlling event that activates more than one sub-events which in their turn activate the participating actors (Figure 20).

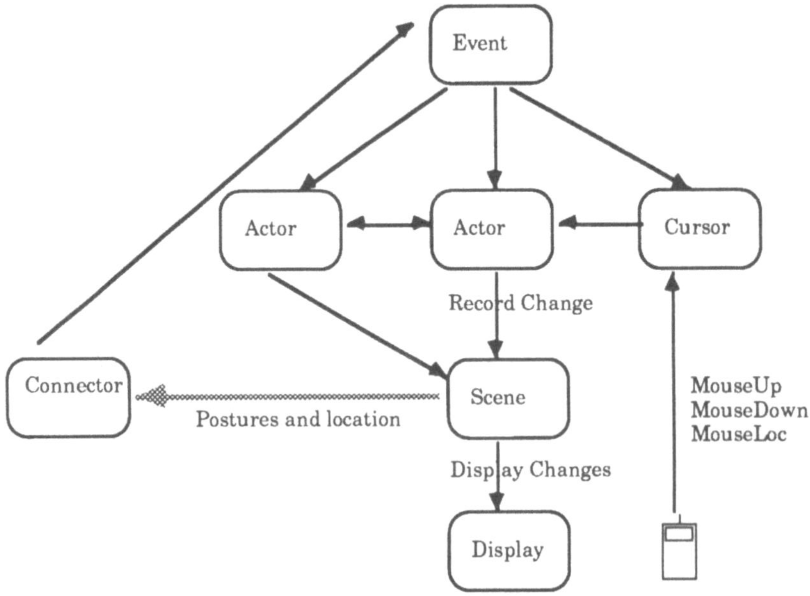

Figure 19. General message-passing structure in the Director's Workbench.

In this way, the behaviour of the actors can be controlled simultaneously by several events. This is useful for generating ambiguous episodes. Maybe one event generates a dance, while another event wants the actors to be courting. The result is a display sequence that is both a dance and a courting. Stories based on the theme of deception can be composed in this way: one event controls the open behaviour, another one the hidden plan of the actor.

In each cycle, a battery of *connectors* inspect the location and postures of the actors, and in certain situations ends the current event and begins a new one.

This concludes the report of the work we have done so far. In the next half year we will collaborate with a dramaturg and a cinema researcher to produce a handful of video clips with real actors; the clips are going to be used in the third gear of our story. We hope to finish a workable prototype of the story during the summer.

So far, the project has been great experience; we feel that we are among the midwives of a new art form. Our story will not itself be great art but hopefully we can make a product that is so good that people that are more gifted than we are will say: "Is this really possible? Well, we can do better!". Our purpose is to help develop an aesthetics of narrative systems, and the last section summarises our current ideas about aesthetics and working methods.

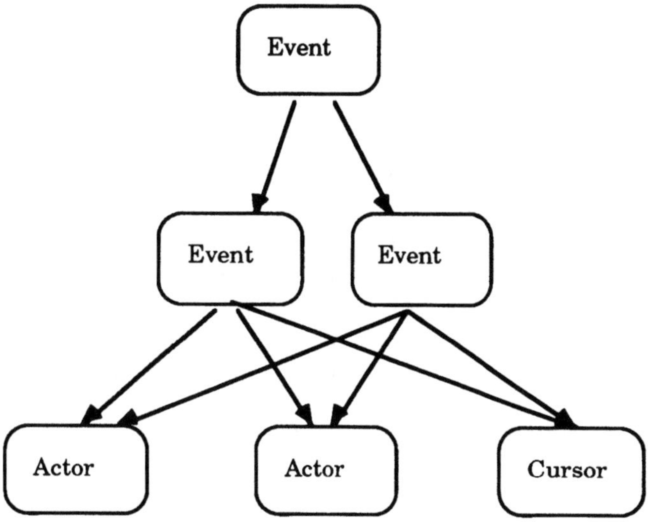

Figure 20. Ambiguous performances. Actors are controller by several events.

10. In search for aesthetic norms for narrative systems

Which kinds of guidelines can be set up for constructing narrative systems? Before we propose some tentative answers, we would like to emphasise that such guidelines will not be psychological laws but aesthetic norms. They are not about the facts of the world, but about how things ought to be done, although of course they should be based upon true assumptions about relevant facts. All the norms we propose rest upon one general norm: exploit the specific properties and opportunities of the medium aesthetically.

Norm: *Formalism* should be the meter and choreography of narrative systems.

Relevant fact: computer systems must be controlled by formalisms. Computer systems must by necessity be controlled by a program that completely describes the data processing. In this sense the medium is formalistic, but this is not unique for computer systems. In contrary, formalism is a necessary ingredient in many art forms. Poetry has its meter, dance its choreography, and music its harmonic schemas and rhythm. Art does not consist in avoiding formalism, but in utilising it as a means of expression.

Norm: The medium should be conceived as a *collage* medium, and naturalism should probably not be attempted.

Relevant fact: it is possible to enter bits and pieces from many different media into a computer, combine them, and present them in a uniform way, namely as pixels on the screen. The computer replicas will normally be of poorer quality than the original, but the new opportunities to juxtapose textual and pictorial material from different genres and historical epochs give exciting aesthetic possibilities that were not present in the originals.

Norm: *Interaction* should be a basic means of expression in narrative systems.

Relevant fact: the computer is the only medium where interaction is possible. Interaction must be a basic ingredient in the composition, and this turned out to be the hardest thing to do for us. During the work we were amazed of how strongly traditional media still influenced our imagination. If we did not take care, we automatically ended up producing an advanced slide-show, where interaction only means that you yourself decide the sequence in which you see the pictures. If nothing else can be achieved, we prefer a real slide-show. It is larger, has better colours, and is not so expensive.

Norm: Narrative systems should be conceived as *inter-textual,* not textual, media.

Relevant fact: if the rhetorical cohesions between the individual runs is not exploited, one could just as well write a normal story, save the expensive equipment, and get a better result.

10.1. System development methods

To do a computer-based novel is system development, and in systems development we normally need a requirement specification. However, we had no such thing, and would have felt it completely unnatural to make one. Who would like to see a movie or read a book based on a requirement specification? On thing is sure: they would be boring to death.

The reason is that the purpose is communication of feelings, atmosphere and information. It is impossible to judge if the purpose is achieved –if the message gets through – by reading a description of the media product. You have to see the thing itself, and the only way forward is trial and error[4] .

You start with an idea, try to realise a little piece, look at the result, discard or accept it, revise the original idea, and so on.

Our experiences of system development can be summarised in three points:

- Make lots of sketches, see to it that you have a large collection of texts and pictures at your disposal, and be prepared to throw away 90% of it.
- Shift between script writing, picture- and text-production *and* coding.
- Avoid copying traditional media, but exploit the computer's own possibilities.

This is not a general system development method. There are lots of system

[4] On second thoughts we realize that film-making is in fact based on detailed paper descriptions: manuscripts, storyboards, shotlists. It is possible that our recommendations simply reflect the fact that we are working with a new medium where lack of experience makes it very difficult to preview the effects on the screen of a written manuscript.

types where this method is neither possible, sensible nor necessary. But whenever the product is a media product that intends to convey a specific message, we believe it to be unavoidable.

11. References

Andersen, P. B. (1986) Semiotics and informatics: computers as media. In: P. Ingwersen, L. Kajberg and A. Mark Peitersen (Eds) *Information technology and Information use.* Taylor Graham, London.

Andersen, P. B. *A Theory of Computer Semiotics. Semiotic Approaches to Construction and Assessment of Computer Systems.* Cambridge University Press, Cambridge. Forthcoming.

Bremond, C. (1986) La logique des possibles narratifs. *Communications,* 8.

Bremond, C. (1970) Morphology of the French folktale. *Semiotica,* 2.

Bremond, C. (1973) *Logique du récit.* Éditions du Seuil,Paris.

DeMarco, T. (1978) *Structured Analysis and System Specification.* Yourdon Inc,, New York.

Eisner, W. (1986) *Comics and Sequential Art.*

Greimas, A.J. (1966) *Sémantique Structurale. Du sens. Essais sémiotique.* Éditions du Seuil, Paris.

Holmqvist, B. (1989). Work language and perspective.*Scandinavian Journal of Information Systems,* 1.

Holmqvist, B. and Andersen, P.B. (1991): Language, perspective, and design. In L. Kyng & Greenbaum (Ed): *Design at Work.* Erlbaum, Hillsdale, NJ.

Hutchins, E. L., Holland, J. D. and Norman, D. A. (1986) Direct Manipulation Interfaces, In D.A. Norman & S.W.Draper (Eds). *User Centered System Design.* Erlbaum, Hillsdale, NJ.

Jackson, M. A. (1983) *System Development.* Prentice Hall, Englewood Cliffs, NJ.

Laurel, B. K. (1986) Interface as mimesis. In D.A. Norman & **S.W.Draper (Eds).** *User Centered System Design.* Erlbaum, Hillsdale, NJ.

Propp, V. (1958) *Morphology of the Folktale.* University of Texas Press, Austin and London (English translation. Quoted from the the paperback edition 1975).

5

A Language-Sensitive Text Editor for Dutch

Gerard Kempen
Theo Vosse
University of Nijmegen

Abstract

Modern word processors begin to offer a range of facilities for spelling, grammar and style checking in English. For the Dutch language hardly anything is available as yet. Many commercial word processing packages do include a hyphenation routine and a lexicon-based spelling checker but the practical usefulness of these tools is limited due to certain properties of Dutch orthography, as we will explain below. In this chapter we describe a text editor which incorporates a great deal of lexical, morphological and syntactic knowledge of Dutch and monitors the orthographical quality of Dutch texts.

Section 1 deals with those aspects of Dutch orthography which pose problems to human authors as well as to computational language sensitive text editing tools. In section 2 we describe the design and the implementation of the text editor we have built. Section 3 is mainly devoted to a provisional evaluation of the system.

1. Some Dutch spelling problems

The three hardest problems of Dutch orthography are easily explained in terms of a comparison with English, French and German:

1. As in English, there are quite a few *homophonous spelling patterns* whose occurrence in specific words is difficult to remember. For instance, the sound /eI/ is spelled as *ei* in some words but as *ij* in other ones. In addition, proper names often spell the same sound as *y*, *ey* or even *eij*. And there are four common ways of rendering the diphthong which sounds like the one in Eng *how*: *ou, au, ouw and auw*. The consonant /k/ is spelled as either *c, cc, k* or *kk*, and as *ck* in many proper names. And many authors forget when to reduplicate a vowel or a consonant (e.g. double *d* and *l* in *onmiddellijk*, Eng *immediately*).

2. As in French, various frequent *inflectional suffixes* are *homophonous*. For example, the verb *gebeuren* (Eng *to happen*) has a third-person singular present-tense form *gebeurt* which sounds exactly the same as the past participle *gebeurd*. Due to word-final devoicing, the endings -*t* and -*d* are both pronounced /t/. If the verb stem ends in -*d* (also pronounced /t/), the third-person -*t* suffix is obligatorily added although it cannot be heard (as in the passive auxiliary *wordt*, Eng *is*). Thus, the third person singular is orthographically distinguished from

the homophonous first person *word* (Eng *am*), which has no suffixes. Since the past-participle suffix is not written after verb stems ending in /t/ (e.g. *besteed* instead of **besteedd*, Eng *spent*), there are three possible spellings of word-final /t/:-*d*, -*t* or -*dt*. In order to select the correct alternative the author must be able to perform a partial parse of the sentence, e.g. identify word classes, finite verbs, participles, person and number of subject noun phrases.

The following examples further illustrate that Dutch orthography often depends on syntactic context. The verb *besteden* (Eng *to spend*) is homophonous with three other spellings, thereby forcing upon the author a choice between four alternatives:

- *Bestede* (inflected past-participle).
- *Besteden* (infinitive; present-tense plural).
- *Besteedde* (past-tense singular).
- *Besteedden* (past-tense plural).

Notice that, although the past-participle suffix -*d* is always deleted, the *d* forming part of the past-tense suffix -*de*, is retained. The choice between homophonous forms *besteed* and *besteedt* is dependent on person of the subject and, in case of second person, on word order of subject and finite verb:

Ik besteeD het geld.	I spend the money.
Je besteeDT het geld.	You spend the money.
BesteeD je het geld?	Spend you the money (Do you spend ...).
BesteeDT je broer het geld?	Spends your brother the money. (Does your brother ...).

The last sentence shows that one cannot simply rely on the presence of *je* after the finite verb: *je* is either personal (*you*) or possessive (*your*) pronoun.

The *o* in *auto* (Eng *car*) is doubled in the diminutive form (*autootje*) but not in the plural (*auto's*) where an apostrophe is mandatory. In all three word forms the *o* is pronounced as the vowel in Eng *road* rather than *rod*. The plural form of nouns ending in -*ie* is either -*ieën* or -*iën* depending on whether or not the word's final syllable is accented (*copieën* versus. *poriën*; Eng *copies, pores*). Again, the pronunciation presents insufficient clues.

3. As in German, compound nouns, verbs and adjectives are written as single words (e.g. *wegverkeer, autorijden, druipnat*; Eng *road traffic, car driving, soaking wet*). The first problem ensuing from this spelling rule is probably caused by interference from English: Dutch compounds are often written as separate words, especially when the compound has low frequency or is a neologism composed by the author.

The third problem derives from two morphological rules which sometimes apply during the compounding process. One rule is the insertion of the shwa phoneme between certain constituent words. A case in point is the second *e* in *perebloesem,* the Dutch equivalent of *pear blossom* (Du. *peer/peren* = Eng *pear/pears;* the bracketed *e* in *pe[e]rebloesem* disappears due to another rule). Shwa insertion only occurs if the first constituent word is singular; if it is a plural noun, one simply writes the plural without an extra shwa, e.g. *perenstroop* (Eng *pear syrup*). However, the difference between *pere-* and *peren-* is not reflected in the pronunciation. The official Dutch-Belgian spelling regulations include an extensive list of composita and simplicia in their correct spelling: the 1954 'Groene Boekje'('green booklet'). Many words are listed with two legal spellings, one of which designated as the word's *Voorkeurspelling* (preferential spelling). Authors wishing to avoid errors or non-preferred spellings such as *perenboom* or *perestroop* need to consult this list.

Another morphological rule inserts the phoneme /s/ between constituent words, e.g. *regerings crisis* (Eng government crisis). In quite a few compounds this *s* is mandatory even though its pronunciation is obscured by a subsequent *s* or *z*. For instance, *regeringssteun* (Eng *government support*) includes an inaudible *s* in analogy with all other compounds having *regering*-cum-audible-*s* as initial member (*regeringsgebouw, regeringsprogramma;* Eng *government building, government program*).

The convention to write compounds as single words has implications for hyphenation. *Between* the word forms which make up a compound, there is always a syllable boundary. *Within* these word forms the normal phonology-based syllabification rules apply. (Any inserted *e* or *s* is counted as belonging to the preceding word form, e.g. *carnavals-hit* instead of **carnaval-shit.*) However, the existence of a morphology-based hyphenation rule can easily lead authors astray. They are sometimes lured into the assumption that other aspects of morphological structure will be mirrored in hyphenation as well. But in Dutch, derivational and inflectional processes do not interact with hyphenation (except for diminutives). For instance, although the plural noun *openingen* (Eng *openings*) contains the morphemes *open+ing+en,* standard syllabification rules nevertheless divide it into *o-pe-nin-gen.*

2. Design and implementation of the text editor

2.1. Design goals

The text editor we have built attempts to identify and correct the kinds of errors described in Section 1 as well as two further error types: unintentional *word reduplications* and *punctuation errors.* So it does not pretend to be a fully-fledged spelling, grammar and style checker.

Word reduplications may arise when the author modifies word order in a sentence by copying a word or phrase but forgets to erase the text at the original position. In Dutch, this easily happens in the course of transforming subordinate into main clauses, or vice-versa, because the finite verb occupies different positions in these clause types (roughly: Subject-Object-Verb in subordinate clauses; Verb-Subject-Object in interrogative main clauses; and Subject-Verb-Object in other main clauses). Other factors are responsible for unintended *contiguous* word reduplications, that is, two adjacent occurrences of the same word –often a function word.

The rules for punctuation in Dutch are very similar to those for English. Typically Dutch are conventions such as the following.

- Never capitalise truncated function words starting with an apostrophe (*'s, 'n, 't*); if they are the first word of a sentence, capitalise the next word instead.
- If a word beginning with the diphthong *ij* is capitalised (e.g. in a proper name or sentence-initially), write *IJ* instead of *Ij*.
- Write a comma between two consecutive finite verbs (the first one belonging to an embedded clause, the second one to the embedding clause).

Punctuation problems also arise in the context of abbreviations and proper names (e.g. *KLM* vs. *K.L.M.* vs. *Koninklijke Luchtvaart Maatschappij* vs. *Koninklijke Luchtvaartmaatschappij* vs. *Kon. Luchtv. Mij*). Although there are not many official rules here, authors will at least strive for consistency within a document. We therefore developed a module which helps authors to maintain consistency in their treatment of abbreviations, proper names, numbers, dates, measure phrases, etc.

We emphasise once again that our language-sensitive editor aims at solving *orthographical* problems. Since Dutch orthography is intertwined with syntax in various ways, the system could not function properly without at least a superficial syntactic analysis of the text. This does not imply that the system is a full syntax checker though.

A final design consideration concerns interaction with users. The system is targetted on texts written by educated authors who are (near-)native speakers of Dutch. Because it makes substantial demands on computational resources and could not run on microcomputers, we have opted for a non-interactive version which processes texts in batch mode[1]. System output consists of a corrected copy of the input text with error diagnostics printed in the margin. A few special editor commands enable the author to inspect corrections and glosses, and to undo or modify any corrections.

2.2. System design

Texts loaded into the editor are processed in four steps:

(1) preprocessing,
(2) word level analysis,
(3) sentence level analysis, and
(4) text resynthesis. The editor's main linguistic components are depicted in Figure 1.

[1] In earlier publications we have described our work on an *interactive* language-sensitive text editor for Dutch. See Kempen, *et al.* (1987) and Vosse (1989).

The *lexicon* is the heart of the system. It contains almost 100,000 lemmas from the authoritative Van Dale dictionary of contemporary Dutch. For each lemma it lists the citation form as well as all current inflected forms ('lexemes'). In total we have about 250,000 word forms. Pointers specify the mutual relationships between each lemma and its lexemes, and between preferred and non-preferred spellings of a word. For the purpose of spelling error correction (triphone analysis; see below), we have computed and stored the pronunciation(s) of every lexeme. The syntactic information in the lexicon also originates from Van Dale and has been enriched in collaboration with the Nijmegen Centre for Lexical Information (CELEX; see Van Gaalen, 1989). Parser and compound analyser need access to the syntactic category and the morphosyntactic features (number, gender, person, case) of every word form. Essential to the parser's functioning is the information about the syntactic valency of lexical entries. Therefore the lexicon includes rudimentary descriptions of the sentence context required by lemmas (in particular the number and phrase type of objects taken by verbs, adjectives and nouns). The lexicon software incorporates interactive tools for semi-automatically adding new words and their inflectional paradigm, and for loading specialised lexical databases, e.g. geographical names or terminology banks.

The *pre-processor* cleans up the input text as follows:

- It removes any characters which do not belong to the text proper, e.g. editing and mark-up commands.
- Characters which do not belong to the set known to the linguistic components, are replaced.
- It corrects punctuation.
- It inserts special symbols marking the beginning and end of abbreviations, proper names, dates, measure phrases, certain frozen idioms which would foul up the parser. These symbols specify syntactic phrase type (e.g. noun phrase, prepositional phrase), thereby simplifying subsequent sentence level analysis.

The pre-processor works on the basis of a string pattern matcher and a dictionary of string patterns to be checked. The pre-processor is an interactive program run by the author. It scans the text for incorrect or undesirable strings. Having discovered a flawed piece of text, it corrects it automatically upon approval by the author. If there are several possible alternatives for corrections, these are shown on the screen. The system then inserts the alternative selected by the author.

Word level analysis comprises a threefold task. First, a list is compiled of all different words ('types') occurring in the text as a whole. This *lexical inventory* obviates the necessity of repeating the full treatment of a word for all its individual occurrences ('tokens'). Second, all words on the list are subjected to a spelling check according to a new technique developed in our institute: triphone analysis. See Van Berkel and De Smedt (1989) for a detailed description.

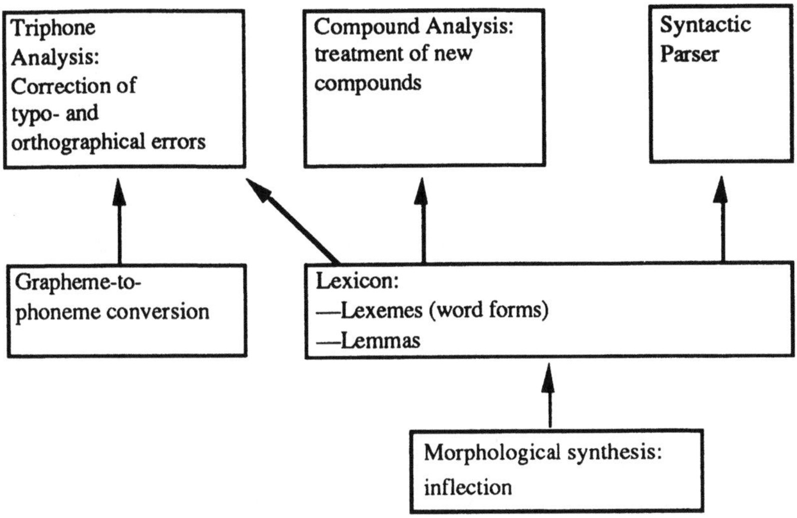

Figure 1. Linguistic components of the text editor

This technique handles both 'look-alikes'(typographical errors, e.g. letter reversals, insertions, omissions) and 'sound-alikes' (incorrect but homophonous spellings). Triphone analysis requires a phonological representation of input words, which is provided by the grapheme-to-phoneme converter (Daelemans 1987). Because a spelling error may very well produce another legal Dutch word (e.g. *zeil* =>*ziel*; Eng *sail/soul*), triphone analysis is applied to *all* words listed in the inventory. The result is a small set of correction alternatives (in the order of 1 to 5) for most of the words. If no suggestions for correction are found, the word is probably an unknown compound or proper name. Third, all character strings in the lexical inventory which are illegal (i.e. cannot be looked up in the on-line lexicon) undergo *compound analysis*. The system tries to interpret these non-words as sequences of two or more word forms that do occur in the lexicon. If this attempt succeeds, the result is added to the list of correction alternatives for the string.

The compound analyser deploys some morphological knowledge of Dutch, in particular concerning the combinability of word forms having certain morphosyntactic features, and about their possible change of appearance in a compound (insertion of shwa or /s/; cf. section 1). Parenthetically, there is no need to decompose word forms into morphemes: the elements making up a compound are themselves word forms having 'wordhood'status.

Sentence level analysis. The syntactic parser does not attempt to reconstruct the sentence structure precisely as intended by the author. Since the editor's goal is to monitor orthographical rather than syntactic quality of documents, many aspects of syntactic structure become irrelevant. This applies, for instance, to the attachment of prepositional phrases and, with the exception of subjects and finite verbs, to the assignment of grammatical function to major clause constituents.

Sentence structures are computed by a Multiple LR(1) parser –a member of the family of shift-reduce parsers – similar in design to the one developed by Tomita (1986). A set of about 500 augmented phrase-structure rules (see next paragraph) was converted to a non-deterministic push-down automaton. Parse trees constructed by this automaton (usually several trees for one sentence) are efficiently represented in memory as 'packed forests'. Spelling errors in the leaves of a parse tree are recognised, diagnosed and corrected by two special mechanisms as follows.

To begin with, the non-terminal symbols of the phrase-structure grammar have been augmented with feature matrices. For example, with symbols S, NP and VP might be associated a matrix specifying number and person features. When the automaton reduces NP and VP to S (cf. the rule S=>NP+VP), it applies a special *unification* algorithm to the NP and VP matrices. Unification succeeds not only in the case when all features match, but also when there are feature violations. In the latter case, a diagnostic flag is attached to the resulting subtree. For instance, if someone types the erroneous sentence *Peter word bedankt* (Eng *'Peter am thanked'*), the NP and VP matrices specify different values for the person feature (NP 3rd, VP 1st). Unification nevertheless 'succeeds' and the S node is marked as violating subject-verb agreement. Later on, during text resynthesis, this diagnostic message triggers the replacement of *word* by third-person *wordt* (Eng *is*) as the desired alternative.

The second technique for dealing with spelling errors utilises special 'error rules'included in the grammar. For instance, there is a rule saying that a clause may consist of two consecutive main clauses: S=>S+S. However, whenever this rule is applied, an error flag is put up at the top S and a warning about incorrect punctuation is put ready.

The parser's diagnostic component employs a system of numerical error weights in order to obtain a quality ranking within a 'forest' (i.e. the set of alternative parse trees computed in response to an input sentence). Any messages, including automatic corrections, are based on the highest-quality tree (least errors).

The parser plays a dual role in the selection of correction alternatives to be communicated to the user. First, if a sentence contains a non-word, the parser is capable of determining which correction alternative(s) fit(s) into the syntactic context. Second, when it fails to produce a fully correct parse tree for a sentence with all words legal, it attempts to construct one by using the correction alternatives.

Text resynthesis. Basing on the results of word and sentence level analyses, the system corrects all words of the document and copies the resulting text to a log file, together with diagnostic messages. The corrections take into consideration certain spelling standards requested by the author in advance, e.g. the preferential spelling as promulgated in the 'Groene Boekje' (cf. section

1), or the punctuation rules in some style sheet known to the system (cf. abbreviations, capitalisation of names of organisations, etc.). The file also contains potential hyphenation points at positions licensed by earlier compound analysis. The author can inspect the log file, evaluate the corrections and undo or modify the ones that are out of place.

3. System evaluation and conclusion

At the time of writing this paper, no detailed evaluation of the language-sensitive editor as a whole is available. However, the individual linguistic modules have been tested extensively over the past few years. We refer to Daelemans (1987) for some quantitative results concerning compound analysis and hyphenation; Van Berkel and De Smedt (1988) present data on triphone analysis. These tests make it amply clear that, although not perfect, the performance of our modules is far better than anything currently available on the market. The parser has not been seriously tested yet because its implementation was finished only recently.

In order to get a first impression of the performance of the integrated system, we have subjected it to an informal Dutch spelling test used to select typists and secretaries. The test consists of 150 sentences, their lengths varying between 3 and 9 words. The total number of words (tokens) was 895 (not counting 10 commas, 15 question marks, 4 exclamation marks and 131 full stops). The text contained 482 different words (types).

In every sentence one word has been underlined, and it is the subject's task to decide whether or not that word contains a spelling error. In fact, 75 sentences are correct. The maximum time to complete the test is 10 minutes. If no more than 5% of the decisions are incorrect, the score is considered 'good'; more than 10% errors means 'failed'.

The 75 to-be-detected spelling errors can be divided into three categories:

- Nonwords (n=59); one of them concerns a punctuation problem (illegal position of apostrophe), three address a diacritics problem (missing or illegal diaeresis), 13 have a verb conjugation problem (illegal but homophonous suffix) and 42 are homophonous misspellings of various other types.
- Legal words which do not fit into the syntactic context (n=14).
- Fossilised multi-word idioms spelled according to obsolete orthographic rules (n=2); an example is *te allen tijden* (wrong) instead of *te allen tijde* (correct; Eng *at all times*); *tijden* is a legal Dutch word which tends to replace the obsolete *tijde* in this expression).

None of the items address the problem of writing compounds as single words or hyphenation.

The editor program (written in C) was running on a DECstation 3100. It took the spelling test without any words underlined. Whenever it discovered a (real or putative) spelling error, it replaced it by the single best correction alternative it could find. No other correction alternatives were logged. The text had not been treated by the pre-processor.

Examination of the log file revealed the following results. The editor scored 140 correct decisions. It overlooked 10 misspellings and gave no 'false alarms'. The 'missing hits'were distributed over the above three categories as follows:

- Of 59 non-words, 56 were detected and 55 were corrected as intended by the test.
- Of 14 legal words *in*compatible with syntactic context, nine were recognised as such and seven were corrected as intended by the test.
- The errors in two fossilised idiomatic expressions were both overlooked.

The editor did not detect any errors in the legal words which were *not* underlined in the original test version.

The 150 sentences took 13.7 minutes of CPU time: 7 for triphone analysis, compound analysis and text resynthesis, and 6.7 for syntactic parsing. Although this is more than the maximum granted to human subjects, one should realise that the editor could not profit from the fact that errors were limited to underlined words, so that it had to pay equal attention to the non-underlined words. Moreover, the human subjects did not correct the misspellings they detected.

The 10 wrong decisions clearly reveal the system's design limitations. Two morphosyntactic errors in the input text were overlooked because they presuppose semantic analysis of the input sentence.

- Ze rende met z'n allen naar huis.
  They all ran home.
- Vroeger beïnvloeden zijn ouders ...
  Formerly his parents influence ...

In (1), the expression *met z'n allen* (Eng *all*) forces a plural interpretation upon the subject pronoun *ze*, which is ambiguous between Eng *she* and *they*. This in turn stipulates plural *renden*, homophonous with singular *rende*, as the correct form of the finite verb. In test item (2), the homophonous past-tense form *beïnvloedden* (with two *d*'s) is entailed by the adverb *vroeger* (Eng *formerly*). Since we do not intend to build any semantic knowledge into the editor, such problems will remain beyond the scope of our editor. Two other errors were overlooked because word-level analysis construed them as legal compounds: *erflijk* was interpreted as *erf+lijk* (Eng *heritage corpse*) rather than as a misspelling for *erfelijk* (Eng *hereditary*) and the editor did not recognise *eigelijk* as a typo for *eigenlijk* (Eng *actually*) but as *ei+gelijk* (Eng *egg-equal*). Such errors, too, are unavoidable in the present design.

We were very pleased with the high error correction rate. Of 65 repair attempts 62 were successful at the first try. Of the three mis-hits, one originated from an infelicitous choice by the triphone analyser, and both other ones from a wrong syntactic parse.

Since there is ample room for improving the editor's diagnostic capabilities and for speeding up its performance, we believe we are close to a language-sensitive editor which can substantially enhance the efficiency and quality of typesetting and proof-reading Dutch texts.

4. Acknowledgements

We thank the present and former members of the Language Technology Project of NICI for their extensive practical and theoretical contributions to design and implementation of the text editing tools described in this paper. We wish to mention in particular Gerben Abbink (pre-processor), Walter Daelemans (compound analysis and grapheme-to-phoneme conversion; presently at ITK, Tilburg), Brigit van Berkel (triphone analysis; now at TNO-ITI, Delft) and Rob Heemels (syntax rules; Océ-Nederland, Venlo).

5. References

Daelemans, W. (1987) Studies in Language Technology. An object-oriented computer model of morphophonological aspects of Dutch. Dissertation, University of Louvain.

Tomita, M. (1986) *Efficient Parsing for Natural Language: A Fast Algorithm for Practical Systems.* Kluwer Academic Press, Dordrecht.

Van Berkel, B. and De Smedt, K. (1988) Triphone analysis: a combined method for the correction of orthographical and typographical errors. *Proceedings of the Second Conference on Applied Natural Language Processing.* American Association for Computational Linguistics,Austin TX

Van Gaalen, M. (1989) De syntactische valentie van werkwoorden, zelfstandige naamwoorden en adjectieven. Paper, NICI, University of Nijmegen.

6

Boxweb: A Structured Outline Program for Writers

Peter Wayner
Cornell University

Abstract

Boxweb is a high-level language for creating outlines. It forces the writer to list both the ideas in an essay and more importantly the way the ideas interact. These lists are compiled by the computer into a traditional, hierarchical outline. The structure of Boxweb is designed to force the writer to think of an essay as not just a set of facts and notions, but as a web of connections between ideas. While the basic structure of the language is adapted from computer languages, the syntax is specifically designed to be very flexible and appear like natural English. The paper will describe the structure of the language, some results from testing it on writers and finally, the algorithms used by the compiler. It will compare the language to some related work done at Xerox PARC, which is primarily visual.

1. Introduction

At the most basic level, Computer Science is the science of organising the world. Programmers take the tasks that need to be done and find the fastest, most logical ways to do them. Some theoreticians use mathematics to prove just what can be attacked systematically while others want to know which solutions are the best. The system designers plan the best way for machines to talk to each other without getting confused. When there are questions about describing a job elegantly, correctly and precisely, the computer language researchers use their bag of tricks to answer them. The problems are mathematical because of the nature of machines. A good computer language makes it easy to cast the problems in a well-defined format so the compiler can convert these expressions into a sequence of instructions for the computer. These must be presented in a logical and carefully designed order so the computer can reach the right conclusion.

The Boxweb project is an attempt to take the ideas and rigour from the development of good, well-thought-out programming languages and use them to help write essays, papers, novels, letters and practically anything longer than a sentence. The project revolves around one admittedly controversial idea: readers are like computers. They like the ideas presented to them in a logical order. Whenever there is a connection between two ideas, readers like the connection made when the ideas are still fresh in their minds. If one idea depends upon another, the dependent one should not appear first. The transitions between topics should be well planned out. If these rules are followed, and the writing is competent, the reader's task should be easy.

The Boxweb software is a compiler for the human mind. The writer composes a list of ideas and then makes semantic connections between them. Boxweb takes these and produces an outline which is consistent and correct. The language gives the writer the ability to order the ideas when connections are made and the outline generator will obey this ordering. The outline is produced in much the same way as compilers generate code for a computer. Much of the internal structure is borrowed from well-known compiler design (Aho *et al.* 1986).

This paper will have several sections. It begins with a description of the language and then discusses the algorithm for creating an outline. After this, several technical details of the structure of the language are presented before the results of testing an implementation of the language are described. Finally, the paper concludes with some comparisons between the "look and feel" of this language and several other similar programs.

2. A description of the language

There are three segments in a "program"for the Boxweb compiler: Ideas, links and connections. The different topics, notions, facts and concepts are listed as tokens in the *Ideas* segment. Boxweb accepts tokens that contain spaces because one word is seldom enough and a hyphenated word is not natural. Some perfectly good ideas might be: "World Peace", "A picnic by the lake"or perhaps, "Sunday Brunch". Parsing problems created by this are discussed later.

The second segment lists the words used to connect two Ideas. These tokens, called *Links*, are usually verb phrases and as with Ideas, they can consist of several words. These links can be as concrete as "depends upon"or as vague as "might be considered related to."The ideas are linked together in the *Connections* segment in quasi-sentences with the basic form: idea token-link token-idea token. If the phrase "makes a nice" was defined as a link, then the sentence "A picnic by the lake makes a nice Sunday Brunch". If parentheses enclose one of these triplets, Boxweb will treat it as another Idea token so large, complex connections can be drawn. Careful planning with the phrasing of these tokens can usually be combined to form simple sentences that approach grammatically correct writing.

There are three different types of Links: Left, Right and Symmetric. These links help the outline generator order the ideas in the final outline. A left link forces Boxweb to place the idea on the left-hand side before the idea on the right-hand side, right Links do the opposite and symmetric Links leave the decision up to the compiler. These designations give the writer some control over the final outline because there are many instances when some order must prevail. A good example is "P=NP implies the polynomial hierarchy collapses". It makes good sense to discuss P=NP (and better to prove it) before attacking the hierarchy. Boxweb presumes undefined Links are symmetric.

The syntax of the programs is simple. The words "IDEAS", "LINKS"and

"CONNECTIONS" begin each segment, periods end the segments and semi-colons separate the different tokens or expressions. Colons separate a Link from its designation as left, right or symmetric. A program should look like this:

IDEAS
$token_1$;$token_2$;$token_3$; .....; $token_i$.
LINKS
$token_{i+1}$:*orientation* ; $token_{i+2}$:*orientation* ; .... ; $token_m$.
CONNECTIONS
$expression_1$;$expression_2$;$expression_3$; ... ; $expression_n$.

orientation can be either "LEFT","RIGHT", "SYMMETRIC" or left out altogether.

Each expression is generated by the following grammar:

S --> SCS | (S) | I=S | $token_1$ | ..... | $token_i$

C --> $token_{i+1}$ | ... | $token_m$

I --> $token_1$ | ..... | $token_i$

The tokens are the terminals.

Boxweb encourages the writer to break the program into simpler parts in two ways. First, the equals sign lets a single idea token represent a complex expression. Second, Boxweb accepts many Ideas, Link and Connection segments as long as no token occurs in a Connection before it is defined. Finally, comments can be included in brackets. A sample Boxweb 'program' and its outline are shown in Figure 1.

```
{Death be not Loud---}
IDEAS
Roger Rotlinger; {Grey-suited, manicured businessman. Never seen without
  his Lear Jet.}
Slimey Oil; {Isn't it all...}
The Oil Cartel; {A secret group of powerful oil companies who meet to set
  the prices for oil artificially high!}
Turk Longfinger; {Cowboy-cum-Oilman. Still wears his spurs. Used some of
  the oil profits to buy New Mexico for a ranch. }
Sagebrush Oil; {A down-home gas company}
Dudley Scott; {Petroleum Engineer...and part-time detective.}
The Murder.

LINKS
owns;
works for;
wants control of;
and;
```

belongs to;
solves;
murders.

CONNECTIONS
The Murder= Turk Longfinger murders Roger Rotlinger;
Roger Rotlinger owns Slimey Oil;
Turk Longfinger owns Sagebrush Oil;
(Slimey Oil and Sagebrush Oil) belongs to The Oil Cartel;
Turk Longfinger wants control of The Oil Cartel; {!}
Dudley Scott works for Roger Rotlinger;
Dudley Scott solves The Murder.

Figure 1. A sample program describing a movie plot.

3. The algorithm for creating the outline.

Creating the "best"outline from a collection of ideas and connections is a problem of efficiency, rigour, style and aesthetics. Boxweb attempts to encapsulate several quantifiable matters of style in its algorithm, while leaving the writer enough flexibility to resolve questions of taste. Boxweb's guidelines for the outline are:

- Linked ideas should kept close together.
- Dependencies must be preserved. Ideas that depend on others should not be placed in the outline until the ideas upon which they depend are included.
- Dependent expressions should be kept close together if possible.
- If all other factors are equal, the order of ideas in the Idea segment should be used to break the ties.

Boxweb starts to create an outline that fits these guidelines by building a directed acyclic graph (dag). The Idea tokens are the leaves and the links between the Ideas are nodes with two directed edges pointing to the nodes they connect. Since Ideas can be used over again and expressions can be used as sub-expressions, the graph does not have to be a tree. The nodes with no incoming edges are called the roots. The root and its decedents correspond to a complete expression. A sample graph is shown in Figure 2.

There are two parts to this algorithm. The first part schedules the Ideas within expressions so they come near each other and the second part schedules the expressions so dependencies are honoured and the dependent expressions are kept in close proximity. They are heuristics because the scheduling problem here is easily shown to be NP-hard by a reduction from the scheduling problem for one register machines. It is strongly influenced by work on register allocation and scheduling algorithms for RISC machines (Gibbons and Muchnick 1986).

```
IDEAS
poverty;war;injustice;oppression.
LINKS
leads to: left;
and.
CONNECTIONS
(oppression and injustice) leads to poverty;
poverty leads to war.
```

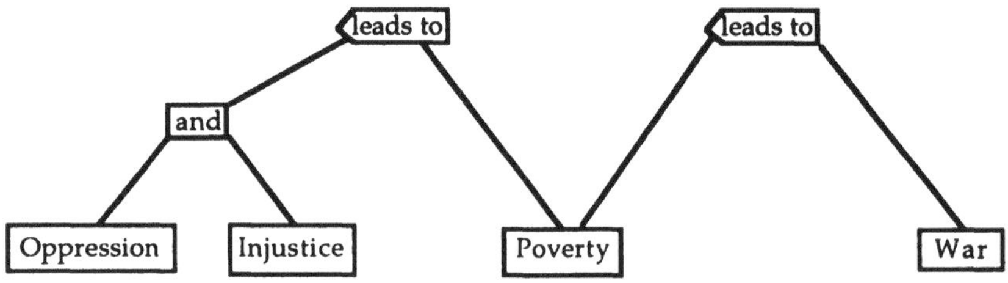

Figure 2. A BOXWEB program and its' directed acyclic graph. (dag)

4. The basics of outline generation

The first part of the algorithm is a straight-forward depth-first walk down from the root of each expression. It lists the nodes in a combination pre- and postfix order. When it comes to a node representing the expression $idea_1$ *link* $idea_2$, Boxweb prints:

Introduce: $idea_1$ link $idea_2$

Describe: $idea_1$

Describe: $idea_2$

Show how: ideal link $idea_2$

If the link joins sub-expressions instead of ideas, Boxweb does not add a "Describe:" entry to the outline. It tackles these sub-expressions recursively. For instance, when Boxweb encounters an expression of the form: *(*$idea_1$ *link* $idea_2$*)* *link* $idea_3$, it produces:

Introduce: ($idea_1$ link $idea_2$) link $idea_3$
Introduce: $idea_1$ link $idea_2$
Describe: $idea^1$
Describe: $idea_2$
Show how: $idea_1$ link $idea_2$
Describe: $idea_3$
Show How: ($idea_1$ link $idea_2$) link $idea_3$

In the previous example, Boxweb chose the left branch first. The orientation of a link affects this choice. If it is a left link, the left side will always be described or recursively searched first. The opposite holds for the right links. If the link is symmetric, Boxweb chooses the branch that leads to the reachable token with the lowest subscript, i.e. the first in the order imposed by the user in the Ideas segment(s). This last rules gives the user some control over the final order.

Boxweb only asks the writer to describe an idea once. After that, it leaves that line out of the outline and does not search that branch again. It presumes the reader is already familiar with the concepts in that section of the graph. For instance, if the previous example *(*$idea_1$ *link* $idea_2$*) link* $idea_3$, was changed to read *(*$idea_1$ *link* $idea_2$*) link* $idea_1$, Boxweb produces:

Introduce: ($idea_1$ link $idea_2$) link $idea_1$
  Introduce: $idea_1$ link $idea_2$
    Describe: $idea_1$
    Describe: $idea_2$
  Show how: $idea_1$ link $idea_2$
  {There is no description of $idea_1$ *here.}*
Show How: ($idea_1$ link $idea_2$) link $idea_1$

This straight-forward heuristic solves the problem of scheduling expressions rather well. Whenever a connection is made in an outline and Boxweb asks the writer to show how something affects something else, the depth-first search guarantees that one half of the connection was just examined. Smooth transitions are a great benefit to an outline.

5. Ordering expressions around

The second part of the algorithm schedules the order the first part compiles expressions and ensures that no dependencies are violated. The basic scheduling algorithm uses the order of the idea tokens in the idea segment to order the expressions. The expressions are sorted by the earliest defined idea tokens. The ideas which come first are presented first. This gives the writer some more control over the final outline.

This simple rule, though, can come in conflict with directed links. For instance if "->"is a directed link, and "*B*->*C*"and "*C*->*A*" are connections, made then the ideas should be presented in the order *B*, *C* and then *A* regardless of their order in the IDEAS segment.

Definition: Expression *B* is *dependent* upon expression *A* (*A* must precede *B*, or *A*>*B*) if expression *B* contains $idea_i$ and in expression *A*, $idea_i$ is either on the right side of a left link or on the left side of a right link.

This dependency analysis can sometimes form deadlocks. If there is a circular system of dependencies, then Boxweb will not be able to find a way to preserve the ordering. In this case, Boxweb arbitrarily breaks the circular dependencies by using the first idea rule to choose an expression. In these cases it notifies the user.

This scheduling algorithm is similar to algorithms for organising operations for RISC machines and register scheduling, but it is specifically tuned for keeping dependent expressions close to each other. In pseudo-code it reads:

Begin with a list of expressions.
Find which expressions depend upon which other expressions.
    while expressions are not scheduled **do**
        begin
          Choose an unscheduled expression which is not dependent upon any other unscheduled expression. Use the order of the ideas in the Idea segment to pick the first one.
          Add this expression to the outline with the first part of the algorithm and mark it scheduled.
          Find all other unscheduled expressions which contain the same ideas.
          Schedule the expressions which are not dependent upon an unscheduled expression.
        end.

Computing the dependencies efficiently can be done as the dag is constructed. Each node must contain a list of all dependent tokens which are part of the expression. As the dag is constructed, the lists are merged. When this is complete, the list of the expressions can be ordered with set operations on these lists. Figure 3 contains an example of the output.

The Outline:

Introduce: The Murder =Turk Longfinger murders Roger Rotlinger
Describe : Roger Rotlinger
Describe : Turk Longfinger
Show how: The Murder =Turk Longfinger murders Roger Rotlinger
Introduce: Roger Rotlinger owns Slimey Oil
Describe : Slimey Oil
Show how: Roger Rotlinger owns Slimey Oil
Introduce: Dudley Scott works for Roger Rotlinger
Describe : Dudley Scott
Show how: Dudley Scott works for Roger Rotlinger
Introduce: (Slimey Oil and Sagebrush Oil)belongs to The Oil Cartel
Introduce: Slimey Oil and Sagebrush Oil
Describe : Sagebrush Oil
Show how: Slimey Oil and Sagebrush Oil
Describe : The Oil Cartel
Show how: (Slimey Oil and Sagebrush Oil)belongs to The Oil Cartel
Introduce: Turk Longfinger wants control of The Oil Cartel
Show how: Turk Longfinger wants control of The Oil Cartel
Introduce: urk Longfinger owns Sagebrush Oil
Show how: Turk Longfinger owns Sagebrush Oil
Introduce: Dudley Scott solves The Murder
Show how: Dudley Scott solves The Murder

Figure 3. The output from the compiler from the Boxweb input in Figure 1

6. Tuning the parser and the lexical analyser

Parsing the expressions is not difficult. The grammar describing them is easily handled by any recursive descent parser. Allowing several words to serve as a token, however creates ambiguities because there is no special character or set of characters that always signifies the end of tokens. For example, the expression "Fruit flies like bananas"can be parsed in two different ways if "Fruit", "Fruit flies"and "bananas"are Ideas and both "flies like"and "like"are Links.

Several solutions were considered. The simplest requires the writer to enclose all ideas in parentheses. Parsing this is as easy as LISP. The second solution relies upon a rule barring the same word from appearing in both Ideas and Links. Finding the end of a token can be found by scanning for a change from words that are part of Ideas to words that are part of Links. This rule is not particularly constricting, because Links are usually verb phrases and Ideas are usually noun phrases.

This third attempt stores the tokens in lexicographic trees and uses this forest as a finite automaton to find the identity of the tokens. Thinking of the lexical analyser as a finite automaton is a well-established paradigm discussed in Aho *et al.* (1986). The lexicographic trees are trees with one letter attached to each node. The letters along every path from root to leaf make up one token. Since there are 26 letters in the English alphabet, each node can have up to 26 branches leaving it, but there are seldom this many. The identification number of each token is stored at the last node of the path that makes up the word. If the token is a prefix of another token, this node is not a leaf. These nodes with ids are "accepting states" and verifying that a string is a token is as simple as starting at the root and seeing if there is a path to an "accepting state". The parsing algorithm is as follows:

```
function parse (string, position,idea?) returning a list of token ids;
local variables: linked list of pointers to "accepting states"encountered in
the graph, current position, current node, new list

current position := position ;
current node := root of lexicographic tree;
while a path exists from current node with label string[current position] do
        begin
          take the path and update current node and current position;
          if the new  current node  is an accepting state matching
          idea?  then
             add it to the linked list.
        end
if no accepting states were found then
        return an empty list
else if current position= the end of the string then
        return the id number of current node  as a single element list
```

```
else
    loop: if the linked list of "accepting states"is empty then
            return an empty list
          else
            begin
              newlist:=parse(string,current position, not idea?);
              if newlist is empty then
                discard the last "accepting state"on the list and
                goto loop
              else
                return concatenate(the last "accepting state"on
                linked list, newlist)
            end
```

This recursive algorithm begins with call parse (string,1,true) where string contains a list of non-punctuation characters to be matched with tokens. The variable *idea?* is a Boolean that is set to true if the algorithm is going to try to match the beginning of the string with idea tokens and false if it is searching for link tokens. The language requires the ideas and the Links to alternate making this pruning of the search possible. (If the algorithm was just searching for unspecified tokens, then this variable could be safely left out.)

The algorithm will only have to make repeated recursive calls when it is matching tokens that are prefixes of others. This recursive iteration can be removed by adding a rule that requires the lexical analyser to return the longest possible token that matches the string. Under this rule the parser will find "fruit flies"as the first token when presented with the example "fruit flies like bananas."

7. An implementation and reactions to it

This project was implemented in PASCAL. It currently runs on the VAX, IBM-compatible PC's and the Macintosh. Both the Macintosh and the PC version have windowing interfaces with editor shells. An extensive manual for beginning users describes the features and presents many examples. Both versions have been available in a limited shareware market for some time. The Macintosh version was used in an introductory course in computer science which included an essay-writing component.

The students and testers who used Boxweb were asked to describe their feelings about its usefulness. I chose not to utilise more sophisticated analysis because I found it impossible to find a valid scientific test. Some software programs gather statistics and use them to rate the "reading level" of writing, but these are based upon strictly syntactic measures and their accuracy has been a topic of wide debate. Another approach, asking neutral readers to rate the quality of the "structure" of a group of essays, is obviously problematic. Not only is the scale and rating system hard to define, but any statistically significant conclusions would require a prohibitively large test section. For this reason, I chose to simply ask the users for their impressions.

The users were divided about the usefulness. About half welcomed the structure and enjoyed thinking about the essays in this way. One said that, "Boxweb makes sure you cover all the angles." Several felt that it was very useful for a technical document. Another felt that Boxweb "was useful for developing scenarios like screenplays and setting all the parameters". Students, over all, reacted quite favourably. The response was also generally much more positive from the testers who had a good technical base and were willing to experiment with new software.

The others seemed to feel that the structure was not worth the work. This attitude was much more prevalent in the more talented and accomplished writers who had developed their own techniques for organising an essay. One professional writer from the English department contended that all communication was contained in the narrative texture not the structure and that Boxweb was missing the point. Another published author said, "Do you think anyone actually writes an outline?"

Given the scope of these reactions, I think that Boxweb is more ideally suited to a beginning writer who has not yet formed a successful style for writing. These students need much more help keeping their ideas focused and their conclusions sound. The structure is much more of a help than a hindrance for people who are not sure what they want to say and how they should go about saying it.

8. Comparisons to the CoLab project[1]

A group at Xerox's Palo Alto Research Centre built a visual version of an outliner similar to this language independently of my work. They were primarily interested in studying the way people work together CoLaboratively on a project and one of the tools they built was a visual sketchpad for diagramming ideas. The icons on the screen corresponded to the phrases used as ideas in Boxweb. These icons were joined by lines which represented the links. The icons and the lines between them both had phrases attached to them which would identify what the icons and the lines between them represented. This drawing could be turned into an outline with a set of rules much like the ones governing Boxweb's outline production. Later versions of the software also added some spatial ordering to the screen which enforced an ordering that was observed in the outline generation.

In the end, the principle difference between the two experiments is that one is visual and the other is textual. The basic concept of representing the thoughts as a web of ideas not a hierarchical outline is the same. The question I have wondered about is what differences the medium makes to the process. To a large extent, the comparisons are mainly based on matters of taste. The systems are similar enough so that what can be represented in one can also be represented in the other. Some people like to think visually, others think

1 Demonstration of the CoLab at PARC. A Xerox PARC videotape.

semantically. I tried, though, to isolate some of the differences in style that would govern people's taste and the way they think about thinking.

First of all, the links in Boxweb are entirely semantic, while the links in the CoLab project are also spatial. By this I mean that when two ideas are linked in a Boxweb connection, they are joined in a sentence-like group. The bond is formed in the domain of the word. In the CoLab project, the link is heavily visual. The two ideas are paired by a line and the words next to this line explain the qualities of the link. The line is often more visually dominant than the words and the link is more a pairing then a semantic relationship. This difference may be the result of the original direction of the project. Boxweb was intended for writers while the CoLab was intended to be used by people collaborating on a project. An entirely textual medium is more conducive to writers who work alone. Visual communication, on the other hand, is more natural for people working together.

A second difference emerges because CoLab encourages the organisers to place items spatially near each other, while Boxweb does not. The CoLab screen is filled with icons with lines linking the items. If a link is made between two icons on opposite sides of the screen, then the line passes over all the icons in between. The users are encouraged to add a spatial dimension to their organisation and place the linked icons near each other to keep everything clean. While Boxweb does allow the user to segment the outline, the language is not constrained by the fact that every link must be physically represented. An idea can be used in many different places throughout the Connections segments and Boxweb will organise it eventually.

The effects of the lines, though, also give the CoLab drawing a scale-dependent quality. If a CoLab drawing is viewed from a distance, the eye can break the drawing into basic groups by looking at the lines alone. The words are too small to see and the mind concentrates on the visual relationships. This is not possible with Boxweb because there are no larger clues to organising the outline. All of the information is contained in the words.

Are these differences real? Do they have any quantifiable effect? I am not willing even to begin to guess. I have tried to elucidate several of the differences which might be the basis of any differences in taste.

9. Differences between Boxweb and a traditional outline

Throughout this entire project, I have experimented with the language and with the thought processes involved in planning a piece of writing. Boxweb has one substantial difference between it and a traditional hierarchical outline. Anyone who plans an essay with Boxweb must think about the transitions and the logic before writing. Moreover, they must consider the terms they will use to describe these transitions and syllogisms before beginning. Some writers may do this in the outline phase, but they are not forced to think about these connections before writing. This process of "pre-thinking" has saved me several times when I was writing essays which were based on untenable wording. If I had begun writing and not discovered halfway through that my word choice could not be substantiated, I would have had to rework the essay. Thinking all of the assertions through semantically is important.

10. Conclusions about the design of the language

The Boxweb language is an attempt to apply many of the techniques from computer languages to writing. Forcing writers to list their thoughts and the ways they affect each other imitates the strong typing of languages like PASCAL. The algorithms for creating the outline grew as imitations of code generators and optimisers, although the requirements of writing made them different.

Boxweb's parser was specifically designed to allow the user a great deal of freedom to use phrases and clauses that are grammatically correct. This has two effects. First, it makes the 'programs' easy to read and more acceptable to everyone. Second, it has the interesting affect of changing the level the compiler 'works.' To the computer, the connection between two ideas is very concrete; it is a node in a graph. The writer, though, sees it on a textual level. The meaning of Link carries all the strengths, weaknesses, connotations and denotations given to it by the language defines the link. It can be as strong as "forces"or as weak as "just might have something to do with". The natural languages allow the software to operate both logically and linguistically. Of course Boxweb never understands the words it uses, but it is flexible enough to accept literary programs. It is, at the very least, an attempt to find common ground between the logical and the linguistic and tap the strength of consistent thought without constraining the writer.

11. References

Aho, A., Sethi, R. and Ullman, J. (1986) *Compilers: Principles, Techniques and Tools.* Addison-Wesley, Reading, MA.

Gibbons, P. and Muchnick, S. (1986) Efficient Instruction Scheduling for a Pipelined Architecture. *Proceedings of the Sigplan Compiler Construction Symposium.*

7

An Author's Cross-referencer

Harold Thimbleby
Stirling University

Abstract

A cross-referencer permits an author to refer to parts of his document, for example, to the page or section number where some subject is discussed. This paper describes the design of a flexible cross-referencer, with particular emphasis on its user interface and the benefits of its helpful diagnostics. The cross-referencer has been used in earnest to help with the production of various documents, from brief papers, a heavily cross-referenced handbook, to a major book of 500 pages.
This paper describes certain useful features that a cross-referencer should provide for its author, and how such features influence the author's style and creativity. For example, good diagnostics encourage the author to 'refer' to text he has not yet written: the diagnostics remind the author of his outstanding commitments. The problems of writing large documents – with a high probability of clashes –is addressed.

1. Introduction

A cross-referencer is a text-processing tool to facilitate authors referring their readers to other parts of their document. Often the author will want to refer the reader to equations, figures, tables or sections, as in "Graph 4 on page 73 shows the data ..." The problem is that when the author writes his document, he may not know what number the graph is, nor which page it will be on. And subsequent revisions to his document might mean he adds more graphs or changes their order to make a better arrangement. A cross-referencer permits an author to use names in place of explicit references, and it supplies their correct values (for example, the text "Graph 4" and "73" in the case above).

This paper is about an author's cross-referencer, called **xr**. We stress *author's* since **xr** is not only extremely easy to use and flexible, but provides powerful diagnostic facilities. These provide much-needed support for the author and enable him to take on more complex writing tasks with confidence.

Xr is aimed at users of markup typesetting systems, such as $\mathrm{T_EX}$, SGML and **troff. Xr** as described in this paper may seem complex to use simply because we have illustrated, in a rather condensed fashion, some of its more arcane capabilities –capabilities that few authors would wish to exploit fully. **Xr** must also be seen in the context of the systems the author would normally be using: **xr** is not only trivial in comparison, but provides the author with more support!

2. Why is cross referencing of general interest?

2.1. The general problem

To justify an interest in cross-referencing, it is useful to separate (1) arguments based on style and convention, from (2) arguments based on the needs of the reader, from (3) arguments based on the needs of the author and publisher. What stylists consider good taste may in part be determined by convention and cost, rather than objective measures of style. What makes life easy for an author is not necessarily best for a reader.

We will conclude that whether **xr** (as an example of an automatic author's tool) is 'good' or 'bad' depends on a variety of factors. However, what is uncontentious is that cross-referencing is an appropriate candidate for automation. And as with all cases of automation, the arguments for or against must shift their focus from how difficult a task used to be, to the utility of the outcome. When cross-referencing becomes trivial for authors, the only valid arguments have to be based on the needs of the readers in each particular case.

2.2. Arguments based on style and convention

Conventionally, cross-references have been difficult and costly to provide. Conventional cross-referencing makes a document very much harder to revise (the editor needs to keep track of all references and what they previously referred to). Excessive cross-referencing is often a sign of a badly organised text.

Easy-to-read documents typically have a purely linear structure with no need for cross-referencing. Conversely, complex documents often contain cross-references. Not surprisingly, there is folklore that cross-referencing is undesirable and unreliable –despite the obvious fact that complex documents might be even worse *but* for cross-referencing!

2.3. Arguments based on the needs of the reader

The needs of the reader cannot always be anticipated, or (for economic reasons) a single document may be aimed at several classes of reader.

The *Informal Introduction to Algol 68* (Lindsey and van der Meulen, 1973) is a case in point. It has a two-dimensional table of contents and directly supports so-called 'horizontal' and 'vertical' reading styles.

Vertical readers follow an in-depth instructional route; horizontal readers follow a survey route. Many sections end with a directive, "Vertical readers, please turn to section ..."; whereas horizontal readers simply continue on to the following section. As with many reference books, many sections contain conventional cross-referencing like, "For more details see sections ..." or exceptions, "but see section ..." Furthermore, the *Introduction is* cross referenced to another book, the *Algol 68 Report,* itself heavily cross-referenced.

As it happens, the *Introduction* merely refers readers to section numbers: the reader has to search for the relevant text (or use the table of contents). Had an automated cross-referencer been available, the section numbers could easily have been augmented by their page numbers or other more helpful information.

If the *Introduction*, a computing book, seems a contrived example, there are many and various examples from other fields where cross-referencing is used to great advantage: the Bible, mathematics books, user manuals, encyclopaedias and reference books generally, adventure stories, programmed learning texts, legal documents. A surprising number of documents are 'twin' in the sense that they present two actual documents together. Thus, a commentary on Aristotle might have two columns, one in English, one in Greek. A chemical catalogue might have safety data for each chemical (referring the reader to the appropriate safety section for the chemical) and the safety section conversely refers the reader back to the necessary chemical antidotes and neutralisers.

It should be noted that providing a cross-referencer tool does not require a text to be intricately cross-referenced even a single cross-reference can be very useful, as in a newspaper article that 'continues in column 3, page 6.

2.4. Arguments based on the needs of the author

One of the most important advantages of an automatic cross-referencer, apart from the assurance that cross-references are correct and readily determined, is that it permits the author to postpone commitment to a particular order of exposition. The order an author chooses to write a document in is unlikely to be the best order for reading it; a cross-referencer facilitates rearranging the order of a text without losing its connectedness.

Adventure story and programmed learning books are cases in point: the author can write a story (or sequence of lessons) with decision points. Later, when the story is to be printed, it can be jumbled up so that the reader cannot 'cheat'. A cross-referencing system would write in the correct page details in directives like, "If your answer is *yes*, turn to page 324".

An automatic cross-referencing system allows the author to use his own names for cross-references. Thus, a chemistry book might have cross-references that are section names and page numbers, but the author may prefer to refer to the sections for his own purposes by the chemicals to which they relate. The author could write '<<CO2>>', but the reader would see 'section 2.4 on page 25' or perhaps '§2.4' (carbon dioxide)', rather than have to refer to the contents or index to determine where the topic is discussed. Furthermore, a cross referencing system would be of considerable help when developing the book; it could inform the author if the section called CO2 had not yet been written.

3. Cross-referencing styles

3.1. WYSIWYG

A WYSIWYG system simply shows the author what his document will appear like when it is printed. The advantage of this is that issues such as layout, fonts and so on (and details such as placement of graphics) is very straightforward. On the other hand, common features within a document (its so-called styles) are not normally visible to the author (since they would never be visible as such to the reader of the documents). It is therefore very difficult to maintain consistent styles and relationships between various parts of a large document. Thus, WYSIWYG systems tend to provide no specific support for cross referencing.

3.2. HyperText

HyperText creates interactive documents, in particular cross-references become active components of the document. The reader of a hypertext can point at (e.g. with his finger) a cross-reference and is then 'taken to' the referenced information.

Although removing all manual effort from the reader, the disadvantage is that the reader can easily become lost in the network of cross-referencing. In a conventional document, of course, each cross-reference would be an explicit signpost, the reading of which would help the user navigate and maintain a 'map' of the document in his head; this map is reinforced by the table of contents and other explicit signs. (A hypertext document typically has no obvious linear structure for which the ordering of a table of contents could be related by the reader).

3.3. Markup

In a markup system, the author writes textual commands to control the format of his document. Examples of markup systems are SGML, T_EX and **troff.** The disadvantage of a markup system is the slow learning-curve for the author: often the control languages are exceedingly complex, and, because markup systems tend to be slow and non-interactive, there is a considerable lack of feedback of success (or failure!) to motivate the author. On the other hand, a markup language can express many things, and in particular, commonalities and relationships that cannot be described explicitly in WYSIWYG and hypertext systems. Markup, then, is of considerable advantage for documents requiring significant cross-referencing.

4. L^aT_EX

For comparison purposes, we briefly examine the cross-referencing facilities provided by L^aT_EX (Lamport, 1986), a widely used typesetting system based on T_EX. L^aT_EX provides explicit and implicit forms of cross-references. Users are normally only aware of the explicit kind, and can therefore be taken by surprise when the support for implicit cross-referencing falls short.

4.1. Explicit cross-referencing

L^aT_EX allows an author to write \label {*name* }in any section, or captioned display item. Anywhere else, the author may write \ref {*name* }to get the section number (or display number) where the label was defined, or he may write \pageref {*name*}to get the page number.

Bibliographic citations are handled by a similar mechanism, but using a different syntax. A bibliographic item is labelled instead by \bibitem [*name*] and cited by \cite {*name* }.

4.2. Implicit cross-referencing

Less obvious forms of cross-referencing are also provided in L^aT_EX. The table of contents is a series of entries that cross-references section names and pages; the index is a lexically-sorted list of topics and references back to the pages (or perhaps sections) on which they occur.

More subtle still are the mechanisms L^aT_EX uses for managing multiple files. If a document is split between several files, it is important that page numbering and section numbering is continuous. L^aT_EX carries forwards these numbers onto the next file in the sequence.

4.3. Diagnostics

L^aT_EX provides very little diagnostic support. It is remarkably easy for page numbering to go awry, with no warning whatsoever. When explicit cross-references change, L^aT_EX warns that 'LaTeX Warning:Label (s) may have changed. Rerun to get cross references right'. This is not very specific, and only increases the author' s worries!

5. Why does the author need more support?

Imagine the author is writing a modest book. For convenience this will be split between a number of files. A typical text book may have several cross-references per page, so the author can soon lose track of the cross-references used in his book and where they are defined. If he wants to use a new cross reference, he must be careful to avoid using an existing name. If he wants to refer to a particular section, he needs to know what its cross-reference name is, out of the possibly hundreds of names available. He is also very interested to know when cross-references change (e.g. if he inserts a new section into the document): in this case, the document must be reprocessed for the cross references to be sorted out. And which files are affected, which use or define what?

Sorting cross-references out, the problem of *stability*, is a serious problem for authors, especially when writing large documents, since the problem can consume a large amount of apparently unproductive time. The Appendix shows that the time overhead for the **xr**-style approach to cross-referencing is negligible.

6. The cross-referencer xr

In contrast to L^aT_EX, **xr** has a very simple cross-referencing mechanism, which we will see can serve a variety of purposes.

6.1. Syntax

A cross-reference is defined in **xr** by writing #define *name value.* The value bound to any name can be obtained by writing <<*name*>> at any point in the document, before or after the definition of the name.

Notice that the form of *value is* unrestricted: it will often be section or page numbers, but can equally be bibliographic citations (e.g. "(Aho and Sethi, 1988)") or other text. Special effects can be readily obtained by making the cross-reference value some text that the typesetter in turn processes, to format text in a footnote, to convert to the words 'above' or 'below' as appropriate, or perhaps a collection of values (page number, section number, chapter number) that the typesetter can 'take apart' to obtain the reference required.

Since **xr** is a separate program from the author's markup system, the markup system typically generates cross-reference definitions: the author writes cross reference definitions in a standard form. For example, in L^aT_EX the \label command may still be used, provided it is defined something like:[1]

```
\def\label#1{\string#define #1 \the\section}
```

6.2. Diagnostics

The diagnostics of **xr** are *very* detailed and specific. The author can request a summary of cross-reference usage (and any problems identified by **xr**) to be formatted along with his document. Diagnostics also specify any files using or defining cross-references –this is invaluable for any document involving more than one file!

Diagnostics can be entered in-line within the document, for example to appear as marginal notes in draft printings.

To a large extent, the diagnostics of **xr** are programmable, this not only allows **xr** to work with a variety of markup systems, but can also be used for surprising purposes, as we shall see.

Xr directly supports such tasks as carrying forward page and section numbers between separate files within a large document as a special case of cross-referencing. The advantage to the author is that this obtains the high-quality diagnostics, for example necessary if the ordering of files within the document is changed. An example of this will be given below.

---

[1] This ignores the T_EX \write command and details to store the page number so that it can be recovered with \pageref.

6.3. Non-standard uses

We simply give a brief list of 'non-standard' uses that xr may be used for in addition to the examples mentioned above.

- **xr** is frequently used to place reminders in documents. Simply by writing <<finish this>> (apparently a reference to a mysterious section) results in **xr** reporting that a cross-reference finish this is undefined, hence indicating to the author that he has more work to do and where to do it;
- similarly, the author may write sections that are intended to 'follow up' discussion elsewhere in the document. Here the author can define a cross reference, and **xr** will report that it is unused, until the author fills in the other text;
- we shall describe a sort-of WYSIWYG way of using a cross-referencer in a markup system below;
- document version control: the author wants each version of his document to be printed with a version number. **Xr** can treat the version number as a cross-reference, and the markup system is only required to add one to the last used value. Thus, each time the document is formatted, its version number is incremented appropriately;
- **xr** can be used to compensate for some deficiencies in the markup system. For example, in **troff** macros can only have names of two characters. In xr there is no such limitation. The author (or a library of definitions) might define unix **as** U\s-1NIX\s0\(tm, which typesets as UNIX™. The author then has a mnemonic name, and no worry about its possible conflict with other names in **troff** (and if there was a conflict, **xr** would say so);
- finally, **xr** is, of course, a persistent macro-processor, and it may be used as such.

6.4. Comparing Xr with a 'software tools' solution

It is very interesting to compare **xr** with a 'competitor', a software tool written by Aho and Sethi for the UNIX system (Aho and Sethi 1988):

	Xr	Aho & Sethi
Language	C code	Grep, shell, awk, and sed code
Lines of code	1868	20ish
Housekeeping	20%	90%
User interface	30%	10%
Error handling	50%	0%

The important points to note are that **xr** is *enormous* in comparison, but devotes a significant part of its implementation to diagnostic support for the user. (The percentage figures for Aho and Sethi are estimates). Of course, the actual size of a program (so long as it runs on the author's machine!) is of no real concern to the author. **Xr** is in fact very much faster than Aho and Sethi's system, but since I am a user of **xr**, maybe the time I took to implement **xr** should be weighed against the time Aho and Sethi took?

7. Examples

The examples below are based on **troff**. Details of **troff** can be largely ignored, except to note that \f3 is the command to start bold text, and \fP reverts to the previous font, typically roman (non-bold) text. Thus 'a\fBb\fPc' typesets as 'a**b**c', with a bold **b**.

7.1. Conventional cross referencing

Suppose the document being processed contains the following text:

```
.NH 1
Example
.xr example
.LP
This section gives the example mentioned in <<mention-example>>.
. PP
This section (<<example>>) needs writing.
<<so-write-a-conclusion!>>
```

We assume that the **troff** macro '.xr' has been defined to generate #define instructions for **xr**. The call here will cause the cross-reference example to be defined to refer to this section.

First, the text above is filtered by **xr**:

```
xr database - example
New database: database
example: uses some undefined names
```

Xr is told to save cross-references in a database, called simply database, which is here created for the first time. At present, the file example uses undefined names, because **xr** has not yet processed any definitions. If we were to print the output of running **xr** at this stage we would get:

```
.NH 1
Example
.xr example
.LP
```

This section gives the example mentioned in \f3mention-example undefined\fP.
.PP
This section (\f3example undefined\fP) needs writing.
\f3so-write-a-conclusion! undefined\fP

Every reference is undefined! But formatting this document will generate appropriate definitions, perhaps

#define mention-example 1.2 (on page 2)
#define example 4.3 (on page 10)

Suppose these definitions are stored in a file example.out.[2] They must now be processed by **xr:**

xr database + example.out
example: reprocess, but still uses some undefined names

If now we run xr to expand the definitions we obtain:

.NH 1
Example
.xr example
.LP
This section gives the example mentioned in 1.2 (on page 2).
.PP
This section (4.3 (on page 10)) needs writing.
\f3so-write-a-conclusion! undefined\fP

At this stage, **xr** could generate the following summary. Note that this has been typeset, as it would have been if the text had been included along with the rest of the document. (**Xr** generates the appropriate formatting instructions).

Comments:
so-write-a-conclusion! undefined

Files:
example: uses some undefined names standard-input: OK

Cross-references:
example
→ "4.3 (on page 10)"

---

[2] In general the author doesn't want to know what files are called (indeed, files may be processed in such a way that their final name is unknown). **Xr** provides facilities (which are not described in the present paper) to attribute the definitions or usage of cross-references in any way that makes sense to the author.

Defined by: standard-input
Used by: example
mention-example
➡ "1.2 (on page 2)"
Defined by: standard-input
Used by: example
• so-write-a-conclusion!
➡ Not defined
Used by: example

The symbol '•' indicates that some error or inconsistency has occurred; in this case that a cross-reference has been used by the file example, but has not been defined.

If the definition of the reference mention-example now changes from '1.2 (on page 2)' to ' 1.2 (on page 3)', say, but we have not yet reformatted the file example, xr's diagnostics would look like this:

Comments:
mention-example (as used by example) has changed
from "1.2 (on page 2)"
to "1.2 (on page 3)"
so-write-a-conclusion! undefined\par **Files**:
example: uses some undefined names
standard-input: **OK**

Cross-references:
example
➡ "4.3 (on page 10)"
Defined by: standard-input
Used by: example
• mention-example
➡ "1.2 (on page 3)"
Defined by: standard-input
➡ "1.2 (on page 2)"
Used by: example
• so-write-a-conclusion!
➡ Not defined
Used by: example

Notice how the diagnostics clearly show how the cross-reference value for mention-example has changed, and that the file example is still using the obsolete value.

7.2. Version numbering

The following troff-wizardry ensures that the troff number register \nV is incremented by one each time the document is reformatted. It can therefore serve as a version number.

```
.nr V <<version-number>>+l
.tm #define version-number \enV
```

The first line here sets the value of the **troff** number register v to the carried forward version number, plus 1. This will be its value for this printing of the document. The second line causes **troff** to output a new definition of version-number for the next time.

7.3. Importing data

Suppose the author wants to know how many words his document is. Under UNIX, there is a simple utility, **wc**, that counts words. **Xr** can provide a simple way of getting the word count from **wc** into the document, and can warn the author when the word count changes. Essentially, the output of **wc** is massaged in the usual UNIX ways (in this case by writing, echo \#define-word count wc - w file'), and this text is processed by **xr** to define the 'cross reference' word-count.

Wherever the author writes <<word-count>>, then, the document will show 2344 or whatever, as required. If the word count changes, then the author will be warned along with any other cross-reference diagnostics. Similar techniques can be used to get any information into a document, and to track when the information changes.

7.4. Using templates

All parts of **xr** are programmable: the user can assign arbitrary strings to any of **xr**'s many so-called templates. Thus, the **troff**-specific strings \f3 and so on can easily be modified for T$_E$X or other typesetting needs.

When a cross-reference value is substituted for the author's <<name>>, **xr**'s normal template (called $normal) is used. This can be reset by writing, for instance, <<$normal *v [*r] >>, where *v and *r refer to the value of the name and the name itself. In this case, instead of simply getting the cross-reference value in the typeset document, the author also gets the cross-reference's name following it in square brackets.

Similarly, by writing <<$multiple *v [*r is multiply defined] >>, the author can easily see which cross-reference names are multiply defined. If the author does not want to spoil his draft text, the following might be more appropriate:

```
<<$multiple *v\foonote{*r=*v is multiply defined.}>>
```

where TeX has been used in the normal way to footnote the diagnostic (note that the *v occurring twice is acceptable).

Templates are provided for the symbols << **and** >>, so these can be changed as necessary. For example, writing <<$start \ref {>>\ref {$stop}>> changes the **xr** default style to look like LaTeX's. (Note that the second '<<' has to be written as \ref {, since we are already part-way through changing the symbols!) The remaining **xr** symbols, $, *, £define, and so on may also be changed in the same way.

7.5. Multiple file handling

Large documents are generally split between several files. This makes the author's document management much simpler, and (given the way most word processors are implemented) also much faster and reliable. However, splitting a document between files causes problems –for instance carrying forward page and section numbers from file to file. **Xr** can handle such problems in a uniform way as a special case of cross-referencing.

Before describing multiple file handling, we need to describe how **xr** handles cross-reference scoping. Generally, cross-reference names should be unique, but (especially in long documents) this restriction is tedious and places an unnecessary burden on the author. **Xr** allows two levels of cross-references (rather like FORTRAN). Essentially, a cross-reference name is either global or local. A global name is defined in another file; a local name is defined in the file where it is used. Thus a name that is defined twice must be defined in two different files, and must be used in at least one of them—to be global in one, and local in the other: otherwise the two definitions would constitute a multiple definition. The effect of this distinction is that any file can refer to its *own* conclusion (say) by using the cross-reference name <<conclusion>>, whether or not other files use the same name.

The local/global scheme has the very useful property that if a file has correct cross-references, then it may be made part of a larger document and it will *still* have correct cross-references – irrespective of any name clashes. Any redefinitions of cross-references will automatically be treated as local cross-references.

More complex scoping schemes could have been devised, but they were avoided because the corresponding diagnostics when things go wrong become complex and daunting. It is not obvious that more powerful scoping would have any practical benefits that could be offset against the greater costs of learning it, and coping with it when it is incorrectly used!

A special cross-reference name, $header, is provided. The reference $header works in a special way: it may be multiply defined, but its 'locality' is the *next* file in the document sequence. In other words, $header is defined in one file, but its value is picked up in the next. For this scheme to work, xr must of course be given the order of files the author requires.

Suppose the document is composed of the files chapterl, chapter2, chapter3 and chapter4 in that order, and that chapterl defines $header as froml, chapter2 defines $header as from2, and chapter3 defines $header as from3. Clearly, in a real situation, each chapter would define $header as some text that specifies the page, section and other information, but for the present illustration it is clearer to use trivial text.

We suppose that at this stage that chapter4 has not yet been processed, nor that **xr** has been told what the correct file order for the document should be. **Xr** is now told the file order by writing

xr database -o chapterl chapter2 chapter3 chapter4

and it immediately responds by producing the terse diagnostic, 'chapter4: reprocess', since chapter4 has not made use of the $header definition from chapter3.

Now suppose the author decides that chapters 2 and 3 should be exchanged. **Xr** will produce the following diagnostic.

```
chapter2: reprocess
chapter3: reprocess
chapter4: reprocess

header used by chapter4 has changed
    from "from3"
            to "from2"
header used by chapter3 has changed
    from "from2"
            to "froml"
header used by chapter2 has changed
    from "froml"
            to "from3"
```

Since **xr** keeps a database of cross-reference usage, there is no problem if the author changes his mind and prefers to reinstate the original file order. **Xr** will simply produce the diagnostic 'chapter4: reprocess', which reflects the original situation.

Other features to help with managing many files. An author may, for example, combine two files into one; **xr** provides an option so that file names in the database may be merged. Or an author may delete a file – xr provides an option so that all information concerning a file can be removed from the database. Or an author may rename a file; **xr** provides an option so that all information associated with a file is associated with a file of another name.

Finally, xr provides a useful feature where the author has an automated document processing system (as in UNIX): xr can be asked to provide a list of all files requiring reprocessing, and this list can be used to instruct the typesetting system to take appropriate action.[3] The same facility can be used automatically to determine when no further typesetting is required for the sake of getting cross-references consistent. (The Appendix has more discussion of this issue).

7.6. Default values

Xr's templates can be used ingeniously to provide default values for undefined cross-references. We simply set the undefined template to the text <<$undefined #define *r >>, and then generate a file of lines, "<<$name_i$>> $value_i$" for each cross-reference whose value should be defaulted.

Running this text through **xr** produces a list of definitions only for those cross-references that are not otherwise defined: since any undefined cross-reference <<x>> is converted to the text #define X, which is followed by x's intended default value. Running *that* text through **xr** then defines those cross-references to the desired default values.

7.7. WYSIWYG feature

The text the author writes soon becomes full of cryptic cross-reference names, such as <<dial figure>>, and the author will lose track of what refers to what. **Xr** can be used so that cross-reference names show their value, for example, <<dial figure = Figure 3 . 4>>. This 'what you see is what you get' feature was inspired by Aho and Sethi who provide a somewhat similar mechanism (Aho and Sethi, 1988), but is implemented entirely by **xr**'s templates. The fact that it can be done at all is an argument in favour of the template approach! (It should be noted that the complexity of the WYSIWYG templates can be completely hidden from any author who wants it: but for the present purposes we wish to explain the mechanism in detail).

We simply arrange for **xr** to process the following template definitions, which may conveniently be stored in a file:

```
<<$undefined <<*r = undefined>*&>*&>>
<<$normal <<*r = "*v">*&>*&>>
<<$multiple <<*r = "*v" multiply defined>*&>*&>>
<<$parameter <<*r *v>*&>*&>>
<<$comment =>>
```

The last line simply specifies that henceforth **xr** will use the character = for comment. The first three lines give suitable replacement texts for undefined, normal and multiply defined cross-references. The template $parameter is the template for processing the template-setting commands themselves; normally, of course, it is null, but in this case we want them to be retained. Setting

[3] In UNIX, we could write:for i in 'xr database -u'; do troff $i. . . done.

$parameter **to** <<*r *v>> simply causes any template settings to be copied faithfully by **xr**.

If our demonstration text now follows these definitions, **xr** produces the following text, showing cross-references together with their definitions:

```
.NH 1
Example
.xr example
This section gives the example mentioned
in <<mention-example = "4.3 (on page 10 ">>) needs
writing.
<<so-write-a-conclusion! = undefined>>
```

(The detail '* &' is a null character, and is used here to stop **xr** recognising >*&> as the actual end-of-name symbol, >>. Other *-symbols are provided, for example *n for a newline, as well as the symbols *r, *v, and so on).

8. Possible extensions

Xr is at present no more than a persistent macro processor with high quality diagnostics. It could, however, be extended to analyse the relations defined by the author's use of cross-references. We give three examples here:

- *Symmetry* . If section x refers to section y, does y symmetrically refer to x?
- *Transitivity* . If section x refers to y, and y refers to z, does section x refer to section z?
- *Reflexivity* Does section x refer to itself? (Reflexive references happen when the author moves text from a section to another section that was previously referenced by it).

One imagines that the author would indicate to **xr** what sort of properties each reference should obtain. For example: a 'continued from <<place>>' probably requires a symmetric reference; whereas reflexive cross-references are typically erroneous and should be reported (see Section 2.2).

It would be possible to perform a topological sort on the *defines* > *uses* ordering, and hence for **xr** to recommend a section ordering that (for instance) minimises forward cross-references.

8.1. What did I do wrong?

Xr is the third cross-referencer I have designed (at a rate of one every three years!), and I still have a lot to learn. When I designed **xr**, I made a fundamental distinction between *using* cross-references and *defining* them. Their syntax is very different, and **xr** has to be run in two different modes to process uses and definitions. Although the program code of **xr** would be simplified if this distinction was removed, I think that the distinction makes

xr somewhat easier to explain. (On the other hand, changing templates might be more natural if they were treated as cross-reference definitions).

Viewing **xr** as a persistent macro-processor suggests all sorts of possibilities: hauling in features that are provided by macro-processors would of course provide an enormous flexibility. On the other hand macro-processors are notoriously complex things, and it is not clear that the author should be burdened with yet another complex system! In summary, **xr** as an author's cross-referencer is ideal; as a contribution to software tools technology, it could be simplified, but that is a different game altogether.

9. Summary

Although this paper may have appeared overly-technical in places, it has shown that **xr** solves the cross-referencing problem very flexibly, reliably, and provides the author with lots of helpful support. **Xr** is a 'clean' author's tool: it does just one thing and it does that very well. Though it has no specialised features, its deliberate flexibility also opens up interesting applications beyond the normal realm of cross-referencing. **Xr** can be harnessed for a variety of interesting information processing tasks –of which WYSIWYG cross-references is but one example.

Because **xr** does a good book-keeping job for the author, the author is freed to write using or not using cross-references as he wishes, happy in the knowledge that all conflicts and other problems will be accurately and precisely reported. The result is that **xr** changes the way authors write.

The guidelines for designing **xr** were: first, that its explanation should be simple; secondly, that it would be flexible and uncommitted to any particular markup system; thirdly, that it should be simple and reliable to use. This last point required extensive effort in providing diagnostics, and in fact **xr**'s diagnostics may be read directly by the author or included within a document. Overall, these guidelines have resulted in a powerful cross-referencer that can do all normal cross-referencing with virtually no effort or training on behalf of the author, yet, **xr**'s flexibility means that it can tackle some useful and interesting 'cross-referencing' problems.

9.1. The paradox of good (writing) tools

Good tools identify and separate tasks. Thus, a good typesetting system separates the tasks of writing from presentation. This allows the user of the tool –the author – to concentrate his attentions to whichever part of the task concerns him, without worrying about the other. Thus, the author can add a paragraph or two, and does not need to worry about pagination. Yet because the tasks are made separable, the user can combine them! In the typesetting example, the author can, if he wishes, fiddle with running headings, pagination, and so on more-or-less at the same time as he edits the textual content. (Such blurring is more obvious in WYSIWYG editing systems).

The paradox of good tools is this: because they identify tasks and allow the user to pursue those tasks independently, the user can (when he wants to) do the tasks in any order or combination he wants, without worrying about strange interdependencies. The effect seems to be a blurring of the user's tasks distinguished by the tool!

The same paradox is manifest in **xr**: cross-referencing becomes a separate and distinct activity from content writing. The author does not have to plan what sections go where, or know what pages they land on. In this sense cross referencing is separated. Yet the author can now write his document as if the cross-references were actual text, for they surely will be when he prints the document. Thus, although **xr** has separated cross-referencing, because it is now automated the user does not have to consider it a separate activity (to be done at the last possible moment) as it would have been in a conventional system (the author would have had to await page proofs before he could write in the actual cross-references) .

Note. Science depends on, and encourages, the repetition of investigations and the full disclosure of methods. To this end the source code of **xr** is available from the author in machine readable form, subject to normal copyright restrictions. The author's JANET email address is: harold@uk.ac.stir.cs.

10. References

Aho, A.V. and R. Sethi, R. (1988) Maintaining cross-references in manuscripts, *Software—Practice and Experience,* 18(1).

Lamport, L. (1986) *L^aT_EX Document Preparation System,* Addison Wesley, Reading, MA.

Lindsey, C.H. and van der Meulen, S.G. (1973). *Informal Introduction to ALGOL 68.* North-Holland, London.

Szymanski, T.G. (1986). Assembling code for machines with span-dependent instructions, *Communications of the ACM,* 21(4).

Appendix: How many passes?

An author may want a forward cross-reference to have the general form 'see above!below on this page' or 'see *pn*' depending on whether the cross-reference IS defined on the current page, or on some other page *n*. Suppose that initially the use and definition occur on the same page. It is quite possible that the length of the text 'see below on this page' is long enough to cause the definition (if, perhaps it is already near the bottom of the page) to be pushed onto the next page. Thus a second pass is required, to substitute the new value. Now the author wants the form of text 'see *pn*'. Since this is a shorter piece of text, the definition may be pulled back onto the current page, and the author will then want the original form. Clearly, the reference is unstable and it cannot be resolved by any number of passes.

Another pathological case is where the author uses the cross-referencer to keep track of a document version number. Each time the document is processed, the author *wants* the version number to increase. It therefore never stabilises, though its value is correct for each version when it is used.

These two cases, one accidental the other intentional, show that automatic handling of non-stable references would be difficult even if feasible.

A special case of formatting cross-reference values is the 'span-dependent instruction problem', shown to be NP-complete by Szymanski (1986). Some machine codes have different forms of instruction depending on the value of their operands. For example, a jump instruction may have a compact form for near labels (e.g. using small relative values for operands) and a long form for far labels (e.g. using large absolute values). The problem is that the assembler cannot know which form of instruction to use until it has a value for the target label, and that in turn depends on its choices for all intermediate instructions. Szymanski also shows that stable allocation of instruction forms may not be achieved if instruction operands can be arbitrary expressions.

The span-dependent instruction problem can be simulated by a programmable text formatter and cross-referencer; so, even when the set of cross-references is in principle stable, stability might only be obtained after exponential time (and with typically slow formatters, the constants of proportionality will be huge).

We gain a more optimistic view by making realistic but conservative assumptions. We suppose that cross-reference values are the character positions of their definitions (this is conservative: normally the author would want a page number, maybe a line number –but neither changes as fast as a character number). We assume that all values are substituted as numerals in any base *b* greater than 1; therefore the change in the length of a definition on substituting a new value will be approximately logarithmic in the ratio of new to old values.

It is possible that the author may wish to refer to pages by name (e.g. by chapter title) and the length of a name need be neither logarithmically nor even monotonically related to its defining character position – a symbolic name is however, less subject to change brought about by its earlier substitution Another confounding possibility is that the author might reasonably want to refer to positions using natural language (e.g. as in, 'see page fifty seven').

We now show that surprisingly few passes are required, approximately three, and (except in extreme cases) approximately independent of the number of cross-references.

The very first pass will have arbitrary values substituted; so a second pass is clearly necessary.

The second pass substitutes

either a now correctly known and fixed value (if the arbitrary value has no effect on its own definition, as would happen for a reference to a chapter or section number). If only fixed values are substituted no further passes are required.

or a preliminary value (if the original arbitrary value might have had an effect on its own definition, as could happen with a forward reference to a character number). In this case, at least one further pass is required.

If preliminary values are substituted, we need to show that they are normally close enough to their final values for one more pass to be sufficient. Suppose that the preliminary value has d digits. No more than a third pass will be necessary if the text between the start of the use of this value and its definition changes within the bounds b^{d-1}, $b^{d}-1$. This gives considerable latitude (the numeral base b is normally 10), considerably greater than d or expected changes in d. After the first pass (when an arbitrary value was substituted, but it could have been 0), cross-reference values will tend to increase until they stabilise.

Since the document is finite (and therefore no longer than b^{n} where n = max (d)) reference values will tend to be at the low end of each interval $b^{d-1}, b^{d}-1$, and large increases will be necessary to require an extra digit. If there are many cross-references between a forward reference and its definition, the situation is not much worse. The effect of changing the values of references is again logarithmic. The more references, the longer the document and the greater the stable range of values covered by the necessary number of digits. In particular, for any numeral base b >1, there is no finite number of forward cross-references that indefinitely postpone stability (though in unary, with b = 1, Just one forward reference is sufficient –pathological uses of Roman numerals may cause intermittent trouble).

It should be noted that a document almost always has to be processed many times in the normal course of revision –thus the apparent overhead of each pass is distributed through the conventional format-revise-format cycle. It is highly likely that the cross-reference definitions will have stabilised before the time of the final revision, so the overhead of using a multi-pass cross-referencer is generally negligible.

8

Text to Hypertext and Back Again

Claude Ghaoui,
Steven M. George,
Roy Rada,
Martin D. Beer
University of Liverpool.

Janus Getta
University of Kuwait.

Abstract

The establishment of hypertext as a usable medium has raised problems when confronted with the transition to and from more traditional methods of writing documents. If hypertext is to become a viable and widely used methodology, the process of transferring from linear to hypertext forms and back again must be satisfactorily achieved. This paper mainly describes work investigating the hypertext to text transformation but the reverse process (text to hypertext) is also examined. Three experiments are reported, the first looking at document structures for guiding the linearisation process, the second looking at document content and semantics. The third experiment is the MUCH experiment where a semantic net is used to investigate the linearisation process. Finally methods will be described to quantify the success of the linearisation process and some conclusions on the role of semantics and structure within hyperdocuments are presented.

1. Introduction

Documents are produced, in the vast majority of cases, for production in linear hard-copy form. The printed page is the most widespread method of passing information within and between the generations of our societies. The increasing complexity of information and the need for faster and more direct access to it, have demonstrated that the traditional method of storing and presenting information in linear form is inadequate.

With hypertext we have a different way of organising documents, which is highly suited to the greater flexibility offered by a computer for browsing and creating semantically richer, more complex documents, and at its best aims to imitate the thought processes of the human mind. In recent years however, the computer has increased in its power to create and distribute electronic documents which may take this new format, that of hypertext, with the majority of these documents also meant for paper distribution. A recent example was the July 1988 edition of the journal *Communications of the ACM* which was produced both in hypertext and linear text forms.

Many different systems are now available in the market for both specialist and non-specialist people. A closer look at any hypertext system shows that it is in fact *nodes* and *links*. The nodes constitute a database of concepts and the links join these concepts together to form a network of information. Nodes and links are in fact the secret behind the great power of hypertext and yet at the same time the reason for some of the difficulties for its effective use.

The following question arises. What system is best suited to the handling of both text and hypertext, and is able to effectively convert between the two? Since all hypertexts consist of nodes and links, the main issue, which differentiates between the systems, is how nodes and links are structured and defined so that information can be organised and stored effectively, the aim being, later on to, enable efficient access to this information. The informality in hypertext causes some serious problems, one such being the disorientation problem, another, the production of linear documents, known as the *"linearisation process"*.

Disorientation occurs when readers who browse hypertext networks become 'lost', unaware of where they are in relation to the document, and thus unable to achieve a sense of text, i.e. an intellectual feel for the substance of the document. This is analogous to starting at a particular word in a thesaurus and passing from one similar associative word to another. Soon it is likely that the reader would be examining a word that is completely different from the original word, with no notion of any meaning to the derivation that has just taken place.

However, this paper is concerned with another major problem for hypertext, that of linearisation, i.e. the production of linear documents from non-linear ones. Linearisation is a transition from one state (the non-linear) to another state (the linear) and is important for the several reasons. Linear documents are the *de facto* representations of text and the printed page is still the most popular method for passing information, thus for publication of even hypertext documents they should be able to be translated into the paper format. Also `good' linear documents guide the reader to relevant information smoothly and interestingly instead of asking "where to search for what?", as can happen searching a hypertext. The feeling with some hypertext systems can be like trying to find one's way through a maze, that is, try every path until the goal is found – be it exit or final document. However, one of the more exciting possibilities offered by hypertext is that of flexibly created documents from a single hypertext database. Hence, people could carve out documents to suit their own personal needs for complexity and subject, rather than have just one level of general text. An example might be the production of two documents from a medical database, one concentrating on diseases and their causes whilst the other concentrates on diseases and their treatments, information which would be linked in the database. This would allow different perspectives of a linear document generated from one non-linear document as the source.

2. The processes of writing

In this section we shall look briefly at the process of writing and describe some existing systems which have been developed to aid the author. Writing can either be undertaken by a single author or can be a collaborative activity, each requiring some common and some different support techniques

Writing is a conceptual activity, Flower and Hayes (Hayes and Flower 1986) said that writing is a problem solving act. The composing process (in its simplest terms) can be seen to approximate to the following:

- Plans for generating ideas (building up a knowledge network).
- Plans for producing a paper (transformation of ideas).

With these simple methods we can successfully turn ideas into a written paper, taking into consideration the writer's purpose, conventional form, reader-based plans and producer-based plans.

A simple model of writing is that an author makes notes about a topic on which he is going to write. In these notes the author establishes the basic information on which the document will be based. This process then leads into an organisational stage when a writer will decide on the general skeletal structure of the document which is then fleshed out in the third stage, that of writing the text of the document within this framework. Given this very crude model for writing, we wanted to see how, if at all, writers would go about preparing a document if we offered a fixed set of link types for their documents.

A study of 35 potential writers, ranging from experienced (lecturers, postgraduate students) to novice writers (undergraduates, manager of a newsagent, even a golf professional) was undertaken to try to ascertain how people go about writing and how they would see a hypertext schema (as being investigated at Liverpool) fitting in with their respective methods.

Although our simple writing model described above still fitted in with virtually all of the people interviewed, we realised that within each of the separate categories of the model there were almost as many subtlely different methods as the people asked. Each person seemed to have their own particular idiosyncrasy regarding their writing method. Some people made copious notes on paper before transferring to computer, others planned out in graphic form and then transferred that to an outline and then to the computer to type the document in. Only two people used the computer solely when going about their writing, that is, to plan organise and produce their work.

Once the interviewees had described their writing styles a hypertext schema was explained to them and their reactions, feelings and comments duly noted. One interesting point that arose out of the study was the way people reacted to the concept of link types. Not one author said that they explicitly think about link types, when creating an outline of a network when initially planning the document. However, 7 out of the 35 did identify with the fact that they implicitly attach meaning to the links when they used them. The feeling was very much, "**well I know what it means!**". Most people felt that for collaborative work, they could see a real benefit from more explicit and descriptive links. The possible use of this is proposed in the Discussion and Conclusion section.

The interview described here simply questioned people on their writing styles as single authors, a similar investigation is currently being attempted, looking into collaborative authoring methods. It will be described more fully in George (1990). We shall look in more detail at the properties and differences between linear and hypertext documents bearing in mind some of the points that the last study has brought up.

2.1 Linear documents

Linear documents may take many different forms from poems to newspapers, and from novels to scientific papers. The type of document suggests the method with which this document should be represented and handled, the type and the subject of a document suggest its *structure* (syntactical view) and its *semantics* (semantic view).

The syntactic view considers the physical layout, i.e. the ordering of the components of a document which suits its type. For example search paper has the following ordering: Title; Authors; Abstract; Introduction etc.... The semantic view considers the smooth flow of ideas and the logical connection between them (McEnery and Oakes 1989). The subject of a document suggests the semantic order of its components, for example historical events require chronological arrangements. For this view, *styles of writing* should be considered, examples are: chronological order; spatial order; inference; classification; comparison and contrast; examples and illustration.

Some documents have a hierarchical structure (like a medical handbook), others have a hierarchical structure with rich cross-referencing (like a course catalogue) and others have a purely linear structure with fewer cross-references (like essays). This shows that even in linear documents there exists *degrees of linearity*.

2.2. Non-linear documents

The linear form of storing and accessing information has been demonstrated to be inadequate (Weyer 1982). The term *non-linear text* refers to *hypertext*. This general term can include many multimedia systems, including at a more advanced level, sound, voices, animation, pictures as well as text and graphics.

Vannevar Bush first expressed his vision of a Memex system for connecting units of information with associative links that could be then indexed and accessed directly (Bush 1945). Bush's vision was then computerised by Nelson and known as hypertext. Several systems have some of the attributes of hypertext but do not qualify, examples are: window-systems; file-systems; outline-processors and text-formatting systems. In the simple case a hypertext system has three main components.

- A database of text.
- A network which connects the text components.
- Tools for creating and browsing the database and the network.

Examples of hypertext systems are: NLS, Augment, gIBIS, Synview, Zog, KMS, Notecards and Hypercard (Conklin 1987). Hypertext systems were grouped according to applications into the following four classifications: macro-literal systems, problem-explorations tools, browsing systems and general-hypertext technology. For each different application, we notice the rich use of different types of links and nodes. The capability of creating links between and within documents allows the writer to make references and allows the reader to make his own decisions about which links to follow and in what order. Links can have names and types and can be turned on and off. They can be used for several functions, for example referential purposes (reference or non-hierarchical). These links can be directed forward and backward to give more details on relevant information. Links are also used for organisational purposes (hierarchical links), they connect a parent node with its children and form tree subgraphs within the hypertext network.

A hypertext *node* represents a single concept or idea. Deciding about its suitable size is a problem in order to make it a discrete object which can fit with its neighbours (coherence of a network). Some systems sort nodes into different types (typed nodes) and using semi-structured nodes simplifies the writer's and the reader's job. Some systems allow the use of composite nodes, in which several nodes are treated as a single node. Other systems allow the use of hierarchical nodes (e.g. table of content).

No standard exists, so each system defines its own set of nodes and links. In most of these systems, the user is totally in control. He decides what information to include in a node, and the links in the network, at the risk of creating meaningless links, worthless database and following obscure paths.

The benefits of hypertext are many, an example is direct and immediate access to information. More importantly, the selectivity of access offers a freedom to pinpoint relevant information without the need to wade through a mass of irrelevant information.

The informality of hypertext represented by the features of the links and nodes, together with the increased accessibility of information, raises some interesting queries, for example:

- Picking a good starting or entry point.
- Disorientation or wrong selection.
- The (semi) automatic production of linear documents –*linearisation*.

All of these problems have a common theme. It is the problem of how to construct a logical path which flows between ideas smoothly? The following section addresses the problems and features associated with the *linearisation process*. Linearisation is the process of traversing a hyperdocument in order to convert it into a linear form. There exists *Degrees of Linearity*. Some documents are totally linear, i.e. there exists no cross-references between its components while other documents are less linear, i.e. they contain few cross-references to other documents, sections, chapters etc. until we reach the level of non-linearity, i.e. like a hyperdocument in which the textual information is divided into small chunks which cross-reference each other. Linearisation is important for several reasons. Humans prefer reading a printed paper rather than a screen version although studies have shown that speeds can be comparable for high quality VDUs, the preference is still for paper. Paper-based "good" documents offer the reader a sensible guide through a network of interrelated topics i.e. keeping the coherent stream of ideas between subtopics in a stricter manner than the more flexibly browsed hypertexts. We envisage different perspectives of a linear document could be generated from one source network, enabling different readers to obtain a document tailored for their particular needs, more specific than a general document. For example, given one medicine database, information of different expertise and/or subject could be obtained.

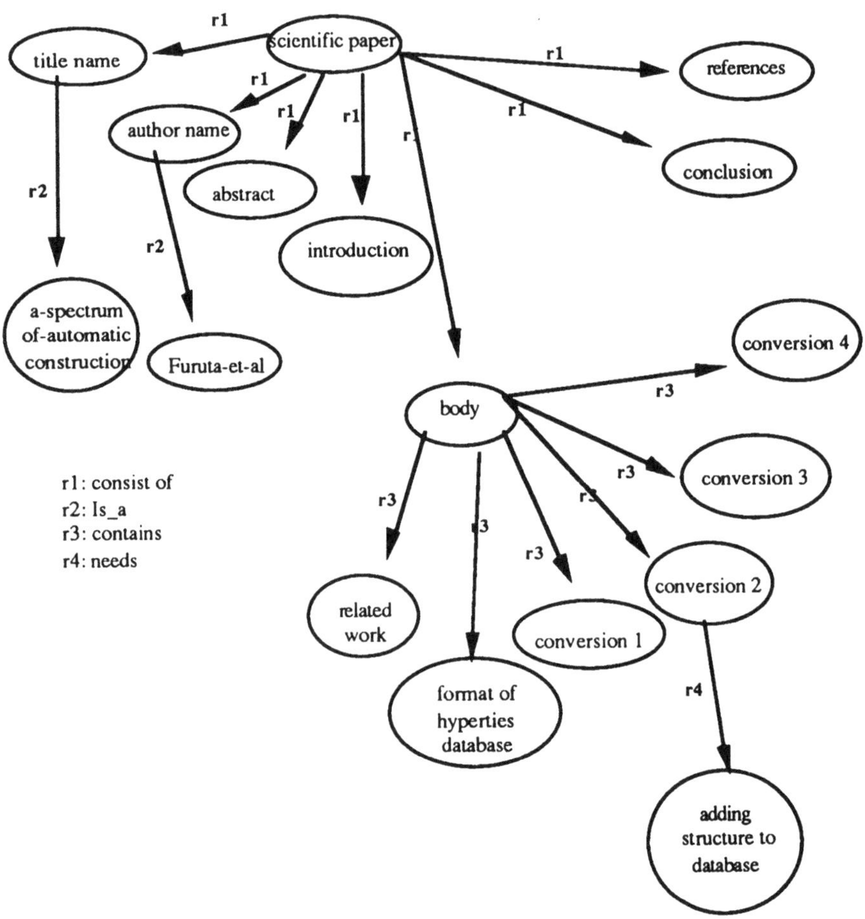

Figure 1. Network of nodes extracted from structure.

3. Text to hypertext: A structural approach

A study by Furuta *et al.* Frisse (Frisse 1989), Nunn *et al* and Egan *et al* (Egan *et al* 1989) has shown that the structure of documents has a great impact on the success or failure of automatic construction of hypertext databases and links. Automated or semi-automated conversion is possible for a document which falls under one of the following categories:

- Regularly-structured. Examples: course-catalogue and medical handbook.
- Documents which contain many relatively short paragraphs cross reference each other.
- A document with a markup language e.g. **TROFF**.

In the absence of any of these marks, the general recognition of a document structure is still a research problem, thus the possibility of automated conversion in this case is very weak.

This examination uses *only* the *structure of a document* , i.e. its physical ordering as a guidance to build up a network of interrelated nodes. A directed graph structure is used for representation. Nodes are primitive and contain just text information. Each node has a name which represents a section or subsection title in the original document and sets of attributes and keywords could be attached to nodes –organisational binary relations are used.

Figure 1 shows a possible directed graph based on the structure of the scientific paper. The nodes represent the main components of the paper, while the edges reflect the structural logical relations between the nodes. The edges could be assigned some labels, in figure 1 the labels are chosen randomly to give a meaningful sense for the relations between the nodes.

Two main traversal techniques for the graph are used, depth first and breadth first. Assuming that the graph is ordered, traversals are trivial; but for unordered graphs both techniques generate a number of different possible linear documents (number produced < ($N!$), where N is the number of nodes in the graph). Figures 2a and b are samples of the possible output. We notice that at least one of the depth-first traversals produced is very close to the original document and thus suggests that we do have some, albeit simple, algorithms to be used to generate the original document from a hypertext interpretation (see Figure 2).

This study shows us that the structure of a linear document affects the construction of the graph representing its non-linear form, which in turn affects the traversal algorithm needed for successful and efficient linearisation. Also, we see that a number of different linear documents are generated using one traversal algorithm and one graph. In order to force the generation of a document which is close to the required document, some rules could be imposed. This is applicable for documents with regular structures, for other documents, in which the structure is not clear, the following study is concerned.

```
Scientific Paper
        Title-Name
                A-Spectrum-Of-Automatic-Construction-of-Hypertext
        Author-Name
                Furuta-et-al
        Abstract.
        Introduction.
        Body.
                Related-work.
                Format-Of-Hyperties-Database.
                Conversion1.
                Conversion2.
                        Adding-Structure-to-database
                Conversion 3.
                Conversion 4.
        Conclusion
        References
```

Figure 2a. Possible depth first traversal of graph in Figure 1.

```
Scientific-Paper
                Title-Name
                Author-Name
                Abstract
                introduction
                body
                conclusion
                References
        Title-Name
                A-Spectrum-Of-Automatic-Construction-Of Hypertext
        Author-Name
                Furuta-et-al

        Body
                Related-Work
                Format-Of-Hyperties-Database
                Conversion 1
                Conversion 2
                Conversion 3
                Conversion 4
        Conversion 2
                Adding-Structure-To-Database
```

Figure 2b. Possible breadth first traversal of graph in Figure 1.

4. Text to hypertext : A semantic approach

In this work, the *content* of a document is used to extract its main concepts and the semantic relations between them. Some automated techniques could be applied for this purpose and work for automatic abstraction (Bucher and Driscoll 1989, Luhn 1958) are two examples. Another example is the use of some Natural Language Processing techniques for understanding and representing knowledge as a conceptual network. Since this work is out of the scope of this paper, a human expert and small documents like the abstracts of scientific papers are used. The human expert uses his natural expertise to understand the content of an abstract and construct a graph that represent this abstract.

The graph produced here could be called a *Semantic Network.* Primitive nodes that contain text represent concepts, each node is assigned the name of that concept and to each of these nodes, a set of keywords and attributes can be attached. Directed binary semantic relations exist between each two concepts: independent type; referential embedded links can also exist, an example of which are the keywords. Figure 3 shows a possible semantic network constructed from the abstract in paper and breadth first techniques are applied on this graph. Figures 4a and b show possible traversals of such semantic network[1]. A comparison between the original abstract and the output in Figures 4a and 4b shows that while the linear document is very close to the original one, the produced output still needs some manual re-editing by the human expert. It is very difficult to get as close to the desired target format, more so than encountered in the last section, where the study was based on structure.

This study is based only on semantics which might work for small documents like abstracts but is difficult to apply to larger documents. An experiment with the MUCH (Multiple Users Creating Hyperdocuments) system has shown that constructing a network based on semantics is a very difficult task for a large document, e.g. a book. Due to this difficulty, the constructed network may be misleading and thus very difficult to be managed and then traversed to give us a meaningful linear form.

In the two experiments above, a digraph structure is used to represent a network of hypertext. Primitive textual types of nodes and binary relations of organisational and referential types are used. These experiments do not consider composite nodes, revisions and n-ary links which might be experimented on in the future. The two experiments suggest that *both* structure and semantic analysis are important for hypertext construction and linearisation processes. Based on the previous theory and experiments, the following two sections suggest some theory for linearising a hypertext graph based on structure and semantics. Some evaluation for such linearisation is also given.

---

1 In these figures, The ordering generated by the traversal algorithm is shown. The repetition of nodes' names are just for readability purposes since after the depth and breadth algorithms visit a node, this node will not be visited again.

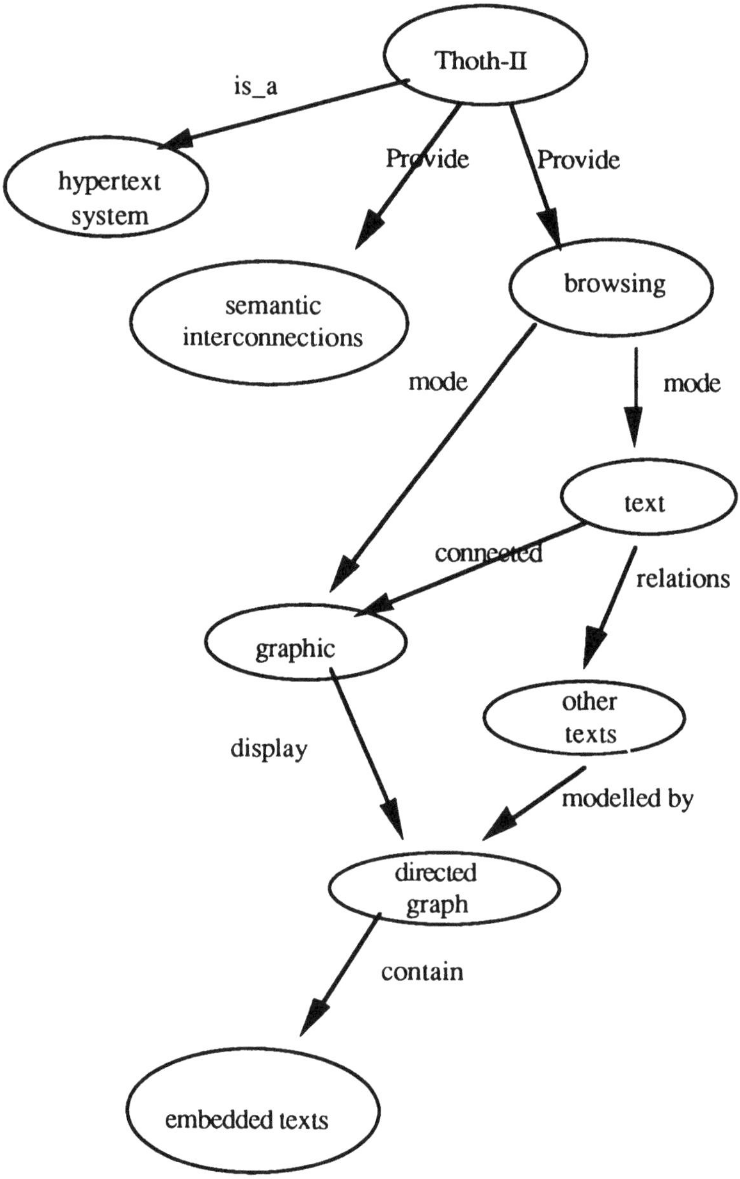

Figure 3. Network of nodes extracted from the semantics of abstract.

Toth-II **is_a** hypertext system
Toth-II **provide** Semantic interaction
Toth-II **provide** Browsing
Browsing **mode** graphic
Graphic **Display** directed-graph
Directed-graph **contains** embedded texts
Browsing **mode** text
text **relations** other text

Figure 4a. Depth first traversal of semantic network in Figure 3.

Toth-II **is_a** hypertext system
Toth-II **provide** Semantic interactions
Toth-II **provide** Browsing
Browsing **mode** graphic
Browsing **mode** text
Graphic **Display** directed-graph
text **relations** other texts
Directed-Graph **contains** embedded text

Figure 4b. Breadth first traversal of semantic network in Figure 3.

5. The evaluation of linearised text

As discussed earlier, the nodes and links play an important role in the flexibility of hypertext systems and at the same time are behind many of the serious problems. In fact, nodes and links have a great impact on both the structure and semantics of a hypertext network. This means that information represented by the nodes of concepts must be organised in ways that prove useful later on. Links leading to relevant information must be distinguished from less fruitful ones. Since many paths are generated, we would like to develop a measure of the *"best path"*, i.e. the path which generates the more coherent and meaningful document.

The traversal algorithm as mentioned earlier considers only the structure of the graph, whether or not the graph itself was constructed via semantic or content guidelines. Therefore, the following evaluation is in fact for two reasons, first of all, to help in measuring the best path which would enable us to secondly, impose some semantic restrictions on the traversal algorithm so that at the end we have a traversal algorithm which is capable of considering the two views (structure and semantics) and serve our purposes better.

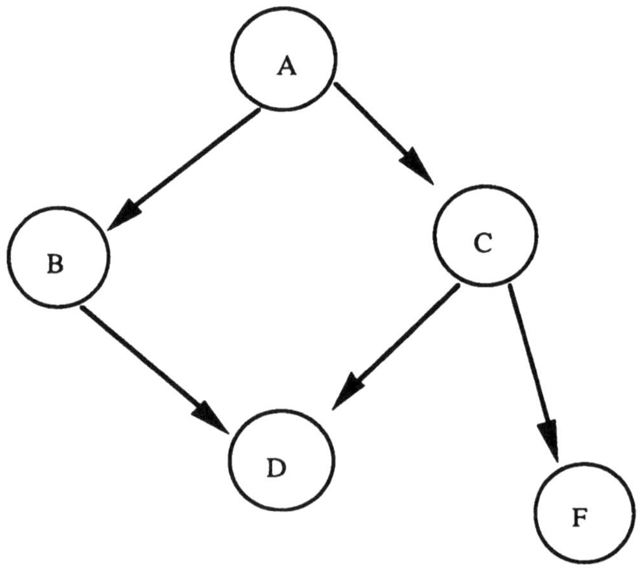

Figure 5. A graph of interrelated nodes.

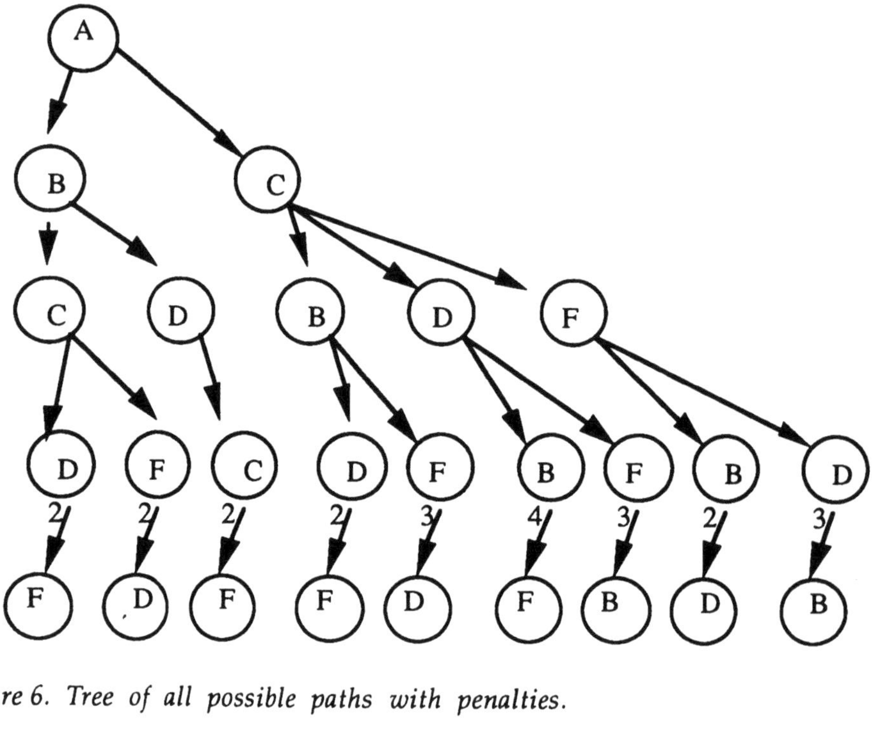

Figure 6. Tree of all possible paths with penalties.

5.1. Structural view

In this study, it is suggested that the path with the *minimum jumps* is the best, where jumping means moving from one idea to another which is not strongly relevant. Typically a jump may mean backtracking in a traversal algorithm, if the method requires us to backtrack 5 levels up a network, then we will have two concepts in the linearised text adjacent here, but actually 5 levels apart in the network. We believe this is a bad idea so to evaluate jumps, some *penalties* are suggested:

> **CASE 1.** Moving in the reverse direction from a visited-node to a non-visited node, assume *Penalty = 2.*
> **CASE 2.** Visiting a node for the second time, assume *Penalty=1.*

Other cases can be considered to suggest some other penalties. In Figure 6, the penalty for traversing each path of the simple graph from Figure 5 is shown. The *best path*\ is the path with the smallest penalty number. For the paths with equal values of penalties, other measures should be considered (under study). Taking the measure of jumps to reflect the relatedness of the ideas in a hyperdocument graph, suggests that the path with no jumps is the ideal path, and if it exists it is called *Hamiltonian Path.* This path suits the generation of some linear documents like *essay,* but does not suit documents with hierarchical structures, or which richly cross-reference other documents.

Since applying the jump-measures to choose a best path sometimes gives more than one alternative having the same penalty total, additional help should be suggested. For example, we can impose a set of partial order rules while traversing a graph. Figure 7 shows an example of a graph and a set of rules that are hoped to be satisfied in the generation of a linear path. Here the partial order rules enable certain paths to be ruled out. As Figure 7 shows, the partial rule $D > B$ means that (even though penalties are encountered) concept D must appear after A and before B. A tree of possible paths that satisfy the given set of rules is given in Figure 8.

5.2. Semantic view

Since the measure of jumps is not completely sufficient, the need to impose some partial order rules is useful, to increase the ability of creating such "good" linear documents by decreasing the number of possible linear traversals. Such rules could be formulated based on the features and properties mentioned in section 2. For example to express that two concepts are *contrasted,* a possible rule is $< c1, c2 >$ i.e. the two concepts $c1$ and $c2$ should follow each other *directly* . Similar rules could be formulated in the same way to impose a semantic and structural connection between the ideas and to generate meaningful linear documents.

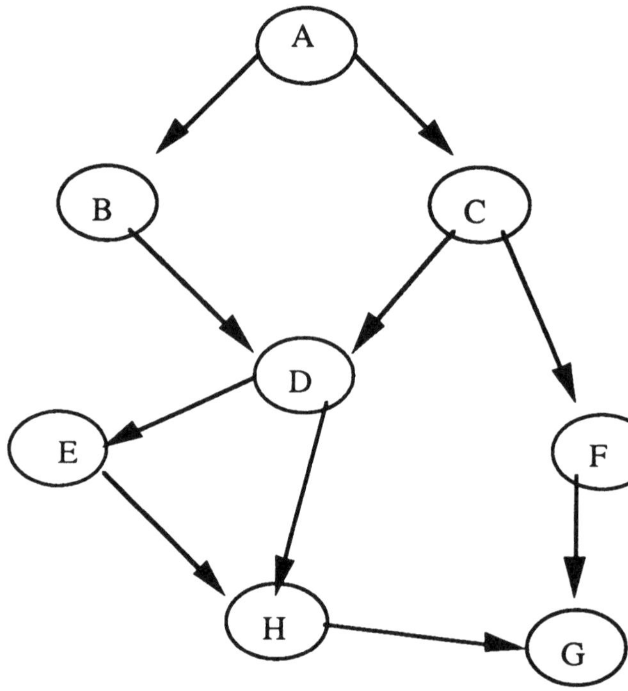

Figure 7. A graph of interrelated nodes with partial order rules.

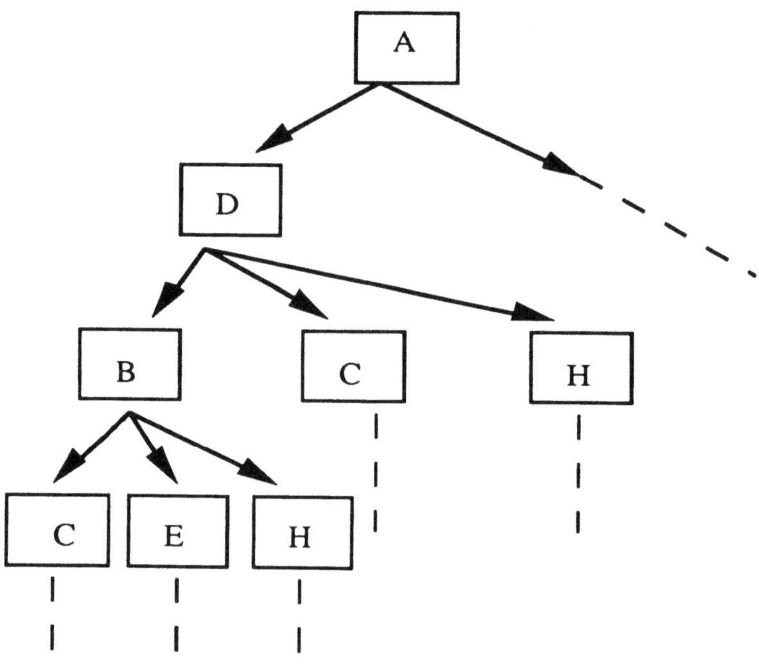

Figure 8. Paths available from partial rules.

6. MUCH system

6.1. Description

The MUCH system is being developed under the UNIX operating system, running on series 300 Hewlett Packard workstations. The code for the programs comprising the system is written in Mock Lisp under the Emacs editor.

Gnu Emacs offers a multiple window interface to the user, giving the ability to look either at different documents within buffers of the editor, or the user can see multiple views on the same document (or even a mixture of both). On the Hewlett Packard workstations, we can run the Emacs editor under the X Windows interface, and thus can have several, simultaneous copies of the Emacs editor being used on one workstation concurrently. Each of these instantiations can have access to the same files and the editor will provide elementary version management to bring the user's attention to the fact that certain versions of a document may have changed during the current working session.

Although this may seem obvious when the different copies of Emacs are on the same workstation, this principle is very important when considering collaborative work where the simultaneous copies of the editor are on distributed workstations. Indeed, this very problem had led to work on document version control and management, for the MUCH writing method, within the department at the moment.

6.2. Semantic net structure and implementation

The representation chosen for the hypertext was that of a simple semantic net comprising node-link-node triples. The nodes represent concepts within the network (also concepts within a document) and the links represent the relationship between the concepts. The links are uni-directional and we have only one way of constraining the search by the method of marking the links as not being able to be traversed.

The semantic net's structure was stored in the form of many small files within a directory, each file being called a `frame' and an example is shown here:

```
(collaborative_writing
        (has authors 1 2 3)
        (requires communication 4 5)
        (requires organisation* 6)
        (produces collaborative_documents)
        )
```

Each frame represents the information about a single node in the semantic net, showing the name of the net, the links to other nodes in the semantic net (these being names of other frames in the directory) and also the names of any paragraphs which should be associated with the node. The path of the search within the network was controlled by the order of the target nodes within the frame. If we wish a node to be visited ahead of another at any particular level, then they must be swapped around in the frame representation. This system places the onus of directing the traversal on the author and such a method is also used in a similar manner in another writing method (Wayner 1988), that of APT.

In the latter example we are looking at the structure representing a fictitious node called *collaborative_writing*. This has four links to other nodes. Lets look at the first link, this gives us the relation, *"collaborative_writing"* has *"authors"* and the associated paragraphs (which may comprise pictures) are enumerated as 1, 2 and 3, should explain this relationship. The second link gives a similar structure but the third link shows how the search can be constrained. The '*' at the end of the target node name signifies that even though we can print out the paragraphs associated with this triple we cannot go to the node being referenced and we must examine the next link at this level. Hence, paragraph 6 would be amended to our output and we would then continue with our investigation of the current node. The final link, which signifies that the node has been fully explored after it has, shows that we can have a link from the current node to a new one without necessarily having to have any associated paragraphs. The paragraphs were stored in their own directory in a similar way to the frames, each of which represented a basic building block (either paragraphs or figures) of the document.

Programs were written to aid the creation of a document for this prototype, which allow the author to create a paragraph which may be referenced by the semantic net frame whilst automatically ensuring consistency in names between the two, in other words that the frame does actually point to a paragraph of a particular name which does exist. However, we did find that deletion of paragraphs sometimes left holes in the semantic net and tools have been developed to find these and take care of them. The programs also produced contents pages, traversal paths listings, documents started from any point in the network, and lists of the relationships that had been explored.

6.3. Linearisation of MUCH network

Having created this schema of text and structure we could continue to develop the programs written in Mock Lisp to perform the traversal of the MUCH network and produce a linearised text. We experimented with two main traversal techniques for the semantic net, similar in nature, yet producing a marked difference in the end document. We examined the resulting documents with the authors ideal in mind and tried to draw comparisons between them, and explain any differences. The different orderings of the paragraphs produced by these different traversal algorithms were assessed to indicate where the most useful improvements where necessary.

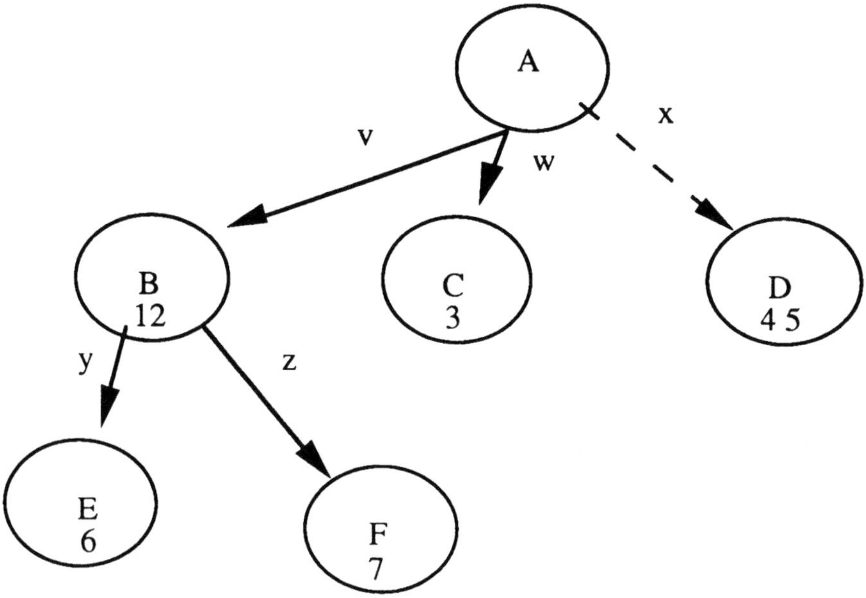

Figure 9. Semantic net example.

Briefly, we can describe the different algorithms as follows and Figure 9 shows example traversals of a very simple hierarchy, represented in the MUCH system in the following manner:

```
(A
        (v B 1 2)
        (w C 3)
        (x D* 4 5)
)
(B
        (y E 6)
        (z f 7)
)
```

The first algorithm searches through the semantic net (via the frames) in a depth first manner. When we arrive at a node, *all* of the paragraphs associated with the children of the node are printed out –this can be likened to a breadth first expansion of the contents of the node. Once the associated paragraphs have been printed out, the search then continues in a depth first manner and the next node is expanded in a similar way to that above. From Figure 9, we see that the search would start at the node called *A*. Immediately, all of the paragraphs associated with targets nodes from this one are printed out, giving us paragraphs 1, 2, 3, 4 and 5 in our output. The depth first part of this algorithm then takes over and we move to node *B*. Again the breadth first expansion of the paragraphs takes place, appending paragraphs 6 and 7 onto the output. Backtracking and further searching visits all of the other nodes in the tree, but no more paragraphs are printed out.

The second method simply searches through the semantic net and expands the contents of the nodes (prints the paragraphs) in a depth first manner. Hence, in Figure 9, we start at *A*, and print the two paragraphs (1 and 2) associated with the next node, *B*. We then move to *B* and produce paragraph 6. Backtracking then takes place and paragraph 7 is the next produced and so on. From the text at the bottom of Figure 12, we can see that although we visit the nodes within a network in the same order, we get the text associated with them differently. The paragraphs would be produced in the following order:

Depth first traversal gives - 1 2 , 6 7 , 3 4 5
Breadth first traversal gives - 1 2 3 4 5 , 6 7

The commas between the numbers representing the paragraphs in the figure are to show the reader at one point we move from one level to another when grabbing the paragraphs.

The programs were written to produce the same layout in order that any comparisons should regard the contents of the text rather than its visual representation. Hence, we had produced a text from the collection of paragraphs making up the original network (or a subset thereof) and we were left with the problem of obtaining a measure of quality and coherence within this synthesised document.

6.4. Observations on different outputs

Initially it was seen that the contents page produced by the programs were identical, confirming that each method traversed the network in the same depth first manner. The difference between the two resultant documents lay in the order of the paragraphs below this. In the first method, that of the breadth first expansion of paragraphs at any node, we see that any section of text is preceded by paragraphs introducing each of the topics within that section, before we go into more detail. This is similar to introducing the concepts that will be talked about and then fleshing them out in turn, although we should note that fleshing out each concept may in fact repeat the process by producing more introductory paragraphs from further down the tree. This approach seemed to give a traversal more akin to an overview of each level within a document rather than concentrating on a particular topic.

The second method, the depth first traversal of the nodes and the paragraphs associated with the nodes, gave us a more focused approach. One topic within a section was fully introduced and described before we reached any of the other parts of this section. It was felt that this was more in line with a book, in which we do not necessarily get an overview of the chapter before the main text. This method gave us a tighter, more focused view of the document under investigation.

Both of the methods described above seem to be at the extremes of the traversal possibilities. On one hand we produced a broadly based, overview of the subjects within the text, whilst the second method produced a detailed look at each topic. When different classes of document and reader models are considered, we see that each method may be applicable for a particular domain but not for others. Indeed, in the case of scientific reports we may wish to use a hybrid of the first and second methods, overviewing early on and focusing later in the traversal.

7. Discussion and conclusion

Based on this study, the problems of converting hypertext to text and text to hypertext are strongly related, in both processes **the content and the structure** are important. Study of the internal structure of hypertext represented by its links and nodes is needed. The almost random nature in defining nodes and links is one of the problems. Some models have succeeded in defining a structure for a hypertext graph that is capable of resolving some of these node and link problems. A good example is the Petri Net structure (Leland *et al.* 1988), which is targeted for the browsing problem, but are less useful for linearisation.

One possible solution might be to allow both representations to exist at the same time within a document. Figure 10 shows how we could have a structure comprising, in the simplest view, of structural links and semantic links. Some of these could be the same in position, but we would see them as separate entities. For linearising purposes we could have a structural set of links which would unambiguously define the structure (possible in a hierarchical form) of the printed version of the document. For hypertext browsing and documents, we could have a set of links which the author bases on the semantics of the text, which may be used for browsing and hypertext document production.

This basically divides the document between two domains, one the printed page, the other the computer-based electronic form. The addition of comments could be handled as semantic links, which may be read on line and yet not wanted in the final printed version. It may even be that at some point we may wish to traverse some of these semantic links (and so should be allowed) in order, for example, to print out all of the comments and discussion relating to a document. Figure 10 show a possible way of using such a structure, with the numbers showing how the bodies of text would be referred in an outline. This graphic shows sections of text which are linked together both structurally and semantically by the different line types. The dashed line represents the purely structural links whereas the solid types represent sections within the text which have semantic links to smaller sections. In this model we have both representations at the same time, and it is possible that a single link would function both semantically and structurally.

It could be possible then to extend this model to give us a very useful method for handling documents. The nature of links can be either semantic or structural. Link types, we feel, should not have static ordering of their relative priorities, but should be dynamically alterable, for instance, in one part of a document a link which corresponds to **example_of** may be of a higher priority than **is_a**, but the priorities may be reversed in another part of the document. Such dynamic *link values* are similar in nature and functionality to the rule values of Knowledge Based Systems. With alterations of these values, parts of the document can be carved out and even private segments to work in can be established within a parental hypertext network, important for collaborative authoring.

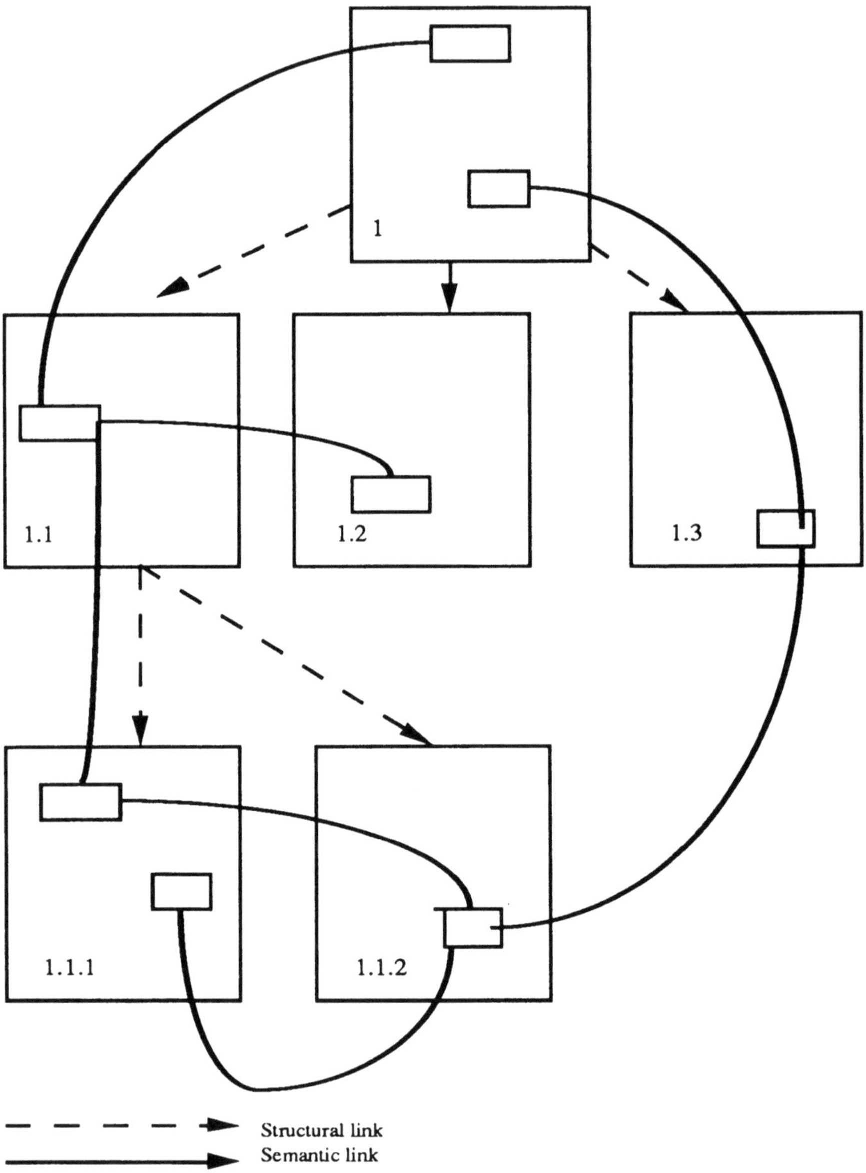

Figure 10. Structure and semantic links in one document.

If we move away from the traditional link-type prioritisation discussed earlier, then we can also move away from the staid, shortlink descriptions which have been shown to be unattractive to authors of many standards (George 1990). We can let the computer handle the updating of the links purely from a link value basis, thus freeing the writers to use link types in a more constructive and meaningful manner. The link types can become more descriptive, helping certainly collaborative authors, to understand what each of the others is trying to convey.

Two authors who may be collaborating over a hypertext network may wish to ascertain the thoughts of each other. If we allow for partitions to be created, by suitable alteration of link values, but allow for user defined, expressive link types then we can linearise and achieve more meaningful outlines, for example:

> (((Gary Player **is_a** Golfer) **excels_at** bunker play) **is_better_than** Jack Nicklaus)

Here it is more clear what the co-author's thoughts and intentions are regarding the subject under discussion. Obviously it is suggested that Gary Player is a great bunker player and is in fact better at this than Jack Nicklaus. However, ambiguities can still arise and we should be able to create comment nodes in the network whose link value would stop it being produced during linearisation. Our network then becomes a set of nodes and links, some of which are printable and others not. However, the key thought is that any node can have its link values altered to make it printable, hence even comments, discussion and meta-discussion will be produced during linearisation which may help in certain stages of a discipline such as software engineering.

The study currently undergoing sets out to test this idea and try to provide some information as to a schema which we can implement, to enable support for single or collaborative document authoring. This study is equivalent to the one mentioned earlier studying writing styles or single authors, but is being undertaken to ascertain the usefulness of more descriptive links combined with link values and hypertext partitions for collaborative authors.

With the results of this survey, it is hoped to be able to formulate a practical system to support the writing process from the point of view of the issues discussed previously.

8. References

Bucher, L. E. and Driscoll, J. (1989) An AI approach to automated abstracting. *Fourth Annual Rocky Mountain Conference on Artificial Intelligence Augmenting Human Intellect by Computer Conferencing --Proceedings*. Denver, Colorado.

Bush, V. (1945) As we may think. *The Atlantic Monthly,* 176, 1 (July).

Conklin, J. (1987) Hypertext: an introduction and survey. *Computer,* 20, 9 (September).

Egan, D. E., Remde, J. R., Landauer, T. K., Lochbaum, C. C. and Gomez, L. M.

(1989) Behavioural evaluation and analysis of a hypertext browser. *CHI '89 Proceedings,* ACM, New York.

Frisse, M. (1988) From text to hypertext. *Byte* (October).

George, S. M. (1990) Writing styles and link types. Internal report, Department of Computer Science, Liverpool University.

Hayes, J. R. and Flower, L. S. (1986) Writing research and the writer. *American Psychologist,* 41 (October).

Leland, M. D. P., Fish, R. S. and Kraut, R. E. (1988) Collaborative document production using Quilt. *Second Conference on Computer-Supported Cooperative Work: CSCW '88,* ACM, Portland Or.

Luhn, H. P. (1958) The automatic creation of literature abstracts. *IBM Journal of Research Development,* 2, 2 (April).

McEnery, A. and Oakes, M. (1989) Defining hypertext with reference to medium and method. *Proceedings of Information Retrieval* 1989, Sheffield (July).

Wayner, P. (1988) It's APT to write. *Byte.*

Weyer, S.A. (1982) The design of a dynamic book for information search. *International Journal of Man-Machine Studies,* 17.

9

Word Frequency Based Indexing and Authoring

Mahmoud Mhashi
Roy Rada,
University of Liverpool

Hafedh Mili
University of Quebec at Montreal

Geeng-Neng You
Akmal Zeb
Antonis Michailidis
University of Liverpool

Abstract

Can word frequency indexing be helpful in hypertext authoring? The MUCH (Multiple Users Creating Hypertext) system has been developed to support document creation, starting from the exploring phase through the organising and ending with the encoding phase. We address the problem of providing authors with access paths to the contents of a textbook. Building an outline for the textbook might provide such paths. A method developed by Mili (Mili and Rada 1987) was intended to construct a hierarchical semantic net from patterns of words across abstracts in a document database automatically. We applied this method on the entire text of an on-line textbook of 600 paragraphs by treating each paragraph as a separate document. The hypothesis was that the hierarchical semantic net so derived could support the construction of alternative access paths to the textbook. Our results suggest that the semantic built automatically is not a hierarchy. Authors may, however, use the index terms and the 'semantic net' relations to go from one paragraph to another related paragraph. Thus, the word-based indexing of paragraphs and the automatically derived semantic net have proven useful as browsing and searching aids.

1. Introduction

Hypertext systems are notorious for lacking adequate tools to support the early cognitive phases of writing, and the need for tools that help people organise their thoughts and text is a pressing one, as hypertext systems are witnessing an ever expanding popularity. Systems that support the early stages of writing are currently under development in companies and research facilities. One such system, called *MUCH* (*M*ultiple *U*sers *C*reating *H*ypertext), is described in section 2. MUCH is being developed on a network of graphical workstations to provide an environment where multiple authors can collaboratively create hypertext. The discipline of hypertext has many facets. Links within a document might be considered as microhypertext, while links among documents form macrohypertext. Traditionally, macrohypertext supports searching, while microhypertext supports browsing. In browsing, one looks through the document by jumping from one place to another and reading only small segments of text in each one of those places. Searching occurs when a reader knows the label for some information and wants only that specific information. The consensus from the founders of hypertext (Bush 1945) to the current pioneers of hypertext is, however, that both browsing and searching facilities should be supported in modern hypertext environments –environments that merge microhypertext and macrohypertext (Halasz 1988). This paper explores a new method for searching and browsing a single document by: (l) using word-based indexing of paragraphs for searching, and (2) automatically arranging the so-derived index terms in a hierarchical semantic net for browsing. Both searching and browsing are important in collaborative authoring environments. A semantic net whose nodes point to blocks of text may support both microhypertext and macrohypertext. In the microhypertext case the blocks of text may be of paragraph size, while in the macrohypertext case, the blocks of text are entire documents. The semantic net of hypertext is an important foundation for browsing and searching, but is also notoriously difficult to develop (Rada and Martin 1987). It is this difficulty which motivated our search for strategies based on word-frequency (Rada *et al.* 1989c) . While the knowledge in people's mind is structured more like a semantic net than like prose (Kintsch 1988), people have little training in directly representing semantic nets. Researchers in natural language processing have been working for decades on the problem of translating documents into semantic nets or other knowledge representations. The parsing of natural language has been successful in narrow domains where the computer could be provided with a substantial knowledge of that domain (Carbonell and Frederking 1984) and some success was attained in the automatic augmentation of knowledge bases from text (Lebowitz 1986). Research in information retrieval has shown the value of word-frequency strategies for indexing and searching (Salton and McGill 1983). Word-frequency indexing takes advantage of the observation that terms which occur relatively frequently in a document are important indicators of that document's content (Luhn 1958). Also, patterns of co-occurrence of terms may give important indicators of relationships among terms (Raghavan and Yu 1979). Mili went a step further and proposed an algorithm that organises a set of index terms in a hierarchy based on their frequency of co-occurrences in documents' descriptions (Mili and Rada 1987). We applied Salton's algorithm (Salton and McGill 1983) to index the paragraphs of a draft textbook entitled *Hypertext* written by Roy Rada using MUCH. Then, we used Mili's algorithm (Mili and Rada 1987) to organise the so derived indexing vocabulary in a semantic net. We hypothesised that: (l) the statistically derived index terms were important indicators of the paragraphs' contents, and (2) the relationships represented in the semantic net were truly hierarchical. A first set of experiments proved the accuracy of the frequency-based index terms. However, an analysis of the relations generated by Mili's algorithm revealed only a small fraction of hierarchical relations. This led us to the following hypothesis: the word-based indexing of paragraphs and the automatically derived semantic net could be helpful in hypertext searching and browsing. Two additional experiments were performed to assess the usefulness of the statistically-generated index terms and relations between them for searching and browsing. The results suggest that word-based indexing of paragraph and the automatically derived semantic net are useful for browsing and searching. In section 2, we describe the MUCH system. The semantic net building experiment is described in section 3. In particular, we describe the algorithm developed by Mili, and discuss its application to the case of hypertext. The experiments are discussed in section 4. In view of the results, the strengths and weaknesses of the methods are discussed in section 5.

2. MUCH system

The *MUCH* system is a prototype collaborative writing environment that enables multiple authors to collaboratively create hypertext. The MUCH system supports document "authoring", "accessing", "discussing", and "annotating". An overview will be given in subsection 2.1. The data model will be described in subsection 2.2, followed by a description for the above functions and the implementation issues in subsection 2.3.

2.1. Overview

The MUCH system has been developed to support the phases of writing a document: *exploring, organising,* and *encoding.* The exploration phase includes brainstorming and making unstructured notes. The organisation phase includes organising the unstructured notes and ideas into an outline or hierarchy. The encoding phase includes writing the prose for the final document (Rada 1990). *MUCH* is being developed on a network of graphical workstations using public domain software tools including UNIX, X Windows, Emacs, UNIX Document Workbench, and Xdvi. The MUCH system has three main functions. They are accessing, writing and annotation (with discussion).

We use a five-window screen as a common user interface. All the functions have some variations on the usages of windows for their own purposes. The system also provides a key menu within the whole screen to indicate the meaning of function keys under different functions. A skeleton of the entry screen is shown in Figure 1. In the next section a description of the system's data model is provided. Then, we will describe the three main functions. Some implementation issues will be discussed in the final section.

2.2. Data model

With the MUCH system multiple authors can create text collaboratively by creating a semantic net and linking it to text blocks. The semantic net consists of frames and links which connect these frames. The directionality of the links is defined by the author by specifying a source and destination frame for each link. The text blocks are stored in the links. There is no restriction on the number of lines that a text block might contain. The collaborators can create notes as well as annotations. Notes are neither connected to the semantic net nor to each other. The authors create annotations by creating frames and linking them to frames in the semantic net. The annotation frames have predefined names in order to distinguish them from the frames in the semantic net. The text of annotations is stored within the annotation frame. Annotations on annotations are allowed by creating annotation frames and linking them to existing annotation frames. The links which connect annotations to frames (within the semantic net) or to other annotations have a predefined directionality. That is, the newly created annotation is always the source of the link. The destination of the link can be either a frame or an existing annotation.

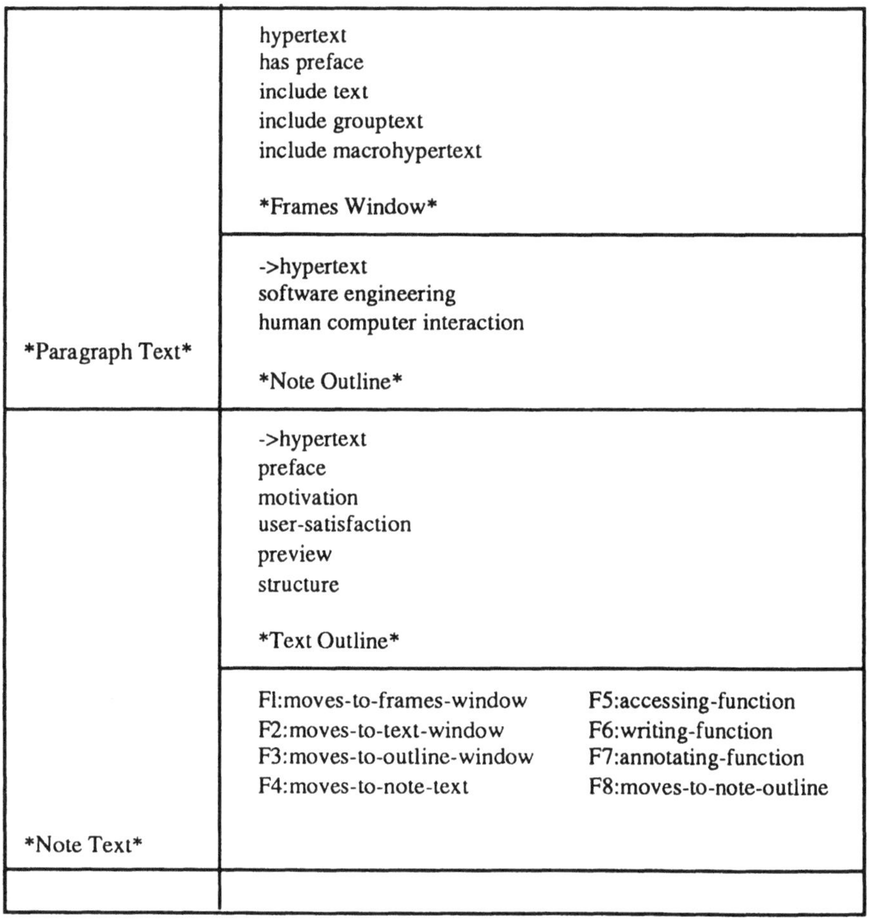

Figure 1. First MUCH screen display.

The MUCH system is based on a relational database model. The database holds the frames and links of the semantic net, the text blocks, annotations attached to frames, notes, and information about the authors and the dates of text blocks which have been created. Text blocks are stored in tables, one tuple per line. The database model of the system consists of 5 entities: *text block, note, link, frame,* and *annotation.* An entity/relationship model of the system can be seen in Figure 2. The solid straight lines indicate a 1:1 (one-to-one) relationship. The delta notation indicates a 1:*n* (one-to-many) relationship. The dashed straight lines imply that occurrences of adjacent entities may exist without taking part in the relationship.

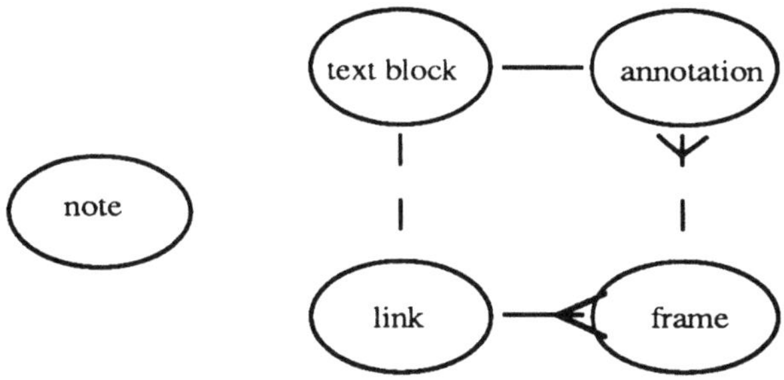

Figure 2. The MUCH entity/relationship model.

The above entities have been further refined through normalisation and their internal representation consists of tables in 3NF (Third Normal Form). These tables along with their attributes are listed below.

Table names	**Attributes**
Text_Inf	link name, author, date, index_terms
Text_Block	link_name, text line, line_order
Link	link_name, author, source_frame
Link_Date	link_name, date, destination_frame
Frame_Author	frame_name, author
Frame_Date	frame_name, date
Note	note name, author, date
Note_text	note_name, text_line, line_order
Annot_text	frame_name, annot_name, text_line, line_order
Annot_Date	frame_name, annot_name, date
Annot_Author	frame_name, annot_name, author
Annot_Frame_Link	frame_name, annot_name, annot_link_name
Annot_Link	frame_name, source_annot, destination_annot, annot_link_name

The above tables have common attribute names. Some of these attributes have different interpretations, depending on the entity. The link_name attribute has the format "source_frame -link - destination_frame", it is unique and indicates the link where the text block is located. In the annotation tables annot_link_name is merely the name of the link. The author attribute is the author's login name and it has the same interpretation within all the tables. The date attribute indicates the date that an author created a text block, a link, a frame, a note, or an annotation. The index_terms attribute consists of a sequence of index terms associated with a text block. The text_line attribute contains a line of a text block, note, or annotation. The line_order indicates the order of appearance of each line of text within the text block, note, or annotation. Source_frame, destination frame, and frame name represent the name of a frame in the semantic net. The note name is a unique identifier for a specific note. Finally, annot_name indicates a predefined name for an annotation.

2.3. System functions

2.3.1. Accessing

Accessing a document in MUCH consists of three functions: (1) reading, (2) browsing, and (3) searching. The following operations can be performed in the accessing part of the MUCH system:

- Browsing annotations. This operation can be performed by selecting an annotation from the annotation outline.
- Reading an annotation for updates.
- Browsing a text block. A text block can be either a paragraph of the original document or a note. Browsing a paragraph can be performed by selecting a frame either from the *Text Outline* window or from the *Frames Window*. A note can be browsed by selecting a note name from the list provided in the *Note Outline* window.
- Reading a text block for update. The text block, in this case, can also be a text paragraph or a note.
- Searching a specific block of text. An outline of the index terms is provided in a window *Index Terms* (which replaces the *Note Outline* window). If the user selects any index term from that outline, all the text paragraphs are searched for that index term and a list of frames is displayed which contains that index term. The user can now look at any or all the text blocks which contain that index term.

Authors provide an outline (a hierarchical table of contents) of a document to help readers and writers visualise the structure of that document (Rada 1990). The traditional outline consists of terms or headings in a hierarchy. In collaborative authoring, generating an outline in further detail enables the authors to discover the missing parts of the document, the sections of the document which require more work, and the inconsistent sections. In the current version of MUCH, the text outline (displayed in the *Text Outline* window) and the index terms are both generated manually. We intend to develop a dynamic outline generator. Similarly, a word-frequency based indexing system will be introduced to create index terms automatically. These index terms will also be used as a *cross-reference* in order to make the browsing of related text blocks easier and quicker.

2.3.2. Writing

The writing function incorporates several features to help the writers creating and updating hypertext. It aims to support writers who are involved in large and complex document generating tasks. Its multi-window user interface is consistent with other MUCH functions and allows the writers to view various referential information like frames, outlines, and other texts while entering the target text paragraph. It also provides notes processing facilities for the writers to put their notes into the system. Other features are the outline generating capability and comprehensive indexing support for the writers.

To utilise these features, the writers can have their ideas recorded by using the notes processing tools to create, update and reference them. When the writers want to write the real text paragraph for the document, they have to create frames and link names for a specific paragraph before entering text for this paragraph. These steps allows the writers to explicitly organise the hypertext as they wish. There are also functions to handle the updating of the structuring entities like frames and links, and real texts entities like notes and text paragraphs as well. Under such writing environment, the support for the writers in the whole writing procedure becomes more organised and further strengthened.

The following is a brief description of the operation of this function:

- The five windows for the writing function differ from the entry window by the *Note Text* window being replaced by the *Write Text* window. The *Text Paragraph* window is used for reference texts and the other three windows are still used for displaying referential information about the frames and outlines for the writers to manipulate during the writing process.
- The referential information on the windows other than the *Write Text* window should be brought up or generated to help the writer obtain a clear idea about the current status of the hypertext document. The writer can thus select the write-function entry from the main menu to get into the writing function. The whole function is divided into two major part, writing and updating.
- Suppose the writer selects the creating function. The writer can choose to either enter the notes first by selecting the create-note option or be more straightforward by directly entering frames, links and the associated actual text paragraphs through the help from the manipulation of the referential information in other windows. Options

to enter indices before storing the text paragraph is also available.
- If the writer chooses the updating function, functions to modify notes, text paragraphs, links or frames are provided. Again the updating process can be assisted from the manipulation of the referential information windows.

2.3.3. Annotation and discussion

Annotations are meant to be interpreted by others as a guide to changing a paragraph, link, or a frame. The annotation facility enables users to write comments about specific parts of an evolving document. The annotations are argumentative. Accordingly, there is a need for supporting the creation of "Link" instances. Annotations can be connected to the "annotated"blocks of text using simple labelled links. Both the destination and the link type should be determined by the user. Each annotation can be linked to more than one annotation. In this system, there is no restriction on the link type.

Allowing the users to see all the annotations made by a specific author over a specified period of time is very helpful (Mhashi 1989). Accordingly, it is important to record the *author* and *date* for each annotation. For each hypertext function several interface alternatives may be considered (i.e. a given function may have several interfaces). An annotator of a paper document makes comments either on the original paper or on a separate paper. Computer annotation facilities may vary radically in the interface style (Rada 1990). In this system, each annotation is separated from the others. The author can create one or more annotations to the text and can also annotate annotations. A relatively straightforward alternative to annotative windows involves allowing an annotator to copy some material from the original paragraph and make changes to it.

The 'annotation mode' option brings forward a screen through which the user can perform the annotation operations. For creating an annotation the cursor should be in one of the two windows '*Frames Window*' or '*Annotation Outline*'. The output of all reading operations will be displayed in a window called '*Annotation Text*'. The following operation can be performed during the annotation mode:

- Creating an annotation.
- Reading an annotation.
- Displaying annotations created by a specific author.
- Displaying annotations created by date.
- Creating a link between any two annotations.
- Modifying an existing annotation.

The annotation function can be used as a discussion function. The discussion phase of hypertext creation reflects discussion among people in the early phases of document construction or critiquing. people collaboratively. The discussion will include blocks of text which are connected by links. The discussions which people may have in working with grouptext may require a unique set of node and link types. The name attribute of an annotation is set by the system as 'annot$_j$'. The user is given an option to change the name attribute. In the discussion, the system suggests the following type of links: *responds-to, supports, objects-to, questions, suggests, replaces, generates, decision-makes, decision-postpones,* and *views.* Also, it suggests the following type of nodes: *Issue, Position,* and *Argument.* (Mhashi 1989). The user can choose to use these links and node types Also, these links and node types can be used in the annotation phase.

2.3.4. Implementation issues

The MUCH system is a homogeneous distributed collaborative authoring system, that has been developed on HP-9000/300 workstations. Emacs and X Windows constitute the front end while Ingres serves as the back end of the system. The user interface is controlled by an Emacs-Lisp program. This program makes calls to a C program which runs on the file server along with Ingres. The C program contains embedded SQL commands that are used to access, store, and update data kept by Ingres. The Lisp program sends requests to the C program. The C program translates these requests into SQL queries which are sent to Ingres. Ingres executes the queries and returns any required data to the C program which, in turn, sends it to the Lisp program. The Lisp program manipulates the data and displays it on the screen.

3. Generating the semantic net

A key feature of hypertext systems is that they enable users to browse through semantically related parts of a document. To this end, one must provide means for: (l) describing the contents of the various parts of a document to allow direct access to those parts, and (2) describing the various semantic relationships that exist between the parts of a document to allow a content-based browsing. In this section, we show how: (l) frequency-based methods can be used to extract content descriptors from textual units, and (2) Mili's algorithm can be used to organise these content descriptors in a hierarchical semantic net, thus providing semantic access paths between the parts of a document. In section 3.1, we describe a frequency-based content analysis method that is commonly used in information retrieval systems, and discuss its applicability to our case. In section 3.2, we describe Mili's algorithm. In section 3.3, we describe the result of applying the above methods.

3.1. Frequency-based content analysis

Two of the existing basic approaches to document content analysis are the *interpretative* and *structural* approaches. With the interpretative approach, semantic information is provided about the domain and often about the English language itself, so that the document may be understood before it is indexed (Kaplan and Maarek 1990). In contrast, the structural approach uses the frequency of usage of words in natural text as an indicator of content relevance, and no semantic interpretation is assigned to any word. The index selection can also take into account other structural information such as word adjacency. The structural approach is based on the observation that writers usually repeat certain words as they advance or vary their arguments and as they elaborate on an aspect of a subject. This approach has motivated a number of automatic indexing algorithms for information retrieval systems (Salton and McGill 1983). The advantages of these algorithms are practicality and ease of implementation. We propose to apply a structural approach, and use a variant of frequency-based indexing.

A typical frequency-based indexing algorithm goes as follows (Salton and McGill 1983):

- Identify all the unique words in the document set.
- Remove all common function words included in a stop list (Rijsbergen 1979. (such as "a", "the", "and", "is", ... , etc..
- Remove some suffixes and combine identical word forms (stems.. This reduces a variety of different forms such as analysis, analysing, analyser, and analysed, to a common word stem "analy."
- Determine the frequency of occurrences of the resulting word stems.
- Give a range of frequencies for terms to be considered for indexing. All terms that are within the range are used as index terms.

More elaborate filtering mechanisms exist that use entropy-based measures that attest to the extent to which a given index term discriminates between documents in the document set (Salton and McGill 1983). Terms with poor discriminatory power are disregarded.

Variations of the above algorithm have been used extensively in information retrieval systems, despite harsh criticisms from the proponents of knowledge-based interpretative indexing. Salton argued that the interpretative methods have yet to justify their added complexity, both computationally and conceptually, by provably better retrieval performance (Salton and McGill 1983). However, there remains a major problem in our case: while frequency-based indexing generates a flat descriptions, i.e. an unordered set of index terms for each document, MUCH documents are indexed by binary relations between terms. For example, a document that defines semantic nets might be characterised by the phrase "*a semantic net* IS-A *graph*", where *a semantic net* and *graph* are both frames (see section 2). Salton's algorithm might identify *a semantic net* and *graph* as index terms for that document, but it would not specify the relationship between them. Therefore, we chose to index our documents in two stages:

- Identify the important content descriptors for each document.
- Apply Mili's algorithm to identify the relationships between co-occuring index terms.

Mili's algorithm is described in the next section.

3.2. Mili's algorithm

The algorithm developed by Mili (Mili and Rada 1987) is based on the widely accepted hypothesis that words (or terms) that often co-occur in textual documents tend to be related according to some relationship important for the document space (Lesk 1969, Soergel 1974, Raghavan and Yu 1979). He goes one step further, and uses empirical data related to the effect that the most commonly used content descriptors within a document collection tend to be more general (Kaplan and Maarek 1990, Sparck Jones 1980) to hypothesise that the most dominant relationship between related terms with different scopes (or degrees of generality) is "Broader-Term." However, he provides no heuristics for identifying other kinds of relationships, both hierarchical and non-hierarchical, that may be equally important to the document space. His algorithm – called STATBUILDER, organises a set of content descriptors (or index terms) into a hierarchy using the above hypotheses.

STATBUILDER relies on the availability of frequency information consisting of:

- The number of times each content descriptor was used in the document set. This information is used to infer the "scope"of the various content descriptors.
- And the number of times two content descriptors are used jointly to describe a document, for all pairwise combinations of content descriptors.

Here information is embodied in a matrix MAT, where MAT(i,j) is the frequency of co-occurrence of term t_i with term t_j. MAT(i,i) is the number of documents in which t_j was used. The rows and columns of the matrix are organised by decreasing order of MAT(i,i) so that for j < i, t_j has a broader scope than t_j. The algorithm goes as follows (assuming N index terms):

1. Normalise the elements of the matrix M by dividing M(i,j) by the square root of M(i,i)x M(j ,j)
2. Choose the terms to be include in the first level of the hierarchy. Make these terms point to the root of the hierarchy. The purpose of the root node is to connect the 18th level terms. The root node can be called anything; call it KBROOT (Knowledge Base ROOT). Assume that the terms t_k through t_{k1} were chosen to be included in the first level.
3. For i = k_l + 1 through N.

3.1 Find the maximum of the elements M(i,l) through M(i,i-l). Note that because of the ordering of rows and columns (step 2), these are the frequencies of co-occurrences of t_i with the terms whose occurrences are higher than that of t_j.

3.2 Create a link between the term t_i and all the terms t_j such that j<i and M(i,j) is the maximum found in 5.1.

Mili reported an experiment where STATBUILDER was tested on a set of index terms used to describe articles from the biochemistry literature (Mili and Rada 1987). The resulting hierarchy – call it STATKB, was inspected for the predominance of "Broader-Term"relations. About 50% of the hierarchical links were indeed "Broader-term". To assess the significance of the remaining links, STATKB was evaluated for the extent to which it could be effectively referenced by a semantic-net based concept-matching algorithm, called DISTANCE, which measures the relevance between documents and queries (Rada and Bicknell 1989). DISTANCE's measurements were compared to people's relevance assessments for the same set of documents and queries. The DISTANCE evaluation correlated well with the human evaluation and suggested that the statistically-derived relations were cognitively meaningful (Mili and Rada 1987).

In our case, the relationships generated by STATBUILDER would be used to replace the statistically-derived flat set of index terms used to describe each document by <$term_1$ BroaderTerm $term_2$> triples. For example, if a document D were indexed by the set I={*a semantic net*,*graph*}, and if STATBUILDER identified a broader-term relationship between *a semantic net* and *graph*, then I would be replaced by the singleton I'= {<*a semantic net*, BroaderTerm,*graph*>}. While this would account for neither all the terms in an index set, nor all the relationships between these terms, it would provide a useful partial description of the document's contents .

3.3. Experiment

The frequency-based indexing algorithm was applied to the 600 individual paragraphs contained in Rada's book *Hypertext*. The initial number of potential index terms was 1737, with frequencies ranging from 1 to 157. We eliminated terms that occurred more than 70 times, and less than 7 times, which reduced the set of index terms to 270 terms. STATBUILDER generated a five-level hierarchy, with 273 relations; some of these relations can be seen in Figure 3. These relations were given to two people who had read the book, and they were asked to mark the hierarchical relations. Only 33 of the 273 relations were categorised as hierarchical by the subjects, i.e. about 12% as compared to Mili's 50% (Mili and Rada 1987).

The discrepancy between our results and Mili's could be due to several factors, including the indexing strategy. For instance, Mili applied his algorithm to manually assigned index terms. However, while Mili's main goal was to build a *thesaurus-like broader-term hierarchy,* we are not committed to a particular kind of relationships between index terms as documents may describe a variety of relationships between their index terms. What the 12% fraction means in our case is that we cannot confidently label the relationships identified by STATBUILDER as "BroaderTerm." However, these relationships may nevertheless prove useful in the context of hypertext systems, in the same way that Mili showed the usefulness of his hierarchy in the context of information retrieval (Mili and Rada 1987). In the next section, we describe a set of experiments to assess the accuracy of indexing and the usefulness of the semantic net generated by STATBUILDER for typical hypertext tasks.

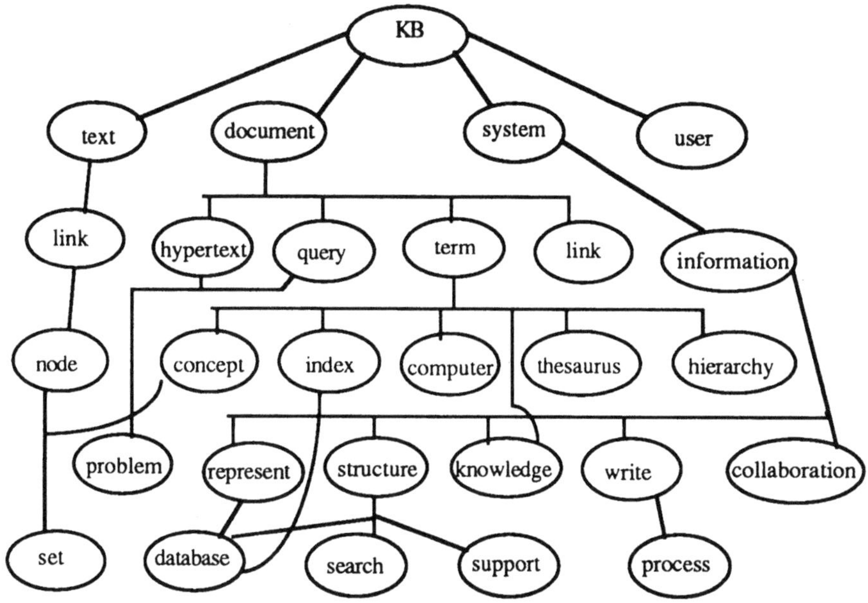

Figure 3. Part of the hierarchy generated by STATBUILDER.

4. Experiments

In this section, we describe three experiments using the index terms generated by Salton's algorithm and the relationships identified by Mili's algorithm. In the first experiment, we test the accuracy of indexing by trying to answer the following question:

> Given that a document D was assigned the index terms t_1 and t_2 by Salton's algorithm, and given that Mili's algorithm identified a relationship between t_1 and t_2, does D "talk"about a relationship between t_1 and t_2?

A positive answer would validate both the index terms generated by Salton's algorithm, and the relationships between them identified by Mili's algorithm. The remaining two experiments test the usefulness of the index terms and the relations to support a variety of hypertext tasks. The second experiment tests the value of flat index sets to measure the similarity between two documents. Such a measure may be used to support searching. The third and last experiment tests the usefulness of relations generated by STATBUILDER to relate documents. Such relations may be used for browsing.

4.1. Accuracy of indexing

This experiment tests the accuracy of indexing derived from the combination of Salton's algorithm and Mili's algorithm. We used a random sample of 20 paragraphs that were assigned index terms by Salton's algorithm, such that Mili's algorithm identified a relationship between two of the terms. For example a document D with index terms $\{t_1, t_2, t_3\}$ such that STATBUILDER generated the relation $<t_3$ Broader-Term $t_1>$ was a candidate for this experiment. The purpose of this experiment was to determine the extent to which D *truly* described a relationship between t_3 and t_1.

We gave the 20 paragraphs and their related pairs of index terms to human experts who are familiar with the topic area. The subjects were asked to read each paragraph and to decide whether that paragraph described a relationship between the pair of index terms. The subjects found that 15 of the 20 documents did, indeed, describe relationships between the related pairs of index terms. To determine the significance of this result, a binomial distribution test was applied. The hypothesis that paragraphs describe relationships between their pairs of related index terms was supported, and we conclude that the indexing obtained by the combination of Salton and Mili's algorithms is fairly accurate.

4.2. Usefulness of index terms for similarity measurements

Searching involves concept matching. In key-word based searching, the user enters one or more keywords, usually separated by logical connectives, and the system returns the set of documents that have those keywords in their indices. When none of the documents of the database completely matches the query (i.e. has all the required keywords), a retrieval system might rank the documents that match the query partially, by degree of match, and present them to the user in that order. Depending on the quality of indexing, that order may correspond to the order in which the user might have like to consult the documents.

In this experiment, we tested a variation on the above argument, and explored the extent to which word-frequency based indexing could support similarity measurements between paragraphs. We defined a similarity measure "SIMILAR" between two documents as follows:

Let doc_1 and doc_2 be two documents with index sets I_1 and I_2, respectively. We measure the similarity between doc_1 and doc_2 by:

$$\textbf{SIMILAR}(doc_1, doc_2) = \frac{2 \times (card(I_1 \cap I_2))}{card(I_1) + card(I_2)}$$

where card(X) is the cardinality of set X.

Note that this measure is normalised, i.e. SIMILAR(doc_i, doc_j) = 1 when $I_1 = I_2$, and less than one otherwise.

We selected a random sample of 20 paragraphs, P_1 through P_{20}, and computed SIMILAR(p_i,p_j) for all $1 \leq i < j \leq 20$. The values ranged from 0 and 0.26. The same 20 paragraphs were given to human subjects who were asked to read the paragraphs and to assign a measure of similarity between 0 and 1 to each pair of paragraphs. Thus, for the 20 paragraphs. The 20(20-1)/2 numbers produced by SIMILAR were compared to those produced by people using a correlation coefficient test (Alvo and Cabilio 1985):

Let X = the similarity produced by the experts.

Let Y = the similarity produced by the machine.

$$r = \frac{\Sigma XY - \frac{(\Sigma X)(\Sigma Y)}{n}}{\left[\left(\Sigma X^2 - \frac{(\Sigma X)^2}{n}\right)\right]\left[\left(\Sigma Y^2 - \frac{(\Sigma Y)^2}{n}\right)\right]^{\frac{1}{2}}}$$

By substitution in the above formula, r = 0.45. Thus the correlation between the manual method and the automatic method is significant at the 5% level. Therefore, we conclude that the word-based indexing can be used as a reference to measure the similarity between documents.

4.3. Usefulness of relationships for browsing

In this experiment, we hypothesised that an author with a set of index terms for a paragraph and the derived semantic net could find a related paragraph. To validate this hypothesis, we took a random sample of 18 pairs of paragraphs (P_1, P_2) such that STATBUILDER identified a relationship between a term indexing P_1 and a term indexing P_2. We gave these pairs to human subjects familiar with the topic area, and asked them to assess the relatedness of the paragraphs within a pair. The subjects found that 15 pairs of paragraphs were, indeed, related. We conclude that the relationships generated by STATBUILDER may be used by browsers to consult related text.

5. Discussion

Hypertext augments text by connecting it to a semantic net. In MUCH (*M*ultiple *U*sers *C*reating *H*ypertext), a collaborative authoring hypertext system developed by the authors, text points to *links* (instead of *nodes)* in the semantic net. Building a semantic net, or a knowledge base, is a time-consuming, conceptually challenging task (Rada and Martin 1987). Further, connecting text to a semantic net consists of no less than conceptual content analysis, an equally challenging task. Information retrieval research has shown the value of indexing strategies based on word frequencies in textual documents (Salton and McGill 1983). Such methods have the advantage of practicality and ease of implementation. However, they describe documents by a flat set of index terms, instead of relations between concepts as required by MUCH. An algorithm developed by Mili organises a set of index terms in a hierarchy based on frequencies of co-occurences in document indices (Mili and Rada 1987). In this paper, we explored the extent to which word-frequency indexing may be augmented with Mili's method to provide both a relational indexing for documents, and a semantic net for browsing. Word-frequency indexing was used to analyse the contents of 600 paragraphs, part of a textbook entitled *Hypertext* written by one of the authors. Mili's algorithm called STATBUILDER, was applied to the resulting indexing vocabulary to build a hierarchy. Mili predicted that the relations generated by his algorithm are "Broader-Term"-like. Given a document D such that STATBUILDER identified a relation between two of its index terms, say t_1 and t_2, we were interested in whether D did, indeed, describe a relationship between t_1 and t_2, and whether that relationship was truly "Broader-Term."Our results showed that only 12% of the links generated by STATBUILDER were "Broader-Term"-like. They also showed that 75% of the documents whose set of index terms included the end nodes of a link generated by STATBUILDER described a relation between those nodes. Thus, while we cannot reasonably assume that the relations generated by STATBUILDER were "Broader-Term"-like, we can be fairly confident that whenever a pair of related index term appear in the index set of a document, the document describes the relationship between the pair.

The ability to rank paragraphs according to their similarity to a specific paragraph using the word-frequency based indexing was tested. Our results illustrated that it was feasible to use this method of indexing to measure the similarity between paragraphs. Word-frequency based indexing and the derived semantic net were used to attempt to find a related paragraph to another paragraph. This experiment indicated that the relations in the derived semantic net were sufficiently accurate to support browsing and thus enable the user to consult a related block of

Many researchers are recognising the potential value of word-frequency indexing for microhypertext purposes (Frisse 1988, Dumais *et al.* 1988). This is in accord with the growing combination of microhypertext and macrohypertext technologies and methodologies (Ritchie 1989). Our experiences have supported the value of this combination. Therefore, we are interested in pursuing extensions to this work. In one extension the *interpretative approach* which is described in sections 3.1 for building a hierarchical semantic net will be tested. In another extension, we will employ simple natural language processing tools. Since grammars of natural language are now well established and lexicons are widely available, we may exploit these to improve our ability to detect meaningful index terms for paragraphs and to suggest relations among those terms.

6. References

Alvo, M. and Cabilio, P. (1985) Average rank correlation statistics in the presence of ties *Communications Statistical Theory Methods,.*

Bush, V. (1945) As we may think. *The Atlantic Monthly,* 176, 1 (July).

Carbonell, J. and Frederking, R. (1984) Natural language interfaces to knowledge-based systems, in D. Reddy (Ed)*The Factory of the Future,* Digital Press.

Dumais, S. T., Furnas, G. W., Landauer, T. K., Deerwester, S. and Harshman, R. (1988) Using latent semantic analysis to improve access to textual information, *CHI'88 Conference Proceedings.* ACM Press, New York.

Frisse, M. (1988) Searching for information in a hypertext medical handbook, *Communications of the Association for Computing Machinery,* 31, 7, July 1988.

Halasz, F. G. (1988) Reflections on Notecards: seven issues for the next generation of hypermedia systems, *Communications of the Association of Computing Machinery,* 31, 7.

Kaplan, S. M. and Maarek, Y. S. (1990) Incremental maintenance of semantic links in dynamically changing hypertext systems University of Illinois at Urbana-Champaign.

Kintsch, W. (1988) The role of knowledge in discourse comprehension: a construction integration model *Psychological Review* 95, 2.

Lebowitz, M. (1986) Integrated learning: controlling explanation, *Cognitive Science,* 10.

Lesk, M. E. (1969) Word-word associations in document retrieval systems, *American Documentation,* 20, 1, January

Luhn, H. P. (1958) The automatic creation of literature abstracts, *IBM Journal of Research and Development* 2, 2, April.

Mhashi, M. (1989) Tool for reasoned discourse, Technical Report, Department of Computer Science, University of Liverpool, Liverpool, September.

Mili, H. and Rada, R. (1987) Building a knowledge-base for information retrieval, *Proceedings Third Annual Expert Systems in Government Conference,* Computer Society of the IEEE, Washington, DC.

Rada, R. (1990) Multiple users creating hypertext (MUCH) Department of Computer Science, Liverpool University.

Rada, R. and Bicknell, E. (1989) Ranking documents with a thesaurus, *Journal of the American Society for Information Science,* 40, 5, September.

Rada, R. and Martin, B. (1987) Augmenting thesaurus for information systems, *ACM Transactions on Office Information Systems,* 5, 4.

Rada, R., Mhashi, M. and Barlow, J. (1989a) Hierarchical semantic nets support retrieving and generating hypertext, Department of Computer Science, Liverpool University.

Rada, R., Keith, B., Burgoine, M., George, S. and Reid, D. (1989b) Collaborative writing of text and hypertext, *Hypermedia,* 1, 2.

Raghavan, V. and Yu, C. T. (1979) Experiments on the determination of the relationships between terms *Association Computing Machinery Transactions on Database Systems,* 4, 2.

Rijsbergen, C. J. v. (1979) *OCCURI Information Retrieval* Butterworths, London.

Ritchie, I. (1989) HYPERTEXT –moving towards large volume *The Computer Journal,* 23, 6, December.

Salton, G. and McGill, M. (1983) *Introduction to Modern Information Retrieval* McGraw-Hill, NY.

Soergel, D. (1974) *Indexing languages And Thesauri: Construction and Maintenance* John Wiley, New York.

Sparck Jones, K. (1980) A Statistical interpretation of term specificity and its application in retrieval. In B. C. Griffith (Ed). *Key Papers in Information Science,* Knowledge Industry Publications, White Plains, NY. Also appeared 1972 *Journal of Documentation,* 28, 1.

10

Text Indexing: The Problem of Significance

C. Korycinski
A.F. Newell
Dundee University

Abstract

Authoring of long and complex texts such as books or major monographs frequently requires the production of a back-of-the-book index. This can be left as a task for the author, but the production of an index requires specialised skills of which they may be unaware. Some major, but very common, problems associated with indexing are discussed, and performance of both computer generated and computer assisted indexing is assessed by comparison to manual systems. Finally, the authors present recent progress in determination of *significance* of sentences and paragraphs -a key criterion for the creation of a subject index - based on probabilistic analysis of style, mark-up and word frequency.

1. Introduction

1.1. The indexing process

Indexing, whether manual, computer-assisted or entirely computerised, suffers from problems of definition. Indexes for databases, for free-text retrieval systems, for Prolog databases, and for current-awareness style journals will have little resemblance to each other, except in that they all serve as pointers to information stored in texts. Thus as 'indexing' means different things to different people, depending on their previous exposure to the term in a specific context, it would be useful to clarify exactly what is to be considered in the following discussion. Specifically, the model of indexing which is to be considered is the creation of subject indexes - often known as 'back-of-the-book' indexes - to large, homogeneous documents. Exemplars of these may be books (where the style and subject matter written about are the product of one person), collections of monographs (where there are multiple authors, but the subject matter is normally very limited in its scope) and technical documentation (where both scope and authors may be wide-ranging, but the description of the underlying processes and the purpose of the text impose a rigid limit on the vocabulary and imagery which can be used). This focus is entirely practical, as indexed books represent the most common example of an information retrieval system.

1.2. The purpose of indexing

What is the purpose of an index? McColvin (McColvin 1958) claims that the purposes are manifold.

- To facilitate reference to a specific item.
- To compensate as far as possible for the fact that a book can only be written in one sequence, according to one plan.
- To disclose relationships.
- To disclose omissions.
- To provide a living for indexers.
- To limit wear and tear on the items indexed. This can be quite a problem in newspaper and similar archives, where text has been published on flimsy or poor quality paper.

To these Borko and Bernier (Borko and Bernier 1978) add the following.

- To answer questions of discovery and foster serendipity.
- To provide a comprehensive overview of a subject field.
- To give nomenclature guidance.

All these items share the feature that the index acts as a form of guidance system by which the tedious search of the specific section of text under consideration can be bypassed. This is accomplished by using some form of surrogate for the item or subject we wish to discover. This requires a content analysis of documents followed by characterisation of such content by descriptive labels (Pao 1978). This, in turn, requires the following steps (Dutta and Sinha 1984).

- Conceptual analysis of the significant content of a document.
- Expressing the analysis by a set of words or phrases to represent the subject.
- Translating the relevant subject descriptions into standard language.
- Arranging the standardised subject descriptions according to the syntax of the indexing language used in the information system.

The ease with which the problem can be expressed does not imply ease in providing a computer-based solution. For example, a human indexer reads a section of text and is normally able to determine its subject content (the 'aboutness' of the text) with no conscious thought –reading the text normally involves understanding, and understanding, in turn, implies that content analysis has been accomplished. If this solution is to be a model for a computational approach to indexing, however, it has to be expressed in algorithmic form. This is a major problem, but one which demands a solution. Indeed, the ever-increasing volume of material being published produces problems both in the time required, and in the number of people needed, to index full texts and abstracts. Furthermore, with increasing specialisation the task of determining the 'aboutness' of scholarly texts becomes ever harder for the non-specialist.

2. Index preparation

2.1. Types of indexes

Assuming that we require a form of guidance system, we need to analyse our needs more precisely to determine which type of guidance system is to be chosen.

2.1.1. Word indexes and concordances

If the guidance is to specific words or constructions in the book, then we use a word index, or concordance. The difference between the two is that word indexes do not use the full text, but only a section of it – commonly the title of a book, paper or abstract. A concordance is a word index to the whole text. An example of a word index is KWIC (key word in context) and its variants, e.g. KWOC (key word out of context). The former was proposed by Crestadoro (Crestadoro 1856), and finally realised by Luhn over 100 years later (Luhn 1959). The purpose of both word indexes and concordances is not to guide the user to a particular subject, but rather to guide them to a word used in a given context. Thus a concordance would typically give each and every sentence or phrase in which the desired word occurs together with its location (page number, etc.). in the text. Both word indexes and concordances are, in essence, unselective. All occasions of the word are referenced without regard to the significance of the context in which the word is found. This can be accomplished automatically fairly easily as word boundaries are clearly marked in many languages by spaces. Thus most individual words can be identified in a very straightforward way, and exceptions such as hyphenated words, abbreviations, formulae, etc. can often either be catered for or an allowance made for them. This means that these types of indexes –particularly word indexes –have a considerable amount of popularity.

2.1.2. Classificatory

An exemplar of this type of index is the library catalogue. Although this is often consulted by some sort of alphabetical ordering (author or title), its underlying order is classificatory. As it is used neither in conventional book indexing, nor in computer systems which attempt to produce indexes automatically, it will not be considered further.

2.1.3. Subject

If the guidance required is to a particular subject of a given text, then the format exemplified by a 'back of the book' index would be used, irrespective of whether the index was, in fact, used in a book, or stored in a computerised information retrieval system.

The definition of the 'subject' of a piece of text may be intuitively obvious, but somewhat harder to define. Borko, for instance, distinguishes between subject, concept and topic indexes (Borko and Bernier 1978). Thus when an author uses examples, or introduces topics which are assumed to be well-known to the potential readership, an indexer who maintains a strict subject index would omit these areas from the index. They are peripheral to the main thrust of the argument (they merely bolster it up), and thus do not form the essence of the subject of that particular section of text.

Although this point of view has merit, it appears that in research fields, if not generally, a broader picture should be painted (Weinberg 1988). A researcher may be well aware of the subject matter of a piece of text, but may want to find precisely those arguments which are used to bolster it up. However, a fine line would need to be drawn by the indexer between strict subject indexing and indexing all matter peripheral to the main argument, thus leading to an unwieldy index which the user may find tiresome to use as they are constantly directed to matter which may be of little interest.

2.2. Creation of a subject index

This type of index is often in the form of an alphabetically arranged list, though there may be partial departures from alphabetisation if the subject matter warrants it. It is important to note that the purpose of this type of index is to guide the enquirer to new and significant subjects, and not to all mentions of a particular subject, concept or topic. This, of course, is a major difficulty with any automatic indexing system, as the concept of 'significance' is purely a mental one based on the relationship of text, intended audience of the text and the specialised knowledge and experience of the indexer. However, it does appear that there are aspects of most texts which can be used to guide indexers towards the identification of significant subject matter. As this is an area of considerable importance for all computer-based indexing as well as for human indexing, it will be considered in detail subsequently.

Having indexed significant subjects and having avoided sending the reader to trivial mentions of the subject, all that remains to complete the index is to arrange the entries in alphabetical order. Although this is not particularly hard to do, there are pitfalls which need to be avoided. A short, and by no means exhaustive list, would include the following.

- Words where the 'plural' may (or may not, depending on context) have an entirely different meaning: e.g. 'damage' and 'damages', 'service' and 'services'.
- Problems of alphabetisation. These would include:
    - Word-by-word or letter-by-letter ordering?
    - Should sub-headings of historical books be arranged in alphabetical or chronological order?
    - Modifiers of chemical names such as alpha, beta, gamma, delta (g before d!) in chemical names need to be ignored during the creation of main headings, but not in sub-headings.

All these, and many others, are well-known problems, and, in nearly all cases, have precedents laid down for their solution. These are contained in a number of British Standards which deal with the correct alphabetisation of index entries (BS 3700: 1988 and BS 1749: 1985). The indexer does, however, have to be aware of these difficulties. Furthermore, so does a computer program which attempts to create an index automatically.

2.3. Syndetic structure and implicit information

Another factor an indexer has to consider is the creation of syndetic structure and of multiple entry points. Looking at the latter, we could see that if a text had the term 'capacitor', then it might be useful to have a reference saying: 'condenser see capacitor '(the two are equivalent). And this reference would be put in whether or not the word 'condenser ' appears in the text in order to create an entry point for the casual reader. In this example, we also see the need for expert knowledge: it is only an indexer who has the broad background of knowledge of a particular subject who might see both need and opportunity for this addition to an index.

This latter point shows the need to index implicit information. In this case, the information was implicit in the knowledge base of the indexer. However, in many cases information may be implicit in the text itself. This means that the indexer has to subject the text to content analysis, and then try to guess which terms a hypothetical searcher would be likely to use when they wished to access the information. These problems are particularly severe when one moves away from the hard sciences towards the arts. Keywords as content descriptors virtually cease to exist, and the vocabulary is much more limited due to the absence of jargon words (Rowbottom and Willett 1982). Indexing a book of literary criticism may be a daunting task.

3. Computerised indexing

3.1. Probabilistic/frequency based systems

How have computers aided the production of indexes? This clearly depends on the criteria one wishes to use. The advantages of word indexes such as KWIC and KWOC are undeniable. Here the computer is being used to its best advantage – that of pattern matching. Large portions of text may be scanned easily and the resultant index produced ready for publication very quickly indeed. This rapidity is the great advantage of a KWIC index.

On the negative side it is clear that pattern matching is hardly suited to the indexing of long texts. The resultant index would be a concordance of keywords, and would be considerably longer than the book itself. The use of a KWIC index has been restricted to short texts (usually titles and abstracts) for precisely this reason.

Other computer-based indexing systems depend on frequency analysis of the text under consideration. It is assumed that word frequency (after the removal of function words) is related to text content. This may appear to be a reasonable assumption; as an author expands and develops an argument then it is likely that the word or words expressing the kernel of that argument will be repeated, providing us with a ready-made content descriptor. As shall be seen subsequently, this is only partially true. These systems have, however, been developed as practical, working indexing programs, but only for titles and abstracts. The 'index' consists of an inverted file of keywords and searching the index for a particular abstract consists of a Boolean search of matching keywords. Thus this is an example of a post-co-ordinate index and is, consequently, unsuitable for use in texts which are likely to be printed at some time in the future as its structure is oriented towards machine-based interactive searching.

3.2. Computational linguistic approaches to indexing

Although the common form of automatic indexing is by keyword extraction, in longer texts keywords may form poor identifiers for the subject matter. Recourse still has to be made to the intellectual (human) indexing process in order to identify correctly the 'aboutness' of a particular section of text (Maron 1978). Thus it is reasonable to suggest that some form of natural language processing should be performed to enable textual content analysis.

3.2.1. Content analysis

It may seem curious that so little progress appears to have been made in content analysis of texts, when human indexers do such analysis with seeming ease. This apparent lack of progress certainly implies neither lack of effort nor lack of desire to attend to needs expressed by those involved in the literary field. Many of the problems are well-known, if not well understood, and it is the challenge of natural language processing that a text in its entirety is far less ambiguous than its individual parts may be. So natural language processing (NLP) has to resolve this ambiguity by applying context to select from the various possibilities which are available, and which are governed by the lexicon and grammar. This is hard because the very information which we wish to have in order to resolve ambiguities may, or may not be, present in the text itself and also as it is present in knowledge of the real world which is implicit in the shared background of the author and the reader. (For a more extensive discussion of this area see Grishman 1986, also Korycinski and Newell 1990).

Traditionally, NLP has been broken down into three main areas:

- Syntactic analysis.
- Semantic analysis.
- Discourse analysis.

Syntactic analysis

Many of the problems of syntactic analysis have been solved. Programs such as CLAWS2 (Garside *et al.* 1987) can parse most sentences with a reasonably high degree of reliability. It should be borne in mind that errors in parsing do occur, and that a very considerable amount of work needs to be undertaken before accurate parses can be assumed as the norm. For indexing purposes they are unlikely to be stumbling blocks, as the majority of index entries consist of nouns or noun phrases which will probably be repeated throughout significant portions of the text. Thus errors in parsing of one section of text are unlikely to affect the overall outcome, as they could be allowed for and corrected in the light of subsequent analysis.

Semantic and discourse analysis

The dual problems of semantic and discourse analysis have, so far, been resistant to generalised solutions. Clearly, a number of well-known strategies, such as frames (Charniak 1978), scripts (Schank 1980) and plans (Schank and Ableson 1977), have been developed to cope with the task of inferring aims and goals from situations where the full data is not given explicitly.

It has been suggested (Sparck Jones and Kay 1974) that the task is to examine the semantic component of:

- Methods of identifying meaningful units in the input document.
- The derivation of document descriptions from them.
- The construction and use of classifications and other forms of index language organisation based on these descriptions.

Unfortunately none of these aims are achievable without the addition of substantial quantities of outside knowledge. Part of this may come from the text itself, but many more assumptions of common knowledge (common to the author and their intended audience) are made than may initially be obvious. A moment's consideration will show that the database of rules needed is very large indeed even for what one would normally consider as fairly trivial situations. A system will require considerable development effort if it is going to 'understand' even those episodes which consist of a relatively few number of sentences, or indeed of only one sentence.

Though one must be careful not to generalise, it can be seen that if there are a large number of sentences all of which deal with essentially the same concept, then extraction of significant subjects becomes easier than if the sentences had rapid changes of content which would necessitate the implementation of a large number of plans in the system. Hence it is possible to imagine a natural language indexing system which could use semantic analysis of text to produce suitable index entries but this would only be possible when the domain of discourse was very restricted. Unfortunately this is also the very area where statistical analysis techniques, discussed later, can be applied quite successfully. It is the more diffuse areas which are proving intractable both for statistical analysis and for discourse analysis. The former is unsuited to this work as keyword extraction may well have little relevance to the production of useful index entries, whereas the very vastness of the domain in the latter poses very difficult problems in spite of efforts to produce generalisations of text.

3.2.2. NLP and Indexing: Conclusion

What is implicit in both semantic and discourse analysis, when tackled by creating plans and scripts, is a particular world view: a view that rules can be stated and scripts designed which, by logical extension, may be applied to new events, making it possible to produce plausible assumptions about novel situations, or situations which, though based on current knowledge and experience, possess a novel component. This view is not without its critics (Winograd and Flores 1986, also Hayek 1952). It is claimed that the proponents of a NLP approach are victims of scientism. This latter view is based on the fallacies of objectivism (the attempt to dispense with subjective knowledge), and collectivism (the treatment of abstract wholes, such as 'language' or 'society', as definitively given objects about which we can discover laws). However, the presence of an objective reality outwith the confines of a specific environment of concerns, actions and beliefs is contrary to experience. And once a subjective reality is accepted the implication is that questions cannot be answered without reference to the context in which the question is made. With this alternative framework in place, the underpinnings of the frames, scripts and plans approach to discourse comprehension are removed and any attempt to apply such methodology must fail in many circumstances. This will especially be true where superficial similarities exist between the script and the text of a particular event, but with no cognisance being taken of the wider circumstances in which the script is being used. These are the very areas where the human ability to have an overall view of the text, and thus be able to select and reject selectively, shows the limitations inherent in present computer-based linguistic analysis systems.

An example which shows many of the problems discussed in these sections would be the phrase 'black hole'. Clearly, the meaning of this phrase could be:

- Literally a black hole.
- Astronomical reference –here it is neither a hole, nor is it black.
- Historical reference –the black hole of Calcutta.

It can be seen that straightforward semantic analysis would make little headway. If background knowledge in some form were to be added to the system, then the problem of distinguishing between the possible meanings would arise.

Despite these problems, the only way forward for those engaged in long-term research into indexing is to make at least limited use of computational linguistic techniques. For as Borko said (Borko 1985), 'During the past decade a great deal of progress has been made. .. Parsing deserves our attention, for it is an essential element of question answering, fact retrieval, decision support and expert systems. If information retrieval is to progress beyond the simple retrieval of bibliographic references, it will need to analyse and restructure text, and it will need effective parsing procedures.' More fundamental research work on the nature of indexing itself does, however, need to be done, as 'The trouble with indexing is that even today we are still at the elementary stage of learning how to do it. We do not know enough about its technique ... each one thinks he knows better than anyone else how an index should be arranged and what should go into it'(Collison, 1969).

3.3. Computer-assisted indexing

An approach which uses the computer as an indexer's aid rather than as a replacement, presents us with a more reasonable goal than that of creating an entire index automatically as a partial solution to the problem is acceptable.

There are, broadly speaking, three approaches to this problem. In dealing with them, systems which attempt to create indexes with little or no human intervention, but need such intervention in practice are excluded. The systems to be considered are specifically geared to assist –and no more –the creation of an index.

3.3.1. Text markup systems

The first approach is one with which one meets most frequently. Index creation is controlled by the incorporation of markup into the text itself. This markup determines which word or phrase is to be used as an index entry, and it normally also determines its indexing level; i.e. whether it is a heading, sub-heading, or even lower than that. Many word-processors have a system which matches this description. WordStar, a program dating from CP/M days, has an add-in called StarIndex. Scribe, another well-known word processor available on larger systems, has an indexing option. Ditroff documents can use programs called indx and findphrases (Abe and Berry 1988). Furthermore the specifications for SGML also provide for index creation in this manner.

The advantages of this approach are clear. As authors type in their text, important aspects of it may be indexed 'on-the-fly'. This ensures that references are not missed, and that the tedious work of index creation is not left until the end. Once the document is complete, the final index is produced automatically. Furthermore, alteration of the text by insertion or deletion will not affect the final page references, as these are generated from the current working copy of the text. This idea is so delightfully simple, that some words of caution might be in order. Specifically, the following points should be borne in mind:

- Creation of syndetic structure (see, see also, see under) is likely to be poor as to succeed in this it is necessary to have an overall view of the whole document.

- If the index is created over a long period of time, then the index is likely to be very patchy and unbalanced. The author forgets the previous structure they have imposed on the index, and may start to ignore items which were referenced in earlier portions of the text, or use different words for the same concepts. Authors do the latter as a matter of course in their writing –it avoids boredom in the reader –but it is not desirable in the creation of an index.
- Every author has a particular axe to grind, but some authors express their opinion more forcibly than others. It is likely that not only are the index phrases picked out by these authors likely to be more biased than those chosen by an indexer, but also the author is likely to forget to index some of the counter-arguments they might introduce in the course of developing their position.

3.3.2. Professional Indexing systems

Most professional book indexers still work with some form of page proofs which are sent to them by the publishers. These are usually galleys or paste-ups and are not available in machine-readable format. They proceed as follows:

- The whole text is read –or at least scanned in order to get the balance of the book.
- Each page is marked up with possible index entries.
- The index entries are written down on cards called slips. These may either be kept sorted, or may be sorted at the end of the index. The advantage of the former is that the indexer can see how the index is shaping up. The advantage of the latter is that of convenience –the slips do not have to be manipulated constantly. A fresh entry demands a fresh slip.

There are a number of professional indexing programs which attempt to remove the tedium of sorting and manipulating the slips (reviews of these appear from time to time in MicroIndexer –a supplement to the journal *The Indexer*). The indexer's task is still to mark-up the text and to type in the index entries, but from then on, the computer will keep a sorted list, will permit straightforward amendation and will print out the final index in almost the correct order with many of the divisions into sub-headings correct.

As the indexer (who might well also be the author) is dealing with the page proofs, it is likely that the problems of balance and syndetic structure mentioned above will not be as severe as when the index is being created in parallel with the text. The problem of bias will, of course, remain.

3.3.3. Expert system indexing systems

There is yet a third computer system for aiding the production of book indexes. But as this relies on an expert system approach and has been tailored for a particular environment (the production of medical indexes for use on an on-line database (Humphrey 1989 also Humphrey and Miller 1987)) it is of little help in the broad problem of index production to texts in general, though it does show that expert knowledge can be used effectively to increase indexing consistency. The assumptions behind creation of such expert systems are likely to have great relevance to furtherance of automatic indexing of texts; after all, if an indexer has expert knowledge in the field of mathematics, it would be unreasonable to expect him to produce a highly competent index in the field of law. There might well be a number of basic approaches to index creation which are similar in the two cases, but for creation of an index which reflects the underlying assumptions –often implicit – of a particular discipline requires expert knowledge. Thus it should not be considered a shortcoming of an indexing program designed to assist the indexer in choosing relevant entries if it performs best only in one environment.

4. Significance

Manual indexing, computerised indexing, and computer-assisted indexing all have one basic problem – that of determining the significance of the text under consideration and of assigning suitable descriptors for it. Possibly the harder of the two is the determination of significance, whereas the assignment of descriptors is likely to be the area in which greater inter-indexer inconsistencies arise. However, it is the former problem which has to be solved before further progress in automatic indexing can be made.

There have been a number of attempted solutions, each based on different underlying assumptions about the nature of language and the nature of the indexing process. As progress in computer-based indexing has been the result of accretion of developments and modifications on top of old ideas, rather than a number of novel developments, it is profitable to examine not only current ways of determining significance, but also a few of the earlier methods. Fuller details may be obtained in Edmundson and Wyllys (1961), in Bourne (1966) and in Stevens (1965).

4.1. Probabilistic systems

4.1.1. Frequency-based

Luhn's Study

Luhn's pioneering work set the stage for the practical realisation of many automatic indexing systems based on purely probabilistic criteria (e.g. the SMART system). In his study (Luhn 1958) he realised that the significance of sections of text had to be determined in order to have a criterion on which to select possible keywords. He determined that significance of a sentence was a function of the following:

- Significance of words in a sentence.
- Relative positions of words in a sentence.

In turn, the significance of a word was to be determined by their frequency of occurrence within a document (the 'document' was assumed to be an abstract):

- Common (i.e. high frequency) words were not significant.
- Very low frequency words were not significant.
- Significant words were the ones left (i.e. those occurring in the middle frequency range). (It is of interest to compare Luhn's ideas with those of Salton as described in his Theory of Indexing mentioned previously).

Regarding word position, Luhn argued that 'the closer certain words are associated, the more specifically an aspect of the subject is being treated. Therefore, whenever the greatest number of frequently occurring different words are found in greatest physical proximity to each other, the probability is very high that the information being conveyed is most representative of the article ...'. The practical application of Luhn's strategy was as follows:

- Calculate word frequency.
- Conflate words which have less than seven dissimilarities after their identical beginnings.
- Common words are not counted.
- Calculate significance (using whole text).
- Words which have a low frequency (determined empirically) are not significant.
- Significant words separated by more than four non-significant words are isolated and not considered significant.
- The significance S = p(squared) / q where p = number of significant words in cluster under consideration q = total number of words in cluster.
- The significance of a sentence is the highest-value cluster in that sentence.

Although it was found that many of the assumptions of Luhn were somewhat simplistic (for example only single keywords were extracted), they are important insofar as they have formed the underpinnings of many of the current IR systems. Furthermore, they were seminal in asserting the importance of a probabilistic approach to the determination of keywords, and consequently to the determination of significance of a sentence.

The Oswald experiments

Oswald's work was performed with the prime aim of obtaining abstracts in an automatic fashion (Oswald *et al.* 1959). They are, nevertheless, of interest. This is primarily because they also attempt to address the problem of significance, but have extended Luhn's ideas to encompass the utilisation of groups of words. Thus once again, the question was to obtain some measure of significance of a sentence.

The following technique was employed:

- Function words were discarded.
- The remaining words were frequency counted.
- Every juxtaposition of two or more words involving a high frequency word was considered as a significant word group.
- Sentences with two or more significant word groups are significant sentences.

The remainder of the technique involved the selection of significant sentences to form the automatic abstracts. The point is that by looking at word groups, rather than at isolated words as Luhn had done, it was possible to pick out some significant phrases. As indexes seldom consist of words, but are nearly always phrases, Oswald's technique demonstrated that extracting them was also a possibility using probabilistic methods.

4.1.2. Term discrimination and vector space models

Gerard Salton has been closely associated with these two approaches to indexing. His 'Theory of Indexing' (qv) discusses these two models in considerable detail. They have proved popular for much of the database IR experiments which have been done over the past decade and a half, but the technique is not without its critics (e.g. Raghavan and Wong 1986) and still has room for improvement (e.g. El-Hamdouchi and Willett 1988). What is of particular interest is observing the effect of applying Salton's technique for indexing free-text in an attempt to obtain content-descriptors which might be used for text indexing. Work by Weinberg has shown that when applied to a limited range of scientific texts which were also manually indexed using a thesaurus, the performance is poor (Weinberg 1981). In particular, some of her findings included the following:

- Humanly assigned index terms do not cluster at one level of frequency. In abstracts, low frequency predominates and in full text high and medium frequency are more common.
- Discrimination techniques break down as a predictor of humanly assigned index terms in full texts.
- Humanly assigned index terms are not characterised by words which have a much higher frequency in individual documents than is to be expected from their frequency in the document collection.
- Terms identified as major or overall content indicators do not cluster at one level of frequency in documents.

Indeed, even in the field of database indexing, it appears that if relevance data is available, the medium-frequency terms used by Salton, and pioneered by Luhn, might not be so useful as previously thought; it appears that low-frequency terms might prove to be more useful (Biru *et al.* 1989). Due to these problems, there has been little progress in attempting to use mainly probabilistic methods in the field of indexing book-type texts. Instead, there have been attempts to merge some of the techniques of syntactical analysis with probabilistic approaches in an attempt to overcome some of the more glaring problems.

4.2. Mixed syntactical and probabilistic systems

Salton's work

Recently Salton has come to consider the production of indexes to books as being a problem which does show differences from the production of indexes to abstracts held in database form. In terms of book indexing, he has suggested that a probabilistic method of text analysis appears to do better than syntactic methods, though some form of syntactic analysis would be needed to generate appropriate phrases (Salton 1988 (bis)). Indeed, the example which was presented in the paper showed poor results from a purely syntactical approach, whilst a mixture of statistical and syntactical analysis was able to produce an index which, though not acceptable, was certainly closer to that produced by a human indexer than pure syntactic analysis was able to furnish.

The approach developed consisted of the following steps:

- Perform a syntactical analysis on the text.
- Use the output from the syntactical analyser as input for a phrase generation system. This works in a rule-based way to create possible noun phrases.
- For the phrases obtained:
- Use phrases exhibiting an occurrence frequency of at least n.
- Use matching components of partly overlapping phrases to construct new phrases (which hopefully contain the sense of those which were deleted in the overlap).
- Use phrases which are: capitalised titles italicised.

The resultant phrases, usually consisting of two words, were then used for the index. It should, however, be noted that this analysis was applied to text with a great deal of manual pre-processing (e.g. knowledge-bases were specifically tailored to the text in question). Thus although the methods used show that a mixture of techniques can profitably be used to produce approximations to indexes, the results must still be treated with caution before attempts are made to transfer the techniques used to working environments.

Earl's study

Lois Earl conducted a number of studies in an attempt to achieve automatic extracting and automatic indexing (Earl 1970). Although this proved unsuccessful, the techniques used could prove of interest if editing of the index entries was to be allowed. Earl decided that both syntax and frequency were to be the criteria on which entries were to be selected. However, the work was hampered by the lack of a suitable syntactic analyser (parser) at that time. One was eventually obtained which was judged to be 'reliable and highly accurate but there is still plenty of room for improvement'.

The technique consisted of the following steps:

- Function words were removed from the text, but noun phrases were preserved unaltered as it was believed that such phrases would form useful entries for an index. These noun phrases now formed the text which was subsequently processed.
- The words were frequency counted. For the purpose of the count, the function words were ignored.
- The frequency corresponding to 10% of the number of total entries in the frequency table was calculated. This formed an (arbitrary) cut-off point. The words and phrases corresponding to all frequencies down to this cut-off were printed out. (In fact another cut-off point was also used, but it did not produce satisfactory results).

A test on a number of chapter-length texts showed that this strategy produced a much longer index than a manual one. In spite of this, and in spite of the fact that the co-occurrence of terms in the manually and automatically produced index was usually less than 50%. However, this figure conceals a range of 40% to 75% of the items occurring in both forms of index. This is not at all bad and shows that development of a mixed syntactic/probabilistic system would be fruitful. What may be a problem is the comment that the automatic system picked up entries which were not indexed manually even though the entry heading was present with another page reference. This 'missing reference' may well have been missed out by the (human) indexer. An alternative explanation might be that it may have been a trivial reference, and that the system failed to distinguish between significant and trivial references to a given subject.

4.3. Thesaurus/dictionary based systems

Klingbiel's Approach

Klingbiel did not attempt to produce automatic indexes, but he rather took the route of assisting the creation of indexes by humans (Klingbiel 1973b).

His approach was basically a word-matching of the input text against a pre-defined dictionary – though the reality of the program was somewhat more complicated than this. Borko has shown that simple inclusion of words (or its converse, the exclusion of unwanted words) does not produce satisfactory results. Neither the dictionary nor the algorithm for eliminating words was reliable (Borko 1970). Under the conditions of its intended use –that of indexing only titles and abstracts – it proved to be capable of assisting in index production, and certainly its performance in a domain-limited field would be of interest. Thus if it was certain that an indexing system were to be used for the indexing of certain types of texts, where there is likely to be a number of keywords which have a high probability of being important, then this research has shown that a modified form of a dictionary lookup would be of considerable value in speeding up the indexing task. However, as a general-purpose indexing system it would be of little use as the relative importance of words input would be changing from text to text and from subject to subject. Ultimately, it is felt that Klingbiel's approach has much to recommend it, but only when used as part of an 'expert shell' which is used consistently within a given text-type environment. The shell would attempt to learn the important keywords, and then use the information so gained to alter the probability of a particular word being used as a keyword. Thus it would act to assist the production of an index by adding information to an existing system rather than being relied on as a stand-alone module.

Dillon's thesaurus-based book indexing project
A somewhat similar system was investigated by Martin Dillon (Dillon 1982). The technique employed required a dictionary of terms which are to appear in the index, along with all text strings that count as instances of the term. The program's function is to search the text for each occurrence of a term or its associated strings and creates an entry to the index when either is found.

Using standard measure of recall (ratio of terms automatically assigned that are correct to the total number of term assignments), Dillon found that the index prepared by his method compared reasonably favourably with that achieved using conventional IR systems; and the performance of these is generally recognised to be good. Needless to say, there are limitations on this type of indexing – the limitations being very similar to those of any lookup system. Unfortunately, these limitations are often the very ones not wanted for book indexing. For example, the fact that a simple comparison is being made between the text and the thesaurus means that indexing exhaustivity is high (all matching terms are indexed). But in a large text this is the very thing which is not wanted. High exhaustivity means that the searcher is continually being sent to trivial mentions of the subject. Thus the proven capabilities of a thesaurus or dictionary system really need to be coupled with some way of determining the significance of areas of text to allow the exclusion of matching, but unwanted, entries. Furthermore, thesaurus or dictionary-based indexing will also suffer from the well-known problems which all such systems have. For example, it appears that terminology changes at the rate of about 4% per year (Harris 1979), so constant problems arise of updating old terms, and of providing suitable syndetic structure to permit access to the older terminology which was used to index previous sections of the text.

5. Current developments

5.1. Subject selection

In 1984 a British Standard, BS 6529 was produced to guide an indexer in subject selection. In it, the suggestion is that indexing consists essentially of two stages:

> "establishing the concepts expressed in a document, i.e. the subject translating these concepts into the components of the indexing language."

In turn, establishing the subject is broken down into the following areas:

> "understanding the overall content of the document, the purpose of the author, etc. identifying the concepts which represent this content, purpose, etc.
>
> selecting the concepts needed for retrieval."

The Standard next considers how subjects may best be extracted by (human) indexers working to a tight schedule. To quote: 'Ideally, full understanding of these documents depends upon an extensive reading of the text. For economic reasons, however, this is not usually practicable, nor is it always necessary. Nevertheless, the indexer should ensure that no useful information has been overlooked. Important parts of the text need to be considered carefully, particular attention being paid to:

- The title.
- The introduction, and the opening phrases of chapters and paragraphs.
- Illustrations, tables, diagrams and their captions.
- The conclusion.
- Words or groups of words which are underlined or printed in an unusual typeface.

The author's intentions are usually stated in the introductory sections, while the final sections generally state how far these aims were achieved.

As has been noted (Piternick 1984), the previous sentence may help to explain why concluding paragraphs are often not very useful as sources for index entries in the way opening paragraphs are. However, they often serve to summarise the main thrust of the author's argument - often signalled by the use of an indicator phrase similar to 'in conclusion...'or 'it has been shown that...'. Some of the issues raised here will now be considered.

5.2. K. P. Jones' theory of indexing

Jones states (Jones 1976) that indexing consists of the following steps:

- The process of extracting words from text.
- Augmenting these words when necessary by other words not in, but which are related to, the original text.
- If necessary the transcription of these words into some form of controlled language (many technologies attempt to employ standardised terminologies and abbreviations - the indexer may decide to comply with these even though the author/s may not have done so).
- The use of words to form an index or as input to an information retrieval system.
- The construction of cross references and thesauri if considered to be necessary.'

Jones then goes on to consider how step 1 –the process of extracting words from text – may be accomplished. It is suggested that a variety of statistical properties of the text are used, either explicitly or implicitly, by the indexer in their attempt to index the document. Thus an indexer is more likely to accept a word for indexing if it occurs fifty, rather than five hundred, or five widely scattered times within a text. If a word occurs very frequently, then it is unlikely to be selected. Thus although the word disease is likely to be very frequent in many medical books, its use as an index entry will have no value, as the entire book is likely to be all about disease. On the other hand, the same word when used more selectively in a text (i.e. restricted to several small sections) is deemed to convey more information, and thus be useful as an index entry. If a word occurs very infrequently then it is possible that they should be indexed, rather than omitted, as they may be important jargon words which are then elaborated and expanded on in the following sections, perhaps without the word being repeated. The indexer's judgement will determine the aboutness of the text, and hence the pertinence, or otherwise, of an infrequently occurring word as an index entry.

Word length and letter frequency also seem to influence the potentiality for selection. In the case of short words, these are likely to be more common, and hence be rejected on the grounds of frequency of occurrence. In the case of a computerised system, then these are the words which would be removed by means of a stop list. Very long words are difficult to incorporate into indexes (a common restriction by the publisher is that the number of characters per line is in the region of 28 - 38, the exact number depending on the book). Unusual letter combinations, bold and italic type when used in moderation, side-headings and sub-headings are all features which are likely to attract the indexer's attention.

There also appears to be a critical density for word selection. If a new term is introduced, it is usually defined, then used quite frequently in expanding and illustrating the definition, and it is at this point that it would be selected as an index entry. Subsequently it may be used incidentally, as part of a vocabulary which is assumed to be understood both by the author and the reader. Such uses are much less likely to form suitable index entries. It is interesting to note that this concept of critical density is implicit in the remarks of Salton (Salton 1988a), when he said that 'For book indexing purposes, a book can be broken down into sections, or paragraphs; the term frequency and document frequency factors are then computed for the individual book components.' It is clear that both term and document frequencies rely on several instances of the term occurring in the paragraph – which is likely to be seen when the term (word) is being defined and explained. Later, more casual occurrences of the term are unlikely to be picked up as being significant by virtue of their low frequency.

Jones goes on to consider the work of Anderson (Anderson 1971) and observes that 'Some parts of a document are especially rewarding to the indexer. Opening paragraphs seem to be particularly rich in indexable words.

Definitions are particularly important and marked by distinctive syntax. They are important as they act as markers for the introduction of new ideas and the word or words associated with these ideas. They also provide clues for the structuring of indexes.'

As all these factors are quantifiable they could form the basis of a theoretic element within the indexing process.

Other factors which need to be considered for the correct identification of definitions are linguistic. Thus a sentence

An A is a B

is likely to be a definition. Other examples would be:

A may be defined as ...
The notion of A-ness ...
The idea of A-ness...
The concept of A-ness ...

and so on.

In a similar way, synonyms may be identified and used to produce index structure. Thus a sentence with the construction 'An A or a B ,' might very well aid the construction of suitable syndetic structure. Jones then goes on to discuss a variety of linguistic strategies which may be used to tease out the underlying structure of a text, and hypothesises that there should be an inferential level in indexing theory – that the meanings of words in parts of the same sentence, or of a succeeding sentence, may be inferred from knowledge of the part under consideration. Indeed, the ability to make these types of inferences enables human indexers to index in unfamiliar subject areas, so it is a matter which needs to be considered if any form of indexing theory is to be at all plausible.

It can be seen that these ideas, those of the British Standard, and those of Salton converge on using certain characteristics of the text itself (for example layout, typeface, illustrations) as well as the previously considered word frequencies and syntactic analysis, to determine the significance of sections of text. If significant areas could be established in a fairly reliable way, the task of creating indexes, or, more realistically, aiding an indexer in the creation of indexes, would be a significant step nearer.

5.3. Indexing long texts

Confirmation of the above ideas has come from some indexing experiments carried out by Jones on short free-texts (articles from a popular science magazine) (Jones 1983). However, work at Dundee University has shown that it appears that the principles hold even when book texts are considered. Although the data has not been fully analysed, preliminary results show that the following observations, obtained from the consideration of texts indexed by professional book indexers, are likely to be valid:

- Sub-headings and headings relating to shorter pieces of text (say 2 –4 paragraphs) are used to assist in the task of content analysis and creation of content descriptors.
- Major headings are little used. This is scarcely surprising, as major headings will cover too large an area of text to act as useful content descriptors.
- When present, diagrams and illustrations may either be used to reinforce the validity of a related descriptor selection, or they may be used in their own right as index entries.
- Tables are often not indexed. This was rather surprising, as a great deal of information is often summarised in tables. It may be the sheer tedium of indexing a large number of tables is too daunting. Discussions with a technical authoring department would indicate that this was certainly a factor.
- In the absence of sub-headings, illustrations and much other similar lay-out material (e.g. when using galley proofs), it appears that index entries tend to come from the beginning of paragraphs rather than the end. In paragraphs from which content descriptors are chosen, roughly twice as many come from the first half of the text as from the second half.

As a cautionary note, it should be added that the sample of indexers was quite small (five indexers with extensive indexing experience and two with limited experience) and that the analysis of large texts was performed on five books (in paste-up or galley form) indexed by two indexers. The rest of the material consisted of 10 page sections of a PhD thesis.

5.4. Role of text markup

The ability to create indexes by means of text markup has been mentioned previously, and a number of pitfalls present in this type of indexing have been enumerated. However, one point often missed is that text markup itself can be a fruitful source of index entries. After all, the creation of a text –here a scholarly or technical text is being considered – usually demands the creation of an outline, with successive refinements until it becomes a sketch for each of the sections of the text itself. Having created this sketch or plan, the author proceeds to develop their argument, following the lines of the plan. It could be argued that the plan, which is usually echoed in the creation of headings and sub-headings in the text itself, can act as a guide to extracting content-descriptors from the text. In the case where headings may occur with a high frequency relative to the body of the text, they themselves could act as content descriptors or even index entries.

As the development of automatic indexing systems has tended to be by the addition of new detail to previous systems rather than a complete re-design, it is likely that an approach incorporating information from markup may help to push forward the capabilities of large-text automatic indexing systems.

6. Conclusions

Several ways of indexing full texts have been examined. Although the intellectual process of subject analysis and the subsequent creation of content descriptors is one which would appear to lend itself to techniques of NLP, these techniques have not been developed sufficiently to be useful in a practical indexing system.

Conversely, probabilistic systems have been found to be surprisingly useful in the creation of indexes to databases, though used in isolation they fail in the production of 'back-of-the-book' indexes. However, they have been improved by a number of workers by a process of accretion –new or modified techniques are added to existing ones so that each layer of the system has to deal with less input, and thus can bring more sophisticated, but computationally more expensive, techniques to bear. At the heart of all these methods is the problem of significance, which has so far proved to be intractable. What is perhaps more surprising, is that with a few exceptions (notably Jones), the bulk of the work in this field has dealt with indexing short texts –normally abstracts – in databases, with a consequent confounding of subject and word indexing. It is suggested that by studying intellectual indexing practices and relating them to aspects of text markup, it should be possible to focus attention on smaller sections of major texts such as books. These smaller sections, assumed to consist of significant references to subjects, could then processed in conventional ways, whilst the sections which have been omitted from processing would consist of references of limited significance.

7. References

Abe, K. K. and Berry, D. M. (1989) Indx and findphrases, a system for generating indexes for ditroff documents. *Software -Practice and experience.* 19 (1).

Anderson, M. D. (1971) *Book Indexing.* Cambridge University Press, Cambridge.

Biru, T., El-Hamdouchi, A., Rees, R. S. and Willett, P. (1989) Inclusion of relevance information in the term discrimination model. *Journal of Documentation,* 45 (2).

Borko, H. (1970) Experiments in book indexing by computer. *Information storage and retrieval,* 6.

Borko, H. and Bernier, C. L. (1978) *Indexing Concepts and Methods.* Academic Press, London.

Borko, H. (1985) (as book reviewer). *Information processing and management,* 21 (2).

Bourne, C. P. (1966) Evaluation of indexing systems. *Annual Review of Information Science and Technology,* 1.

BS 1749: 1985. British Standard Recommendations for Alphabetical Arrangement and the Filing Order of Numbers and Symbols. *British Standards Institution.,* London.

BS 3700: 1988. British Standard Recommendations for Preparing Indexes to Books, Periodicals and Other Documents. *British Standards Institution,* London.

BS 6529: 1984. British Standard Recommendations for Examining Documents, Determining their Subjects and Selecting Indexing Terms. *British Standards Institution,* London.

Charniak, E. (1978) On the use of framed knowledge in language comprehension. *Artificial Intelligence,* 11.

Collison, R. L. (1969) The elements of book indexing, part I. In G. Knight (Ed) *Training in Indexing.* MIT Press, London.

Crestadoro, A. (1856) The art of making catalogues of libraries: a method to obtain in a short time a most perfect, complete, and satisfactory catalogue of the British Museum library, by a reader therein. *The Literary, Scientific and Artistic Reference Office.,* London.

Dillon, M. (1982) Thesaurus-based automatic book indexing. *Information Processing and Management,* 18 (4).

Dutta, S. and Sinha, P. K. (1984) Pragmatic approach to subject indexing - a new concept. *JASIS* , 35.

Earl, L. L. (1970) Experiments in automatic extracting and indexing. *Information Storage and Retrieval,* 6.

Edmundson, H. P. and Wyllys, R. E. (1961) Automatic abstracting and indexing –survey and recommendations. *Communications of the ACM,* 4 (5).

El-Hamdouchi, A. and Willett, P. (1988) An improved algorithm for the calculation of exact term discrimination values. *Information Processing and Management,* 24 (1).

Garside, R., Leech, G. and Sampson, G. (1987) *The Computational Analysis of English.* Longman, Harlow.

Grishman, R. (1986) *Computational Linguistics.* Cambridge University Press, Cambridge.

Harris, J. L. (1979) Terminology change: Effect on index vocabularies. *Information Processing and Management,* 15.

Hayek, F. A. (1952) *The Counter-revolution of Science.* The Free Press, Glencoe, Ill.

Humphrey, S. M. (1989) A knowledge-based expert system for computer-aided indexing. *IEEE Expert.*

Humphrey, S. M. and Miller, N. E. (1987) Knowledge-based indexing of the medical literature: the indexing aid project. *JASIS* 38 (3).

Jones, K. P. (1983) How do we index?: A report of some ASLIB informatics group activity. *Journal of Documentation,* 39 (1).

Jones, K. P. (1976) Towards a theory of indexing. *Journal of Documentation,* 32 (2).

Klingbiel, P. H. (1973a) Machine-aided indexing of technical literature. *Information Storage and Retrieval,* 9.

Klingbiel, P. H. (1973b) A technique for machine-aided indexing. *Information Storage and Retrieval,* 9.

Korycinski, C. and Newell, A.F. (1990) Natural-language processing and automatic indexing. *The Indexer,* 17.

Luhn, H. P. (1958) The automatic creation of literature abstracts. *IBM Journal of Research and Development,* 2 (2).

Luhn, H. P. (1959) Keyword-in-context Index for Technical Literature (KWIC Index). IBM, Yorktown Heights, NY.

McColvin, L. R. (1958) The purpose of indexing. *The Indexer 1 (2).* Reprinted in *American Documentation* 9, 1960.

Maron, M. E. (1978) On indexing, retrieval and the meaning of about. *JASIS,* 28.

Oswald, V. A. *et al.* (1959) Automatic indexing and abstracting of the contents of documents. *RADC-TR-59-208,* USAF. Quoted by Edmundson, H. P. and Wyllys, R. E. *op.cit.*

Pao, M. L. (1978) Automatic text analysis based on transition phenomena of word occurrences. *JASIS* ,21.

Piternick, A. B. (1984) The indexing process (letter). *Journal of Documentation,* 40 (1).

Raghavan, V.V. and Wong, S. K. M. (1986) A critical analysis of vector space model for information retrieval. *JASIS,* 37 (5).

Rowbottom, M. E. and Willett, P. (1982) The effect of subject matter on the automatic indexing of full text. *JASIS,* 23 .

Salton, G. (1988a) Syntactic approaches to automatic book indexing. *Proceedings of the 26th annual meeting of the association for computational linguistics,* Buffalo, NY.

Salton, G. (1988b) On the application of syntactic methodologies in automatic text analysis. *Technical report 88-954.* Cornell University, NY.

Schank, R. C. (1980) Language and memory. *Cognitive Science,* 4.

Schank, R. C. and Ableson, R. (1977) *Scripts, Plans, Goals And Understanding.* Lawrence Erlbaum, Hillsdale, NJ.

Sparck Jones,. K and Kay, M. (1974) *Linguistics and Information Science.* Academic Press, NY.

Stevens, M. E. (1965) Automatic indexing: a state of the art report. *National Bureau of Standards Monograph,* 91.

Weinberg, B. H. (1981) Word frequency and automatic indexing. D.L.S. dissertation, Columbia University, NY.

Weinberg, B. H. (1988) Why indexing fails the researcher. *The Indexer* ,16 (1).

Winograd, T. and Flores, F. (1986) *Understanding Computers And Cognition.* Ablex, Norwood, NJ.

11

Factors Affecting Organisational Acceptance of an Automated Writing Aid

A.E. Winterbauer
DLS Group

Abstract

For an innovation to be accepted by an organisation, the members of that organisation must "buy in." An important element of "buying in" is that they have control over how the innovation is used (Berman and McLaughlin 1978; Havelock and Havelock 1973; Oettinger 1969; Stewart 1982). So, it would follow that for teachers to accept an innovation like a computer program to help students with writing, the teachers should have some say in how the program operates. To test this idea, a computer program, Writeaid, was designed so that teachers could, within limits, modify its operation. However, Writeaid was not organisationally acceptable. The reasons why it failed could be useful to anyone thinking of designing automated writing aids for use in a school curriculum.

1. Introduction

Writeaid was developed to help college teachers work with their students on writing projects. Specifically, it would relieve teachers of the initial prewriting conference with students, a time when they decide upon a paper topic and some ideas of how to develop it, and which usually takes half an hour or more per student. The idea was that subsequent consultations would be more productive because students would arrive at the session with a definite topic in mind and a rough outline of the paper.

It was hoped that Writeaid would prove successful by being adopted by faculty who tried it. An innovation can be defined as adopted when "mutual adaptation" has occurred, a phenomenon whereby the members of the organisation adapt their procedures to accommodate an innovation as well as adapt the innovation to fit their needs (Berman and McLaughlin 1978; Berman, Greenwood *et al.* 1975). For example, word processing software is an adopted innovation. We can modify it to fit our needs (e.g. margins, spacing, and print fonts), and we have adapted the way we work to accommodate the word processor (e.g. learning about computers, special furniture for printers and consoles, and revising text at the keyboard rather than with a pencil).

To promote mutual adaptation, the design of Writeaid and its implementation were based on ideas of what makes for effective writing intervention as well as what makes an innovation adoptable. If mutual adaptation occurred, that is if teachers adapted their teaching methods to accommodate Writeaid and adapted Writeaid to accommodate their teaching practice, then Writeaid could be considered adoptable and potentially useful. There were three questions that, if answered in the positive, would indicate the process of mutual adaptation:

- Would faculty adapt Writeaid to suit their own teaching practice?
- Would faculty adapt their teaching practice to accommodate Writeaid?
- Was, therefore, the fundamental design of Writeaid satisfactory, and was it properly implemented?

2. Design of Writeaid

Writeaid is a computer program, written in Pascal and UNIX shell routines, that runs in a UNIX environment. It draws upon three sets of files that contain (a) questions of a general nature (useful for establishing the main points of a paper); (b) a collection of phrases to search for in students' responses, the conditions for conducting those searches, and questions to ask should these phrases be encountered under the conditions set in the rules; and (c) questions to ask should these searches fail.

After asking as many of the general questions as the student desires to answer, Writeaid returns to the answers that the student provided and looks through them for phrases that might prove useful to pursue, such as "I don't know," "therefore," "I think," and so on. Should such a match occur, either individually or in combination with other phrases, the program can ask further questions for clarification of a point, to narrow terms, or to ask whatever the instructor deems important. After these more general responses have been investigated, the program again goes back to square one, this time with the students' (hopefully) more fully developed responses, and it pursues them. Each pass the program makes through the responses constitutes a level of detail in the paper. These levels are arranged as an outline and given to the student as a file for printing or for downloading to a personal computer (see Appendix 1).

The instructor can modify the supplied top-level questions or substitute new ones. Entire sets of questions for different disciplines or topics can be placed into files and used by Writeaid. Also, the instructor can modify or replace the collection of phrases used by Writeaid for the in-depth interviews of the student and can control how the program uses this collection when interpreting students' responses (see Appendix 2).

The purpose of this design was twofold. First, the program adheres to the theory of writing as a non-linear process whereby the students' attention during brainstorming can be diverted from form and mechanics and focused instead on content (Bannister 1982; Burtis, *et al*. 1983, Odell 1980, Smith 1982; Stallard 1974, Wason 1980). Second, the program adheres to the theory of organisational acceptance of an innovation so that instructors would have ultimate control, allowing them to change the questioning followed by Writeaid.

3. Implementation of Writeaid

Faculty at a private university were asked to participate in a study of Writeaid (Winterbauer 1986). Of 30 university faculty initially contacted, seven agreed to try using Writeaid with their students over two academic quarters (five months). They attended an orientation session that explained how Writeaid works and were given users' manuals. It was made clear to them that they were under no obligation to use the program in order for this study to be considered successful, nor did they need to employ Writeaid in any specific manner or under any certain circumstances. The researcher scheduled regular hours at a convenient location where he could help students and professors with their use of Writeaid. The faculty were asked, however, to maintain certain records that provided data for the study.

Teachers then made arrangements to have orientation sessions provided for their students once the study commenced. The students were given users' manuals as well. How the students were to use the program in connection with their studies was left to the discretion of the teachers. Students were periodically administered questionnaires during the course of the study.

To augment (and to check) the information provided by the faculty and students, software monitors tracked the use of Writeaid: when it was used, for how long, and by whom, and whether the files were modified or augmented by the instructors. Other software stored transcripts of students' sessions. These data were then compared with the material gathered in questionnaires and interviews to help with interpreting how teachers and students were using the program.

4. Results

4.1. Did faculty adapt Writeaid to suit their own teaching practice?

The faculty were not able to adapt the files within Writeaid to their satisfaction.

Adaptation of Writeaid was defined as the enhancement by the teachers of the questions, the phrase pool, the interpretative rules, and the follow-up questions for failed searches. Across all faculty participants, there was a positive movement toward adapting Writeaid, though this movement was more a recognition of the need for adaptation than its execution.

The few teachers who experimented with altering the files in Writeaid were not rewarded with satisfactory student use of the program. Indeed, these teachers were operating in a vacuum, for without much student use (and transcripts of their interactions with the program), the teachers had little information with which to write better interrogative rules. A catalyst was missing that would have powered the cycle of students using the program and teachers modifying it to encourage better use. Because this cycle could not get started, those instructors who remained interested in using the program were forced to try to find situations for which Writeaid was useful rather than to find ways to change the program to make it more useful. Thus, the program became an auxiliary tool for occasional use under particular conditions.

4.2. Did faculty adapt their teaching practice to accommodate Writeaid?

The faculty were not able to find a way to integrate the program with their courses.

The faculty could be said to have adapted their teaching to accommodate Writeaid if they had altered what they taught, how they taught, or how they conducted prewriting consultations with their students. Only one teacher made minor modifications of this type.

The faculty believed that if they had had more examples of how the students reacted to the program, they would have known how to alter their teaching methods to make better use of it. And the students did not use the program because they could not see how it would help them accomplish the goals of the course. Again, the problem lay with that missing catalyst that would have sparked the cycle whereby teachers and students could provide one another with the information necessary to integrate the program into the course.

As revealed by the answers to the last two questions, there was something missing that would have helped faculty to overcome inertia and promote mutual adaptation. Was there something in the design of Writeaid itself that was preventing mutual adaptation or was it the way the program was implemented with teachers and students?

4.3. Was the fundamental design of Writeaid satisfactory?

The faculty liked the idea of a program they could modify, but at the same time they needed a program they did not have to take the time to modify. Also, the students liked a program that would guide them through the prewriting stage, but they did not like having to go through a prewriting stage to begin with.

No matter what changes a person makes to the questions, phrase pool, or the parsing rules of the program, Writeaid cannot be stretched beyond its fundamental design. It is meant to be used during the initial stages of idea formation for a paper. Its open-ended questioning approach guides the writer from general observations to supporting details without reference to the mechanical aspects of writing or to the overall organisation of the paper. The resulting outline then could be used in discussions between the teacher and student. The faculty had no arguments with this design although they did start to come up with ideas of their own for automated writing aids (some of which would have required sophisticated machine intelligence). Generally, due to constraints on their time, they wished somebody could modify the program files for them so they would not have to think about them.

Students generally thought the approach was interesting but they objected to the time required to develop a topic. They believed that the approach was too exhaustive, and it caused them to spend more time than they wanted on an activity (prewriting) that they did not particularly enjoy. Additionally, most of the students had little or no computer background and had problems with the lengthy procedures required to log on to a network of VAX minicomputers in order to gain access to Writeaid. Although having the program on a such a network negated the problems encountered with distributing the different files of questions and parsing rules on diskettes, it complicated the means of using the program by students and apparently contributed to their anxiety about using it. In summation then, the overall design of the program was generally acceptable to both teachers and students, although numerous modifications were suggested to the program itself (and not just the files). However, the core of the problem seemed to be that students were unwilling to devote "extra" time to using an innovation that did not seem to have a direct relationship with the rest of the course requirements, and the teachers did not want to devote the "extra" time to tinkering with an innovation that did not pay off in increased student use and noticeable improvement in students' paper planning. It is ironic that a program that could have made teacher-student prewriting conferences more efficient was actually perceived as using up too much time. The problem then was how the program was implemented with its intended audience so that wasted labour was reduced in the prewriting process.

4.4. Was Writeaid properly implemented with teachers and students?

No. A program like Writeaid is more complicated to use than, say, a word processor. It is an automated liaison between faculty and students and calls for a significant, initial investment of time to work out the issues involved in its use, and then requires a continuing investment of time for its maintenance.

It was not enough simply to show the faculty the procedures for using Writeaid. Although they were made aware of what steps to take to add or replace questions in the different files and how to modify the parsing rules, they needed to develop strategies for using the program in their courses. In other words, they needed to pay less attention to the program *per se* and more attention to the problem of anticipating students' answers to questions and pursuing them.

Additionally, too little attention was given to implementing the program with students in the belief that the faculty would handle that matter themselves and that most of the students were familiar with computers. Although it would eventually be the teachers' responsibility for establishing a strong relationship between the program and the course so that the students would see a link between their efforts at using the program and the goals of the course, more could have been done to ease the students' anxieties with the computers.

5. Recommendations and conclusions

5.1. Initial Implementation with faculty

Once the faculty were aware of the mechanical aspects of operating Writeaid, then they should have had assistance in determining first if the program would be useful in their courses and, if so, how to use the program effectively in their courses. Perhaps if the teachers could have gathered periodically with similarly interested faculty to brainstorm methods of:

- Inventing and categorising general, leading questions that would help students with various prewriting strategies.
- Anticipating students' responses to these general questions and what would be likely key phrases in the responses that would call for follow-up questions.
- Pursuing a line of questioning based on these key phrases.
- Using the resultant outlines in consultations with students.
- Examining the students' responses in the outlines to look for additional problems the students were having with their plans and concoct more strategies to build into Writeaid's files.

Perhaps with such preparation, the faculty could then have made a better start with linking the program to their different courses, leading off with some better questions and parsing rules within Writeaid and with some better ideas of how to alter instructional methods to take advantage of the program to meet course goals.

5.2. Implementation with students

Given that the faculty could show the students ways to use the program to meet the goals of the course so that the students wouldn't feel that any work they did with the program was just so much effort over and beyond course requirements, then other steps could have been taken to alleviate the students' anxieties over using the computer network. First, a series of orientation sessions could have gradually introduced them to using the computer network. After they were comfortable with the mechanics of the computer system, then they could have been introduced to Writeaid itself, first telling them the purpose of the program and linking it to the goals of the course, and finally showing them how to use it. In addition, a better, more succinct manual could have been written that was divided into five sections: an overview of the program, a sample session, procedures for program use, a quick reference section, and a generous appendix. Also, the manual should have offered very detailed instructions for using the computers in the network.

5.3. Maintenance

It may be that these steps would have provided that catalyst necessary to establish a cycle of give and take between faculty and students which in turn would have pushed forward the process of mutual adaptation. It should have been recognised that computers do not necessarily save time, that often their use just merely shuffles about how that time is spent. Although one of the attractive ideas about Writeaid originally had been that teachers would not have needed to spend so much time on those initial, wheel-spinning prewriting consultations with students, and that teachers would have then been able to use that freed block of time for other activities than writing projects, such may not be the case. They may need to spend that time instead trying to figure out how to change the innovation, and the world around that innovation, to help their students learn more about the prewriting process than they could with individual consultations. That adds up to maintenance, and that leads to the last recommendation.

Administration

Because this was a modest study, it was not possible to secure administrative backing in the form of faculty release time. However, the volunteer faculty were interested in investigating this program, and they might have made more progress had they had assistance in rearranging their schedules to experiment with it. Similar steps were being taken on campus at the time of this study to assist faculty with word processing and with using the computer network for communication. It also became increasingly clear that introducing an innovation like Writeaid into an already established system is like tossing a stone into a pond and watching the ripples spread. Once the faculty and students were made aware of the program, one could see the participants contending with established routine. Essentially, a method must be devised by either the participants or other interested parties to secure administrative support before and during the trial of something like Writeaid. At least in some colleges and universities, there is a growing recognition that investigation of new pedagogical methods is as important as research within a discipline.

To sum up, these factors influenced the adoptive process in this case study:

- A computer-based writing aid that faculty can adjust to suit the writing requirements in their courses.
- "Grants" of time to allow initial and continued experimentation with the program to establish links between use of the program and courses.
- Relief of students' (and teachers') anxieties over the use of the writing aid by gradual orientation to the computer as well as to the program, and well-written, succinct documentation.

One final realisation of this study was that the successful adoption of an innovation can mean a change to the recipient culture. Since the culture is not exactly what it was before, then it too can become an innovation itself with which the members of that culture must contend. If the adoption of Writeaid had been successful and use of the program had spread beyond the volunteer faculty, the change to the culture would have been modified instructional techniques and different ways to organise time. This new culture would have then either succeeded or failed depending upon its members' abilities to adopt it through mutual adaptation.

6. References

Bannister, L. A. (1982). Writing apprehension and anti-writing: a naturalistic study of composing strategies used by college freshmen. Doctoral dissertation, University of Southern California. Dissertation Abstracts International, 43-A 1436.

Berman, P., Greenwood, P. W., McLaughlin, M. W., and Pincus, J. (1975). Federal programs supporting educational change, Vol. IV: A summary of the findings in review *(R-1589/4-HEW(Abr). Washington, DC. US. Office of Education, Department of Health, Education, and Welfare.*

Berman, P. and McLaughlin, M. W. (1978) Federal programs supporting educational change, Vol. VIII:Implementing and sustaining innovations *(R-1589/8-HEW). Washington, DC. US. Office of Education, Department of Health, Education, and Welfare.*

Burtis, P. J., Bereiter, C., Scardamalia, M., and Tetroe, J. (1983) The development of planning in writing. In G. Wells (Ed)., *Explorations in the Development of Writing*. Wiley, Chichester.

Havelock, R. G., and Havelock, M. C. (1973). *Training for Change Agents: A Guide to the Design of Training Programs in Education and Other Fields.* University of Michigan, Ann Arbor, MI.

Odell, L. (1980) Teaching writing by teaching the process of discovery: An interdisciplinary enterprise. In L. W. Gregg and E. R. Steinberg (Eds)., *Cognitive Processes in Writing* Erlbaum, Hillsdale, NJ.

Oettinger, A. G. (1969) *Run, Computer, Run.* Harvard University Press, Cambridge, MA.

Smith, F. (1982). *Writing and the Writer.* Holt, Rinehart & Winston, New York.

Stallard, C. K. (1974). An analysis of the writing behaviour of good student writers. *Research in Teaching of English, 8.*

Stewart, D. W. (1982) The diffusion of innovations:a review of research and theory with implications for computer technology. Paper presented at the annual convention of the American Psychological Association, Washington.

Wason, P.C. (1980) Specific thoughts on the writing process. In L. W. Gregg and E. R. Steinberg (Eds)., *Cognitive Processes in Writing.* Erlbaum, Hillsdale, NJ.

Winterbauer, A. E. (1986). Writeaid: A case study approach to monitoring the adoption of an automated writing aid at a private university Doctoral dissertation, University of Denver 1986. Dissertation Abstracts International, 47-A 1214.

Appendix 1

Outlines produced by Writeaid sessions

When used by the student on a new topic, Writeaid begins with a series of general questions. The student answers those he wishes to. These general questions constitute level 0 of the interview process. When finished, the student can print out the results or continue into deeper levels.

Below is an outline from level 0 only. Writeaid's questions, drawn from the "general" question file, are displayed between asterisks. Responses to those questions are shown immediately below each question.

TITLE OF PAPER:
News from Short-wave Radio
----

(1) 1.*What is the single, most important concept about "News from Short-wave Radio" to get over to the person unfamiliar with the topic?*
That it's an important source of information.

(2) 2.*Who would be most likely to disagree with you about "News from Short-wave Radio"?*
People who do not care for news.

(3) 3.*Complete this sentence: I think that News from Short-wave Radio....*
Can offer a person a different perspective on events.

(4) 4.*Why did you pick "News from Short-wave Radio" for a topic anyhow?*
I like listening to short-wave stations.

(5) 5.*Of what significance are the important words in "News from Short-wave Radio?"*
News is important.

When finished with the general questions, the student can elect to continue the interview. Below is an outline of an interview conducted through level 1. The level 1 questions (1.1 1.2, etc.). are generated as a result of Writeaid looking through the student's responses to the level 0 questions. If Writeaid can find a match between something the student said and a word or phrase in the phrase pool, under the conditions set for that match, then Writeaid responds with the associated question or remark. Should there not be a match, then Writeaid responds from another file of random questions and remarks to keep the interview going. The student has the option to terminate a line of questioning and go on. There can be any number of levels, with the program searching through the student's responses from the previous level (although after 4 levels the formatting looks peculiar).

TITLE OF PAPER:
News from Short-wave Radio
----

(1) 1.*What is the single, most important concept about "News from Short-wave Radio" to get over to the person unfamiliar with the topic?*
That it's an important source of information.

(2) 1.1.*What does that have to do with anything?*
We need more than one cultural perspective on events.

(3) 1.2.*I understand. Go on.*
We can't just be satisfied with news from our domestic networks.

(4) 1.3.*Why not?*
That leads to a parochial point of view.

(5) 1.4.*Oh? Why?*
We need to hear how people from other cultures interpret an event to get a rounded impression of it.

(6) 2.*Who would be most likely to disagree with you about "News from Short-wave Radio"?*
People who do not care for news.

(7) 2.1.*No? Why not?*
Some folks do not believe that knowledge of contemporary events is necessary.

(8) 2.2.*Why not?*
I do not know.

(9) 2.3.*How would you obtain the requisite knowledge? Why not?*
I guess I could ask them.

(10) 3.*Complete this sentence: I think that News from Short-wave Radio....*
Can offer a person a different perspective on events.

(11) 4.*Why did you pick "News from Short-wave Radio" for a topic anyhow?*
I like listening to short-wave stations.

(12) 4.1.*Can you add to that?*
I enjoy listening to more than just the short-wave broadcast stations.

(13) 4.2.*Keep going please. I'm almost interested now.*
I listen to radio teletype news broadcast to ships at sea from different news agencies.

(14) 5.*Of what significance are the important words in "News from Short-wave Radio?"*
News is important.

With this outline, a student might make a further attempt on his own to come up with an outline before consulting the teacher. For example:

I. Short-wave news is an important source of info.
    A. Offers perspective on events from different culture.

B. Reliance on only domestic news is parochial.

II. Variety of news sources on short-wave radio.

A. Short-wave broadcasters (BBC, VOA, etc.)..

B. Other media available with appropriate equipment.

1. Radio teletype and Morse code broadcasts of news to ships at sea
2. Weather information around the world (code, teletype, and fax)

Appendix 2

Files used by Writeaid

General question files

One set of files contains general, leading questions which students answer on their first pass through the interview. Each of these general, or leading, questions can be written three different ways, and the program will select one of the three when questioning students. This prevents the student from always seeing the same question whenever using the program. Also, the instructor has the option of inserting a special symbol (the "@") into the questions. Whenever the program encounters this symbol in a question, it will replace the symbol with the student's paper title supplied earlier by the student when he first fired up Writeaid. Some examples of general question groups are:

1. Of what interest is this topic to the world in general? Why did you pick "@" for a topic anyhow? Do you think that the subject is important? Why?
2. Can you describe your topic like one could describe a baseball or anything concrete? Off the top of your head, give me a quickie description of "@." Is "@" just too abstract to be thought of in concrete terms? Why?
3. Do you think "@" can best be talked about in abstract terms? Why? Of what significance are the important words in "@?" Perhaps we cannot think of the topic in abstract terms?
4. Do you think "@" could be described as a process or series of events? If you had to, how would you describe the topic as a set of occurrences? Why should we think or not think of "@" as a process?
5. Is the major element in "@" part of a group of class? Against what background can "@" be best discussed? If a collie is a member of the canine family, then "@" is a member of....
6. What is the real issue in relation to @? Is "@" a cause or effect of some other problem or issue? How? What issue or problem is analogous to "@?"
7. What can you tell me of the history of "@" as a topic? Where did this issue come from? For how long has "@" been a topic worth consideration?

8. Complete this sentence: The problem with @ is.... Complete this sentence: I think that @.... Complete this sentence: The major issue in @ is....
9. How would you explain "@" to someone not familiar with the topic? I suppose just about everyone is familiar with "@", right? What is the single, most important concept about "@" to get over to the person unfamiliar with the topic?
10. Who are you writing this paper to? Can you describe the person most likely to read your paper? Who would be most likely to disagree with you about "@"?
11. Can you relate @ to your school experiences? Is there any correlation between @ and what you've learned in school? Can you relate @ to your school experiences?

Phrase files
The instructor can create files that contain the phrase pool or key words to look for in students' responses to questions, the conditions under which a match is made, and the questions to ask if a match occurs. There can be any number of these files, any one of which the student can be told to call for when initiating the program. The following examples are taken from such a file. The numbers in the left margins are record numbers.

Pattern searching
Writeaid can be made to look for phrases in two ways. It can search for simple words and phrases, like "am confused" or "thus," as well as for parts of words, like "tion" or "ing."

```
        +---------        Note the space. Will only match on "thus"
        |                 if preceded by a space. Will still match
        |                 on "thusly" because there isn't a following
        |                 space.
        |
        v
 9  @ :& thus
```

Please provide more evidence for this conclusion, if you can.
Who else can you think of would support a similar conclusion?

```
        +--------         Will match "therefore," "Therefore,", "Wherefore,"
        |                 and "wherefore" because of no space.
        |
        v
18  @ :-herefore
```

Can you add to this conclusive remark? If you have further support for such a conclusion, let's hear it.

The teacher can also embed symbols in the key words or phrases to make searches more flexible. An asterisk ("*") allows for non- essential verbiage to be skipped as in "I*am*lost."

```
        +     +--------------     The * means any number of characters
        |     |              or words can go between "I", "am," and
        v     v              "lost."
1   @ :&I*am*lost
```

Are you having problems with the computer or with your topic? I need more specific information in order to help.

The only restriction is that the words "I," "am," and "lost" must occur in the order shown.

To get around this, the slash symbol ("/") tells Writeaid that the words can be encountered in any order.

```
                +-----+----------          The / means to accept "trouble,"
"with,"
                |     |  and "computer" in any order.
                v     v
2  @ &trouble/with/computer
```

Press the @ key, exit, and use the mail facility to tell system operator what's wrong (leave a phone number).

When you exit the program, you can send the system operator a detailed note of what's wrong.

And of course, it's possible to react to students who simply press the RETURN key.

```
                         +---------        The $ will match if the student presses
the
                         |                 RETURN key without providing a
                         |                 response.
                         v
31                 @ :&$
```

Please provide an answer. Did you hit the return key by mistake? You gave no answer.

For every key phrase or word, the teacher can assign two remarks or questions, one of which the program selects when responding to a student.

```
 1   @ :&I*am*lost
Are you having problems with the computer or with your topic? I need more
specific information in order to help.                         ^
^                                                         |
|                                                         |
|                                                         |
One response                And another response to make
to make if
"I*am*lost" found
in student's
response.
```

When to match

In addition, the teacher can tell Writeaid at what level in the interviewing process to cause matches to occur. Since the program makes successive passes through the students' responses using the key phrase pool, and thus making deeper levels, the teacher can cause the program to react in a variety ways at different depths. In the example below, if the word "thus" is found in a student's response to a general question, Writeaid could respond with "You appear to be rather confident. Please provide more evidence for this conclusion, if you can." The first sentence comes from the match at level 0, and the second sentence from the "everywhere" match "@." However, should "thus" be encountered in a student's response below level 0, then Writeaid might simply respond with "Who else can you think of would support a similar conclusion?"

```
          +---------          Match only if "thus" found at level 0 (responses
          |                   to general questions).
          |
          |
          v
4         0 :& thus
You seem to be coming to conclusions early.
You appear to be rather confident.

          +---------Match at all levels.
          |
          |
          v
9         @ :& thus
Please provide more evidence for this conclusion, if you can. Who else can you
think of would support a similar conclusion?
```

What phrases are found

To help the teacher keep track of what key phrases are more useful than others, it records next to each phrase a symbol indicating if it has ever been encountered in a student's response.

```
                      +--------          The & means that this phrase has been
                      |                  encountered in a student's response.
                      |
                      v
1                     @ :& I*am*lost
Are you having problems with the computer or with your topic? I need more
specific information in order to help.

                      +-----------------  The - means that this set of words
                      |                   has not been found in any student's
                      |                   response. Could delete this phrase.
                      v
```

4 @ :-trouble/with/topic
That could actually be a good sign. You might want to press the @ key, and think for a while.
You might be ready for a chat with your instructor then.

Random response files
The teacher can create a file of questions to be used by Writeaid if it fails to find a key phrase in a student's response to any given question. These "random" questions again are general and should be designed to draw more information from the student. They are equivalent to the psychiatrist's "I see. Please tell me more."

1. Please continue.
2. Can you think of an argument against your position?
3. I do not agree.
4. I'll grant that. Goon.
5. I can't take your word for that. Have you provided sufficient evidence?
6. Can you elaborate?
7. I still haven't picked up on any words I'm looking for. Please continue.
8. I do not follow.
9. Why should I believe you?
10. What do you mean?
11. What does that have to do with anything?
12. I understand. Go on.
13. Oh? Why?
14. Do you want me to take your word for that? Why do not you explain in a bit more detail.
15. Okay. Continue with your response please.
16. Can you add to that?
17. Keep going please. I'm almost interested now.
18. You could have fooled me.
19. Can you add to that?
20. Please clarify that for me.
21. I suppose that sounds logical. Goon.
22. Why would you say that?

12

Supporting Writing with an Undo Mechanism

Yiya Yang
Appleton Rutherford Laboratories

Abstract

Current word processors fail to support the way writers go about composing text because they fail to allow writers to consider their excisions and revisions alongside the current state of their text. In order to support the writing process more transparently a revision tracing facility is proposed for incorporation into software for writers. This paper argues that an undo mechanism can be used to support this new feature, describes how it can do this, and discusses interface issues concerning its presentation.

1. Introduction

Writing is an everyday activity. Almost everyone writes. Creating a book is writing just as much as penning a letter is writing. However, this paper is concerned with the serious composition of texts by writers. Writers can be journalists, academics, poets or novelists. Nowadays many writers use word processors to help their writing. Since writing is an important activity of modern society, it is interesting to assess how aptly such techniques of automation can assist writing and its cognate, thinking.

Writing is a creative, an expressive and a communication skill. Writing is different from most processes open to automation by computing technology. It is not a mechanical process but an intelligent one which involves many different cognitive activities. Researchers are actively seeking new ways of presenting information and constructing knowledge with various on-line tools for writing (Barrett 1988, Catano 1985, Cherry 1982). Researchers are also studying how to use computers to model the cognitive processes of writing in the hope that computers can have intelligence themselves and can intelligently assist with writing (Flower and Hayes 1981, Gregg and Steinberg 1980, Quere 1986). This has resulted in software which has been designed to help writers with a broad spectrum of writing activities; sketching, drafting, revising, and editing; while recognising the recursive and idiosyncratic nature of writing processes (Von Blum and Cohen 1983, Smith *et al.* 1986, Quere 1986). However, no research has yet proved this software's effectiveness. In the real world computing technology which supports writing processes appears to be predominantly in the form of word processing. In the near future, no matter how clever a computing environment is designed to be, it will not automate writing but will serve in an assistant role in making it easier for a writer to review, revise, backtrack, and when needed, back out of his creative endeavours. This paper considers how current word processors are used as aids to support writing activities and how existing undo facilities provided by word processors can be used to facilitate writing in a more transparent way.

2. Writing and word processors

Writing is the textual and contextual process of externalising thought. Writing consists of three major processes: planning, translating and reviewing. The function of the planning process is to take knowledge from the task environment, which includes everything external to the writer that influences the performance of the writing, and from his long-term memory and to use it to set goals and to establish a writing plan to guide the production of a text that will meet those goals. The translating process acts under the guidance of the writing plan to produce language corresponding to knowledge in the writer's memory. The function of the reviewing process is to improve the quality of the text produced by the translating process (Gregg and Steinberg 1980). These processes interact with one another through writing processes. Computers have been used in all stages of these processes: before drafting to brainstorm, outline, list and generate ideas; while drafting to add, delete, substitute, and move text around; and after drafting to polish and proof-read the papers.

Although writing involves idea gathering, categorising, organising, drafting, revising and editing, revision is one key to good writing. Revision is an indispensable way to making writing better. Skilled writers revise constantly, trying to resolve the tensions between what they want to say and what the sentences actually record. For many skilled writers, revising is the crux of the writing process. It is the way they shape prose into meaning for an audience, and the way they discover what they want to say, sometimes to their own surprise. They know they cannot do it right the first time, and they live with temporary chaos in the meantime. Through revision they move from semi-formed ideas to elaborated texts, create what they believe they want to say and then change their minds, probably more than once. Thus how adequately a word processor supports revision is crucial to its ability to facilitate writing.

A word processor is a software program that enables a computer to accept text which can then be revised, saved, changed again, then saved again. A word processor offers a user the ability to create and edit text, permits a user to format and print the text as the user wants it to look, and allows a user to store and retrieve files of text. Most writers, who use word processors, agree that word processors have speeded up their composition, made revision easy instead of being a chore, and improved the quality of their writing. Word processing also improves attitudes toward writing. It gives writers more motivation to write and to revise their writing. It helps them transform thought into detailed, coherent texts without getting discouraged. They realise they can add information much more easily and make corrections and revisions more quickly that if they were using only pen and paper and had to make a fresh copy by hand each time a major set of corrections or revisions was necessary (Collins and Sommers 1985).

Although a word processor enhances a writer's ability to explore, to articulate and to reshape, it is not a panacea. Word processing does no make its user more creative, more imaginative, or more intelligent. Currently word processors present something for writers to think with and not to think for them. They do not possess intelligence to think for the writers but objectify or trace the activity of thought in writing. Writers use word processors to archive each proposition as it is created, so that it can be reviewed, speculated upon, and facilitate in turn another tentative entrance of an idea. It can be regarded as a stage for acting out ideas. Revision is not an end-of-the-repair process, but a constant process of "re-vision" or re-seeing what goes on while a writer is composing (Sommers 1980).

Writing can be viewed as a process of generating and editing text within a variety of constraints. The constraints come from three sources: structure (what are good sentence forms, paragraph forms, and text forms), content (what ideas are to be expressed and how are they related), and purpose (what are the goals of the writer and what is the author's model of the reader). The traditional way to use typewriters to write allows writers to refine their ideas relatively transparently. When a writer crosses something out on the paper, he can still read the crossed out content. Being able to see the crossed out content and its position within the text provides a natural context for the writer to consider refinements. Since writing is a process of exploration and elaboration, it involves many refinements on the first draft. A refinement process can be illustrated by the many rough drafts for Yeats' poems (Stallworthy 1963). The following is part of the rough drafts of Yeats' "A Prayer for my Daughter".

Nor am I
~~I am not~~ the first father that has
~~Many another father may have stood~~
~~Where And weighed ( )~~
~~As I stand now beside~~ this cradle-hood

Time

And judged by the ~~blast~~ beside

And as all times have trouble, this own
the world fell
Thought the ~~storm beaten~~ stone upton stone
and that the masters of the world ran
~~The world fell while its masters are gone wild~~

And racked his brain to think of all

That might that sleeping child befall
~~And what were the best prayer to pray for the~~
~~And prayed as I some charmed gift for his child~~

And what to ask of heaven for the child
~~And what prayer might be best~~

Yeats' excisions and abandoned alternatives are not merely of interest to textual scholars. They were clearly cues and aids to Yeats' own process of creative writing in his struggle to find the most apt turn of phrase to propel his poem forward. Most word processors do not allow an author to see the deleted or changed text, especially in its position with other text. For example, when the Macintosh editor MacWrite is used, once text is deleted a user cannot see it in its original position. A user can only see the last text change in the clipboard. This suggests that in order to support writing more transparently, current word processors need to be improved further by a facility which allows a user to see what changes he has made in producing his current draft alongside the current draft. Such a capability will be termed a revision trace facility.

3. Undo support

Currently good word processors provide an undo facility which allows users to reverse the effects of executed commands. Such an undo facility provides a recovery and usability feature which permits ready recovery from many simple errors. It avoids creating frustration where a user discovers that an unexpected result of a command cannot be reversed and encourages safe exploration of unfamiliar options. It can also be used to deal with mode errors, interactive deadlocks, and changing one's mind (Carroll and Mack 1984, Darlington *et al.* 1983, Monk 1986, Norman 1983).

Research into undo support (Archer *et al.* 1984, Gordon *et al.* 1985, Leeman 1986, Vitter 1984, Yang 1989) suggests that two general requirements for it are that every user command should be undoable and that a system should provide *n*-step undo support to allow a user to reverse the effects of the last command whereas *n*-step undo support allows a user to reverse the effects of the last *n* commands. A common feature of techniques to implement the mechanism of *n*-step undo support (Yang 1989) is that some information has to be recorded for each undoable command which is executed to enable it subsequently to be undone. The variants are what information is needed and how it can be saved efficiently.

An undo mechanism can be used to support a revision trace facility to enhance word processors for writers. Since revision is done by the insertion and deletion operations of a word processor, this means that deleted and changed text has to be saved to allow a writer to trace his revision. Delete and insert commands are undoable with respect to undo support, so the saved information for these commands by the undo mechanism can be used here. Thus, word processors with undo support have already saved the information needed to allow a writer to trace his revisions. Since the revision trace facility is mainly used by a writer at the revision stage of text composition and word processors are used at all stages of writing processes, it would be desirable to have a switch to turn this facility on or off. However, information gathering to support such revision must be kept on all the time.

4. Presentation issues

When a writer conducts a revision, he takes actions; *addition, deletion, substitution* and *rearrangement* to make surface and structural changes in his work (Sommers 1980, Hairston 1981). These actions are realised on a word processor by the commands, *insert, delete, substitute, and cut and paste.* Thus, the presentation issues for the revision trace facility are how to present these operations of inserting, deleting, substituting, and cutting and pasting on the display screen and hard copy.

Since the purpose of the revision trace facility is to allow a writer to see what changes he has made and the writer was interested in which commands cause which changes, the essential presentations issues are how to maintain changes as new text and old text in their original position in the whole text and how to differentiate new text from old text in this context. The differentiation if new text from old text can be done through its appearance and relative position in the whole text. For insertion, the position of the inserted text is where it is and the only thing for the revision trace facility to do is to make the appearance of the inserted text different from its surrounded text. For deletion, if the deleted text is kept in its original position, the only thing for the revision trace facility to do is to indicate that the text is deleted. For substitution, it can be seen as the combination of a deletion and insertion. The resulting appearance, the deleted text followed by the inserted text, are differentiated by the same methods of deletion and insertion. For cutting and pasting, it can be seen as deleting in the cutting position and inserting in the pasting position with separate presentations for the deletion and insertion. This method does not indicate that the deletion and insertion are a single operation, especially when the cutting position and the pasting position are on different pages. However, this lost information may not matter much because a writer is more interested in the deleted text within its context and the inserted text within its context. Using this analysis, operations to cause revisions are categorised either as insertions, deletions, substitutions or cut and paste operations and the four operations can be further reduced to two operations; insertion and deletion. Since the original positions of inserted text and deleted text are maintained naturally, the revision trace facility only needs to differentiate the inserted or deleted text within its context.

The appearance of inserted or deleted text can be differentiated by colour, or by special fonts such as italic or bold, by background highlighting or by special marks (scoring out or underlining) on the text. If a polygon with right angled vertices is used to surround inserted text and a scoring line is used to cross out deleted text, the following examples show how to present a single revision.

1. <u>Insertion</u>

Bananas are green and striped , Bananas are green, blue and striped.

↓

Bananas are green, blue and striped.

2. <u>Deletion</u>

Bananas are green, blue and striped. , Bananas are blue and striped.

↓

Bananas are ~~green,~~ blue and striped.

3. <u>Substitution</u>

It discusses the procedure to choose an evaluation method. ,

It discusses how to choose an evaluation method.

↓

It discusses ~~the procedure~~ how to choose an evaluation method.

4. <u>Re-arrangement</u>

The needed information has to be recorded for each undoable command. ,

The information needed has to be recorded for each undoable command.

↓

The ~~needed~~ information needed has to be recorded for each undoable command.

The above four examples illustrate how to present a single revision to a writer. When a writer conducts a revision, he is likely to make multiple revisions to a piece of text which are a combination of several single revisions. The presentation issues for multiple revisions are how to present the initial text and final text of a multiple revision and how to present the transformation process from the initial text to a final text. Analysing all the combinations of the four operations indicates that they are either independent of each other or their dependencies can be reduced to two combinations, inserting part of or the whole deleted text, and deleting part of or the whole inserted text. In order to have clean text after multiple revisions, the multiple revision of inserting part or the whole of deleted text is presented by removing the scoring line on that part of the text and the multiple revision of deleting part or the whole of inserted text is presented by scoring out part of the text surrounded by the insertion marking polygon. Furthermore where insertions (deletions) are adjacent to insertions (deletions) the separate marks are coalesced into a single insertion box (deletion stroke). The following examples show how to present the two dependent combinations of operations for multiple revisions and coalesced insertions (deletions).

5. Inserting after deletion

Bananas are green, blue and striped. ,

Bananas are striped. ,

Bananas are blue and striped.

Bananas are ~~green,~~ blue and striped.

6. Deletion after insertion

Bananas are green and striped. ,

Bananas are green, blue and striped. ,

Bananas are green and striped.

Bananas are green ~~, blue~~ and striped.

7. Adjacent insertions

Bananas are striped.,

Bananas are green and striped. ,

Bananas are green, blue and striped.

↓

Bananas are green, blue and striped .

8. Adjacent deletions

Bananas are green, blue and striped. ,

Bananas are blue and striped. ,

Bananas are striped.

↓

Bananas are ~~green, blue and~~ striped.

The transformation process from an initial text to a current text can be represented by undoing and redoing within the revision trace facility from the initial text to the current text. The following gives a scenario to illustrate how such a revision trace facility might work.

5. A scenario

It is assumed that the word processor of the scenario has a direct manipulation interface style. One of its menu item is *revision trace* and another is *undo.* The default form for the revision trace facility is off. A writer can turn the revision trace facility from off to on or from on to off by clicking the menu item *revision trace.* When the revision trace facility is off, normal text is displayed after every command. When the revision trace facility is on, the display feedback for each revision will indicate the changes made by the revision. They are shown by examples 1 to 4 of the previous section. If the writer has made n single revisions and the initial text is called text 0, the current text is called text n. If the revision trace facility is currently on and the writer issues m step undo ($m \leq n$), the system will take the writer m single revisions back. The display feedback is text n-m with the change made by the (n-m)th command which is indicated by methods of examples 1 to 4 in the previous section. Assuming the present text is text i ($0 \leq i \leq n$) and the last command is undo if the writer issues a j step redo command ($0 < j < n-i$), the system will show text ($i+j$) with all changes made by commands i to j indicated by the methods of examples 1 to 8 in the previous section.

6. Conclusions

This paper has discussed the nature of the writing process and argued that current word processors fail to support part of the way writers go about writing. It has explained how an undo mechanism can be used to support a new feature called a revision trace facility in software for writers to support writing more transparently. How this feature can be supported internally by an undo mechanism has been described and interface issues concerning its presentation have been discussed. A scenario has been given to show how a revision trace facility works. This revision facility not only facilitates writing but can also be used in conjunction with an undo history to help research on the composing process. Future work for this research is to evaluate empirically this revision trace facility, especially its presentation choices.

7. Acknowledgements

The author would like to thank her husband and her colleagues at the Rutherford Appleton Laboratory for their help and support.

8. References

Archer Jr, J. E., Conway, R. and Schneider, F. B. (1984) User recovery and reversal in interactive systems. *ACM Transactions on Programming Language and Systems*, 6 1.

Barrett, E. (1988) *Text, ConText, and HyperText: Writing with and for the Computer.* The MIT Press, Cambridge, MA.

Carroll, J. M. and Mack, R. (1984) Learning to use a word processor: by doing, by thinking and by knowing. In J. Thomas and M. Schneider (Eds) *Human Factors in Computing Systems.* Ablex, Newark, NJ.

Catano, J. V. (1985) Computer-based writing: navigating the fluid text, *College Composition and Communication*, 36.

Cherry, L. L., (1982) Writing tools, *IEEE Transactions on Communication*, 30.

Collins, J. L. and Sommers, E. A. (1985) *Writing On-line.* Boynton/Cook.

Darlington, J., Dzida, W. and Herda, S. (1983) The role of excursions in interactive systems. *International Journal of Man-Machine Studies.*

Flower, L. and Hayes, J. R. (1981) A cognitive process theory of writing, *College Composition and Communication*, 32.

Gordon, R. F., Leeman Jr, G. B. and Lewis, C. H. (1985) Concept and implications of undo for interactive recovery. *Proceedings of the 1985 ACM Annual Conference.*

Gregg, L. W. and Steinberg, E. R. (Eds) (1980) *Cognitive Processes in Writing*, Lawrence Erlbaum, Hillsdale, NJ.

Hairston, M., (1981) *Successful Writing.* Norton, New York.

Leeman Jr, G. B. (1986) A formal approach to undo operations in programming language, *ACM Transactions on Programming Languages and Systems*, 8, 1.

Monk, A. (1986) Mode errors: a user-centred analysis and some preventative measures using keying-contingent sound, *International Journal of Man-Machine Studies.*

Norman, D. A. (1983) Design rules based on analyses of human error, *Communications of the ACM.*

Quere, M. (1986) Expert systems: toward the CAI of the future. In K. Duncan and D. Harris (Eds) *Computers in Education.* Elsevier.

Smith, J. B. *et al.* (1986) WE: a writing environment for professionals, *Technical Report 86-025,* Department of Computer Science, UNC, Chapel Hill.

Sommers, N. (1980) Revision strategies of student writers and experienced writers, *College Composition and Communication,* 31.

Stallworthy, J., (1963) *Between the lines: Yeats' poetry in the making,* Oxford University Press, Oxford.

Vitter, J. S. (1984) USandR: a new framework for redoing, *IEEE Software,* 1(4).

Von Blum, R. and Cohen, M. (1983) WANDAH (writers' and authors' helper), Technical Report of the Word Processing Writing Project, Department of Psychology, University of California, Los Angeles.

Yang, Y., (1989) User-Oriented Design of Undo Support, PhD Thesis, Department of Computer Science, Heriot-Watt University, Edinburgh.

13

Internationalisation: The Programmer, the User and the Writer

Lindsay F. Marshall
University of Newcastle upon Tyne

Abstract

Recently considerable interest has arisen in the problems involved in internationalising software and its documentation. Much of this attention has been directed either at problems of character set representation or at large texts such as user manuals. However, it is probable that the various messages produced by computer systems are the texts most often seen by users. It seems as though little thought goes into their design, preparation and realisation. This paper looks at various guidelines for internationalisation and suggests a better method for implementing messages. The proposed method allows programmers and writers to work together to produce systems that are easier to configure for different language environments.

1. Introduction

Computer folklore has it that it takes about ten years for a new idea to become established in the mainstream of computing. For example, after some twenty years the (unproven!) advantages of modular structuring of programs are now universally accepted and programmers are now starting to pay more attention to portability and software re-use. Object Oriented programming is just starting to gain ground and it looks as though internationalisation will be the next bandwagon, Juggernaut, good idea – call it what you will –to come along. Manufacturers are aware of the need for support for localised variants of their systems, but few go out of their way to do much about it. The most likely concession is the appropriate national keyboard, display of at least some accented or non-latin characters and the translation of the manuals. Some systems go much further than this, for example the Xerox ViewPoint office system and the Apple Macintosh®. Others do not even go this far. The collapse of national computer industries and the overwhelming influence of the USA has meant that, until recently, considerations of any language other than English were of little commercial value. After all doesn't *everyone* in computing speak English? Surprisingly, and sadly, this attitude is prevalent in non-English speaking countries as well so there has been little struggle against it. However, the continued penetration of the computer into every aspect of life everywhere is slowly turning the tide and manufacturers are starting to respond.

Hardware is not really the problem. It is simple to display non-ideographic writing and progress in Japan shows that the making of cheap displays with enough resolution for more complex writing systems is also easy. Software is where the problems really lie. At its lowest levels there are many assumptions about internal character representation and at the higher levels, system messages and ultimately the design of command languages all reflect an Anglo-centric viewpoint. Nevertheless, the large software producers, most of them based in the USA, are realising that their products are increasingly likely to be used by people who cannot be assumed to speak English (or French, or German, or Korean ...). They do not wish to drive this potential market away and so are starting to consider seriously ways by which they can improve the situation. Many of them have already produced internationalised versions of their products though most of these still leave much to be desired.

In this paper I shall look at internationalisation from the point of view of the programmer. My concern is with ways in which the programmers can be freed from the need to worry about those aspects that are of no relevance to them. In particular it looks at how best to cope with the problems of internationalising system messages which are texts that users cannot avoid seeing –unlike system manuals which often gather dust in corners, still in their shrink wraps. I also consider the design of command languages, for those systems which still have such things, but I offer no solutions to their problems here!

2. The problems

It is a salutary experience, that should be mandatory for every system designer, to sit and use a system configured for another tongue, if they can find one. The keys you hit are not what you think they are because of the keyboard layout. Touch typing turns out not to be such a useful skill after all. You cannot understand the messages. Is that an error, a warning or just some useful but unimportant information? You cannot find your way around the menus with any certainty. You are lost. Just like the rest of the world when they try to use the systems that you design. Of course, this is not just a problem with computers – have you ever burned yourself by unthinkingly using the tap marked C on a French sink? Nevertheless, the world of computing does seems more of a minefield than others and there are almost no international standards for the high level parts of user interfaces. Certainly nothing that could be compared with the highly successful system of icons used for road signs which most of us take so much for granted.

A good, but short summary of some problems involved in internationalising programs occurs in (Apple® Computer 1987). This does tend to make the difficulties appear less severe than they really are and the wide ranging discussion in (Kirkman 1988) of the writing of documentation and the problems it presents for the translator opens up areas that the Apple manual does not consider at all. Taken together, these two sources provide complete coverage of the major issues involved.

The most obvious problem – that of internal character set representation and collating sequence can be approached in two ways. Both share the characteristic that nothing should be assumed about the chosen representation. The first, "closed" approach, chosen by Xerox for their ViewPoint system, is where all character codes are allocated from a large space with different alphabets represented in convenient, contiguous sections. This works well and allows considerable flexibility of use[1] but does present significant portability problems when information must be moved to other systems. The more usual, "open" approach uses the ISO standard representations for characters (BSI 1984ab, 1985, 1986). Programs that use this have become known as *8-bit friendly*. Unfortunately an astonishing number of programs turn out not to be 8-bit friendly when put to the test and it often takes considerable effort to remedy this.

Taken alone the ISO based approach does not solve all the character set problems. The arrangement of the characters takes no account of the collating sequence of the languages that use them, nor of any rules for the capitalisation of accented letters. To cope with these, programmers should be provided, as they are on the Apple Macintosh, with a set of standard procedures to carry out all necessary operations on text strings (Apple Computer 1985, 1988). Porting these procedures to a new environment then becomes a simple process provided the local rules are well-defined. Note, however, that where multi-lingual working is important, a simple, standard scheme for selecting the language rules that should be applied at any given time would be desirable. This has not yet appeared. For instance, the Macintosh decides which rules to use based on a flag set in the system which is not particularly easy to change and which only has values defined for those countries in which the Mac is for sale.

Starting at the other end of the system, it is common for manuals to be translated into the native languages of the target country, though the programs often still work in English. The next step is for the messages from the program to be translated. Older style systems that produce cryptic, IBM-style error codes rather than messages are easy to deal with as the translation of the error message happens when the rest of the manual is translated. Of more modern systems, the Macintosh, or at least some applications written for it, is probably the best performer, though it is interesting that the ubiquitous UNIX[2] "?" message is remarkably international. From the user's point of view this is fine, but for the programmer things are not so simple and I shall deal with these issues in a later section. However before doing that it is worth briefly considering the question of the interface by which the user drives the system.

Internationalisation of menu driven systems comes as part of the global message translation but command driven systems are another matter. For a very simple example take the shortcut keys provided as standard by the Macintosh – Z for undo, X for cut, C for copy and V for paste. The only obvious reason for the choice of this set of keys is that they are close together on the keyboard. The QWERTY keyboard. They are not nearly so convenient to use on systems

[1] However the size of the problem may cause problems in the long run. Osterrmann (1952) identifies 220 different uses of accents of which 28 apply to the letter 'A'.

[2] UNIX is a trademark of AT&T in the USA and other countries.

that support the French AZERTY layout. However the Apple standard says that these are the keys to use, so they are. Looking at truly command driven systems like MSDOS, VMS[3] or UNIX the situation is much worse for the non-English speaker. Most of the strings that must be typed to drive the system have some mnemonic significance in English, but at best they probably will have none at all in other languages, and at worst might be offensive or imply the opposite of the intended meaning. Providing localised versions of command language interpreters is probably impractical and it would make command files and scripts much less useful as exchanging them between countries would be difficult. Much better to move towards WIMP style interfaces for applications meant for international, non-specialist use. By providing ways to define shortcuts and macros, each user can then tailor the system to their liking. For computer users forced to travel without their personal machine, this will mean that they must carry their profile" with them, but this is of no real consequence as it is likely that they will be taking some kind of storage medium with them anyway. When truly portable, low cost machines that run reasonable operating systems finally arrive in the shops many of these problems will vanish. The computer will finally become, as Van Renesse has wished (Renesse 1989), just like your toothbrush. You take it with you when you go somewhere, you do not share it with anyone and you get a new one when you need it.

3. Message handling

I should now like to look in more detail at message handling, with particular emphasis on the role that the programmer plays and ought to play in its implementation. Irrespective of internationalisation issues, the design of every message has five stages. By looking at these we will obtain a clearer picture of who should be doing what and when. Questions of target language can then be isolated and dealt with much more effectively.

GR:	EpanakollhtikeV tainieV pou anoiyokleinoun polleV joreV.
E:	Cintas adhesivas reutilizables.
NL:	Hersluitbare kleefbandies.
I:	Nastri Adesivi.
D:	Widerverschließbare Klebebänder.
GB:	Refastenable Tapes.
F:	Elle facilite le collage et le décollage des adhésifs.
S:	Återförslutbar tejp
SF:	Uudelleenkiinnittyvät teipit

Figure 1. Translations of a simple phrase

[3] VMS is a registered trademark of Digital Equipment Corporation

4. Semantics

Even if their only purpose is to provide reassurance to users, messages should convey information. The need to display a message can either be part of the original specification of the program or else it can become apparent to the implementer that a situation could arise (perhaps not covered by the high level design) about which the user should be informed. Thus the responsibility for message origination lies both with the design team and the programmer, but in the latter case there should always be consultation with the designers to verify that the programmer's perception is correct. However, what is most important is that the information that is to be conveyed must be precisely specified and should not allow the possibility of ambiguous interpretation. Unfortunately, there currently is no easy way to do this and so carefully checked natural language specifications probably must suffice.

5. Lexis

Once the meaning of a message is clearly specified, the words (or symbols) used to express it must be chosen. This is not always easy as the choice of words will determine the reaction of the program's users to the message. Both human interface and language specialists are needed here –the former to decide the tone of the message and the latter to provide the words in the target language. Programmers should be rigorously excluded from this process because normally they do not have the necessary skills. Note also that word selection for each language must always start from the message's specification and should avoid direct translations from other. Figure 1 illustrates this process with a simple example taken from the instructions contained in a box of disposable nappies. The notion of "refastenable tapes" is complex and though most of the examples show considerable similarity, those that do not are very different. An examination of multi-lingual packaging and instruction material for everyday products is instructive and highlights the kinds of cultural and linguistic differences that may be encountered. (Note that the Greek text in the figure is missing some diacritical marks as my UK Macintosh would not allow me to add them ...).

6. Syntax

Having chosen the "best" words, they must be arranged in correct, grammatical order and must be in the appropriate form for their tense, mood, gender etc. Word forms and order vary greatly between languages and it may be necessary dynamically to change these to take account of any values required to be displayed. The knowledge needed to do this is essentially linguistic. However, some basic programming skill will be required if dynamic changes have to be made as the choices must be built into the program. This is unavoidable, though it would perhaps be desirable to devise a better way of specifying these than the use of a conventional programming language.

7. Presentation

The effect of a message can depend as much on its presentation as on the words that go into it. This is very much the domain of the HCI expert. For some messages it is better to dispense with words altogether and use iconic forms instead. Look and feel –the "corporate image" of the total product – also plays a part here. This is best left to the skills of the graphic designer, though the environment in which the program is to run may already have dictated it, for example the Macintosh or MOTIF. Besides, due allowance also must be made for the expected skill level of the user. It may be necessary to incorporate some means of controlling the density of the information presented. This also must be considered in the preceding phases of message design, especially lexis, and may mean the existence of several forms. Some systems also allow user control over such things as fonts and display colours. It is important to be aware of this to avoid any assumptions that could prevent users from making those changes that might be necessary to prevent eye strain or cope with colour blindness.

8. Implementation

Finally the message is ready to be displayed and this *is* the realm of the programmer. The target environment may well place constraints on the implementer, but most modern systems are so rich in primitives that it is always necessary to make some kind of choice. Issues of portability between environments will play an important part here as will questions of efficiency and the avoidance of undesirable interactions between message display and other parts of the running program.

9. The present state

Unfortunately the programmer is frequently expected (and expects) to be responsible for each of these phases and, as with documentation, many companies will not employ people with the appropriate skills to do the job properly. For small organisations this is reasonable, but large, multinational companies are just as guilty and the inadequacies of their products are all too obvious. Even their English versions of programs do not show any real care in message design. This is often due to programs living longer and having wider distribution than their originators intended. The poor quality of many UNIX messages is due to this, though little effort seems to have been made to improve them even when it became obvious that the system was going to have a wide market (this may of course be the very reason no work took place).

Inevitably we come back to the Macintosh (and its inspiration the Xerox Star (Smith *et al.* 1982)) for an example of a system that really does try to provide the support needed for the international market. However, even the Mac does not go far enough. It would be unreasonable to expect much concrete support for the first two phases of message design, though it might be possible to provide some kind of crude word selection mechanism in environments where many technical terms occur. The difficulties start to show when considering syntax and presentation.

The primary mechanism for divorcing messages from the code of a program is the use of *resources*. Essentially these are named items that can be loaded and manipulated by a program but whose values can be altered after the program's compilation using system utilities such as the program *resedit*. There are many kinds of resources but *Strings* and *Dialogues* are the ones of most concern for message creation. The recommendation to programmers is to store in string resources all text that might need to be modified when porting a program. The system then loads them when the program references them. Dialogue resources are templates for the layout of windows. They describe the arrangement of the stuff of user interaction – texts, buttons, etc. This makes the presentation aspects of message handling easy to deal with and means that redesigning a layout to cope with variations in string lengths caused by translation does not present significant technical difficulties. Programmers can create dialogue on the fly and many programs do so, but this does seem to miss the point of the use of resources in the first place.

Also provided is a means of parameterising dialogue so that values can be substituted dynamically and it is here that the problems start to arise. When the program needs to display a message whose syntax changes depending on the values it is showing (for example "1 error" against "2 errors") the temptation is to code this right where the need for the message has arisen. This makes internationalisation even harder as the whole program must be examined to find every place where it displays a message to ensure that such syntactic variations are found and translated. For large programs, such as many word processors, this can be time consuming and fraught with error as it is easy to miss an instance, particularly if the code is "clever".

10. The solution

The solution is obvious, but all too often ignored – modularisation. Message generation should be isolated from the rest of the implementation and accessed only through well defined interfaces. Even better is to go further and adopt a fully object oriented approach. The essence of object oriented programming is the correct assignment of responsibility and much of what I have said above is concerned with just that. The programmer should be provided with instances of a message class and can cause their display only by using the interface provided by the message class. The details of the implementation of the class can then be ignored and can be tailored to many environments without any changes being necessary to the calls. Internationalisation is then the responsibility of the message implementers who need only concern themselves with the code of the message class they created. The language specialists can deal with those aspects which are of concern to them and need have no involvement with the rest of the implementation.

Most messages are simple and will share the same implementation, but where matters are more complex, new classes that re-implement some aspect of the display can be derived from the message class *without the message user being aware of this fact.* Thus, even when a particular message turns out to be more involved in another language, the invocations will not need to be changed. The simplicity with which this can be done is the great benefit of using OO languages and is one reason for their expressive power. The improvements in maintainability and reliability that go with this approach are a welcome side effect.

Many implementers seem to have a blind spot about messages and do not see that the techniques that they use elsewhere in their programs can be applied equally well there. As I said above, the solution is obvious, but people often need to be reminded of the obvious.

11. Conclusions

This paper has looked at some problems for the programmer in trying to produce a software product that copes with the language problems inherent in today's international marketplace. The ideas proposed, besides the technology that now exists can go some way to alleviating the difficulties encountered. If only by passing the buck to those more qualified to deal with language issues – the technical writers and translators. We shall be using the object based system for message handling that I have proposed in the ESPRIT funded, multi-national TOBIAS project (No. 2294) and it will be interesting to see how well it works in actual practice. It also should be said that whilst language skills often come hand in hand with programming skill, just as often they do not. No programmer should feel ashamed that they do not have the competence to deal with general language issues. The educational systems in most western countries enforce the bogus arts/sciences divide. This, combined with the "macho" hacker image espoused by many programmers and the historical supremacy of the English language in computer science, has had much to do with computing's failure to respond to the needs of the everyday user. As a native English speaker who is not a very good linguist I often feel embarrassed at my inadequacy when faced by conferences full of people who speak my language fluently but whose own languages are a closed book to me. Strangely, enough very few of these fluent speakers to whom I have mentioned this see it as a problem. Many of them seem to feel it natural and right that everyone involved with computing should speak English. I suspect that there is an element of brainwashing in this. If computers really are to become as common as we have been promising everyone for years, then something must be done to help change these attitudes. To quote from a Berlitz advertisement – "The language of international business isn't English ... it's the language of your customer". We could, of course, all learn Esperanto as a second language and thus solve some of our problems, but just think of the mess when gestural interfaces become more common!

12. References

Apple Computer, Inc. (1985). *Inside Macintosh.* Addison-Wesley Inc. Reading, MA.

Apple Computer, Inc. (1988). *Inside Macintosh.* Addison-Wesley Inc. Reading, MA.

Apple Computer, Inc. (1987). *Human Interface Guidelines: The Apple Desktop Interface.* Addison-Wesley Inc. Reading, MA.

BSI (1984a)*Coded Character Sets for Bibliographic Information Interchange. Part 1: Specification for Extension of the Latin Alphabet Coded Character Set.* British Standards Institute., BS 6474 Part 1: 1984 ISO 5426 –1983.

BSI (1984b) *Coded Character Sets for Bibliographic Information Interchange. Part 3: Specification for African Coded Character Set.* British Standards Institute., BS 6474 Part 3: 1985 ISO 6438—1983.

BSI (1985) *Coded Character Sets for Bibliographic Information Interchange. Part 2: Specification for Greek Alphabet Coded Character Set.* British Standards Institute., BS 6474 Part 2: 1985 ISO 5428—1984.

BSI (1986) *Coded Character Sets for Bibliographic Information Interchange. Part 4: Specification for Extension of the Cyrillic Alphabet Coded Character Set.* British Standards Institute., BS 6474 Part 4: 1986 ISO 5427—1984.

Smith, D. C., Harslem E., Irby, C. and Kimball, R. (1982) The Star User Interface: an overview. *Proceedings of the 1982 National Computer Conference,* Houston.

Kirkman, J. (1988). How "friendly" is your writing for readers around the world? In E. Barret. (Ed) *Text, ConText, and HyperText.* The MIT Press, Cambridge, Mass.

Ostermann, G F. von (1952). *Manual of Foreign Languages.* Central Book, New York.

Renesse, R. van (1989) *The Functional Processing Model.* Vrije Universiteit Amsterdam.

14

Controlled English (CE): From COGRAM to ALCOGRAM

Dirk Schreurs
Geert Adriaens
University of Leuven

Abstract

In order to increase the consistency and to reduce the reading difficulty of technical documents, the Louvain Department of Linguistics is currently developing a 'controlled English' grammar. Such a grammar is based on a limited vocabulary range and 'controlled' sentence structures. Besides lexical and syntactic control strict rules concerning style, punctuation and layout are taken into account as well. At the Bell-Alcatel Training Centre in Antwerp engineers will be able to conform to the writing rules set out in the CE grammar and restrict their choice of words to the limited lexicon. Consequently they will be able to write in a clearer way so that the technical documents and reports are less difficult for an ever wider public to comprehend. Moreover, documents written in CE become accessible to readers who would normally need a translation. Additionally, machine translation can benefit from the linguistic reductions so that standardisation of terminology and consistency of translation is ensured. The rules for using CE are the frequently stated foundations for effective technical writing. The use of CE can bring benefits in efficiency, economy and standardisation as it transfers technical prose into readable and accurate documents thereby increasing comprehension and accessibility.

1. Introduction

The continuous expansion of international industries has inevitably led to the need of standardisation and conformity in the field of written communication. Not only have multinational corporations faced the problems of language incompatibility – especially with respect to translation of documents into other languages, they have also experienced that the language used in many industrial documents, from the largest report to the smallest hand-out, needs a thorough revision in order to be used efficiently by both native and non-native writers.

To ensure that the language of technical documents is unambiguous, well-structured, economical and easily translatable, "controlled" language has been thought to be the solution. However approachable this phenomenon seems to be at first sight, it has been marked with some kind of mysterious isolation: controlled grammars appear not to exceed the confines of industry. International companies protect their own controlled grammar to enhance the internal functionality of personal business matters without attempting to co-operate with other multinationals, or even universities.

To maximise the power of controlled language usage it is indispensable to accurately examine the phenomenon of controlled vocabulary, syntax, and stylistics. Linguistic study and detailed comparison of controlled English manuals undoubtedly will bring about more insight into their structural organisation, expressive tone and linguistic bases. In discussing the essence of controlled language, it is also important to consider the roots from which the present state of controlled English has evolved in order to understand its current characteristics. Moreover, machine translation can certainly benefit from the linguistic confines and standardisation of terminology resulting from Controlled English approaches as done, for instance, in the Dutch BSO/DLT machine translation project.

To reveal the identity of controlled English, the Department of Linguistics has been doing intensive research into this particular domain. In addition, after a preliminary analysis of three representative grammars, a prototypic controlled grammar was developed which aimed at covering the fundamental qualities of English grammar. This model, which we call COGRAM, was tested extensively to find out about the pros and cons. From that prototypic grammar several more complete and thus more convincing versions have emerged, until eventually a linguistically well-founded grammar appeared that is to be structured into an operative algorithmic grammar. The final version can be used at any company producing large amounts of technical texts. Consequently, their experts will increase the consistency and reduce the reading difficulty of technical documents in their field of interest: the contents of technical hand-outs, manuals, and reports will be less difficult to comprehend.

The following sections will deal with the Controlled English project in a chronological way, starting with a brief historic description of its roots, then discussing the outcomes of the preliminary research, the evolution from a prototypic version (COGRAM) to an algorithmic grammar (ALCOGRAM) and, finally, ending by focusing on possible advancements in the future.

2. The roots of CE

The foundation for most of the existing CE manuals was laid by the Caterpillar Tractor Company (Peoria, Illinois, USA) in the mid-1960s. This company introduced Caterpillar Fundamental English (CFE), upon which two significant derivatives, i.e. J. Smart's Plain English Program (PEP) and B.T. White's International Language for Serving and Maintenance (ILSAM) were based. PEP gave birth to grammars used by Clark, Rockwell International and Hyster a.o., while ILSAM can be considered the roots of grammars used by the AECMA (Association Europeenne de Constructeurs de Materiel Aerospatial) See e.g. AECMA (1988), IBM[1], Rank Xerox and Ericsson Telecommunications (see e.g. Ericsson group 1983).

---

[1] Examples can be found in a number of IBM in-house Information Development Guidelines on content, on-line information, style and vocabularies for customers and service information.

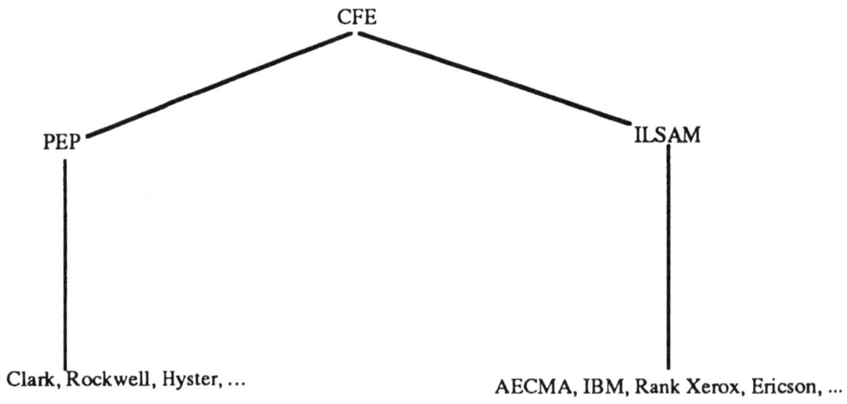

Figure 1. The CE heritage tree

Since the above-mentioned grammars have been adapted to the individual needs of each company, they might – to some extent- differ from one another. Unfortunately, we were not able to get hold of any grammar from the PEP branch. Despite this limitation, three of the above-mentioned grammars, namely AECMA, Ericsson English and the IBM manual, were taken as suitable representations in order to determine the starting point from which our research and development in the domain of CE could evolve;

3. Preparatory linguistic study

In the following abstract, a rough outline of the preliminary research will be concisely depicted. Although the study does not claim to be exhaustive, it gives a good impression of the structural dissimilarities between the three grammars used by AECMA, Ericsson, and IBM. Furthermore, this investigation underscores some of the qualities and deficiencies of each manual.

At this phase in the controlled English project, the grammars used by AECMA, Ericsson and IBM were thoroughly examined and evaluated with respect to spelling, syntax, style, and other information such as completeness and readability. After careful examination, it became clear that, although the English language used in all three grammars was of good quality, the grammars differed in structure overtly.

Although the IBM hand-out is the most compact, it tolerates more than the other two grammars. The AECMA grammar is at several points rather inexplicit and does not treat some relevant syntactic issues such as subordinate clauses, negation, etc. The Ericsson grammar is the most complex, and the most enjoyable to study. It comprises two levels of Ericsson English (EE), of which only Level 1 was at our disposal. Level 1 "was created for use in basic technical instructions and descriptions" (EE: 3), while Level 2 is intended to write "higher-level documents (such as instructions for computerised testing, technical descriptions and explanations of processes)." (EE: 3) Ericsson advises the writer to stay within the rules of Level 1 as much as possible, though the rules of Level 2 are of higher flexibility.

In the next section, we will comment on structural differences in vocabulary and spelling, syntax, and style.

3.1. Vocabulary and spelling

As far as the lexical organisation is concerned, the following interesting findings were reached. All three manuals contain a controlled vocabulary list. In particular, Ericsson English uses a two-level structure in its lexicon: Level 1 documents may only use those lexical items that are marked 1, whereas Level 2 documents can be edited using a more extended vocabulary. In the IBM word list, a marginal '!' symbol marks some words to indicate that "the word has some restriction, either a restriction to one meaning or a caution that the word is not at eight-grade level and should only be used with care. Cautionary advice is given with the word". Other words are preceded by a marginal X indicating "a word to be avoided". With respect to spelling all three grammars are based upon this very principle: the spelling of words must be conform to the spelling used in the word lists. EE prefers – next to British spelling – the British term if an American and British technical term are interchangeable, whereas AECMA consistently uses American spelling rules as prescribed in the Webster dictionary. Obviously, as they were inspired by individual heritage and international business matters, each of these companies have taken pragmatic decisions that most functionally match their internal organisation.

To check lexical terminology and spelling in their documents, the IBM company supports its writers by means of three computer-assisted instruction programs: WORD CHECKER II, SPELL 370, and PROOF.

The systems required to run WORD CHECKER II are either VS (virtual storage) or the IBM VM/370 (Virtual Machine Facility /370). By this program an unprocessed source document will be transformed into a similar text displaying additional line numbers and a list of all words in the document, followed by remarks such as "avoid", "questionable", "known" and "unknown", and suggestions for correction to the user.

SPELL 370, which runs on VM/370 systems, checks documents for typographic and spelling mistakes in words ranging from 2 to 41 characters. The output text is analogous to the source text but with line numbers. Moreover, it contains a list of additional or misspelled words that do not occur in the dictionary.

Being an interactive computer program, PROOF scrutinises SCRIPT files or other text documents for conformity to the word list. Because of the on-line output, the writer can edit the document on the screen. Not only are possible errors highlighted but also tools are provided to update the input text. Processing options include spelling verification, word checking independent of any reading-grade level in particular, detection of redundant phrases or repeatedly misused word-stock. PROOF uses VM/370 units with CMS (Conversational Monitor System).

The AECMA grammar reveals a remarkable degree of lexical flexibility: "Besides the words in the dictionary, the writer can also use those words which he decides belong to one of two categories: either Technical Names or Manufacturing Processes" (AECMA 1988). (Nevertheless, controlled rules tell whether or not a term belongs to the field of Technical Words or a Manufacturing Processes). "In-house preferences" can be "defined in your company's house rules, or by your editors". (AECMA 1988) In a controlled grammar, however, you cannot deliberately add new meanings to the vocabulary list, and transfer words from one lexical category to another. With respect to this strategy, the Ericsson grammar demands that no new lexical items may be listed, unless the Ericsson Standards Department gives permission to do so. Similar authority holds for the IBM DPPG CUSTOMER and SERVICE INFORMATION. Nevertheless, Ericsson describes a special procedure for using non-listed words: "If you need to use a new word that is useful only in a very specialised context, give a definition of the word in EE, in the document that you are writing. If you need to give several definitions in the document, make an alphabetical list of the definitions at the end of the document." (Ericsson 1983). In the IBM grammar the use of new words is heavily restricted. Writers can, if really necessary, use X-marked words (see above), provided they have been defined and even illustrated in every line where they might be encountered for the first time, and preferably in a glossary, as well.

All three manuals allow noun clusters or compounds, if the number of nouns making up the compound does not exceed three. Adding prefixes or suffixes to items listed in the vocabulary lists is also not allowed; if the item "wash" already exists, the new word "pre-wash" must not be formed, even if the prefix itself is part of the controlled vocabulary.

3.2. Syntax

Besides restriction of lexical items, the three grammars aim at grammar control. In Ericsson English it is of prime importance that "the two fundamental principles of writing are: the meaning must be clear; the language must be simple." (Ericsson 1983) Ericsson, AECMA and IBM control more or less identical grammatical units, notwithstanding each company has its individual way of restricting syntax. For example, all three grammars control the verb forms to be used, but AECMA Simplified English (SE) does not allow either a gerund or a participle. EE only allows gerunds ("EE uses -ing words ... as nouns to describe activities") and it "does not use present participles or the continuous tenses". The IBM company, in its turn, lets the present participle function as an adjective or a noun.

At times, one of the three grammars proposes –besides a rule of control – valuable information, which cannot be found in either of the two other grammars. The AECMA grammar, for example, instructs the writer how to change a passive sentence into an active one, and states that no verbs should be left out to reduce the sentence length. In addition, one particular grammar sometimes does not contain a rule of control which the two others have: the

Ericsson grammar does not refer to control of articles; AECMA and IBM do not take into account subordinate clauses (except for controlling the participial adverbial subclause). Still, although individually focusing on syntax control, all three manuals are incomplete: since EE considers but a few aspects of subordinate clause control, the grammar reveals insufficiency and incompleteness. There are no satisfactory answers to questions such as: What about gapping and elliptic structures? How about using zero-relative markers and zero connectives? Are sentential relative clauses allowed? Can nominal relatives be used? The rules of control are vague as, for instance, in the EE statement: "A comma divides a sentence into its natural components and makes it easier to read". What is the meaning of "natural components"? Numerous other examples of rules that are not well-defined or vague instructions indubitably cause confusion and lead to grammatical errors.

3.3. Style

Next to some elementary rules of punctuation control, the EE grammar does not focus on stylistic control. AECMA Simplified English takes into account some aspects of punctuation, and it discusses sentence length, paragraph length, and structure.

IBM has a special Information Development Guidelines manual called "STYLE". It goes without saying that uniformity of style and layout certainly enhances the overall quality of documents edited in controlled language.

3.4. Conclusion

3.4.1. Discussion

Figure 2 summarises the comparison between the three grammars systematically (Lemmens 1989). First of all, we concluded that "the linguistic foundations of these manuals are at times very weak: oversimplifications often lead to linguistic inaccuracies; ... frequently occurring linguistic structures are not covered; the instructions are at times vague and ambiguous; and often the rules disregard the linguistic reality." (Lemmens 1989).

Secondly, in all three grammars there is lack of clear distinction between descriptive and normative principles. There is not any specification whether the structures to be avoided are ungrammatical or simply non-controlled. Typical of the three grammars is the normative "Do not use" meaning "Avoid". Seldom –if ever — is this phrase used to show that the writer cannot use a particular construction because it is ungrammatical. For example, the rules for distributing "when" and "if' do not mention the incorrect use of "when" in conditional subclauses. Moreover, sometimes descriptive information needs to be included. This kind of description might be a list of alternative constructions in common English not to be used by the writers. Unfortunately, in order to guide the writing of descriptive documents such as course books, reports, hand-outs etc. the rules set forth by the above-mentioned grammars have to be violated regularly. To write a new CE grammar a clear distinction between rules for editing, on the one hand, basic instructive technical documents, and, on the other hand, "higher-level" descriptive documents (cf. EE Level 1 and 2) will be required.

Consequently, "... it is not sufficient to construct a new grammar by just melting together the three grammars, as was mentioned earlier. The new grammar should also be linguistically well founded, unambiguous and, where necessary, descriptively adequate" (Lemmens 1989). This conclusion opened up a new dimension towards the organisation of a controlled grammar.

	AECMA	**ERICSSON**	**IBM**
Spelling			
word list	yes	yes	yes
new words allowed	yes	no	no
free compounding	no	no	no
spelling checker	no	no	yes
Syntax			
verb forms	restricted	restricted	restricted
subclause	nothing	limited info	very little
grammar checker	no	no	no
tense distribution	nothing	nothing	nothing
linguistic basis	weak	weak	weak
descriptive	little	little	little
Style			
punctuation	basic	nothing	basic
sentence structure	+/-	little	little
paragraph structure	basic	nothing	nothing
Other information			
check list	no	no	no
completeness	no	no	no
readability	+/-	ok	good

Figure 2. Comparison of CE grammars

4. Organisation of the COGRAM project

Since the development of the Controlled English grammar (COGRAM) –as it will be systematically presented in this paper –mainly consists of two components, a word list and a grammar, a two-dimensional strategy has to be taken into account.

On the one hand, a limited lexical database is being developed at the University of Antwerp: A basic word list containing 2000 terms has been constituted to be used in vocabulary exercises. Recently, this list has been extended to a vocabulary package of approximately 5000 words. Moreover, another 1000 technical terms were added to make the controlled vocabulary more complete. On the other hand, at the University of Leuven, the Department of Linguistics has been doing intensive research into the field of controlled English in order to generate a selection of adequate grammar rules that pertain to multiple aspects concerning technical writing: lexical structures, syntactic patterns and stylistic features.

At a final stage in the project, both the lexical database and the grammar will be integrated into a powerful tool for writers. To ensure that a possible introduction of the grammar at a company will take place without many users psychologically objecting to Controlled English, we have thought of illustrating the grammar rules by means of straight-to-the-point examples, all taken from the users' field of interest.

5. Organisation of a prototypic controlled grammar (COGRAM)

The general development of COGRAM has been partly directed by a three-fold division into a lexical, syntactic and stylistic component. Also, most of the COGRAM rules can be –conceptually speaking –characterised by the following three models: "Do not use X", "Use only X", "Avoid X". At times "Do not use X"-rules are complemented with alternative suggestions. Secondly, the difference between "Do not use"-rules and "Avoid"-rules is fundamental in COGRAM; "Do not use"-rules mean "You must not use", whereas the "Avoid"-rules denote "Try not to use". Some crucial remarks to be made here are: How is each type of rule related to the others? To which extent do they need to complement one another and how?

Unfortunately, a dilemma makes an adequate solution even more complicated. On the one hand, from a pedagogic point of view it is not useful to add non-controlled forms to a "Use only"-rule. All rules in the grammar should be kept as simple as possible. Moreover, the addition of an non-controlled forms may cause confusion on the side of the users; they might be enticed to use incorrect non-controlled forms. On the other hand, in view of Natural Language Processing applications, it is necessary to take into consideration all correct and incorrect forms in order to develop a powerful grammar checker. The problems that arise with regard to the modelling of rules result from the inability of exactly determining the users' knowledge of non-controlled but correct, and controlled English: What should the level of non-controlled English be, before one starts mastering COGRAM?

In the following sections, we focus on each component with respect to the descriptive approach, linguistic foundations and structural organisation. Each component will be illustrated by means of COGRAM examples.

5.1. Lexical component

To guarantee that the new grammar would systematically cover all major lexical categories in English, the grammatical division by Leech and Svartvik was taken as a starting point. To create the initial frame of the grammar all ten lexical categories as described in the Communicative Grammar of English were divided into four major word classes (nouns, main verbs, adjectives, adverbs) and six minor classes (auxiliaries, pronouns, determiners, conjunctions, prepositions and interjections). All the rules applying to these categories were methodically brought together into a lexical component. Moreover, previous rules were updated, while new rules were formulated to enhance linguistic efficiency.

Example 1: Avoid splitting infinitives, unless the emphasis is on the adverb.

- \- BOM tries to *accurately* list all the subassemblies.
- \+ BOM tries to list *accurately* all the subassemblies.

Example 2: Use short infinitives of regular action verbs.

- \- The secretary *makes a photocopy of* a CAD graph.
- \+ The secretary *xeroxes* a CAD graph.

Example 3: Use a before a noun beginning with a consonant sound for non-specific reference.

- \- Store all numerical information in database program.
- \+ Store all numerical information in *a* database program.

5.2. Syntactic component

Beside the lexical component a syntactic module, which mainly controls co-ordination, subordination, tense, and aspect generates controlled English sentence patterns. It should be mentioned that during the organisation of the controlled syntax two computer-assisted writing programs, Grammatik 4[2] and Right Writer[3] were thoroughly analysed in order to weigh pros and cons with respect to controlled syntactic patterns.

---

2 Reference Software International (1989).

3 Right Soft Inc. (1987)

Example 4: Write all instructions in a chronological order.

- \- Press the button on your right, after you set the switch to the middle.
- \+ Set the switch to the middle. Press the button on your right.

Example 5: Do not use a participle to introduce an adverbial clause.

- \- Using MIC manufacturing, electroplate the housings.
- \+ Use MIC manufacturing to electroplate the housings.

Example 6: Use only **because,** never **since** in a subclause of reason.

- \- *Since* a DBCS manages the System 12 database, physical storage of data is made transparent to the users.
- \+ *Because* a DBCS manages the System 12 database, physical storage of data is made transparent to the users.

5.3. Stylistic component

The third subsection in the grammar comprises controlled punctuation and layout rules to efficiently organise the textual material. Extensive study of Kirkman's manual on punctuation added to the insight into the facilities of style control as well (see Kirkman 1983).

Example 7: Use a question mark only at the end of a direct question.

- \+ Is the component single-sourced or multi-sourced?

Example 8: Do not divide words.

Example 9: Expound major topics. Restrict minor topics.

6. The prototype: test and evaluation

The first version of COGRAM comprised approximately 100 rules. To test the efficiency of this prototypic version, we made an exhaustive analysis of a technical text sample of approximately 450 lines (Schreurs 1989). Because of its linguistic resemblance with other technical text files this segment might be a suitable representation of the crucial grammatical problems to be discussed.

A preliminary remark involves the semantics of the terminology. During the revision of the file several incomprehensible terms and phrases had to be decoded. Since most linguists are not technical experts, an irreproachable contextual-semantic revision could not be guarantied. This is obviously a semantic problem, and thus beyond the scope of this lexical and syntactic analysis. Nonetheless, the English of the sample text had been revised as thoroughly as possible to test our prototypic yet controlled English grammar.

6.1. Analysis of the sample text: results

1. General results

Sentences	187
Mistakes	452
Mistakes per sentence	2.41

2. Specific results

Common English		Controlled English	
Choice of words	78	Punctuation	77
Abbreviations	36	Passive sentence	57
Spelling	21	Wordiness	43
Syntactic construction	7	Noun identification	38
Word position	6	Capital letters	20
Conditional clause	4	Technical compounds	17
Dangling participle	3	Tenses	8
Relative clause	3	Noun clusters	7
Agreement	2	Obligation	5
Co-ordination	2	Ability	3
Plural form	2	Acronyms	1
Subclause of reason	2	Gerunds	1
Subclause of purpose	1	Conjunctions	1
Apposition	1	Terminology	1
	168	Numeric information	1
		Future Tense	1
		Content	1
		Coherence	1
		Singular form	1
			284

Figure 3. Results of the sample text analysis

6.2. Discussion

After examining the analysis of the sample text through the COGRAM prototype (see Schreurs 1989), we concluded that the grammar was still incomplete and not powerful enough to transform technical prose into fully controlled documents. The results, as shown in the table, do not reflect the linguistic contents of the document in a realistic way; obviously, because the rules of the prototype were not explicit enough, a lot of constructions that were acceptable in controlled English were flagged negatively. The rule "Put a full stop at the end of each syntactic unit", for instance, was not accurate enough. It led to flagging of all titles, headings and sub-headings, which obviously do not end with a full stop. Consequently, the number of punctuation mistakes should be considered with caution.

No matter how inflexible the prototype was, the analysis has unquestionably led to clearer insights into the use of authentic and controlled English. Moreover, this analysis should be considered not as a mere criticism on the writers of the sample text, but as a self-critique test, from which new impulses towards the future were given. Therefore, at the University of Antwerp the research and development of controlled definitions of technical terms needed to be extended and adapted remarkably. Furthermore, at the Leuven University, the updated versions derived from this prototype, have definitely brought about more accuracy, clarity and productive power through more efficient rules, more functional examples, and a more structured organisation.

7. ALCOGRAM: the algorithmic controlled grammar

After a few updated versions, the invention and modular classification of approximately 150 grammatical rules categorised over the three components could function as a solid infrastructure from which a new stage can emerge: the organisation of an algorithmic controlled grammar (ALCOGRAM).

The question to be answered with respect to the logical organisation of the grammar is twofold. First, can we keep the three-fold division (lexical, syntactic, stylistic component) unchanged when storing 150 rules of control into a single algorithm? Secondly, how much will an algorithmic structure affect the adequate interaction among the components? In order to find a suitable solution to the above-mentioned questions, the following paragraphs will deal with the internal structure of the ALCOGRAM module.

7.1. Organisation of ALCOGRAM

7.1.1. Level One: preparatory textual control algorithm (PTCA)

Constructing an algorithmic controlled grammar indisputably presupposes accurate composition of rules: careful text control implies specification of the initial stage, from which the limited and exactly defined steps have to be taken. This starting point is to be situated within a preparatory phase i.e. before the actual text is written. When a technical writer wants to write a text, guided brainstorming would be the solution to avoid superficiality from the initial point in the process of writing. This segment of the algorithm will be labelled *Preparatory Textual Control Algorithm (PTCA).* The PTCA may entail introductory control, control through adequacy, writing control, paragraph control, and example control. Furthermore, it will generate a textual frame in which the syntactic component can operate adequately.

Introductory control
Control through adequacy
Writing control
Paragraph control
Example control

Figure 4. ALCOGRAM: PTCA

7.1.2. Level two: syntactic control algorithm (SCA)

The *Syntactic Control Algorithm (SCA)* will then, at a second stage, control syntax in terms of sentence length, co-ordination and subordination patterns, tense and aspect. A variety of syntactic units i.e. titles and headings, statements, direct, and indirect questions will be prepared for lexical control.

Sentence length
Co-ordination
Subordination
Tense
Aspect

Figure 5. ALCOGRAM: SCA

7.1.3. Level three: lexical control algorithm (LCA)

At the third stage, the *Lexical Control Algorithm (LCA) will* operate on all major and minor classes: noun control, verb control, adjective control, adverb control, auxiliary control, pronoun control, conjunction control, preposition control and interjection control. The output of the LCA is a controlled lexico-syntactic unit.

Noun control
Verb control
Adjective control
Adverb control
Auxiliary control
Pronoun control
Conjunction control
Preposition control
Interjection control

Figure 6. ALCOGRAM: LCA

7.1.4. Level four: micro control algorithm (MCA)

Stage four aims at controlling particular micro-features of the lexico-syntactic unit. The *Micro Control Algorithm (MCA)* includes a.o. numeric control and reference control. When each sentence has passed through all four blocks, from macro to micro control, it should be sufficiently controlled.

Numeric control
Reference control
Series control
Omission control
Crucial term control
Expression control

Figure 7. ALCOGRAM: MCA

7.2. Discussion

Note that, in comparison to the prototypic grammar and its derivatives, the structure of three blocks could not be kept unchanged: the stylistic component is not a separate unit within the algorithmic grammar; control of punctuation and style has been accurately merged into the textual, syntactic, lexical and micro control subdivisions. Moreover, the answer to our second question can thus be formulated: the link between the PTCA, SCA, LCA and MCA will definitely be more compact, even more structured and, with respect to the integration of the stylistic component into the algorithmic frame, more functional.

7.3. ALCOGRAM: General algorithmic structure

The modular structure of the algorithmic controlled grammar can be outlined as follows:

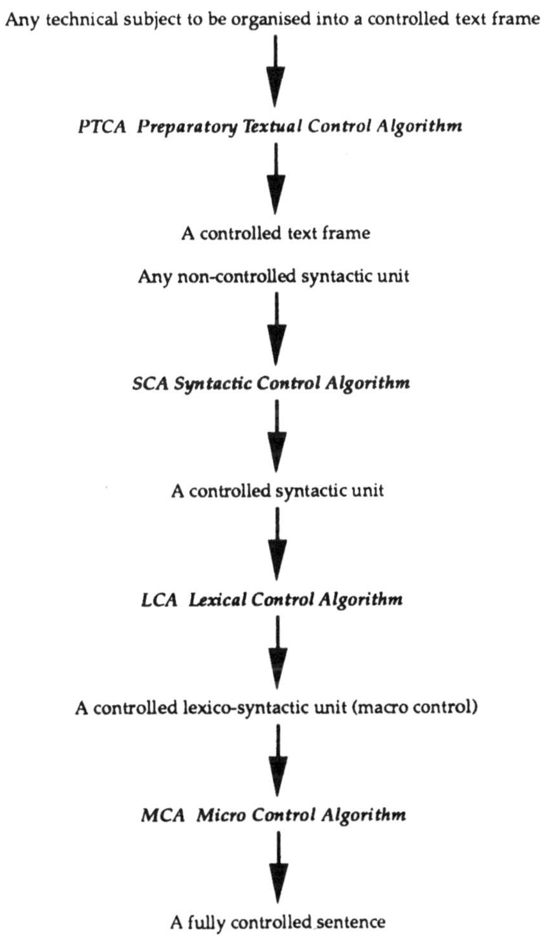

Figure 8. ALCOGRAM

7.4. Flow-chart example of ALCOGRAM

The following algorithmic sample has been taken from the SCA. In this part of ALCOGRAM, adverbial subclauses will be controlled. If the users answer the questions generated by the algorithm correctly, they will be given suggestions for adverbial clause control.

What type of subordinated clause?

1. adverbial 2. relative 3. nominal

↓

What type of adverbial subclause?

1. time 2. purpose 3. condition 4. reason 5. concession 6. result 7. place

↓

What kind of condition?

↓

1. positive 2. negative

↓

Use **unless**

Figure 9. ALCOGRAM: Flow-chart sample

8. Future developments

When the controlled grammar has been structured according to strict algorithmic principles, the notion of applying a computer in the process of technical writing is obviously close. Accordingly, the Department of Linguistics is presently considering the following three-level approach in the on-line presentation of the subject matter.

First, on an initial level, a computer program will operate as a controlled database which engineers can consult when writing technical documents. When they select one particular grammatical item from a menu, the computer will display all the rules applying to that particular item so that they can revise the document manually.

Secondly, we will develop a program that guides the writer through the algorithm by asking questions and giving suggestions on how to control a specific item (see also Beeken, this volume).

Thirdly, an intelligent grammar and style checking program based upon Artificial Intelligence techniques will then transform non-controlled lexico-syntactic units into controlled ones without substantially affecting the semantic content of the units (see also Thurmair 1990, and Wojcik *et al.* 1990).

9. Conclusion

To conclude, at the Department of Linguistics we have analysed, revised and tested all characteristics typical of existing Controlled English grammars in order to construct -starting from an incomplete prototypic yet controlled grammar (COGRAM) – a functional working tool, namely an algorithmic controlled grammar (ALCOGRAM).

In the near future, the system of rules organised in ALCOGRAM will lay solid foundations for the development of an intelligent CE grammar and style checker, based upon techniques of pattern recognition as used in the field of Artificial Intelligence. Since a high degree of interaction between the user and the program is required, we will –from a pedagogic point of view – examine the possibilities of the interactive processes used in the field of CAI to guarantee functional control. The CE checker will guide the writer of controlled English by distinguishing between authentic English structures and controlled patterns. Furthermore, any non-controlled syntactic input will be lexically analysed, syntactically parsed and stylistically checked, before the program transforms it into an acceptable controlled English output sentence.

However fascinating the study of controlled language for linguistics might be, it remains to be seen whether the phenomenon will be widely acknowledged and accepted in international business environments. To discover the potentials of controlled language usage means to comprehend a new resourceful method of consolidating efficiency, economy and standardisation into one active system.

10. References

AECMA, (1988) A Guide for the Preparation of Aircraft Maintenance Documentation in the Aerospace Maintenance Language. *AECMA Simplified English,* Paris.

Ericsson Group, (1983) *Ericsson English Writer's Guide.* Ericsson Group, Stockholm.

Kirkman, J. (1983) *Points on Punctuation for Scientific and Technical Writing.* John Kirkman Communication Consultancy, South Glamorgan.

Lemmens, M. (1989) Controlled English Project –Preliminary Research. Department of Linguistics, Leuven.

Schreurs, D. (1989) Grammatical Analysis of a DATACOM2 Sample through the controlled English Grammar COGRAM. Department of Linguistics, Leuven.

Thurmair, G., (1990) *Parsing for Grammar and Style Checking.* Siemens AG, Munich.

W ojcik, R., et. al. (1990) *On Creating a Practical Simplified English Checker.* Boeing Computer Services, Seattle, WA.

15

Action Centred Manuals or Minimalist Instruction? Alternative Theories for Carroll's Minimal Manuals

Stephen W. Draper
University of Glasgow

Keith Oatley
Applied Cognitive Science
OISE

Abstract

Minimalist instruction, as our replications have demonstrated, is a robust and reliable method for writing documentation that out performs most commercially produced manuals by a large factor in learning time, user satisfaction, user confidence, and reduced printing costs. But why does it work? Recently Carroll offered a theory in terms of human learning. An alternative theory that ignores learning and concentrates on doing –on action supported by information flow – also predicts the main features of the method. It claims that while the minimalism (the savings in space and time for both users and manufacturers) is the motive for using this method, it is being action centred that is the key to both its nature and success. The apparent conflict between the theories highlights the issues that are important to achieving a synthesis, and ultimately casts doubt on the traditional approach of treating action and learning separately. A new combined theory is developed, and some conclusions about how to write minimal manuals are derived from it.

1. Introduction

1.1. The minimal manual research field

Over the last eight years or so, Jack Carroll and his associates have pursued a connected line of research on techniques for designing instructional materials for computer software. These materials are referred to as "minimal manuals" after the latest version of the technique, or "minimalist instruction" after the title of a recent paper (Carroll 1989). By the standards of the field of Human Computer Interaction, this line of research is uniquely well grounded. It is user centred. Beginning with a study of the actual problems of users in practice (Mack *et al.* 1983), it has been a progression of attempts to solve them (guided exploration cards, training wheels, minimal manuals), each in turn tested on users. It is a connected progression, where the problems found in one stage have led to the development of new techniques and the abandonment of old, rather than the elaboration of an original idea until interest in it is lost and effort switched to an unrelated topic. While a number of theoretical ideas have been brought to bear, the driving force has come from the actual phenomena –the difficulties and successes of users at learning new interfaces – in contrast to many projects which have been essentially tests of the applicability of a prior theory rather than the search for a theory to fit prior data. The reward of this approach has been one of the very few practically valuable results in HCI: a technique for writing instructional material which reliably allows users to learn more, in less time, and with a better subjective experience leading to a gain in confidence than if they use the manufacturer's material. Furthermore, as we ourselves have demonstrated, this technique is reproducible by others on the basis of little training other than reading one or two research papers.

We have, then, something comparable to Jenner's development of vaccination against smallpox: an effective procedure of considerable practical importance. As academics, however, we would also like to understand why it works, both as a matter of intellectual curiosity, and in the hope that we might eventually discover generalisations not yet dreamed of (just as Pasteur developed a more general technique of vaccination, based on a better theory of infection as caused by organisms). In this chapter we discuss some alternative theoretical ideas to account for the success of the minimalist approach.

1.2. Overview of the chapter

We begin with a brief summary of the replications and applications which we and our students have done. A typical case is a three month project for a student with very modest training in computer science and HCI, constructing a small minimal manual and finishing with a controlled experiment demonstrating a sizeable and statistically significant advantage over existing manuals both in user performance and preference. It is far from clear however exactly where the root cause of this effect lies. The technique is expressed in four or so principles, written in English. There is as yet no consensus about detailed format for minimal manuals, nor about exactly what to include. This variability almost certainly speaks to the power of the underlying effect, rather than meaning that such details have no effect.

Recently Carroll (1989) offered one attempt at explaining the approach, by linking the principles to characteristics of human learning: we summarise this theory in section 3. We next offer a different explanation based on the idea of user action supported by "information flow" rather than prior knowledge. This is essentially a theory of doing and not of learning, whereas Carroll's theory is one of learning, not of doing; yet both independently offer groundings for the principles that summarise the minimalist approach. This apparent conflict opens up a discussion about whether manuals are for tutorial use or for reference, about what exactly are the cognitive tasks involved in using a manual, and about what learning theory is presupposed by various styles of manual. It is clear that using any manual, whether intended as tutorial or reference, in fact involves both learning and acting on tasks using the manual as a reference source. Thus some kind of synthesis of the two initial theories must be necessary: of considerations of action and of learning. In the penultimate section (7) we re-analyse the design and use of manuals from the start, taking into account the issues raised, and reaching a new provisional theory for this approach. In the concluding section we apply this to derive some more explicit and detailed ideas about how to write manuals.

2. Replications of a robust effect

There are already some reports in the literature of work by others on the minimalist approach: Greif (1986), and work at the Telecom Australia Research Laboratories by J. Chessari, G. Lingaard, L. Perry and others. Carroll (1989) also reports on some applications in industry.

We ourselves have supervised a series of student projects based on the minimalist approach. These each represent three months full time work by the student, and perhaps 10 hours supervision by us. The students had at most 20 hours of lectures on HCI, of which at most 2 hours were on minimal manuals. For the rest, they learned the technique from the published research papers and from pilot trials on users. In no case has a minimal manual failed to out-perform the manual it replaces, but in some cases the tests were not sufficiently well conducted to produce a dependable result. For instance, in one case there were only three new users a year, so insufficient subjects were available in the time span; in another, we were not allowed to run a control group with the manufacturer's manual as the teacher responsible regarded that as "obviously" disadvantaging those users. Here we mention three which directly demonstrated the replication of Carroll's effect.

Meldrum (1987) developed a minimal manual for creating "glossaries" (a kind of user-defined macro) in a Wang word processing system. She compared its success with that of a pilot videotaped tutorial being developed professionally, and with the manufacturer's manual. Her manual had one third the number of words, and she found a performance factor of about two in items learned and speed at tasks. Her study also showed particularly clearly that the minimal manual created a confidence in her users (who were women of a range of ages, who had to learn the word processor as a job requirement) that they could teach themselves further features with little human support; a confidence not shared by those in the control group learning from the manufacturer's manual.

Boo (1988) wrote and tested a minimal manual (of 8 pages) for the electronic mail system running under VME (an operating system for an ICL mainframe), and compared it to the standard manual of 49 pages. After taking slightly shorter training times with less than half the errors (and with a higher proportion recovered from), the minimal manual subjects performed the post test 40% faster, while scoring slightly better than the control group. They also were much more positive on subjective measures than the control group.

Bryce (1990) developed a manual for PageMaker (a sizeable layout program for manipulating the layout of text and graphics for desktop publishing). This demonstrated the technique on a larger system, confronting us with the need to treat different phases of learning separately (first introduction, through to reference-supported exploration). He again found the minimal manual superior to commercially published manuals, and of about the same effectiveness as a lecture based taught course.

3. Carroll: links to characteristics of human learning

It seems clear that there is a strong underlying phenomenon. So far the replications by our group have been based on a set of a few principles, stated in English. In this section, we list those principles and then summarise an attempt by Carroll to account for them in terms of characteristics of human learning.

3.1. The principles of minimalist instruction

The minimalist approach is summarised in a set of principles, different statements of which appear in different papers. The main paper on minimal manuals (Carroll *et al.* 1987/8) lists four, which I have labelled A to D, plus two more (E, F) which are not on the explicit list, but were tested for in the second experiment reported in that paper.

- Focus on real tasks and activities.
- Slash the verbiage.
- Support error recognition and recovery.
- Guided exploration.
- Get the user started fast.
- Promote users' co-ordination of display and manual. i.e. to use text as the basis of observation and action, not only as a story to read.

3.2. Deriving the principles from characteristics of human learning

Carroll (1989) (see also Carroll 1990) develops an argument based on characteristics of human learning (at least in this kind of situation). It links observed problems or features of users' behaviour, to methods of learning, to principles of how to write minimalist materials. The principles listed below are numbered as in Carroll (1989), while the capital letters in parentheses refer back to the list of principles given above, the symbol "->" may be read as "because", and "=>" as "therefore". The general form is thus:

user error type ->
characteristic of human learning =>
minimalist instruction principle

The five specific derivations of principles are as follows:

People tend to jump the gun ->
People learn by doing; they try to act in order to learn =>
1. (E) **Allow the user to get started fast**

People are not always careful planners ->
People learn by thinking and reasoning;
they generate and test hypotheses in order to learn =>
2. (D?) **Rely on the user to think and improvise**

People are not good at systematically following instructional steps ->
People seek to work in a meaningful context and toward meaningful goals =>
3. (A) **Direct training at real tasks**

People's reasoning about situations is often subject to interference from what they know about other, superficially similar situations (abduction) ->
People rely on their prior knowledge when they try to manage and assimilate new experience =>
4.(B, F?) **Exploit what people already know**

People are often poor at recognising, diagnosing, and recovering from errors they make ->
People use error diagnosis and recovery episodes as a means of exploring the boundaries of what they know =>
5.(C) **Support error recognition and recovery**

The most salient, single, concrete technique is to support error recognition and recovery. This is often the most obvious difference in content between a minimal manual and a conventional one, and it is the one which the observation of actual users motivates most directly. The most profound underlying idea, however, as argued in the following sections, is a super-principle of organising the design around user activity: all the other principles (A to E) are related to the aim of supporting action by the user above everything else. The other super-principle that seems to underlie the minimalist approach is to design around the effect of the user's prior knowledge (a theme that is prominent in the science education literature, and in the literature on explanation): whether or not the manual writer wishes it, this will profoundly affect user's actions and understanding, and this is reflected in 2, 3, and 4 above.

We might say, then, on the basis of the two versions of the principles listed above, that there seem to be two underlying super-principles from which they may be derived:

S1 Organise the design around user activity.
S2 Design around the effect of users' prior knowledge.

Carroll's account focuses on learning, and certainly accommodates S2. However, although it is organised as an account about learning it seems to emphasise its dependence on, even subordination to, action. The next section shows how far an account based on action alone can be developed.

4. Action centred manuals: links to theories of action

Carroll and his associates have discussed how computer users strive to learn through active exploration, even when manuals do not support this but penalise it. The success of minimal manuals shows the benefits of building on this pronounced active orientation. We suggest that this orientation to action is more fundamental: that even when people are learning material for the first time, their activity shows the same general organisation as most human interaction with computers. In particular, users treat the manual as an information source subordinated to an external task –in effect their actions do not reflect any "instructional objective", but just the immediate task (such as typing a letter, or creating a glossary to speed future letter creation).

In this they are behaving in a way similar to expert users. Draper (1985) found that even expert UNIX users did not seem to know more than a fraction of the available commands, and suggested that expertise in large systems lies rather in skill in retrieving information when needed, just as a librarian's expertise is not in having memorised the catalogue but in knowing how to use it. Such experts know how to translate goals that they (or those who consult them) may have into ways of retrieving command information and hence into successful actions. We suggest that new users are attempting from the outset to operate in this way, but because they do not (unlike UNIX experts) in fact have special expertise in operating the system's information sources, it is crucial to design manuals to support them more directly. We can understand the minimalist rule of organising material around tasks rather than command names or system structure in this way.

We are suggesting two things here. Firstly, we should understand the behaviour of new users embarked on self-instruction as basically similar to that of experienced users accomplishing their own goals. In both cases the activity is goal directed, but some of the actions are directed at fetching information needed to perform other actions. Secondly, successful action is frequently based not on a previously learned, comprehensive knowledge of the domain, but rather on a timely flow of information picked up just when it is needed (for instance by a reminder contained in a menu item's name, or seeing that you need to move the cursor another character to the right). Such timely "information flow" (Norman and Draper 1986) saves both the amount of information that must otherwise be learned and remembered, and the amount of planning ahead that must be done. Mayes *et al.* (1988) reported that users of a highly visual interface show very poor recall of its details (e.g. number, names, and content of menus), even though these details are functionally important. This is consistent with the possibility that we do not memorise knowledge which is always available (delivered by the interface) whenever it is needed.

Theories of action commonly treat perceptual input as an intrinsic part of action on an equal footing with physical action itself (Miller *et al.* 1960, Norman 1986). This cycle (e.g. a TOTE unit, Norman's gulfs of execution and evaluation) is reflected in the recommended structure for each unit of a minimal manual i.e. each unit will have a description of its purpose (the goal which the user could satisfy by performing the action described in the unit), a description of the method (the plan to be executed to achieve the goal), how to recognise success (that the goal has been achieved), how to recognise problems, and how to recover from them. These features closely correspond to the steps in a theory of action from intention through planning and action to perception, evaluation of the outcome, and possible iteration. Some notions of action, such as those in early Artificial Intelligence planning work, focused on planning and neglected perception. Norman's approach stresses the importance of the perceptual side of the cycle in understanding user interaction, in order to account for evaluation of success. The idea of information flow additionally stresses the importance of perceptual input not only as feedback in the control engineering sense (for testing the degree of goal satisfaction), but for the timely acquisition of the "knowledge" (e.g. of command names and action sequences) that is a prerequisite for the planning and doing side of the cycle. Thus both the internal structure and the whole concept of minimal manuals can be understood in terms of a general theory of action, augmented by an emphasis on the importance of action based on an information flow mode as well as on the more theoretically familiar knowledge based modes.

These ideas of action centredness based on information flow explain many of Carroll's principles and their inter-relations. Principles A, E, and F above are direct corollaries (focus on real tasks and activities, get the user started fast, promote users' co-ordination of display and manual). D, C, and B (guided exploration, supporting error recognition and recovery, slashing verbiage) are implied because minimal manuals are meant to support the discovery of information from action with the interface rather than from reading. They also point to an account of *how* verbiage may be slashed (B) by forcing suitably constrained problem solving (i.e. guided exploration—D) on both a large and small scale. For instance an instruction (in a manual on a word processor) to "open the header and add a phrase" need not be expanded into "go to the Format menu, execute the 'Open Header' command, click in the new window and type a phrase, close the window" if users can be relied on to search the menus for commands they do not know, and already know (or know how to look up) how to insert text. Such instructions are not designed by thoughtless omission however. If users do not already know about opening headers, it is important that the phrase used ("open the header") be a close match to the command name they must search the menus for, or the search will be poorly constrained.

This theoretical approach also draws attention to how tutorials must deliver items at three levels: not only plans (methods), but also what the basic units of action are in this domain (subgoals to the user, basic commands to the system), and how they are combined into typical user tasks (goals). Most manuals are mainly concerned with supplying articulatory information (how to carry out a single domain operation) such as command names and syntax, of the sort often supplied by menus. Just as important is how users are taught new goals (cf. Owen 1986): for instance in word processing, why (and when) a glossary or macro facility might be useful to them in their work. After all, it is not a facility available in the typewriter domain from which they had earlier presumably transferred many of the goals (e.g. letter writing) associated with word processing. Attempting to apply the minimalist approach exposes the importance of this issue in practice, but it is not explicitly dealt with either by Carroll's minimalist principles, or by his proposed instructional theory.

In summary, manuals are part of the overall interface between user and system, created to supplement the informational deficiencies of the bare machine, at least until the user has internalised the missing information. People will try to use a manual to support an information flow mode of operation when the bare interface only supports a more knowledge-based mode. Manuals must be designed to mesh smoothly with this cycle of action, organised almost entirely around goal-directed behaviour.

This approach to instructional material might perhaps be better described as "action-centred" rather than as "minimalist". This is partly to differentiate it from Carroll's (1989) theory of its effectiveness and to refer to this alternative account of why it works. But it is also because we find that lecturing on "minimal manuals" often means that people wrongly confabulate a notion of taking an existing manual and deleting material. This is wrong as a method for generating a minimal manual, wrong because one of the biggest factors (as Carroll *et al.* 1987/8 note) is the *addition* of material on error recovery, and wrong because what feels most different about it to the users is probably not the length but the mode of using it. The length (the minimalism) is an easily noticeable feature, is attractive to manufacturers because it reduces their printing costs, and to users because it is less intimidating; but is not the central feature either for those who wish to write such material or for theoretical explanations of its effectiveness.

5. The conflict between the theories

The two theories sketched above show up a tacit conflict between two roles for a manual: promoting learning vs. promoting successful first time use, and between a tutorial and a reference manual accessible to novices.

The latter would seem to be best served by offering complete recipes to follow that allowed the user not to think. Problem-solving takes time and is error-prone, and so would reduce first time performance. However, Carroll's observation that people follow instructions poorly suggest that there will be difficulties here, perhaps to be remedied by support for error recovery. It is also hard to see how to keep the material brief if no learning is assumed, and any part may be read by a novice with no experience of the rest of the manual. The test of success for this objective would be the success of users in performing novel tasks given the manual. The claim of a strong form of the information flow theory would be that even expert performance is essentially of this kind, and that novices should perform as well as experts if the manual is good enough.

The former theory would seem to be best served by forcing learning i.e. forcing inference, forcing extra exploratory activities so that users discover extra things; dictating tasks to try that the user would not try otherwise. This is familiar from the practice at many educational institutions, and naturally seems to follow from the ideas on learning to which Carroll refers. It seems to conflict with allowing users to choose their own tasks, and to achieve them efficiently. The test for this objective would be one of learning i.e. what do users know (without consulting the manual) that they did not know before the tutorial session?

Work up to now provides little evidence that can differentiate these objectives, and so tell us which theory is closer to describing what "minimalist" materials achieve. They have typically measured the time taken to go through a tutorial, and performance on novel tasks after learning but with continued access to the manual. They have not measured how well a user performs tasks after learning but without a manual to refer to, nor other direct tests of knowledge. Neither have they tested first-time performance with the manual directly, and compared that to how well users could do without the manual, by doing problem-solving on the system itself. Thus they have confirmed the effectiveness of minimal manuals in supporting user performance during and after a learning period; but have not shown how this effect divides into support for learning and support for action without learning.

6. An initial synthesis

In practice it is hard to imagine any real manual that is not a profound compromise between the objectives implied by the two theories. With no learning by the user the manual must be bulky because simple instructions (e.g. about how to hold down a shift or control key) must be repeated; but forcing learning actively violates the principle of letting users get on with achieving their goals ("real tasks") especially in the light of evidence that even experts do not learn more about an interface than is strictly demanded by getting things done. Moreover, supporting use not learning seems to be a vote for providing recipes—but Carroll observes that people follow recipes badly i.e. people seem to use their understanding anyway. This generative problem solving and creation of novel behaviours seems closer to learning. Furthermore we could not in any case spell out recipes for everything. All manuals in fact rely on being able to express general rules at some level. Finally, manuals are always likely to be a slower information delivery medium than the interface, so there is always likely to be a small but continuous pressure favouring learning, if only in the SOAR style of automatic rule compilation through practice (Laird *et al.* 1987). Does this view of learning in fact undermine the distinction between learning and performance? Certainly SOAR proponents seem to see learning as something that *only* occurs during performance.

Part of the solution must be understanding how to support learning in a way that does not make users feel they are being held up. Another part is the issue (not apparently discussed by Carroll) of how to merge strictly tutorial material with reference material: in particular, instructions to do a task whose only purpose is that the user will learn something that might be useful later.

6.1. Theories of learning

A large part of the problem is that none of the above offers an explicit theory of how learning takes place, or even of what exactly is to be learned. To begin with traditional manuals; they typically describe facilities command by command, perhaps with exercises. The implicit learning theory seems to be that if you read a statement or type in a command, then you are likely to remember what you read or typed, and furthermore to be able to apply it when appropriate. Carroll's instructional theory is more sophisticated, in that it has some ideas founded on experience of the kinds of situations and activities most likely to promote retention of material. Its implied claim is that minimalist material creates those situations, and hence promotes learning. Its problem is that there is a tension between knowing that retention is helped by the user feeling that the activity furthers their own goals directly, and wanting to teach material the user may not know they need. The information flow theory in its basic form is a theory of action, with nothing to say about learning. Indeed there is some evidence that experts know rather little, in which case learning would seem not even to be a desirable objective of the design of manuals!

In fact we do not yet know much about what people need to know or actually know to support practical action (the ultimate aim of manuals for computer programs, and other devices). Mayes *et al*. (1988) offered some evidence that experts and novices differed little in what they remembered about a visual interface, both recalling surprisingly little. That work derived in part from Nickerson and Adams' (1979) study of memory for coins. They too had found much poorer memory than they or their subjects expected for coins, and concluded with the suggestion that people remember only what is functionally necessary. In fact their own data refute this: their subjects clearly did remember more than a minimum. For instance, functionally you could remember nothing and just read a coin's denomination; or remember size and colour in order to discriminate coins at a glance, and forget even that they have a head depicted on them; yet their subjects clearly did remember the presence of features like the head. The question then is how much more than the functional minimum do people spontaneously (or "incidentally") learn? Applied to menu-based systems, near-novices can perform well by re-scanning a menu each time for the target word, but highly practised users in fact seem to remember and use an encoded form of some spatial aspects of the display (O'Malley *et al*. 1991; O'Malley and Draper 1991). This suggests that a menu system can support good performance by information flow rather than learning, but that with practice, performance comes to be supported by learned knowledge instead, i.e. the basis for performance invisibly shifts. It seems likely that tiny improvements of performance provide a small but effective pressure for learning in such situations.

Until further research on this has been done, we may apply this suggestion to advancing the basic information flow theory. If manuals really did achieve information delivery as smoothly as a good user interface, then we should see no learning even after many trials: just smooth pickup, use, and forgetting of information. However, it is likely that although one important test of a manual is whether it can support action based on information delivery, the basis of action is likely to shift with experience. Another test therefore will be of learning: of the learnability of the interface given the scaffolding of the manual. The information flow idea can be used to suggest the nature of what constitutes good scaffolding for this kind of learning. New studies will be needed to see how this works in practice. Existing data does show impressive first time performance, but does not really bear on gaps in retention because the information delivery is so good that task performance times do not readily show whether the necessary information is being recalled or picked up when needed: different tests are needed for this.

7. A fresh analysis

To find a resolution to these issues it seems best not merely to try to find a synthesis, but to analyse the use of manuals more completely: how they are used, what learning we should expect them to promote and how, how they relate to normal user performance after initial learning.

Scharer (1983) suggested that users do not read manuals at all. This observation can be interpreted as evidence that conventional manuals are not found to be useful, and so for the need for an improved kind of manual. It is perhaps best taken to represent the fact that users do not read manuals when manual writers might expect them to: they often fail to find the information that they need, even though it is present somewhere in the manual. Providing it in print does not mean that it is accessible in practice. (This is continually rediscovered during the debugging of each minimal manual.) Draper (1985) suggested a somewhat different interpretation: that using a manual was in fact characteristic of expert (rather than novice) use of large systems like UNIX. This would be predicted by an analogy to librarians, who also know only a fraction of the items (books) available, but whose expertise lies in knowing how to get the information needed, when it is needed. This theory suggests that expertise does indeed make a big difference to performance, but does not consist of encyclopaedic knowledge but rather of meta-knowledge of how to get information when needed. One (but only one) source of knowledge is reference manuals. Expertise, then, essentially includes knowing how to find what you need to know in a reference manual. Novices may not use manuals much, but that is not only an indictment of the manuals but also a measure of their lack of a necessary skill. To achieve even an information-flow-based performance requires knowledge of a kind: of how to pick up information.

Experts take information from the environment when they need it, as discussed in an earlier section. In interactive software, this may well be from menus and screen prompts. Knowing how to use menus, learning search procedures such as scanning all the menus in turn looking for a suggestively named command, is an example of the kind of meta-knowledge that a user acquires. Guided exploration consists of making the user develop and exercise such search procedures (after perhaps some initial explicit training in them). Draper (1985) suggested that a mixture of consulting the manual, doing experiments, and searching various system files and source code were the kind of information-fetching procedures characteristic of experts in UNIX. Whatever they are in a given system, they are the most important kind of knowledge to teach a new user. The principle of using real tasks suggests that they should be taught (only) in the context of doing real and motivating tasks.

This idea of skill residing in knowledge of how to find information can be applied in two places; to what it is to be an expert (and so to modelling the state of knowledge a tutorial should aim to give a user), and to how a user will be operating within a tutorial.

The first question to be asked in trying to analyse the issue of writing manuals is what the aims of the manual are. Is it to be a tutorial or a reference manual? Most of the minimal manuals written to date set out to be instructional materials i.e. to be tutorials. However, in the light of the arguments above, we see that the distinction is not so self-evident. On the one hand, minimalist or action centred principles can (and should) be applied to both reference and tutorial manuals. On the other, the state of competence which a tutorial should aim to create in a learner is one of knowing how to use reference materials (including the reference manual) fluently. Therefore on this analysis, the design of a manual should begin by the adoption or (re)design of reference material, whose use will be the intended target of user competence. In a highly visual and interactive system, it may be that the menus (say) will comprise the whole of this material; more usually, it will include some printed material, perhaps a "cheat sheet", i.e. a one-page quick reference card, or a larger reference manual, or an integrated tutorial and reference manual. The test of successful learning from the tutorial materials will be performing tasks using this reference material, not the tutorial material if that is distinct.

The design of the tutorial material must include training in using reference material. Deliberate exercise in this will presumably form part of the tutorial. This is of course entirely consistent with the idea of guided exploration, where problems or tasks rather than solutions are given to the user. The tutorial material must also train the user in how to use the tutorial itself as well as the final reference material: it must be self-explanatory, as well as explanatory of the system and the final reference material. This necessity leads to the introductory material being bulky: for instance with explanations of notation, of how to press keys, of what basic terms mean. In contrast, quick reference material is typically just a list of command names and one or two word meanings: all the rest is left to the user to know e.g. how to combine commands, how to read the notation used. One design solution is to have a graded series of kinds of material, beginning with very full material, somewhat more minimal material for the middle of the tutorial, and only quick reference for the remaining, rarely used commands. This is possible because in most systems, a lot of necessary information is common across it and need only be learned once: both low level articulatory conventions (how to use the control key, how to use the menus), general syntactical rules (e.g. objects are selected first, then commands), and general error recovery procedures. This design has been adopted in a couple of cases - by Bryce (1990) in a manual for PageMaker, by ourselves in a manual for the UNIX editor "vi".

Our pedagogical objective, then, is to support the acquisition by new users of skilled performance at the interface given some specific reference manual. That reference manual may itself be designed using the same principles, and will be used during the tutorial (just as the program will be), but the tutorial manual may be distinct, or include parts that will not be referred to by experts. The test of learning will be successful task performance, given access to the reference (part of the) manual.

The next thing to analyse is what needs to be learned, and how we suppose learning will take place. One thing that needs learning is task-action mappings i.e. how to go from an internal mental specification of something you want to do (a goal or task) to the sequence of actions that will accomplish it (Payne and Green 1986). Ordinary manuals, especially reference ones, are like dictionaries i.e. they go from command names to meanings. This mapping is the wrong way round to support action. Thus a reference manual needs to be organised like a thesaurus, not a dictionary i.e. to have a way of going from meaning to command name or procedure. Similarly, a tutorial should not merely be a sequence of exercises of each command in turn. Performing those exercises will at best (and this is unlikely) leave a set of associations in the user's mind from command to effect: but can never give any practice in going from need to action, from goal to plan. Thus if our pedagogical aim in writing tutorial material is to allow users to perform tasks, then they need to be exercised in being given a task and having to find and execute a plan to achieve it. It is not enough merely to execute the plan by following a recipe, and to be told (or rather to have one's eyes pass over a printed assertion) that it achieves a goal. This will not even exercise, much less cause the learning, of task-action mappings.

A complete theory would need to be a theory both of content and mechanism for learning. Task Action Grammar (Payne and Green 1986) is a theory of content, showing part of what is wrong with traditional manuals that fail to provide this content because they offer only action-effect information. Carroll's (1989) theory offers some ideas about learning mechanisms or at least the occasions for learning. The information flow theory is a theory that the main content for supporting action is items such as command names (not generalisations), but that the important learning is a few generalisations (rules) on how to pick up and how to use the bulk of such items. It has no theory of learning mechanism; but is consistent with an expectation that learning will happen as a side effect of action, as in the SOAR model. However it might be possible to develop it to predict what features of an environment are good for exploratory learning, not just because they promote action (e.g. by being safe, fast, self-revealing and good at information delivery) but because they tend to give experiences from which general conclusions can be drawn (cf. Lewis 1988, Lewis *et al.* 1989). Learning from action is presumably sensitive to this: if the environment is unpredictable but with a good help system, the user might always be able to get through the task, but not to learn what actions would have worked without help.

To understand this in more detail, consider the experience of doing a tutorial. The actual task for the user is that of going through the tutorial: of obeying the instructions. It is not of learning anything by creating and executing a plan to discover the information, nor of some task they independently wish to achieve, such as writing a memo. This task of "doing a tutorial" is satisfied by reading printed instructions and executing them. Learning facts, or even noticing them, is not part of this. If the tutorial gives recipes –detailed instructions of what to type – then you do this. The checks that are natural to apply to this are to check the keystrokes if possible (if they are echoed). You are usually not told what to expect to see, and are not trying to achieve a goal of your own, so no other checks are possible. You may at most harbour a private hope that the result will be some entertaining visual demonstration. There seems to be a powerful effect of inducing an almost zombie-like mode of trust; of doing what you are told, and trusting that this will somehow benefit you. You have no way of checking that following instructions will teach you anything, since you have not created or been told the plan of how it will do that. In any case, your attention is typically fully occupied with finding the right line in the manual, working out what it might mean, and doing that. Furthermore, none of this involves any task-action mapping in the sense of tasks the system is designed to support (e.g. writing a letter of your own, in the case of a word processor), so it is unlikely to offer practice in the mental operations that are important to the practice it is supposed to teach.

Mack *et al.* (1983) describe an instance where "one learner misread the instructions for typing in a letter and found herself moving the cursor from place to place on the screen but not entering the actual text of the letter". The subject felt that this was a little odd, but constructed a story to make sense of it. A number of points can be made from this, such as people's facility at abduction – at constructing explanations to suit the observed facts. However perhaps most basically it illustrates the compliant frame of mind induced by tutorials based on following recipes. We ourselves find it a subjectively powerful effect, and despite thinking and working on these issues, fall into it when we act as subjects for a badly written tutorial. Largely independently of training and personality, following recipes seems to suppress constructive thought and with it, most learning.

In conclusion, we have seen that an action-centred approach can be extended to include ideas about learning, and so to provide a better theory of how minimalist instruction works. Furthermore, whereas Carroll's account considered only learning as the objective of minimalist materials, and the initial information flow account considered only action, in fact both need to be considered together. This conclusion is perhaps unsurprising: the traditional divide between learning and action in cognitive science is now being widely discarded, for instance both in connectionist theories and in the latest views of cognitive architecture based on production rules, such as SOAR embodies (Laird *et al.* 1987). Applying this to the development and study of minimal manuals does, however, mean some departure from practices up to now. For research, it implies a study of what exactly is being learned, as opposed to information that is necessary for action but is picked up, used dynamically but not retained. We need to understand both what information is needed to support action, and how much of it can be effectively delivered on demand (and by what techniques): the difference is what must be learned by the user. The next section tries to recast this into a more explicit set of directives for writing manuals, but first we summarise the theory proposed.

7.1. Summary

The principles comprising the "minimalist" approach flow from two unstated underlying (or "super") principles - organise the design around user activity, and design around the effect of users' prior knowledge. They might be seen as concerned with doing and learning respectively, but as we have seen these cannot be considered separately in practice. We derived a theory consistent with these from two related sources; a theory of action, and the idea of supporting such action by just-in-time information delivery instead of by previously learned knowledge alone. This theory is essentially action-centred, and is so in two respects: it asserts that manuals should be organised around user tasks and actions using the system, and that they must be designed with a view of how they themselves fit into and support action, e.g. when and why the manual will be opened, how users find the part they need, how this manual use relates to using the system and to the user's overall goals. Minimalism is a consequence (not a cause) of this. All action is dependent on information about what to do and how, and this information must be either known already, delivered by the machine, or delivered by the manual. Any deviation from minimalism will tend to overload the user's ability to find and pick up the information.

8. Conclusion: How to write a minimal manual

Carroll *et al.* (1987/88) offer a general three stage prescription:

- Design analysis –observations on needs and problems existing prior to designing a MM
- Subskill testing –systematic testing of each bit of the manual against what you expect it to achieve. Basically this is systematic iterative design using think aloud protocols.

- Criterion testing –final experiment on the overall effect in controlled conditions.

This is a high level prescription for designing a manual: a framework within which we must fit the actual design activity.

8.1. Designing a single item

One component is relatively clear from published work, at least by example, i.e. how to present an item within a minimal manual. An item is a unit of user action (often corresponding roughly to a system command). The manual item will usually contain the following components (although in particular cases one or more of these may be omitted):

The purpose or goal of the action.

This tells the user what the action will accomplish, but it thus also tells them the reason for reading and using this item, and so acts as a title for the item and is the user's method for selecting the item from the manual. Although often in one-to one correspondence to a system command, it will NOT usually be the command name. It might be "typing something" not "the insert command"; "getting rid of files" not "how to use **rm**".

How to perform the action.

These are the instructions for executing the action, though it can be almost blank if this is obvious to the user from screen prompts etc. (This does not make the manual item unnecessary: knowing that there is a system command to accomplish a given goal is important information in itself, motivating and constraining a search for it.) This section may have (or mainly consist of) hints about aspects the user is most likely to neglect e.g. "don't forget to press <return>".

How to recognise success.

Often this is obvious, but in principle and sometimes in practice the user must learn (by being told) how to recognise the effects e.g. in UNIX, no message means success; in some Macintosh applications graph output may appear in a buried window and the user must be warned to search for this until it is uncovered.

How to recognise, diagnose, and recover from errors.

This section is perhaps the greatest single source of the superiority of "minimalist" manuals. It is vital to supply information about error recovery *where* it is needed: immediately after the information about executing the action.

Other components.

More variable are some other possible components. For instance sometimes it seems impossible to avoid the wish to give some declarative explanation or "*comment*" even though users seldom read them. For instance, knowing about the hidden "clipboard" buffer that most editors have, makes sense of commands that copy text to and from it. If the manual is intended to support learning by guided exploration, i.e. if it is believed the users will do some experimentation beyond their own urgent tasks, then a component listing a set of *things to try* may be useful.

8.2. The overall design

Designing the presentation of each unit of action is however only part of the design task: the lower level. Above that is the question of how to organise the units into a complete manual, and more generally how to decide on and achieve its overall objectives.

As a first step towards formulating a prescription for how design a minimal manual (how to do the upper level of organisation), we can use the theory above to derive how not to write one, or rather why not to use the obvious and traditional way of creating documentation. That is: to form a syllabus of what there is to know, then to create a manual that follows that list. This leads to a classic reference manual, mainly a list of commands, plus sections on other levels of knowledge (e.g. the meanings of special keystrokes), and a section listing error possibilities. Using the minimalist approach on how to write each item or section would be only a partial amendment, improving the effectiveness of the section, but not of the manual as a whole including whether the user will find the section when it is needed.

To do the upper level of overall design, we should first consider the boundaries of what we must cover. It often turns out that a manual for a text editor, say, must include how to start up the machine, and enough of the surrounding system to allow for copying and deleting files. Omitting such material, on the grounds that it is someone else's documentation responsibility, simply means your users will be unable to use the editor on meaningful tasks. (One of the implications of a user-centred approach is that documentation will not divide along system-centred boundaries.)

We should next consider the final teaching objective: of having the user be able to operate like an expert, with whatever reference materials an expert uses. Then we can think of the stages of tutorial material aimed at moving the user towards that.

Potentially, there are four sequential stages to consider in the material to be presented, though you may or may not decide to mark this explicitly in its structure:

- Preliminary articulatory material, e.g. how to use the mouse, how the manual will denote the control key, what a message box looks like, how errors are signalled. Since this material will be relevant to many sections, it will make the manual bulky (and so support the user less effectively) to repeat it. Furthermore, without it the user is unlikely to be able to do anything. The difficulty is often how to teach it without resorting to special exercises and so failing to get started quickly on goals that are meaningful to the user.

- A minimal core set of commands (often a small subset of all the functions in the system) that is functionally adequate for accomplishing real tasks, presented in such a way that users can see their relevance. With this core, the user will be able to perform any task, even if inefficiently. After gaining access to this core, many users will feel they can use the system, and the rest of the material may be accessed only via reference material, as need arises. Alternatively other users may be prepared to go through further deliberate tutorial material (c) to improve their competence.

- An expanded set to give the user a reasonable efficiency at common tasks. For instance in a text editor, four cursor keys that move one position per keystroke are enough to move around the whole file, but force the user to do (say) 24 keystrokes to scroll on to the next page. At this stage, extra commands for scrolling a page at a time might be introduced. The set chosen here will still be a subset, but instead of being minimal will be chosen from analysis of the most common user tasks.

- The rest of the material. This can and should typically be presented in slimmed down version, perhaps only by a quick reference sheet, or guided exploration hints, or even an "ultraminimal manual" which simply lists tasks to attempt (relying on the system to deliver any information needed), as a way of ensuring users are made aware of what is possible and given a viable order to explore them in. This is reference material designed for expert users: you may wish to adopt existing material, or the desire to include a tutorial element (e.g. suggestions for learning by exploration) may cause you to redesign this too.

Particularly for small manuals, it may be possible to avoid treating these stages separately. The advantage is that then the user must only learn to deal with one format. However writing manuals for larger systems brings greater pressures: some of the material will certainly only be used in reference mode if and when needed, which means that users must be introduced to essential material in some other way. Conversely, the pressure to save space is greater in large manuals, but this is only possible if it is safe to omit repetitive material such as common error recovery procedures, how to use the control key etc. All of this requires a more explicit design plan for how users are expected to move through and use the material, and this seems to demand a staged manual. This is really a particular form of the general conflict between reference and tutorial goals; between authoring a network of material in hypertext and authoring particular paths through it.

8.3. Methods for designing minimal manuals

Given decisions about the overall framework for the (sequence of) manuals, the main design work consists of deciding *what* items (units of action) to include, and then *where*, *how*, and *whether* to present each.

For each item in the manual, *what* to present and *where* can be decided either (a) on the basis of relatively unstructured observation, (b) by systematic empirical data gathering, or possibly (c) predicted by analysis. For instance the original decision to write a minimal manual may be driven by existing unstructured experience (a), as is the case for the informal approximations to minimal manuals written by many teachers of computing who see the problems their students have with supplied material. Similarly, one could just write a manual from intuition and then debug the inclusion of items iteratively, by seeing which were unused or caused only trouble. Alternatively (particularly if the manual writer is not familiar with the application) method (b) may be applied to discover from experts what to put in a set of core commands, and from users in general what problems are common. For example, together with Judy Ramsay, we designed a manual for electronic mail on the basis of feature checklists, semi-structured interviews and incident diaries filled in by existing users. Using task analysis to deduce what commands are vital to achieve the basic tasks would be an example of (c).

System commands are not the only kind of action unit (item) to be sought out and designed into the manual—four main kinds must be considered:

The top level tasks (e.g. writing a letter in a word processor, dealing with the day's new messages in an electronic mail system). Part of the importance of this "semantic" level is that it is this which matches the user's prior goals, and so are the original motivation for using the system. Another part is to inform the user about goals which they have but would not guess were supported e.g. spelling correction. Another is to inform them about goals they will need to learn to adopt e.g. the need for backing up files, for cleaning out unwanted files to save space.

The subgoals corresponding to system commands at the highest level directly reflected in the system (the "central arena"), which are organised into plans (sequences of commands) to achieve the user's top level tasks. These should not be treated separately as a matter of principle (only user tasks are natural units in a user-centred approach), but in practice they are often used in different combinations and so economy is likely to lead to a separate section each for many commands, or sets of commands with similar effects.

Articulatory subgoals corresponding to actions needed to execute a system command. For instance how to invoke a menu command, how to scroll through a document, how to bring the right window to the top, what double clicking with the mouse means. Again, it is a desire for saving words that motivates treating these as separate items in the manual, even though direct support for meaningful user goals together with a desire to accommodate complete novices would itself cause such information to be duplicated in every item of the manual.

Error recovery procedures. Most observed user errors and problems can be dealt with by a component within the relevant manual item: giving reminders or recovery procedures for specific situations. However, in many systems, part of expertise is the acquisition of general recovery procedures to deal with problems that may arise at any time, not just as the consequence of specific user actions. For instance in UNIX, accidentally hitting <control>S may be done at any time, and will lock up the screen. Time-outs and system crashes are similarly not context specific, but manuals should deal with them. This is likely to mean separate special sections in the manual. It also leads to a problem of arranging for the user to find them when needed.

Another issue is *whether* to present an item in the manual. For instance if there is a visible labelled button to execute a whole task, there is no need to waste space in the manual, since users are likely to discover it by observation and experiment. A method for predicting the latter analytically is to draw up a list of what they need to know, and then to perform a rough "information audit" on the interface to see whether the necessary information about that item is already delivered by the interface or must instead be delivered by the manual. If the item is not represented on the screen nor is predictable from some rule the user knows, then there is a gap in information delivery to be filled by the manual. This approach can also be used to treat observations of user problems with manuals in a systematic way: each observed problem or impasse may be analysed for the missing information that caused it, i.e. would have prevented it if it had been effectively delivered. If this is immediately grasped by the observer, then it can be tested on the spot by trying an intervention in the form of a verbal delivery of the missing information. If that succeeds in "unsticking" the subject, then that is suggestive of the correctness of the analysis and of the form and content of an addition to the manual. Often however such interventions fail, and alternative ones have to be made, in effect compressing several design iterations (about *how* to present an item) into one episode with one subject.

8.4. A final word

One problem that emerges is the difficulty of writing a completely sufficient manual for all novices. For instance explaining how to use the mouse or the keyboard is going to create a bad impression of bulky irrelevance on any user who already has that knowledge. Observing novices without that knowledge, however, shows how important it is for them. This points up a little-studied problem that the more successfully a manual is pruned to the minimum, the more it becomes apparent that a manual should be tailored to the exact knowledge state of its intended user. Anything already known by the user should be omitted; but also users with particular prior experience may be vulnerable to errors that others are not, due to the "interference" (erroneous reasoning by analogy) from that experience.

9. Acknowledgements

This paper would not have been possible without the students who have worked with us, allowing us to pursue our interest in this subject: David Batchelor, Boo King Song, Craig Bryce, Julie Cairns, Frank McElhinney, Mary Meldrum, Judy Ramsay, and Christine Wilson. This work has also benefited from funding for work on developing user interface performance measurement methods by the Science and Engineering Research Council and the Department of Trade and Industry's Information Engineering Directorate, grant GR/F 39171/ IED4/1/1109.

10. References

Boo, K. S. (1988) A comparative study of self-training materials for novice users learning to use the electronic mailing system, M.Sc. dissertation, University of Glasgow.

Bryce, C. R. (1990) Minimal manual on Aldus PageMaker, M.Sc. dissertation, University of Glasgow.

Carroll, J. M., Smith-Kereker, P. L., Ford, J. R. and Mazur-Rimetz, S. A. (1987/88) The minimal manual, *Human-Computer Interaction* 3.

Carroll, J. M. (1989) An overview of minimalist instruction *Technical Report RC 15109*, IBM, Yorktown Heights.

Carroll, J. M. (1990) *The Nurnberg Funnel: Designing Minimalist Instruction for Practical Computer Skills* MIT Press, Cambridge, Mass.

Draper, S. W. (1985) The nature of expertise in UNIX. In B. Shackel (Ed) *Interact '84: First IFIP Conference on Human-Computer Interaction* North-Holland, Amsterdam.

Greif, S. (1986) Job design and computer training. *Bulletin of the British Psychological Society*, 39.

Laird, J. E., Newell, A. and Rosenbloom, P. S. (1987) SOAR: an architecture for general intelligence. *Artificial Intelligence*, 33.

Lewis, C. H. (1988) Why and how to learn why: analysis-based generalization of procedures. *Cognitive Science*, 12.

Lewis, C. H., Hair, D. C. and Schoenberg, V. (1989) Generalization, consistency, and control In K. Bice and C. H. Lewis (Eds) *CHI'89 Proceedings*, 1-5, ACM Press.

Mack, R. L., Lewis, C. H. and Carroll, J. M. (1983) Learning to use word processors: problems and prospects *ACM Transactions on Office Information Systems*, 1, 3.

Mayes, J. T., Draper, S. W., McGregor, A. M. and Oatley, K. (1988) Information flow in a user interface: the effect of experience and context on the recall of

MacWrite screens In D. M. Jones and R. Winder (Eds) *People and Computers IV*(conference proceedings of HCI'88). Cambridge University Press, Cambridge.

Meldrum, M. C. R. (1987) A comparative study of self-training materials for experienced users learning to use an advanced feature of word processing. M.Sc. dissertation, University of Glasgow.

Miller, G. A., Galanter E. and Pribram K. (1960) *Plans and the Structure of Behaviour.* Holt, Rinehart and Winston, New York.

Nickerson, R. S., and Adams, M. J. (1979) Long-term memory for a common object *Cognitive Psychology,* 11.

Norman, D. A. (1986) Cognitive Engineering. In D. Norman and S. W. Draper (Eds) *User Centred System Design.* Erlbaum, London.

Norman D. A. and Draper S. W. (1986) Introduction to the section on information In D. Norman and S. W. Draper (Eds) *User Centred System Design.* Erlbaum, London.

O'Malley, C. E., Bibby, P. and Waterson, P. (1991) What users know about menus in display based interactions (submitted to CHI'91).

O'Malley, C. E. and Draper, S. W. (1991) Are mental models in the mind? In Y. Rogers *et al.* (Eds) *Models in the Mind.* Academic Press, London.

Owen, D. (1986) Answers first, then questions In D. Norman and S. W. Draper (Eds) *User Centred System Design.* Erlbaum, London.

Payne, S. J., and Green, T. R. G. (1986) Task-Action Grammars: a model of the mental representation of task languages. *Human-Computer Interaction,* 2.

Scharer, L. L. (1983) User training: less is more. *Datamation,* .29, 7.

16

A Dictionary View of Technical Writing

Agnes Kukulska-Hulme
Aston University

Abstract

It is possible to view a technical field through the prism of its terminology and dictionary definitions provide a particular kind of description of a field. Traditionally, the dictionary has remained separate from the specialised texts, and has followed certain conventions as to content and form. Computer writing environments which provide access to on-line dictionaries and terminological data banks are making it possible to review the way that these tools are organised, bringing them closer to the organisation of texts. Dictionary look-up methods are also under review, and include information gathering strategies which go far beyond headword look-up. This paper explores the nature of the changes which have come about in the process of accessing dictionary information in the writing of technical texts, and proposes more effective ways of incorporating specialised background knowledge into the dictionary reference tool.

1. The relationship of dictionaries to writing

As someone who has been working on the design and development of computerised dictionaries for a number of years, let me firstly confirm what many of you will already know – namely, that the concept of a dictionary has undergone revolutionary change – and let me further say that in the context of writing, the most significant change is this: never before has the dictionary been allowed to get so close to text.

When you consider a typical defining dictionary, with its alphabetically ordered entries describing individual words, it is hard to see what affinity it might have with either the processor or the products of writing. Its segmented appearance leads one to believe, quite naturally, that it gives solutions to problems which concern individual, specific words. This obvious aspect conceals, however, a more important truth: that it is in practice impossible to consider one word in isolation from others, not only because words belong to a language system, but also because, when used in writing, they are the smallest fragments of a text, and are woven into its fabric. In the dictionary itself, words are defined through the use of other words; when in addition you take the view that it is in fact concepts rather than words that are described, it becomes clear that the first impression created by the dictionary is a deceptive one. Like all first impressions, it tends to linger, and hampers the development of a successful interaction between the dictionary and its user.

As soon as we suggest that the dictionary is not an assortment of entries but a system or structure made of interrelated parts, and that this view has implications for writing, we should hasten to add that the structure has gaps, and superfluous parts: missing or obsolete headwords, descriptions of meanings which are incomplete, or which are irrelevant to the task in hand. It is an imperfect structure, and one that doubtless can never be quite perfect.

The technical dictionary is a special case, and also a case in point. Specialised dictionaries are often compiled by people who are not lexicographers by profession but rather specialists in a particular field of knowledge. This means that the selection of information may be biased in favour of personal interests or idiosyncratic views. On the other hand, a subject specialist has the subject knowledge necessary for a systematic description of a specialised domain, where gaps and superfluous information are less likely to appear.

Let it also be said that there is no such thing as a 'perfect fit' between a dictionary and a target text. Typically, a dictionary covers a wider field than a given text, but then again a text will often straddle two or more subject fields. A technical dictionary represents a domain of knowledge, and so does a written text, but the chances of a good match between the territories they cover are remote. The dictionary will always be of limited use unless its data is derived from highly relevant textual material – a point which will be taken up again later.

It is possible to view a technical field through the prism of its specialised terminology, and dictionary definitions provide a particular kind of description of a field. A dictionary has the makings of a shortcut to knowledge, particularly if it is encyclopaedic in character, or if it is written specifically for students. A so-called 'student's dictionary' (e.g. Stratton and Hayes 1988; Watson and Hill 1984) will be written in clear, unambiguous language, with illustrations to clarify difficult points, and will include definitions of basic terms, explanations of methodological terms, and longer entries on topics representing significant areas within the subject field, providing summaries of these areas. It will aim to relate a number of seemingly diverse topics, and to draw together a range of subjects into an intelligent whole. It will consciously try to overcome the difficulties associated with the fragmented structure of traditional dictionaries.

If you look upon the dictionary as being a kind of technical reference manual, it can be said that, in one sense, the traditional dictionary is not the ideal technical manual, because the web of relationships between its terms and concepts remains implicit in its cross-referencing system and in its genus-differentiae definitions. It does, of course, have the advantage of coming straight to the point.

2. The functions of dictionaries

Dictionaries have always responded best when called upon to elucidate meanings. To aid understanding has been their first and foremost calling, but their application to text production is now being highlighted (see e.g. Sinclair 1987). If understanding is a forerunner to writing, then we have a secondary, indirect role for the dictionary. Synonym dictionaries more obviously play a dual role, since synonyms explain a headword and at the same time provide alternative words for writing (proscribed terms in the context of technical writing). Dictionaries specifically for encoding have often had the non-native speaker or language learner in mind, and have included valency dictionaries (e.g. Helbig and Schenkel 1973), dictionaries of word combinations (e.g. Dzierzanowska and Kozlowska 1982; Mel'cuk 1984; Benson *et al.* 1986), and dictionaries of contexts (e.g. Friederich 1979). There are just one or two examples of technical dictionaries which address the problems of usage (e.g. Godman and Payne 1979; Petrov 1983). (Further information on dictionary types can be found in Knowles 1988; Hartmann 1982).

When specialists write in their own technical area, it is assumed that they know their subject, and that they know the language in which they are writing. Both assumptions could be wrong ! Much of technical writing is communication between a specialist and a layman, or directed at an expert in a different discipline. For a subject specialist, deciding how to convey knowledge at the right level using the appropriate terminological and lexical elements of language is a process which requires support (it may even be more appropriate for the reader, not the writer, to determine those levels at the reading stage!). On the other hand, for a technical writer who is not fully conversant with a subject, clarification of concepts and background knowledge are needed, and can be provided by a dictionary reference tool.

Writing in a foreign language or for a foreign readership puts new demands on the writer. Writing for members of a different culture is writing within another conceptual framework - not just another set of words and sentence structures, although those are important, too. The support needed here is both of a linguistic and a conceptual nature, incorporating information on the cultural differences which must be taken into account. In a paper on writing for readers around the world, John Kirkman (1988) makes the point that it is not usually specialist jargon that causes most difficulty for foreign readers, but thoughtless use of "ordinary" language in between the specialist terms, often in a humorous or whimsical tone (one example he gives is the sentence: 'software is a fancy name for a computer program', written to try to alleviate the intimidating tone of computer jargon. Most foreign readers would sooner understand the word 'software' than 'a fancy name'!)

When we examine the nature of support that is required for technical writing, we can see why the standard bilingual or defining dictionary falls short of the mark. Siting it on a computer presents some advantages, but its usefulness remains limited unless more fruitful access routes to the information are made available, or unless the basis of its organisation and its content are changed, in recognition of the needs of different writers. The computer environment only potentially changes all the rules.

Dictionaries have always remained separate from writing, and have been compiled according to certain lexicographical conventions as to content and form. Giving access to a dictionary on the screen, even within writing software, does not bring it essentially closer to the process of composing text.

3. Complex and flexible searching

One way of tackling the problem of the remoteness of dictionary information is to make every element of it directly searchable, and to increase the information potential of the dictionary by making complex queries possible. This commendable approach is being championed within the CD-ROM versions of established dictionaries such as the Oxford English Dictionary and Harrap's multilingual dictionaries, and technical term banks like the Swedish TERMDOK CD-ROM. The OED's definitions and quotations are all open to key word search, and it can be queried on fields like specialist subject label and etymology, separately or as a combined search criterion. Harrap's 18 dictionaries may be searched for instance by parts of headwords, by key words of idioms, and by 'reverse' searching of the target language information of a bilingual dictionary. All 18 dictionaries, which are contained on one disk, can also be searched as one database; this is also true of TERMDOK, which consists of seven terminology databases (including AFNOR's NORMATERM, and the Canadian TERMIUM database).

The advantage of these search facilities is that they give much more pertinent information to the user. They also go some way towards adapting to a particular user's style of searching. Nevertheless, the length of time spent on formulating queries makes such strategies more suited to the discovery of meaning, or other 'research' activities, than to the process of writing, which shuns lengthy interruptions. Unresolved as ever is the conflict between, on the one hand, the need for appropriateness, accuracy, and subject knowledge (which can be fulfilled by the dictionary), and on the other, pressure of time to complete a piece of technical writing in order to keep down costs.

The 'flexible search approach' puts the onus on the dictionary user to formulate queries, to indicate where and how to search, and to make sense of the results. Even a 'knowledge based' dictionary may not solve that problem, since:

> "the farther we move away from 'data' towards 'knowledge', the more complex is the world that we want to be able to ask questions about. This means that not only the computer representation of the data or knowledge becomes more complex, but so too does the communication with the user in order to provide answers." (Waern 1989).

What must be recognised is that dictionary consultation is a skilled activity within the skilled activity of writing (see Kukulska-Hulme 1988). It is a complex, intentional (goal-oriented) activity, which involves a sensory-motor component as well as cognition, and shows learning effects over time. Its efficiency is assured by quick decision-making and by dextrous co-ordination with the other component skills of writing. The implications for dictionary design are two-fold: it should be possible to get to a search goal quickly, and without disrupting the business of writing.

4. 'Reusable' dictionary information

We have established that an improved dictionary for conveying information would be one that was much closer to the process and product of writing. It should not slow down writing, and ideally, it should speed it up. It could also improve the quality of the resulting text, making the text easier to understand (not just easier to write).

One way of speeding up writing and at the same time maintaining accuracy is to provide ready-made or reusable "chunks" of text. This is the basis for commercial programs like LinguaWrite (by Multilingua) which give users a database of phrases out of which business letters can be put together. It is also the thinking behind recent initiatives (e.g. by the Commission of the European Communities –McNaught 1987) to make available to translators databases of texts already translated in a given subject area. Examples of contexts and sets of collocates from the dictionary can serve a similar purpose on a smaller scale. The idea here is that the writer browses through dictionary data and 'lifts' relevant phrases without needing to retype, although some editing may be necessary. This is similar in concept to the PAL program (Predictive adaptive lexicon, developed by Iain Murray at the University of Dundee) which displays a selection of words that it thinks the user is about to type, after the first letter has been entered, and allows the user to select the correct word with a single keystroke. Below are examples of 'reusable chunks' for the tasks of (1) writing in English, and (2) translation into French or writing in French. The entry point in these examples is a key word (e.g. 'macro' in the example below).

(1) Word processing manual - macros

One of three types of data can be presented:

(a) 'raw' data extracted from texts

create a macro
edit a macro file later on
use a filename to name a macro
start the Print macro
use a macro to send a memo to the printer
add a macro to the primary file
define the entire macro over again
change the contents of the macro
saved in the macro file on disk
the macro is assigned to ALT-M
a macro lets you record keystrokes

(b) 'edited' data with gaps

create a macro
edit a macro file later on
use ... to name a macro
start the ... macro
use a macro to send ... to the printer
add a macro to the ... file
define the ... macro again
change the contents of the macro
saved in the macro file on disk
the macro is assigned to ...
a macro lets you record ...

(c) 'edited' data with examples

create a macro
edit a macro file later on
use A FILENAME to name a macro
start the PRINT macro
use a macro to send A MEMO to the printer
add a macro to the PRIMARY file
define the ENTIRE macro OVER again
change the contents of the macro
saved in the macro file on disk
the macro is assigned to ALT-M
a macro lets you record KEYSTROKES

(2) Printer manual - paper handling

alimentation en papier
chargement manuel du papier
chargement automatique du papier
réalignement du papier continu

réaligner le papier continu
tirer le papier continu vers l'arriére
insérer le papier continu
soulever le papier
déchirer le papier le long du pointilléinférieur
aérer le papier
enlever le papier
enlever le papier coincédans le circuit
charger du papier au-deláde la ligne de chargement

le presse-papier
renfermer le presse-papier

l'encoche de la plaque presse-papier
le bord supérieur de la plaque presse-papier

le guide-papier
utiliser le guide-papier coulissant
le guide-papier latéral
dépasser la languette du guide-papier

le plateau ápapier
insérer le plateau ápapier

les perforations du papier
aligner les perforations du papier
insérer les perforations du papier sur les ergots

As definitions gradually diversify into a profusion of less rigid or orthodox types (e.g. Collins' COBUILD dictionary/database), so too does the definition become a candidate for ready insertion from a dictionary into text. Questions of copyright may interfere, given that definitions will not normally be produced 'in-house'. Nonetheless, consider the following definition of 'fifth generation computer' in this light:

> "a knowledge-information processing system based on innovative theories and technologies, that can offer the advanced functions expected to be required in the 1990's, overcoming the technical limitations inherent in conventional computers. The previous four generations of computers have exploited successive developments of new hardware techniques but all were based upon the same Von Neumann architecture. The fifth generation machine breaks with this tradition and represents a unification of four current separate areas of research: knowledge based expert systems, very high level programming languages, decentralized computing and VLSI technology." (Macmillan Dictionary of Information Technology 1985).

For the technical writer with limited knowledge of a subject, a judicious configuration of terminological units in series relating to the domain's principal actions and objects, along with their attributes, can provide the kind of background knowledge that writers need. A computerised dictionary can be designed so that it highlights the relationships between concepts, and allows the user to focus on this aspect of information: logical, hierarchical, functional links. (For a detailed account of this type of dictionary design (Kukulska-Hulme 1989ab, 1990).

With regard to improving the comprehensibility of texts, reminders of previous uses of words (in current or earlier documents, or uses set down in guidelines, house standards, etc.) are an assurance of consistent usage for the native writer and a reassurance of correct usage for the non-native writer: consistency and correctness facilitate a reader's understanding of a text. Consistency can mean adhering to a given level of vocabulary, in the style of readability grading, and it can also mean transposing jargon terms into plain English or everyday terminology. As an example of this last point, consider the following terminology, encountered in documentation describing the use of a computerised diary application to non-expert computer users:

- Deleting an item from the calendar.
- Inserting an item into the calendar.
- Moving an item.
- Copying an item.

We all have diaries, but we do not talk about them in these terms, not even in formal, business contexts. We are used to 'making appointments', 'changing appointments', 'cancelling' them, 'crossing them out' from the diary, 'scheduling meetings', 'making sure a meeting does not clash with any other meeting', 'seeing if so-and-so is available', 'putting' something in our diaries, and so on. An everyday, familiar activity has been mystified, and the gates to understanding have been shut. Here are two 'translations' of section headings from the same manual:

Adding multiple items to your calendar
= Planning regular appointments and holidays

Viewing calendar items
= Looking at details of appointments

It would have been relatively easy to use the more familiar expressions at least in section headings of the manual, in the list of contents, in an index or a key to the contents page. A program which checked for the occurrence of data processing terms (delete, insert, etc.) and suggested familiar alternatives (cross out/remove, add/write in/put, etc.). would be useful in this context, and could be used by the writer either as a post-writing tool, or as a prompting tool in the course of writing. It should be noted that the reader would not normally consider using a dictionary or comprehension program in such a case: the problem is that to the reader of the manual, the data processing terms are not unknown, but merely abstract, in the sense of being unrelated to his or her experience.

5. A lexicographical contribution to writing

The crucial image conjured up here is that of a dictionary as a source of ready-to-use, appropriate information made available 'on tap', or as a constant trickle in the background, seen through a window on the screen, concurrently with the process of writing. Its main role is seen as prompting the writer. Where applicable, it may be implemented as a lexical analysis program rather than a dictionary of a more static kind – for instance, where the document being worked on is constantly being analysed for previous uses of a word. There are a number of commercially available text indexing and retrieval programs which can produce concordances, words lists and lists of collocations, e.g. OCP (The Oxford Concordance Program), TACT, WordCruncher, BRS/Search, AskSam, GOfer, Micro-concord, Textsearch.

Existing analysis programs specifically designed for writers, such as Writer's Work Bench (Macdonald *et al.* 1982), CRES - the Computerized Readability Editing System (Kincaid *et al.* 1981), Kieras' Advanced Comprehensibility Aid (Kieras 1989), or any of the simple commercial packages for 'style' checking (StyleWriter, Grammatik IV, PCProof/Bilingual PCProof) do not focus on lexis to the extent suggested here, and are largely designed as post-writing tools.

In designing support environments for writing, we should take into account the substantial existing body of lexicographic knowledge and experience. General language lexicography as well as specialised language terminography can contribute to our understanding of what information is needed in the process of encoding, and in what ways native and foreign-language writers, and writers for foreign readers, have different needs.

6. References and bibliography

Bennett, P. *et al.* (1986) *Multilingual Aspects of Information Technology.* Gower Press.

Benson, M., Benson, E. and Ilson, R. (1986) *The BBI Combinatory Dictionary of English - A Guide to Word Combinations.* John Benjamins.

Dzierzanowska, H. and Kozlowska, C. (1982) *Selected English Collocations.* PWN.

Friederich, W. *et al.* (1979) *Dictionary of English words in Context.* Lambert Lensing.

Gellerstam, M. (1988) Studies in Computer-Aided Lexicology, *Data Linguistica 18.* Almqvist and Wiksell.

Godman, A. and Payne, E. (1979) *Longman Dictionary of Scientific Usage.* Longman.

Goetschalckx, J. *et al.* (1982) *Lexicography in the Electronic Age.* North-Holland.

Hartmann, R. (1982) *Dictionaries and their Users.* Exeter University.

Helbig, G. and Schenkel, W. (1973) *Wîrterbuch zur Valenz und Distribution deutscher Verben.* VEB BI.

Ilson, R. (1985) *Dictionaries, Lexicography, and Language Learning.* Pergamon Press.

Kieras, D .E. (1989) An advanced computerized aid for the writing of comprehensible technical documents. In: B. K, Britton and S. M, Glynn (Eds). *Computer Writing Environments: Theory, Research, and Design.* Lawrence Erlbaum, Hillsdale, NJ.

Kincaid, J. P, Aagard, J. A., O'Hara, J. W. and Cottrell, L. K. (1981) Computer readability editing system. *IEEE Transactions on Professional Communications,* 24.

Kirkman, J. (1988) How 'friendly' is your writing for readers around the world

?. In E. Barrett (Ed). *Text, Context, and Hypertext.* MIT Press, Cambridge, MA.

Knowles, F. E. (1988) The role of dictionaries in developing writing skills In D. Ager (Ed). *Written Skills in the Modern Languages Degree.* CILT.

Kukulska-Hulme, A. (1988) Computer-assisted reference skill development. In D. Ager (Ed). *Written Skills in the Modern Languages Degree.* CILT.

Kukulska-Hulme, A. and Knowles, F. E. (1989a) L'organisation conceptuelle des dictionnaires automatiques pour textes techniques. *META,* 34 , 3.

Kukulska-Hulme, A. (1989b) Dictionnaires informatisés et traduction. *META* , 34 , 3.

Kukulska-Hulme, A., Knowles, F. E. (1989c) The Computer as a tool for the writer: the quest for the 'right' word. Paper presented at the *Man and the Media II AILA Symposium* 18-20 September 1989, Goethe-Institute, London.

Kukulska-Hulme, A. (1990) .Subject knowledge in computerised dictionaries. Paper presented at the *Maastricht-Lodz Colloquium on Translation and Meaning in Practice,* 4-6 January 1990, Maastricht, The Netherlands.

Longley, D. and Shain, M. (1985) *Macmillan Dictionary of Information Technology,* (2nd ed.) Macmillan.

Macdonald, N. H., Frase, L. T., Gingrich, P. S. and Keenan, S. A. (1982) The writer's workbench: Computer aids for text analysis. *IEEE Transactions on Communications, COM-30* (1).

McNaught, J. (1987) Round table on multilingual knowledge bases and linguistic applications, Report to the *Agence Linguistique Européenne and the Commission of the European Communities, Directorate-General XIII,* UMIST, Manchester.

Mel'cuk, I. *et al.* (1984) *Dictionnaire Explicatif Ee Combinatoire du Francais Contemporain.* Montreal UP, Montreal.

Petrov, V. *et al.* (1983) *Russian-English Medical Dictionary Phrasebook.* Russkij Jazyk.

Sinclair, J. M. (1987) *Looking up. An Account of the COBUILD Project.* Collins.

Sinclair, J. M. (Ed). (1987) *Collins COBUILD English Language Dictionary.* Collins.

Stratton, P., Hayes, N. (1988) *A Student's Dictionary of Psychology.* Edward Arnold.

Tomaszczyk, J. (1979) Dictionaries: Users and Uses. *Glottodidactica 12.*

Waern, Y. (1989) *Cognitive Aspects of Computer Supported Tasks.* John Wiley & Sons, London.

Watson, J., Hill, A. (1984) *A Dictionary of Communication and Media Studies.* Edward Arnold.

Whitcut, J. (1979) *Learning with LDOCE.* Longman.

Zgusta, L. (1971) *Manual of Lexicography.* Mouton.

17

Textbase Technology: Writing with Reusable Text

Richard A. Buchanan
Boeing Computer Services

Abstract

The Audit Program Generator System (APGS) is used to create technical documents by reusing text stored in the system. The main features of APGS are that the textbase contains reusable text elements; style and page layout is controlled automatically; the system is menu driven with hot-key bypass; an electronic revision trail is provided, authors can browse through the textbase; APGS is a Local Area Network shared resource. The paper describes how a team of analysts and writers (users of the system) developed the APGS software through the stages of requirement analysis, options analysis, functional specifications, design, coding, testing and implementation. The current version of APGS reduces average writing time from 40 hours to 4 to 8 hours.

1. Introduction

The database long ago solved the need to store, retrieve, analyse, and process numbers. While the database does an excellent job of storing and retrieving data and could be forced into holding text, it is not a very useful nor powerful writing tool.

More recently, systems such as hypertext solved the problem of storing textual information and rapidly retrieving it through keyword indexed searches. However, pure word processing prowess is not hypertext's forte.

A technology similar to but yet quite different from these two, the textbase, is now emerging. In the past, writing by reusing text was limited to boilerplate. The writer generally would bring in a large block of text and possibly modify it slightly. But what if you wanted to create new material, on the fly, by reusing text?

The answer is a word processing textbase. A textbase is composed of pieces of text called elements, which, depending on the situation, can be from one sentence to several pages long. The elements are stored in a logical manner that groups similar elements together so the writer can peruse an entire group of candidate elements for the one that comes closest to solving the current need. Similarly, the writer can seek elements that contain a key word or phrase. Thus, the textbase differs from databases and hypertext because it does not use key fields or an indexing system to locate elements. Rather, it uses the associative properties of the elements themselves to locate text. Using the textbase in conjunction with a word processor, the writer can save time by combining and manipulating reused text to create a new document.

The best way to demonstrate how this works is to examine an actual case study. This paper describes the original problem, the textbase system and how it works, and the method used to solve the problem.

2. The problem

A group of seven technical specialists for an audit organisation creates highly structured documents that instruct loaned managers on auditing management control systems for good business practices and compliance with US government and internal Boeing regulations.

An audit program document begins with a scope and objective for the entire audit and is divided into multiple sections, each with its own scope and objective. A section is further divided into subsections containing an objective, expected results, and numbered verification steps. A reference list of recommended reading, a revision history log, and a table of contents complete the document.

Formerly, each specialist used a popular word processor on a stand-alone Compaq 286 personal computer and stored the document files on floppy diskettes with no effective method to locate existing text. Some of the specialists attempted to minimise typing by creating a whole generic document and then modifying it. In many cases, so much research and modification was necessary that it was easier to just start fresh.

Most of these writers were marginally computer literate and none was an effective typist. The average completion time for a program document was 60 hours, of which 75% was clerical in nature. There was no conformity between documents created by different writers because of a lack of any format or style standards. There was a standing rule that every verification step in the document should have a document reference relating its reason for inclusion. Since there was no master reference list and the titles were incredibly long, references were not usually included.

In 1988, they realised the inefficiency and limitations of the current situation and wanted to find a better computer solution. They had identified the following major requirements:

- Store text from existing and future documents.
- Provide multiple means of locating text.
- Provide powerful word processing capabilities.
- Provide data integrity for the text.
- Be menu-driven and easy to use.
- Share text among the specialists.
- Produce documents with a uniform look.
- Compile a recommended reading reference list for each document.
- Create work files compatible with Microsoft Word for field use.
- Have adequate user documentation.
- Reduce the 60-hour writing time to about 35 hours.

3. The solution

The group's first solution was to purchase an off-the-shelf software product, get help in establishing a Local Area Network (LAN), and adapt the system to meet their needs. Much to their surprise, no such product existed. There are several reasons for this. Due to the highly specialised nature of their vocation, data processing professionals would not know what a technical specialist is. They also wouldn't know what the specialist's job entails nor how it is done. Therefore, the solution was not out there waiting for them.

The specialists realised that they needed help and contacted their Boeing Computer Services support organisation, who worked with them as a team to create the Audit Program Generator System (APGS).

3.1. Overview

The system hardware consists of their existing personal computers linked via a LAN to a Compaq 386 server with 300Mb of storage and two laser printers. In addition, there is a Compaq 286 communications server linking the network to Boeing mainframes and networks.

The system software is a high-powered publishing application using XyWrite III Plus by XyQuest, Inc. of Billerica, MA, as an engine. All formatting and page layouts are pre-defined to the system which supplies them automatically, freeing the specialist to be concerned more about content than looks. All numbering, such as section and subsection heads and verification steps, is automatic. If material is inserted, deleted, or moved, all numbers reflect the change instantly.

OPERATIONS	EDIT	PRINT	TEXTBASE	DICTIONARY	WINDOWS	HELP	QUIT

Figure 1. The main menu

	File Handling Hot-Key Assignment
Ctrl + A	Abandon the current document without saving
Ctrl + C	Create a new docu,emt
Ctrl + F	File document away & stop edit
Ctrl + I	Issue a document & start revision record keeping
Ctrl + L	Library document placement and retrieval
Ctrl + N	Name change of document
Ctrl + R	Retrive a document
Ctrl + S	Save document & continue edit
Ctrl + W	Workpaper document creation in MSWord format
	Press Esc for the previous menu.

Figure 2. The operations menu

A menu system provides an easy way to learn APGS but can be totally bypassed with hot-keys by an experienced user. By striking two keys, the writer can request the main menu display. When the user makes a selection, APGS displays the appropriate pull-down menu showing the available tasks. The pull-down menu also shows the hot-key combination that directly performs the task. Figures 1 and 2 show the main menu and a sample pull-down menu.

GETTING STARTED	Escaping	Ordering (.ORD files)	Textbase structure
Abandoning a file	Exporting	Outlining	Thesaurus
Adding directories	Exporting several elements	Pagination	Titles
Additional references	Filenames	Printing	Underline text
Browsing elements	File operations	Quitting	Unzooming windows --------
Bold text	Forced page breaks	Reference request	View a new directory
Bullets	Global changes	Release highlighted text	Windowing
Bypassing menus	Highlighting text	Removing a textbase element	Work in progress(WIP) --------
Cancelling actions	Hot-Keys	Restoring deleted text	Workpapers
Change document name	Importing all	Retrieving a file	Zooming windows
Copying text	Importing elements	Saving a file	
Creating a document	Inserting notes	Search/Replace	
Cursor control	Issuing (.ISS files)	Sections	
Deleting heads	Italicise text	Show/Hide format markers	
Deleting lines	Library (.LBR files)	Spell checking	
Deleting page breaks	Locating text	Steps	
Deleting text	Menu selections	Storing a file	Move highlighting with cursor keys – and press RETURN to select.
Dictionary (Personal) Moving text	Subsections		
Directory structure	Normal text	Substeps	
Editing	Notes	Text modes	Press Esc to exit.

Figure 3. Main help index

A quick reference card is the only user documentation that is not on-line. The help system consists of a main index of topics for the user to select from. A help panel for each topic describes the subject. Related topics appear as a list of key words. With this cross-referencing feature, the users can move from panel to panel until they find the information that they require. Figures 3 and 4 show the main index and a sample help panel.

Browsing through textbase elements

You can browse through related elements in the textbase looking for the best one to fit your needs.

Option 1: Select TEXTBASE from the main menu and choose Browse.

Option 2: Press Alt + B

APGS will ask you to select the Contractor Selected Element (CSE) and also the area of the textbase and type of generic text element that you want to explore. APGS will then display a listing of all the related elements in the directory with the first element highlighted. You can move the highlighting with the up and down cursor keys. When the desired element is highlighted, it is ready to import.

Related topics:

Editing	Importing all steps	Importing elements	Ordering (.ORD files)
Removing a textbase element	Textbase structure	View a new directory	Windowing

Press Esc for the previous menu.

Figure 4. Sample help panel

Accurate, complete reference titles reside in a master list so the writer obtains a reference with a minimal number of key strokes. When the writer prints an audit program, APGS automatically generates a table of contents, a reference list, and a revision log.

3.2. Window environment

The user views APGS through the following seven windows.

The document window (1) is the workspace where the user creates and edits Audit Programs.
The outline window (2) contains an outline of a document currently in the document window.
The locate window (3) displays all files in the textbase that contain a key word or phrase.
The browse window (4) displays all elements in a selected directory.
The export window (5) temporarily holds an element prior to insertion into the textbase.
The reference window (6) contains the master reference list.
The activity window (7) contains a user activity logfile.

3.3. Textbase structure

The textbase is a DOS tree structure divided into thirteen categories. Similar elements are grouped together as separate files in directories. Figure 5 below shows a typical category tree and the type of element stored at each level. In the figure, the directory names relate to a coding system. The EP audit level stands for engineering. EP-1 represents engineering and design management, while the EP1-1 section level is design, co-ordination, communication, and status. The EP1-1-1 subsection holds design, EP1-1-2 is co-ordination, EP1-1-3 is communication, and EP1-1-4 is status. In this manner, a very broad scope is divided into manageable pieces.

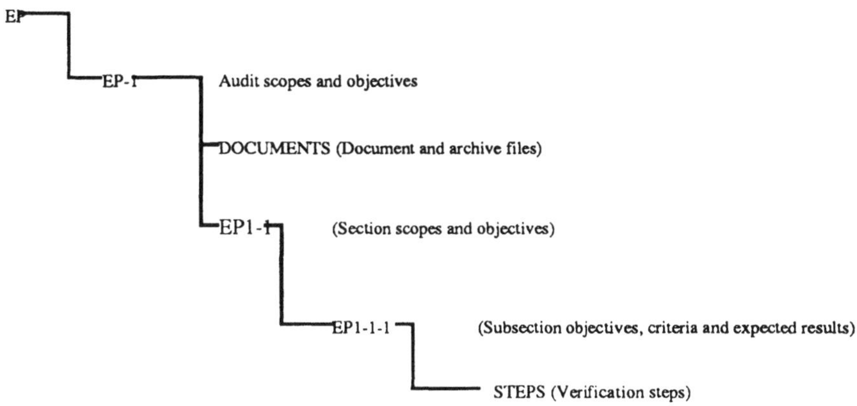

Figure 5. Sample directory structure

3.4. Security

To provide security, a specialist is responsible for one or more categories and is the only one authorised to add, delete, or edit elements in that category. A password-based system ensures that only those authorised have access to particular areas of the textbase. The other writers are allowed to browse through each others' areas but can only obtain copies of text; they cannot alter the element in another specialist's category in any way.

3.5. Data integrity

For data integrity, APGS automatically checks the spelling of an element before placing it into the textbase. A system rule requires that all verification steps must contain a valid reference from the master reference list. APGS enforces this rule and will not place steps without a reference into the textbase.

3.6. Creating a document

When the user wants to create a new document, APGS automatically pulls in several pages of boilerplate material used in every document into a new Work In Progress (.WIP extension) file. In the boilerplate, headings for the audit scope and objective paragraphs act as place holders, ready for the writer to select an appropriate element from the textbase. After the writer informs the system as to which part of the textbase to go to, APGS displays the elements and highlights the first one. The specialist can browse through all these related elements looking for the one that best meets the need. The system will import the currently highlighted text when the writer presses two keys. APGS will place a copy of the text at the current cursor location in the document. The writer can further customise the text to the new documents needs.

The specialist continues to build the document by requesting further sections and subsections and then filling in the blanks with text from the textbase. The user can also type in new text and if desired, export it into the textbase for later reuse. In this manner, the writer creates the audit program document very quickly with minimal typing.

3.7. Issuing a document

The author releases a completed program document to an auditor by issuing it. This process makes the document official and requires the tracking of all subsequent revisions in a log stating the author, date, and the reason for the revision. After making a revision, the specialist must re-issue the document and update an electronic log. When APGS detects that a document was altered since last issued or re-issued, APGS will not print it until the revision log has been updated.

3.8. Archiving a document

When the field auditor completes an audit program and responds with the results of the audit, APGS places the document in an archive library. An archived document may be printed, but because it is an historical document, it cannot be altered in any manner. However, the system will copy the contents of an archived document into a new Work In Progress file to create a new document.

4. The method

The entire development process for this system emphasised team work. The basic team consisted of two systems analysts and all of the specialists working together toward a common goal, the creation of an effective productivity tool.

The Software Development Life Cycle (SDLC) process used to develop this system consists of the following phases:

- Requirements gathering.
- Options analysis.
- Functional specification.
- Detail Design.
- Coding.
- Test.
- Implementation.

4.1. Requirements gathering

All of the specialists and one of the systems analysts attended a facilitated consensus session to determine exactly what the requirements for the new system would be.

A consensus session occurs behind closed doors with each attendee having one vote. A non-voting facilitator (moderator) is present to keep the session on track. The group lays all of the possible needs and concerns on the table and discusses them thoroughly. At the end of the session, the members vote on those issues to be incorporated into the formal requirements document.

This is the cornerstone to a useful outcome of any endeavour. In this case, 95% of the functional features were identified from the outset of the project through this process. The remaining 5% were discovered during the coding phase through prototyping.

4.2. Options analysis

One of the systems analysts took the results of the requirements gathering and identified several possible solutions that were then reduced to five:

- Customised XyWrite III Plus on a LAN.
- A mainframe text retrieval system linked to a personal computer.
- A mini-computer hypertext system linked to a PC-based network.
- A mainframe database system linked to a personal computer.
- Modify the current PC word processor.

An expert on each of the possible solutions, a representative for the specialists, and two systems analysts were voting members in a three-day facilitated consensus session. The consensus team created a matrix for the five potential solutions based on the following considerations:

1. *Requirements satisfaction.*
    - Multiple retrieval methods.
    - Word processing capability.
    - Create reference list.
    - Standardised format and style.
    - User friendly and easy to use.
    - Data integrity.
    - Microsoft Word compatibility.
    - Adequate documentation.
2. *Technical considerations.*
    - Hardware architecture.
    - Software architecture.
    - Communications architecture.
    - Data architecture.
    - Security.
    - Remote access.

3. *Management considerations.*
   - Project complexity.
   - Resource availability.
   - User training.
   - System documentation.
   - Growth of user pool.
   - Compatibility with overall audit plan.
   - Risk.
   - Costs.
   - Schedule.
4. *Major advantages and disadvantages.*

The group completed each matrix and then thoroughly discussed and analysed them. At the end of the third day, a vote indicated the group's consensus for the solution - XyWrite on a LAN.

4.3. Functional specification

The two systems analysts created a document detailing all the functions needed to fulfil the requirements in the selected XyWrite III Plus environment. This document also specified the scope of the project, the responsibilities of all team members, general requirements of the system, and the style and format of the audit program documents.

The following description of the page layout and style definitions shows the level of detail used to cover all the aspects.

APGS will automatically adhere to the following format standards.

Cover Sheet:

Title	Multiple lines in Times Roman 12 pt.type located in a 4"x1-3/4" box whose upper left-hand corner is 3" from the top and 3-1/4" from the left side.
Author, Revision Date	Bold Times Roman 10 pt. located in the lower right-hand corner with the first character of each line aligned in columns.

General Page Layout:

Dimensions	8-1/2"x11"
Top margin	1/2"
Bottom margin	1/2"
Left margin	1-1/4"
Right margin	1"
Maximum lines per page	55

Tab settings	Every 5 characters
Running header	The document title in Italic Times Roman 10 pt., centred 1/2" above the first line of text.
Running footer	The plan number and revision on the far left and the page number on the far right in Times Roman 8 pt. with the first page of the document being Page 1.
Head levels	Level 1 - Un-numbered uppercase bold Times Roman 12 pt. Whitespace 2 lines above, 1 below. Level 2 Numbered (1.1) uppercase bold Times Roman 12 pt. Whitespace 2 lines above, 1 below. Level 3 - Numbered (1.1.1) initial cap bold Times Roman 12 pt. Whitespace 2 lines above, 1 below. Level 4 - Un-numbered initial cap bold Times Roman 10 pt. Whitespace 1 line above, 1 below.
Steps	Numbered (1) in Times Roman 10 pt.
Sub-steps	Numbered (a) in Times Roman 10 pt.
Standard typeface	Times Roman 10 pt.
Emphasis typeface	Bold Times Roman 10 pt.
Bullets	Solid black square followed by a tab.
Table of contents	Follows the title page and contains the first three head levels.
Reference list	Initial cap underlined Times Roman 10 pt. set at tabs 5 and 30. Whitespace 1 line above and below.
Recommended reading	Times Roman 10 pt. set at tab 22.
Footnotes	Not supported. Possible Phase II.

Automatic pagination:
Sections must start on a new page.
A page cannot break inside a verification step or sub-step.
Widow and orphan control set to a minimum of two lines.

Printer:
Hewlett-Packard Series II with Times Roman soft fonts.

4.4. Detail design

The design analyst took the functional specification and determined the design necessary for XyWrite to accomplish all the required tasks.

The design document defined the file naming conventions, directory structure, and the required system files. It described all the program modules required to accomplish the requirements, how they interact, and what data they pass or use.

The most difficult feature was changing the command-line- driven XyWrite product into a menu-driven one. Although not an original requirement, to overcome the 'unfriendliness of a menu-driven system to an experienced user, the designer added a hot-key (macro) bypass system for improved speed.

4.5. Coding

Coding consisted of creating a number of macro files, customising printer drivers and help files, developing a user interface, and writing some Pascal utility programs.

The development occurred in a prototypical environment. As a portion of the system was completed, the analysts would walk the specialists through the new addition. They could get a feel for how the system worked and provided valuable feedback when a feature could be altered to make it work better. This interactive environment spawned innovation for new features not in the original requirements as the systems analysts learned more about the specialists and they more about software development. This method truly gave the users a sense of ownership which helped the developers to provide them with an effective tool. This iterative action continued throughout the coding phase.

To shorten the development time for this project and to emphasise the team approach, all the coding was done at the specialists' work site. Any functional questions were resolved immediately, thus avoiding the problems of inter-site communications.

4.6. Test

Each system function was alpha tested as a unit by the design analyst when coding was completed. Next, the other analyst tested the function in conjunction with other parts of the system, such as the help and menu systems, to detect any ripple effects. Any software problems encountered were formally recorded, tracked, corrected and then retested at block points during this period.

A systems analyst conducted a system test by creating, revising, printing, archiving, and retrieving several complete documents. Next, the analyst tested each individual function for performance as outlined in the functional specification document. The specialists' acceptance and verification test was the final test before implementation.

4.7. Implementation

Boeing Computer Services turned the finished product over to the specialists in September 1989. APGS is currently operational and is approximately 50% populated with text. The specialists estimate that it will take approximately 8 hours to complete a document when the textbase is fully populated, instead of the former 60 hours or the target of 35 hours.

5. Conclusions

Many categories of writers could avail themselves of a system like this. Anyone who creates material with great similarity such as contracts, legal documents, catalogues, sales product specifications, maintenance manuals, or even formula fiction is a likely candidate.

As with many specialised needs, the perfect computer solution may not exist when you need it. With proper computer support and an informed, willing user community, you can build a solution for the problem at hand.

It is relatively easy to design and create an effective system that does the job right the first time, if you adhere to two simple but often overlooked rules.

- Have a structured approach similar to SDLC and follow its intent.
- Work together as a team toward a common vision.

6. Acknowledgements

Just as APGS resulted from a team effort, so did this paper. I want to thank all the team members for their considerable help.

The Team:

Richard Buchanan, *Systems Analyst*
Patia Woods, *Systems Analyst*
Wayne Gunderson, *Technical Specialist Senior Manager*
Jon Brumbach, *APGS System Administrator, Technical Specialist for Manufacturing Operations*
Bill Goff, *Technical Specialist for Engineering/Program Management/Flight Operations*
Ron Schei, *Technical Specialist for Quality Assurance/Safety*
Its Shiotani, *Technical Specialist for Contracts/Finance*
Al Davidson, *Technical Specialist for Materials Management/Inventory Management*
Fred Kulczycki, *Technical Specialist for Compliance Review*

18

A Hypertext-Based Support Aid for Writing Software Documentation

Gary Born
SD-Scicon

Abstract

Medium-sized and large software organisations base their operations upon a body of written standards and procedures. These provide guidance to staff on the appropriate way of handling ordinary business and of filling in forms and other documents. Unfortunately, the written information is usually difficult to understand and interpret.

This results in inefficiencies and errors in applying them, with consequent poor quality and loss of profit. The staff themselves suffer morale problems, as they struggle to understand the complexities of technical and management documentation. Finally, it can result in loss of confidence by the organisation's clients.

Traditional training methods share a common drawback: they are employed separately from the task in hand. As we know from experience, the application of standards in *theory* is very different from the *application*.

Thus, these separated training methods provide a poor understanding of the real standards and are ineffective in improving the poor morale that can accompany their application. It is more effective to provide a tool that is integrated with the application of the standards. A team within SD-Scicon has done so by developing a Software Engineering Support System (SESS) on personal computers.

The essence of the SESS is its integration of three accepted technologies into a single system:

- **Hypertext**, to provide access to the written standards and other assistance as the user carries them out.
- **Knowledge Based (Expert) Systems**, to guide the user through the standards, to produce draft documents tailored to the individual project, and to perform automated quality audits of documents
- **Word processing**, to enable the user to create documents and forms required by the standards

The integration of these technologies results in a system tailored to users' needs. Novice users can browse through the standards and obtain help in completing documents. More experienced users use the system mainly as a word processor, with occasional use of hypertext to reference standards and use of the self-audit capability to check the quality of their documents.

1. The problem of writing software documentation

In producing professional software, developers produce a mass of printed documentation. This is essential to the development process, as documents provide the basis for communication between team members, achieving project milestones, checking the quality of the systems and maintaining the system after it is commissioned. Examples of such documents include quality plans, requirements specifications, designs and test plans. For a large system, the documents can number in the hundreds or even thousands.

In principle, there should be no problem in writing software documentation. As it is at the heart of the process of developing software, relevant documents should be produced with little fuss. Unfortunately, this is often not the case, due to the following factors:

- Software documentation is complex and difficult to write.
- Professional software development organisations have large and complicated procedures which must be followed in writing documentation, yet are hard to understand and to carry out.
- Authors of documentation are often inexperienced and do not understand what they should be writing or the relevance of the documents.
- It is difficult to re-use documents produced on other projects, which would save time and effort.
- It is difficult to check documentation for quality, veracity and consistency.
- It is difficult to maintain documents as the project makes changes and extensions.

This is a long and depressing list of difficulties, and the problem appears even worse from the individual's perspective. First he or she must understand the documentation system and its relevant standards. This requires training or previous experience or both. While they can get by just by reading the standards, this will result in a poor quality document if not supplemented by training or experience.

After understanding the standards, the staff member must identify which standards and which parts of them are relevant to the specific project and document being produced. Then the document must be produced, in accordance with the standards. Finally, the document must be reviewed for quality and conformance with standards, either by a Quality Assurance representative or by line management.

A number of existing, but non-automated, approaches assist this process. Printed guidelines or manuals provide limited guidance in applying the standards, but they mostly are confined to general information which is hard to adapt to a particular project's requirements. Some companies have produced "boilerplate" documents serving as a model for projects. Another method is a set of guidelines indicating how to write documents for a project of a particular type. These methods introduce their own problem, as the author has yet more materials to digest, and may still lack the understanding of the underlying principles necessary to customise an individual document.

When totalled, the problems created by this unsystematic approach to writing documents can be substantial. For a large software organisation (such as my own company), we have hundreds of projects underway at any one time, and each must follow company procedures. The quality plan alone can take several days to write.

For the software industry as a whole, the results are not only substantial extra time and expense, but also morale problems, additional training expense and, if corrective action is not taken, a reduction in quality of the delivered software.

With this background, it is easy to see that the software industry has a great deal to gain by providing computer aided support tools for documentation. SD-Scicon have taken a lead in this area by developing tools for intelligent documentation production, as described later in the paper.

2. Previous work

At present, we are not aware of work specifically geared to documentation in its complete sense. While massive resources have been devoted to CASE tool development, these only provide a part of the documentation needs of projects. Certainly they provide a formal description of the requirements and designs of the system, as well as managing record keeping of documents ("configuration management"). But they do not address the problem of *writing* documents, which involve non-formalised concepts, without a symbolic notation, which can be expressed only in ordinary language.

At SD-Scicon, we have been working on related problems since 1984. Our first efforts resulted in an expert system for reviewing test plans and test organisation (Born 1985). This assisted reviewers of the document, but still could not provide assistance in drafting and editing the document.

Our first breakthrough came early in 1989, when we produced a quality plan generation system as part of an ESPRIT project (Bruce 1989). This system, QPLAN, advised project managers on which standards applied to their project and on the appropriate sections for the document. It also included a word processor to write and edit the quality plan. Later, we added hypertext, so that the project manager could access the standards on-line (Born 1989).

We have continued work on this system, which has been extended to include review of the document and automatic generation of the draft document. This is the system which is described in the remainder of this paper. It runs on PC compatibles of AT performance or better.

3. Intelligent document production

The phrase Intelligent Document Production (IDP) is a general term referring to the production of documents with knowledge-based support. As used in this paper, it refers specifically to the use of expert system, hypertext and other 'intelligent' techniques to enhance the production of standard documents required for project work.

Another key concept in IDP is that all these techniques are fully integrated in a single system. One of the drawbacks of existing manual systems is that they require the author of a document to shift between documents and media. At the least, the author must use two media, the printed standards and the computer-based word processor. In practice, it is worse, with the unfortunate user dealing with the standards, guidelines for applying the standards, examples of similar documents and so on, in addition to the word processor. In IDP, we integrate all the user's requirements on the screen, so that all materials are available together and organised efficiently for referencing and for document production.

3.1. Technologies used in intelligent document production

Figure 1 contains a summary of the technologies used in IDP, the functions they provide and the uses they cater for.

Technology	Functions	Uses
Hypertext	Indexing and referencing information	Structuring standards Rapid reference to standards
	Browsing Referencing the standards	Learning the standards
Knowledge Based Systems	Browsing	Directed, context- specific browsing
	Document creation	Advice on which documents to create and how to write them Generation of draft texts
	Auditing assistance	Auditing texts
Word Processing	Editing texts	Creating documents Editing documents
	Scanning documents	Auditing the document

Figure 1. Technologies and their functions and uses in IDP

3.1.1. Hypertext

Hypertext refers to the storage of documents on-line within a computer system, with the possibility of accessing information with built-in links in the documents. As used in IDP, the standards are always available on-line, and the user can call up the appropriate parts of the standards while working on a document.

Hypertext is used in IDP in the following ways:

Structuring the standards
In order to store texts so that they can be accessed easily, it is necessary to structure the standards coherently. This has considerable side benefits even for paper-based standards, which are easier to read after the structuring process.

Learning the standards, via browsing
Hypertext provides a simple way to understand documents, by allowing the user to browse through them. Jargon words and cross-references are immediately clarified with a click of the mouse.

Reinforcing (refreshing) the standards
If the user has not used a standard for some time, applying it will be difficult. It is awkward and time-consuming to read the whole standard cover-to-cover. Hypertext provides a ready solution to this problem, since the user browses only through the information of his or her choice. In IDP it is particularly appropriate, since the hypertext will be relevant to the document currently being written.

Rapid referencing/indexing
One of the more frustrating aspects of writing project documents is the need constantly to break off and look up information from the standards manuals. First the user must find where the information is contained (and there can be hundreds of different standards in a professional software company!). Then the user must strive to interpret the standard for his or her requirement. Hypertext in IDP radically reduces this problem by referencing only the parts of the standards which are relevant to the section of the document currently being written.

Different views for different user communities
The standards are used by a variety of user communities, not merely for project managers and leaders. These include technical staff on projects, line management and document reviewers. By their nature, paper-based standards can provide only one view. Hypertext can provide as many views as there are user communities, since the computer provides an unlimited number of ways of 're-configuring' documents before they are displayed on the screen.

3.1.2. Knowledge based systems

While knowledge based systems refer to a large number of techniques, in IDP they generally are confined to rule-based systems for guiding the user through the standards and their use. For example, the following functions can be provided with a rule based approach.

Assistance in browsing
Rules can be provided to supplement normal hypertext browsing, by making it context specific. In IDP, this would involve the system keeping track of which

part of the document is currently worked on, and then directing the browsing to concentrate only on the relevant parts of the standards.

Assistance in knowing which documents to create
Rules are provided to guide the user through the documents required for the project. Typically this would always include a quality plan, but other documents will vary. For example, a study may require only a feasibility study or requirements document, while a development project will require many more documents for design, coding and testing.

Assistance in creating documents
Rules can be provided to assist the user in putting together the document, and a number of organisations provide guidelines to direct authors through the standards for a particular project.

The SD-Scicon IDP system automates this with a rule-based system which asks the user questions about the project, and then uses this information to suggest how to write the document. It then takes it another step by preparing a draft of the document based on that information.

Assistance in auditing documents
The job of auditing a project document can be as difficult as writing it, and it requires a similar knowledge of the appropriate standards and how they apply to particular projects. An IDP system can assist this function by providing a rule-based auditing assistant – the system provides the questions about the document, based on the standards. It is still up to the auditor to decide on the quality of the document, based on the supplementary information about quality provided by the system. After receiving answers about the document, the system uses its rules to decide which parts, if any, fail to meet the company's standards.

While such a system does little more than current manual practices, it operates much more efficiently, doing the same work faster and with more reliable and consistent results. It also relieves auditors of much of the routine tasks associated with an audit.

3.1.3. Word-processing

Obviously there is nothing unusual about using word processing to create project documents. What an Intelligent Document Production does is to provide many additional facilities to a normal word processor. These are described above, and include immediate on-line referencing of required information in the standards, guidance about what to write, and auditing capabilities. The IDP system can also use in-built rules to generate rough documents, which the user can edit immediately with the word processor provided.

3.2. The user's view

The following groups of users can make use of an IDP system for software development:

- **Project Managers and Leaders** writing the documents required by company standards.
- **Line managers and corporate staff** familiarising themselves with the standards and how they are used in practice.
- **Quality Assurance** staff and others involved in checking documents and compliance with company standards.
- **Producers of standards** responsible for writing, issuing and maintaining the standards.

They would use the IDP system for the following activities.

Learning and reinforcing the standards
One of the biggest problems currently is familiarising staff with the standards and the procedures for writing project documents. The IDP system would be of great value here, since it automatically adapts itself to the needs of the individual. As he or she becomes more experienced and familiar with the standards, the system's training function is less used, but with full on-line referencing available whenever required.

Creating documents
Project managers and leaders, and occasionally other members of project teams, would use the IDP system to create documents. At a simple level, the system would lead them through the standards appropriate to their project and point out what they require of the documentation. At a more sophisticated level, the IDP system will produce draft documents which are tailored to the project's specific requirements.

Checking documents
Auditing staff would use the IDP system as an automated assistant which provides advice about which parts of the document to examine and which questions to ask about the document. It also provides on-line reference to the standards whenever required. Finally, the system produces a report listing the document's deficiencies.

4. Architecture of an IDP system

The IDP system architecture distinguishes between generic functions and functions and text specific to the initial system implemented. This 'kernel'-based architecture has two main advantages – the system can be changed readily to incorporate new standards and documents, and it enables maintenance to be carried out more easily and by less-trained staff. This follows normal practice in expert system design, where there is a division between knowledge and the way in which knowledge is handled by the system.

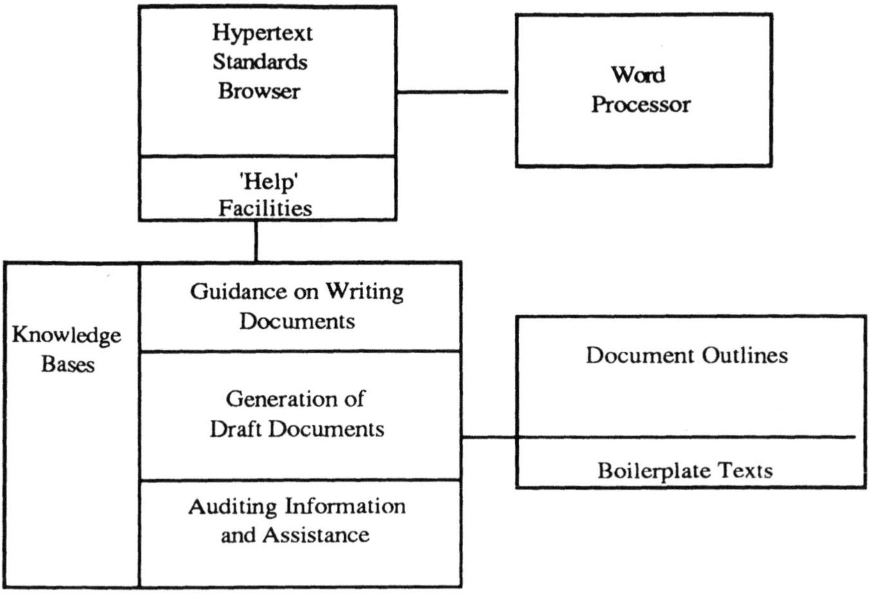

Figure 2. IDP functional architecture

From the system's point of view (Figure 2), the system is built as a number of key functional elements based on a **hypertext-based** core. This core contains the standards texts which users can reference whenever required, and the hypertext means of accessing and displaying parts of the texts.

A **word processor** is also provided, since documents produced will need to be edited. The edited document must share the screen with hypertext functions, since the user will occasionally need to reference the standards while editing the document.

Knowledge bases are provided for several areas of rule-based guidance:

- Guidance on which standards to use and how to write documents.
- A knowledge base which asks details about the project and uses the information to construct a draft document, based on pre-written boilerplate text.
- A knowledge base for auditing, with knowledge about how the document should be constructed, which will compile a list of deficiencies in the document.

The system also contains a number of **texts**, including sample texts for editing into documents and boilerplate texts to be tailored into the draft document.

5. Using IDP for software documentation

The concept of IDP can best be illustrated with examples taken from a current demonstration system which we built for the European Space Agency (ESA), and makes use of the ESA software engineering standards. This system concentrates on the software quality assurance plan (quality plan), although it can also be used on some other ESA documents. As with our other IDP systems, it runs on PC/AT compatibles.

Figure 3 shows a sample browsing screen, where the user can look up relevant information in the standards, using hypertext support.

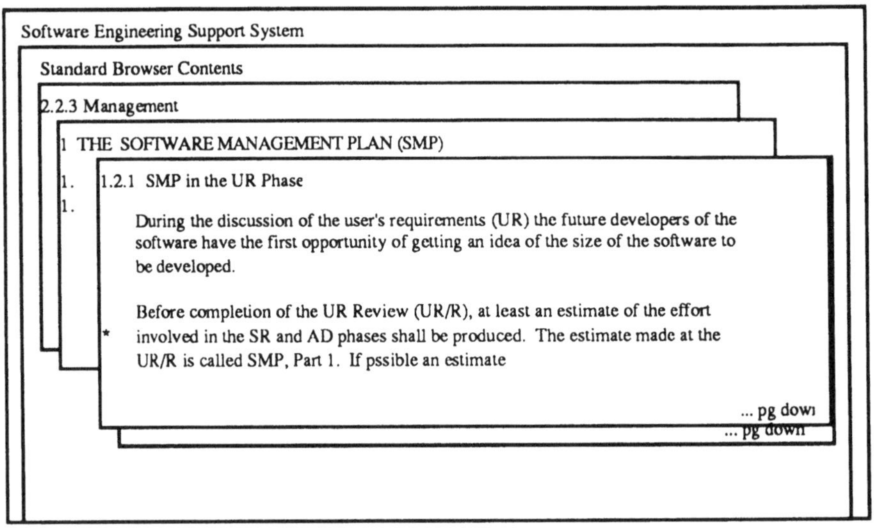

Figure 3. Browsing with the IDP system

Figure 4 illustrates the guidance aspect of the system, where the author is asked questions about the project and given advice about the contents of the quality plan. Hypertext reference to the standards remains available.

Figure 5 extends the guidance aspect to produce a draft quality plan for the project, based on information provided by the user. In the case illustrated, the four questions are sufficient to draft the full text - but if either of the first two answers had been negative, new questions and different draft texts would have been used. (Note that the question about gender is needed to determine text as well!).

As each section of the document is drafted, it is displayed on the screen, and the author is then invited to revise it if desired. At the end of the session, the sections are pasted together into the full document, and the author may again edit the document before it is issued.

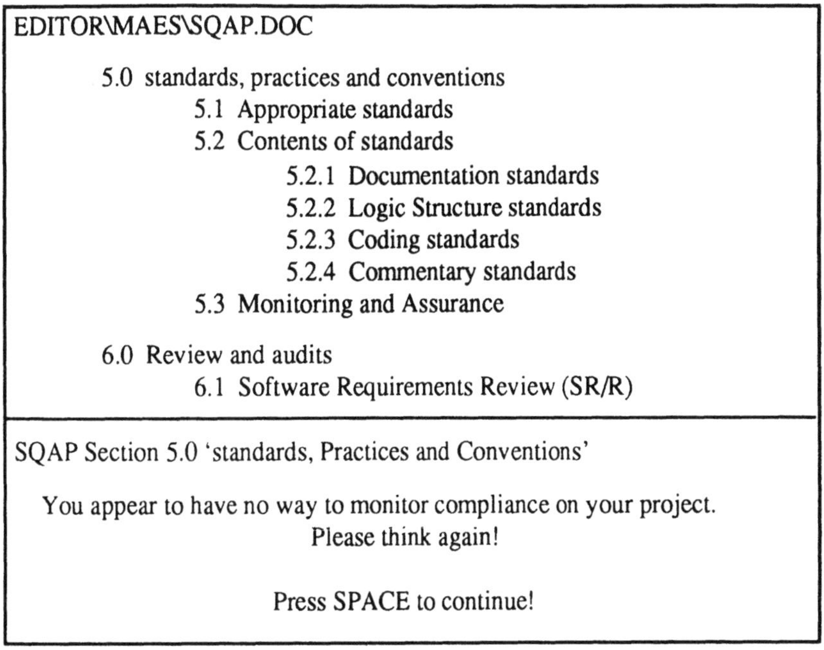

Figure 4. Guidance in writing documents

The final part of the system is illustrated in Figure 6, where the resulting document is reviewed (audited), say by a member of the Quality Assurance Department.

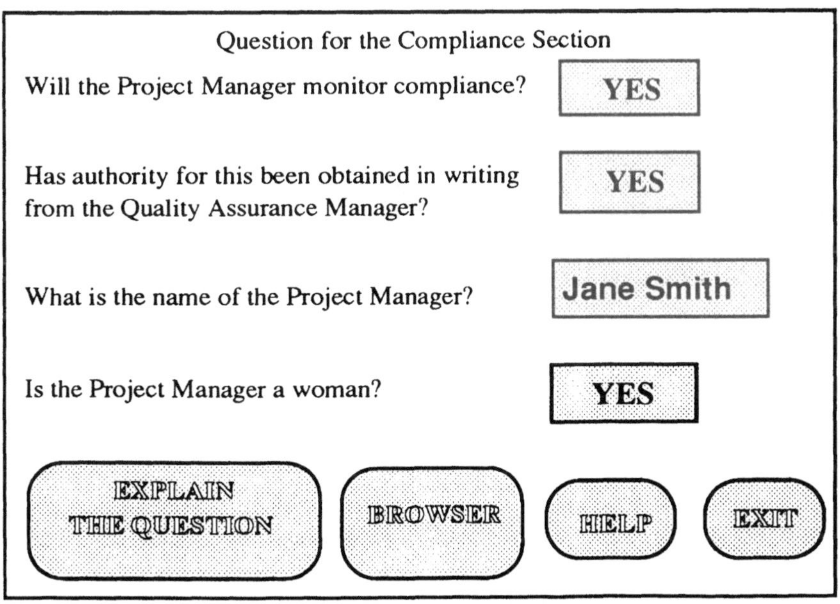

Compliance Section Draft Text

5.3 Compliance

The Project Manager, Ms Jane Smith, will monitor compliance with the standards described in this Quality Plan. The methods she will use are documented in the SD Quality Manual (SD1001) and the SD Quality Procedures Manual (SD1002).

For this procedure to be valid within SD-Scicon, it must be approved by the Company Quality Assurance Division. This authority has been obtained, and a form signed by the Quality Assurance Manger is held in the Approval and Authorisation Section of the Project Filing System.

EDIT THE TEXT   SAVE THE TEXT

Figure 5. Document generation

EDITOR\MAES\SQAP.DOC

5.0 standards, practices and conventions
- 5.1 Appropriate standards
- 5.2 Contents of standards
  - 5.2.1 Documentation standards
  - 5.2.2 Logic Structure standards
  - 5.2.3 Coding standards
  - 5.2.4 Commentary standards
- 5.3 Monitoring and Assurance

6.0 Review and audits
- 6.1 Software Requirements Review (SR/R)
- 6.2 Architectural Design Review (AD/R)

Audit SQAP Section 5.0 'standards, Practices and Conventions'

1. Appropriate standards
   1.1 Are the standards for the Project adequately described...
   1.1.3 For management areas (Project Management, Quality Assurance, Configuration Management, etc.)?

Yes
No

Figure 6. Auditing the document

The reviewer reads the document in the top window, while answering the questions which appear in the bottom window. As with all other parts of the system, hypertext reference to the standards is always available. At the end of the session, the system produces a report on the quality of the document, which may be used by the project to produce a revised version complying with the appropriate standards.

6. Conclusions

Intelligent Document Production as described in this paper provides significant benefits for a certain kind of organisation. The necessary conditions are:

- That there are a large number of standards or procedures.
- These must be applied and adapted to individual projects.
- The organisation requires a considerable amount of documentation, complying with the standards, to be written for each project, and
- Staff have difficulty understanding and applying the standards.

These conditions apply to all large software organisations and to any others wishing to be compliant with the international quality standards (BSI 1987). IDP results in an improved quality of document, with significant savings in staff time.

Fortunately, individuals within these organisations will also benefit. One of the most difficult and stressful jobs is to understand a complicated procedure and apply it, without experience or training. IDP systems, which combine learning with doing, will make their jobs far easier, with the additional satisfaction which comes from producing high quality results.

7. References

Born, G. (1985) Getting quality into your plans: how the expert systems approach can help, *NCC Data Processing Circle Annual Meeting*, March.

Born, G., *et al.* (1989) ESRIN –Study of expert systems in scientific and technical information processing: final report, European Space Agency, December.

Bruce, R., (1989) QA plan generator KBS: evaluation report, ESPRIT Project 1098 (KADS), October .

BSI, (1987) British standard for Quality Systems (BS5750 and ISO 9001-9003).

19

An Automated Grammar and Style Checker for Writers of Simplified English

James E. Hoard
Richard Wojcik
Katherina Holzhauser
Boeing Advanced Technology Centre

Abstract

The AECMA Simplified English writing standard for commercial aircraft maintenance manuals mandates a very restricted style that prescribes artificial limits on vocabulary and grammatical constructions. Simplified English documents are intended primarily for non-native speakers, especially those whose command of the language may be somewhat limited. While manuals conforming to the Simplified English style are easy to read, the writing (and rewriting) task is extremely difficult. At Boeing, we have developed a Simplified English Checker to assist our engineer writers. The linguistically-based Checker uses a sophisticated 350-rule English grammar and parser, which is augmented with special functions that check for violations of the Simplified English standard. We report here on the Simplified English Checker's capabilities and on the error reports that it produces for the engineer writers. We find that the Simplified English Checker has the potential to bring the quality and consistency of the writing in aircraft maintenance manuals to a level that is probably not possible without it.

1. Introduction

Boeing Commercial Airplanes has made a commitment to write its aircraft maintenance manuals in Simplified English, the new international standard for aerospace technical documents. The standard places a heavy burden on the technical writers who produce the documentation, since Simplified English prescribes severe restrictions on grammar and style, forcing the writers to memorise an enormous body of detailed information about word usage.

The purpose of this paper is to give a preliminary report on the capabilities of the Boeing Simplified English Checker, an automated system that provides writers with detailed reports on deviations from Simplified English, reports which they use to help them bring texts into conformity with the standard. Section 2 gives a brief overview of Simplified English – in sufficient detail, we hope, to indicate the magnitude of the learning burden it imposes on the writers who attempt to use it. Section 3 describes the capabilities of the Simplified English Checker we have developed to aid our engineer writers. Section 4 offers the results of a simple experiment we conducted to demonstrate that the Simplified English Checker provides very real help with the writing task. In Section 5 we summarise our work to date on the Simplified English Checker and suggest how on-going research in natural language processing can lead to even more robust grammar and style checking capabilities. The Appendix gives a number of parallel examples of un-Simplified and Simplified English text to give the reader who is unfamiliar with the standard some appreciation of the differences.

2. The simplified English standard

Simplified English is now the international writing standard for aircraft maintenance manuals. The standard was developed by AECMA (Association Européene des Constructeurs de Materiel Aerospatial) in response to requests from European airline companies to improve the readability of aircraft documentation. The standards were formulated over a period of years, beginning in the late 1970s, and were initially released in 1986 as AECMA document PSC-85-16598, *AECMA Simplified English: A Guide to the Preparation of Aircraft Maintenance Documentation in the International Aerospace Maintenance Language.* The Simplified English standard imposes restrictions in three areas: general English vocabulary, technical vocabulary, and grammar and style. The vocabulary and constructions allowed as part of the standard were selected wherever possible for their commonality with the other major European languages and because of their comprehensibility to speakers of these languages.

2.1. Simplified English vocabulary

The general English vocabulary allowed by the AECMA Simplified English standard comprises about 1500 words, fewer than 200 of which are verbs. Each of these words is to be used –with few exceptions – in one, and only one, meaning. Examples of allowed words (from the A's) are:

Nouns:	acceleration, access, accident, acid, adjustment, agent, aid, air, aircraft, airflow, allowance, alternative, analysis, angle, approval, area, arrow, assembly, authority, average, axis
Verbs:	absorb, accept, adapt, add, adjust, agree, align, apply, arm, assemble, attach
Adjectives:	accidental, accurate, acid, adjacent, adjustable, aft, airborne, alternative, analog, angular, apparent, applicable, approved, approximate, automatic, auxiliary, available, axial
Adverbs:	accidentally, accurately, aft, again, all, almost, also, alternatively, always, apart, approximately, automatically, away, axially

Prepositions:	about, above, across, after, against, along, around, as, at
Conjunctions:	after, although, and, as
Articles:	a, an

Examples of disallowed general vocabulary items (from the A's) are:

Nouns:	abnormality, absorption, acceptance, accumulation, accuracy, action, activity, actuation, addition, aeroplane, agitation, aim, airframe, alignment, alteration, amendment, amount, annotation, aperture, application, arrangement, article, assembly, assessment, assistance, atmosphere, attachment, attempt, attendance, attention
Verbs:	abandon, abrade, abut, accelerate, accommodate, accomplish, account for, accumulate, achieve, acknowledge, act, activate, actuate, adhere, admit, adopt, advance, advise, affect, afford, aggravate, agitate, aid, aim, air-dry, allocate, allow, alter, alternate, analyze, anchor, annunciation, appear, approach, approve, arise, arrange, arrest, arrive, ascertain, ask, assemble, assess, assign, assist, assume, assure, attack, attain, attempt, autorotate, avoid
Adjectives:	able, abnormal, abraded, abrupt, acceptable, accessible, accumulated, acrid, activated, active, actual, actuated, additional, adequate, adjoining, adverse, advisable, affected, air-driven, allowable, alternate , another, anticlockwise, any, appropriate, arranged, associated, asymmetric, audible, aural, authorized, aware
Adverbs:	absolutely, anytime, at least, aurally
Prepositions:	according to, among, as to
Conjunctions:	as

Simplified English has many part-of-speech restrictions. To be sure, there are some cases in which both members of a noun-verb pair (or a near pair) is allowed (e.g. 'bend' n., 'bend' v.; 'assembly' n.,'assemble' v). For most pairs, however, only one member is permitted. Rarely, it is the verb that is allowed (e.g. 'help' v., but not 'help' n.). Most often, only the noun use of a noun-verb pair is allowed. For example, 'check, chip, chock, choke,' and 'circle' are permitted as nouns but not as verbs. Similarly, 'analysis' is allowed, but not 'analyse'; 'computer' is allowed, but not 'compute'; 'distortion', but not 'distort'. These part-of-speech restrictions require that many rather ordinary notions be expressed as phrases ("written around", as it were). Thus, one cannot "chock the wheel". Instead, one must "put a chock on the wheel". Because of the limited vocabulary available to the writer of Simplified English, circumlocutions such as this must be used quite often.

To assist the writers of Simplified English in overcoming the vocabulary restrictions, the AECMA dictionary is structured in the manner of a thesaurus. In addition to the allowed general vocabulary items, it lists proscribed words that might be used in aircraft maintenance manuals along with suggestions for alternative choices (and circumlocutions) from among the permitted general vocabulary. The following examples from the AECMA SE dictionary illustrate the dictionary method. Upper case entries indicate the legal words, and lower case is used to denote illegal words. The definitions give the one-and-only authorised meaning for each word and the part-of-speech restriction that applies.

talk (v) USE:	SPEAK, TELL
tamper (v) USE:	MOVE, CHANGE, ADJUST
TASK (n):	"Assigned" work or procedure
TELESCOPIC (adj):	Related to items that retract into each other
TEMPORARY (adj), TEMPORARILY (adv):	For a short time only, not permanent
TEST (n):	That which you do when you operate or examine an item to make sure that it agrees with applicable specifications test
(v) USE:	DO A TEST

The highly restricted Simplified English general vocabulary is to be augmented with technical vocabulary items chosen by the manufacturer. These words fall into two groups, technical names and manufacturing processes. The technical names comprise by far the larger group. The technical names are largely nouns, both single words and compounds. Adjectives can also be technical names, both singly and as part of compound technical names. Some examples of Boeing technical names are: adhesive, aisle, bearing, circumference, countersunk rivets, drain plug, electrostatic, nacelle.

Labels comprise an important subgroup of the technical words. As one might expect, many aircraft components, on the flight deck and elsewhere, have labels. Some examples are: OFF, ON, CIRCUIT BREAKER, SPOILERS, STABILISER.

The manufacturing processes are verbs. Some typical examples are: crimp, drill, insulate, rivet, swage.

2.2. Grammatical and stylistic restrictions

The Simplified English standard has a wide variety of grammar and style restrictions, ranging from broad expository considerations to simple syntactic prohibitions. The following account of the Simplified English grammatical and stylistic restrictions is illustrative and is not intended to be exhaustive.

- *Sentence length.* Sentences should be no more than 20 words long, except that in description and operation texts an average of one sentence in every ten can be 25 words long. The colon and dash are to be treated as full stops, while text inside parentheses counts as a separate sentence. Each word in a hyphenated group is to be counted as a single word.
- *Variety of sentence length.* The sentences in a paragraph should not all be the same length.
- *Instruction sentences.* Sentences can have only one instruction, except for instructions that have to be done at the same time. Instructions must use the imperative verb form.
- *Specificity of instructions.* Instructions should be as specific as possible. Verbs and nouns should not be omitted to make sentences shorter.
- *Paragraph length.* Paragraphs should have no more than six sentences, and only one paragraph in ten can have but one sentence in descriptive text.
- *Paragraph content.* Paragraphs should have only one topic. The first sentence should be the topic sentence. Connecting words should be used to show the relationship between the sentences in a paragraph. The paragraphs must reveal the logic of the text.
- *Tabular layout.* Use a tabular layout where it is appropriate –for example, for steps in an instruction that are closely related.
- *New and complex data.* New and complex data should not be presented too quickly or in an unclear manner.
- *Warnings.* Warnings should be clear and simple and set off from other text. An explanation should accompany a warning to give an idea of possible risk.
- *Compounds.* Noun groups should not contain more than three nouns in a row. For technical names that consist of four or more words, the hyphen is to be used as a joining symbol to show how the words are related.
- *Articles.* Singular count nouns are to be preceded by an article or another determiner.
- *Verb forms.* Only the present tense, the past tense, the simple future, and the past participle forms of verbs are allowed. The past participle

can be used only as an adjective, with a noun or after the verbs 'be' and 'become'. The progressive verb forms and the perfective aspect are not allowed, except that '-ing' forms can be used as part of technical names.

- *Showing action.* The verb should be the action word wherever possible.
- *Passive Voice.* Use only the active voice in procedures. Avoid the passive voice in description and operation sections.
- *Dependent Clauses.* Dependent clauses that begin a sentence must be set off with a comma.
- *Colons and dashes.* Colons and dashes are to be used only in tabular formats.
- *Hyphenation.* The hyphen is to be used only as a joining symbol.

2.3. Effectiveness of simplified English

There is some question as to whether it is desirable to impose a controlled language as restrictive as Simplified English on the writers of maintenance manuals. Do the vocabulary, grammatical, and stylistic restrictions of Simplified English, taken as a whole, actually define a variety of English that is indeed simpler for non-native speakers to understand? It would seem *a priori* that this must be the case. Yet the point is certainly debatable, for we know of no body of experimental evidence to support the claim. Indeed, no definitive tests can be conducted at the present time, since no sizeable body of connected text certified to be in conformity with the Simplified English standard exists. When such texts become available, comprehension tests administered to non-native speakers will help settle the issue.

Further, does the Simplified English standard, as given, constitute a complete and coherent sub-language? In other words: Does the standard allow one to say what needs to be said to provide fully adequate manuals for aircraft maintenance and repair? We know of no reason to suppose that it does not. Yet there may be gaps in the general vocabulary that make it extremely difficult to treat some maintenance topics clearly and effectively. Then, too, it might well be that the proscription of certain forms, particularly verb forms, will result in a very unnatural expository style that is itself a source of unclarity and imprecision. Again, carefully crafted comprehension tests that explore alternative modes of expression, administered to both native and non-native speakers, will help settle such issues.

It should be kept in mind, of course, that the Simplified English standard is an evolving standard, one that is subject to revision by AECMA as the need for changes becomes apparent. In any event, it is clear that the Simplified English style will be very difficult for writers to master, and that an automated grammar and style checker can be of great help in preparing aircraft maintenance manuals that conform to the Simplified English standard.

3. The Boeing simplified English checker

The Boeing Simplified English Checker is based on natural language processing technology developed under an on-going research and development project at the Advanced Technology Centre of Boeing Computer Services. In particular, the research team has developed a sophisticated syntactic analyser consisting of a number of distinct components, including a tokeniser, lexicon, parser, and English grammar.

The tokeniser scans ASCII strings and uses the lexicon, which has entries for over 22,000 items, to identify the words, punctuation, and other tokens in the input stream. The parser uses an English grammar of some 350 high-level syntax rules to analyse the tokenised strings. The parser, which works left-to-right and bottom-up across the token strings, produces full syntactic analyses. The English grammar is based on the linguistic theory known as Generalised Phrase Structure Grammar (Gazdar, *et al.* 1985); the parser is described in Harrison (1988).

In late 1988, Boeing managers and technical staff concluded that it was possible to build a very effective Simplified English Checker using the existing syntactic analysis capability, augmenting it with special functions to check the analyses of texts for Simplified English violations. Since Boeing Commercial Airplanes believed that the proposed tool had a great potential for enhancing the quality of aircraft maintenance documentation, as well as for reducing the cost of converting existing documentation to the Simplified English standard, the development effort was scheduled to deliver the initial version of the Checker within a year of the project starting date. Development was begun in February, 1989, and the first phase of the Simplified English Checker went into production use in early March, 1990.

3.1. Scope of the simplified English checker

Since the Simplified English Checker is based on syntactic analysis of text, it was necessary to separate the Simplified English requirements into those that can be satisfied by syntactic means and to leave aside those that require semantic and pragmatic analysis. Indeed, some of the requirements are quite beyond any foreseeable natural language processing system. Even human editors often have difficulty in deciding whether a paragraph contains only one topic.

The functionalities of the initial version of the Checker are given below. The grammar and style functionalities correspond to the Simplified English requirements listed in section 2.

Vocabulary restrictions.

Vocabulary entries, both general and technical, are checked by lexicon lookup procedures. All vocabulary entries sanctioned for use in Simplified English documents are noted in the lexicon; and for every sanctioned entry, the applicable Simplified English sub-classification is noted. Part-of-speech restrictions are enforced by a combination of lexical lookup and parser-grammar analysis. There is no check of approved meanings, since this would require both semantic and pragmatic analysis.

For unsanctioned lexical entries that have valid Simplified English alternatives, whether single words or circumlocutions, we provide a full listing of the alternatives, in the manner of the AECMA Simplified English dictionary, as an aid to rewriting.

Grammar and style restrictions.

- *Sentence length.* Checked.
- *Variety of sentence length.* Not checked. This is apparently unnecessary. The sentences seem to vary in length as a matter of course.
- *Instruction sentences.* Checked. All conjoined imperatives are flagged, and the writer makes a judgement about simultaneity.
- *Specificity of instructions.* Not checked, since it requires human judgement.
- *Paragraph length.* Paragraphs are checked for a maximum length of six sentences. The Checker does not determine if only one paragraph in ten has but one sentence, as it is unclear if the frequency of one-sentence paragraphs is an overall restriction on a long section of text or a local restriction.
- *Paragraph content.* Not checked, since human judgement is required. But connecting words are flagged.
- *Tabular layout.* Not checked.
- *New and complex data.* Not checked. Human judgement required.
- *Warnings.* Checked. Imperative sentence structure is required for the first sentence. The second sentence must be a declarative sentence.
- *Compounds.* Checked, but no hyphenation is suggested. Adjectives embedded in compounds are counted as nouns (e.g. 'the door frame lower corner').
- *Articles.* Checked, albeit conservatively. Both mass nouns and plural indefinite count nouns are not flagged, even though they might need to be preceded by an article or determiner in the context in which they occur.
- *Verb forms.* Checked. The use of past participles as adjectives receives limited checking. Past participles are marked so that one part of speech (adjective or verb) is always chosen when there is ambiguity. The marking is intuitively based.
- *Showing action.* Not checked. This requires human judgement.
- Passive voice. All passives are flagged. No distinction between the two types of text is made.
- *Dependent clauses.* Checked.
- *Colons and dashes.* Not checked.
- *Hyphenation.* Not checked.

In addition, we introduced several checking functions not directly mandated by AECMA. For example, we check for the double words that often result from writing and editing with a word processor. We check co-ordinated noun phrases for the inappropriate use of semicolons where commas will do. We enforce consistency in the use of labels. And, we check for missing 'it is', as in 'remove the overhead panel if necessary'. This last checking function gives substance to at least a small part of the AECMA injunction not to omit nouns and verbs to make sentences shorter.

It should be apparent that the scope of the Boeing Simplified English Checker goes well beyond vocabulary checking and sentence length checking. We aimed at the outset to bring the full power of the syntactic analyser to bear in determining deviations from the Simplified English standard. In particular, the ability to parse a sentence completely gives us the opportunity to check for such things as part-of-speech violations, passive voice versus passive adjectives, noun group composition and length, and missing articles. These capabilities greatly exceed the abilities of any other grammar and style checker we have seen.

3.2. The development of the simplified English checker

The Boeing Simplified English Checker was prototyped in Lucid Common Lisp on Sun workstations. The functionality of the existing syntactic analyser required only a few modifications to serve as the core of the Checker. The lexicon was restructured slightly to accommodate information about permissible words and alternatives to unsanctioned words. At the beginning of the project, the lexicon had about 14,000 entries. In the course of the development, we added a large number of vocabulary items, over 8,000 in all. We added a modest number of new rules to the grammar to handle special constructions found in aircraft maintenance manuals. In addition, we modified the grammar so that certain grammatical structures would be flagged as violations of Simplified English. For example, the original grammar allowed passive, progressive, and perfect verbal auxiliary constructions (e.g. 'was seen', 'is seeing', 'has seen'), as a grammar of English should. We modified the original rule for building auxiliaries to disallow such structures, and we created a new rule which built the structures, along with a special marking to indicate their illegality in Simplified English. Finally, we added a parse scanner that examines the parse trees produced when text is analysed and collects error markings for output to a report generator. See section 3.3, below, for examples of error reports.

The parser and grammar produce all the parses for a given sentence. Since English, like every natural language, is highly ambiguous from a purely syntactic perspective, our parser includes a strategy for weighting the syntactic rules according to their likelihood of occurrence. The weightings do not, of course, guarantee that the right parse will be selected for a given sentence. Nonetheless, the method succeeds enough of the time to make it quite useful for grammar and style checking, and we incorporated syntactic weighting into the Checker. Thus, the parse scanner examines only the most highly rated parse for each sentence. Sometimes, of course, the wrong parse is selected. For instance, for the sentence "The system supplies evaluation and monitors flight progress," the most highly rated parse has 'monitors' as a noun and 'progress' as a verb. That is, the syntactic weightings favour noun phrase plus intransitive verb over co-ordinated verb plus noun phrase--incorrectly in this case.

The prototyped system was reimplemented in C and tested on both Sun and Apollo workstations. After testing, the production version of the Checker was installed on Apollo workstations. The current version of the Simplified English Checker is used with textual records stored in a data base on an IBM mainframe. The data base does not store actual manuals, but blocks of text that are assembled to form manuals. In this way, Boeing can customise different manuals to meet the needs of different customers. The Simplified English Checker checks blocks of text exported from the mainframe to Apollo workstations, where the actual checking is performed. The Checker uses information associated with the records to determine what type of text it is examining. Thus, the Checker can tailor its reports depending on whether the block is in a procedure or a description and operation section. After the Checker has completed its analysis, an error report is generated and delivered to the engineer who requested it.

3.3. Simplified English checker error reports

The reports generated by the Simplified English Checker list each sentence in the text block that is checked followed by an account of the Simplified English violations that were detected. The reports give alternative words or expressions for all the unsanctioned words for which information is available in the lexicon. The first sentence of each of the four example pairs given below show typical Simplified English Checker outputs generated for unsimplified text sentences. These examples are followed by the revised, Simplified English version of each sentence and its report.

Spring is under extreme load.

```
**Word errors**
   PREPOSITION ERROR: under
      USE: below
         less than
         lower than
   ADJECTIVE ERROR: extreme
      USE: very high
         very bad
         at the limit of
**Missing articles**
   Spring
   extreme load
```

The spring has high load.

No errors detected

If cable slips, rapid retraction can cause serious injury to personnel.

Word errors
VERB ERROR: slips
USE: remove
move
ADJECTIVE ERROR: rapid
USE: fast
ADJECTIVE ERROR: serious
USE: bad
important
dangerous
NOUN ERROR: personnel
USE: persons
Missing articles
cable

If the cable moves, the fast retraction can cause injury to persons.

No errors detected

WARNING: Do not allow hands to contact any of the cables.

Word errors
VERB ERROR: allow
USE: let
permit
VERB ERROR: contact
USE: touch
tell
ARTICLE ERROR: any
USE: all
if

WARNING: Do not touch the cable.

No errors detected

Injury to personnel could occur because of frayed cables.

Word errors
NOUN ERROR: personnel
USE: persons
NON SE words
could

because of
frayed

Damaged cables can cause injury to persons.

No errors detected

The following example shows the ability of the Simplified English Checker to detect an ambiguity in a co-ordinated construction. The sentence means either: "Cover the duct openings and cover the line openings ..." or "Cover the duct and line the openings ...". If it is the latter meaning that the writer intended, then, as the Checker report indicates, some verb other than 'line' must be chosen.

Cover the duct and line openings to prevent the entry of unwanted material.

Structure errors
TWO COMMANDS - POSSIBLE ERROR: Cover the duct and line openings to prevent the entry of unwanted material
Word errors
VERB ERROR: cover
USE: put covers on
give
have
VERB ERROR: line
ALLOWED AS: NOUN

The Checker gives useful feedback on over 80% of the sentences in the maintenance texts that it examines. In a number of cases where parsing fails, the cause is the ungrammaticality of the original text. An example is:

The pressure sense line to the conditioned air check valve.

This "sentence" seems to be missing its verb. The Checker reports:

Can't do SE check

Lastly, we give an example of a missing 'it is' error:

Remove electrical power if no longer required (Ref 24-22-00/201).

Structure errors
MISSING 'IT IS': if no longer required
Word errors
ADJECTIVE ERROR: required
USE: be necessary

In addition to detailed reports on each of the sentences in a test block, the Simplified English Checker also gives a summary report on how well an entire document or document section conforms to Simplified English.

4. A simple test of the simplified English checker

During the summer of 1989, when the prototype of the Simplified English Checker was fully functional, we conducted a simple experiment to determine if the Checker would be as helpful in rewriting existing maintenance manuals as we supposed it would be. A 12-sentence passage from a 737 manual that contained a total of 28 Simplified English violations was selected. The number of deviations was determined, with the help of the Checker, by careful analysis of the passage.

Twenty writers who were completing a three-week course in Simplified English served as our subjects. They were separated into two groups of ten. Each group was instructed to rewrite the passage and put it into Simplified English. One group, Group A, used only AECMA Simplified English to assist them. The other group, Group B, used both AECMA Simplified English and an error report generated by the Simplified English Checker. No time limit was given for completing the rewriting task. Our aim was to check the degree of conformity to the standard the two groups could attain using the two methods, not in the speed with which they performed the rewriting. As it happened each group took about the same amount of time to rewrite the passage (about 40 minutes, on average).

The ten subjects in Group A, who did not have an error report, found an average of 21.2 Simplified English violations in the passage, leaving an average of 6.8 violations unchanged. The number of violations they rewrote ranged from 15 to 24. The ten subjects in Group B, who did have the error report, noted and rewrote an average of 25.3 violations in the passage. That is, they chose not to rewrite on average 2.7 of the Checker's 28 findings. Presumably, the Group B writers either did not trust the Checker's advice in these instances or else the writers made some error in applying the recommendations. The response to the Checker's report for Group B subjects ranged between 22 and 28.

Now, when a writer is rewriting a passage of a maintenance manual in order to bring it into conformity with the Simplified English standard, not only must the writer find and correct violations of the standard that are embedded in the text, new deviations from the standard must not be introduced into the text as part of the rewriting process. Clearly, if one has confidence in the accuracy of the reports that the Checker produces, then one has confidence that those portions of a text that are not flagged in the error report for that particular text already conform to the standard--and need not be changed.

We expected, then, that Group A would introduce more errors into the passage during rewriting than would Group B. This expectation was fully borne out. Group A introduced, on average, 5.5 new violations into the passage. The number ranged from 3 to 14. Group B, who had the advantage of the error report, introduced an average of only 2.9 new violations into the passage. The range was from 0 to 5. It should be noted that we did not expect that no violations, or nearly none, would be introduced into the text on average, since the Simplified English Checker is not always correct in its advice and, in any case, is no substitute for human judgements concerning readability.

In sum, after rewriting the passage, Group A ended up with an average of 12.3 violations of the Simplified English standard. Group B, on the other hand, ended up with an average of just 5.6 violations. The results are displayed below in tabular form for ready comparison:

	Group A	Group B
Violations not corrected:	6.8	2.7
Violations introduced:	5.5	2.9
Total:	12.3	5.6

We hasten to add that no statistical significance should be attached to the results of this simple experiment. We do, however, find the results to be highly suggestive; and we hypothesise that they will be confirmed in statistically significant tests involving a much larger number of subjects.

5. Conclusion

We have described in this paper both the Simplified English standard and the initial version of Boeing's Simplified English Checker. The initial version works in batch mode, analysing blocks of text that are stored in a data base and exported to an Apollo workstation for checking. Future versions of the Checker will perform interactively with text composed and stored on the same Apollo workstations that host the Simplified English Checker. The engineer writers will then be able to analyse sections of text with the Checker and make corrections to the text interactively.

We also plan to implement a version of the Simplified English Checker that analyses text in ordinary word processing formats. A generalised Checker might not be as good at distinguishing among different types of text as the current version, but it might find more widespread use, since many of the texts that could be made more readable by conversion to Simplified English are not stored in special record formats, as our maintenance manuals are.

As part of our on going research in natural language processing, we have designed and implemented major modules of an interleaved architecture that resolves ambiguity by bringing syntactic, semantic, and pragmatic information to bear in a highly interactive fashion. For ordinary text input, the experimental system produces disambiguated semantic interpretations and their associated parse trees. (See Hoard, 1989, for a description of the architecture and semantic representation.) When this technology matures, we intend to apply it to automate the checking of the Simplified English restrictions that require semantic analysis of texts. In particular, it should be possible for an enhanced Simplified English Checker to determine if sanctioned words are being used in the meaning specified in the AECMA dictionary.

With the advent of technically sophisticated grammar and style checkers such as our Simplified English Checker, it is now possible to achieve a high level of accuracy and consistency in satisfying the requirements of a controlled language like Simplified English. For complex and lengthy texts that have multiple authors, such as aircraft maintenance manuals, there may be no way to certify conformity to a complicated standard without the use of automated grammar and style checkers. At the very least, software systems such as the Simplified English Checker will greatly ease the burden that hand editing of manuals would entail.

6. References

AECMA (1989) Simplified English. *AECMA Document* PSC-85-16598, Change 5. Paris.

Gazdar, G., Klein, E., Pullum, G. and Sag, I. (1985) *Generalised Phrase Structure Grammar.* Cambridge. Harvard University Press, MA.

Harrison, P. (1988). A new algorithm for parsing generalized phrase structure grammars. Unpublished Ph.D. dissertation. University of Washington, Washington.

Hoard, J. E. (1989) Natural language processing and advanced a management. *Telematics and Informatics*, 6.

Appendix

Examples of Non-simplified and Simplified English Text

The Simplified English versions of the examples were produced manually by writers who are well trained in the standard. We note two remaining violations of the standard that are detected by the Simplified English Checker.

1. NON-SE.

The bulk cargo door has two cables. The spring cable is the cable between the spring tube and the cable drum. The door cable is the cable between the cable drum and the door.

1. SE.

The bulk cargo door has two cables. The spring cable is between the spring tube and the cable drum. The door cable is between the cable drum and the door.

2. NON-SE.

The purpose of this procedure is to check the spring cable and door cable for damage while the cables are in a slightly preloaded condition.

2. SE.

This procedure gives steps to make sure that the cables are not damaged. The cables are examined when they have minimum tension.

3. NON-SE.

Attach a DO-NOT-OPERATE identifier to door exterior handle.

3. SE.

Attach a DO-NOT-OPERATE identifier to the external door handle.

4. NON-SE.

DO NOT ATTEMPT TO SECURE BALANCE MECHANISM CABLE WITH BLOCKS AND C-CLAMP.

4. SE.

CAUTION: DO NOT TRY TO ATTACH THE BALANCE MECHANISM CABLE WITH BLOCKS AND C-CLAMP.

5. NON-SE.

IF CABLE SLIPS, RAPID RETRACTION CAN CAUSE SERIOUS INJURY TO PERSONNEL.

5. SE.

IF THE CABLE MOVES, THE FAST RETRACTION CAN CAUSE SERIOUS INJURY TO PERSONS.

6. NON-SE.

Secure the balance cable mechanism in place by installing a safety pin in the spring tube.

6. SE.

Install the safety pin in the spring tube to hold the balance cable mechanism in position.

7. NON-SE.

DO NOT REMOVE SAFETY PIN FROM SPRING TUBE. SPRING TUBE IS UNDER EXTREME LOAD. INJURY TO PERSONNEL AND/OR DAMAGE TO EQUIPMENT MAY OCCUR ...

7. SE.

CAUTION: DO NOT REMOVE SAFETY PIN FROM THE SPRING TUBE. THE SPRING HAS A VERY HIGH LOAD. INJURY TO PERSONS OR DAMAGE TO EQUIPMENT CAN RESULT ...

[The word 'THE' should appear before 'SAFETY PIN'.]

8. NON-SE.

Open the door slightly to relieve the load on the cable system.

8. SE.

Open the door a small amount to remove the cable load.

9. NON-SE.

Check cable for damage as follows:

Under bright light conditions, visually check the spring cable and the door cable for damage.

NOTE: Using only a flashlight is not acceptable. The interior of the airplane must be well lit.

WARNING: DO NOT ALLOW HANDS TO CONTACT ANY OF THE CABLES. INJURY TO PERSONNEL COULD OCCUR BECAUSE OF FRAYED CABLES.

9. SE.

Examine the cables for damage as follows:

Examine the spring cable and the door cable for damage with a bright light. NOTE: Flashlights do not give sufficient light. The area lighting must be very good.

WARNING: DO NOT TOUCH THE CABLES. DAMAGED CABLES CAN CAUSE INJURY TO PERSONS.

10. NON-SE.

Stretch a small portion of cheesecloth across the cables and run it along the length of the cables as far as possible. Cable damage can be suspected if the cheesecloth hangs up or tears. Verify the suspected cable damage by visual check.

10. SE.

Run a small piece of cheesecloth along all of the available cable surface. If the cheesecloth tears or is caught by the cable, the cable has damage. Examine any cable you think is damaged again with the bright light to make sure it is damaged.

[The word 'any' is not allowed in Simplified English. The writer might expressed this as:' Examine all the cable you think are damaged ...']

11. NON-SE.

DO NOT ATTEMPT TO CLOSE AND LATCH THE DOOR UNLESS THE CABLES ARE FULLY ENGAGING THE CABLE DRUM AND THE PULLEYS. PAY SPECIAL ATTENTION TO THE ABLE ENGAGEMENT AT THE SPRING TUBE PULLEY SINCE IT IS HIDDEN FROM VIEW BY A PULLEY BRACKET.

11. SE.

WARNING:DO NOT TRY TO CLOSE AND LATCH THE DOOR IF THE CABLES ARE NOT FULLY ENGAGED IN THE CABLE DRUM AND PULLEYS. MAKE VERY SURE OF THE CABLE ENGAGEMENT AT THE SPRING TUBE PULLEY BECAUSE IT IS NOT EASY TO SEE.

12. NON-SE.

Check door operation by opening and closing the door thru several cycles.

12. SE.

Open and close the door to make sure it operates correctly.

13. NON-SE.

Position truck shield under main gear truck and mark locations on truck where truck shield clamps will attach.

13. SE.

Put the truck shield below the truck. Make a mark where the truck shield clamps attach.

14. NON-SE.

CAUTION: DO NOT USE MAIN GEAR SHOCK STRUT RETENTION STRAP ON A PRESSURIZED SHOCK STRUT. STRAP MAY BREAK CAUSING DAMAGE TO GEAR.

14. SE.

CAUTION: DO NOT USE THE SHOCK-STRUT RETENTION STRAP ON A SHOCK STRUT THAT IS PRESSURIZED. THE STRAP CAN BREAK AND CAUSE DAMAGE TO THE GEAR.

15. NON-SE.

Depressurize center hydraulic system (Ref 29-11-00).

15. SE.

Remove the pressure from the center hydraulic system (Ref 29-11-00).

16. NON-SE.

Check that clearance between RAT actuator arm and downstop is a dimensions shown in Fig. 502.

16. SE.

Make sure that the clearance between the RAT actuator and the a agrees with the dimensions shown on Fig. 502.

17. NON-SE.

When propeller speed has stabilized, check that green light on RAT tachometer is on the red light is off.

17. SE.

When the speed of the propeller is stable, make sure that the green light on the RAT actuator is on the red light is off.

18. NON-SE.

Press RAM AIR TURB manual select switch on the pilot's overhead panel P5 to deploy RAT. After RAT is fully deployed, return select switch to OFF position.

18. SE.

Push the RAM AIR TURB switch on the pilot's overhead panel, P5, to release the RAT. After the RAT is in position, move the RAM AIR TURB switch to the OFF position.

19. NON-SE.

If lift fixture A71015-60 is to be used, secure adapter to safety screen support with nut and washer.

19. SE.

If you use the lift fixture A71015-60, temporarily attach the adapter to the safety screen support with a nut and washer.

20. NON-SE.

NOTE: Installation of forward and aft transducer wiring is similar.

20. SE.

The installation of the forward and aft transducer wiring is almost the same.

20

Ruskin to McRuskin – Degrees of Interaction

Steve McGowan
Heriot-Watt University,

Abstract

This paper describes an enhanced version (McRuskin) of an existing style analyser package (Ruskin). The new system has two distinct advantages over the previous system; (a) it has a more interactive interface, (b) it includes a discourse analysis module, both of which are described. The paper then gives several screen outputs from McRuskin, and describes the interface evaluation performed on the system. The conclusions drawn from this evaluation resulted in modifications to the McRuskin interface; these are also presented.

1. What are style analysers?

It is generally accepted that writing is a difficult process involving the management of several simultaneous activities and constraints (Flower and Hayes 1980b). The 'juggling' of these processes often leads to 'cognitive overload' when developing substantial, unfamiliar or complex documents, resulting in poorly-worded text, ill-conceived goals and inappropriate end text. For this reason many researchers have developed computing tools to help writers in the writing process. These tools are generally referred to as *style analysers* or *writer's aids.*

Typical tasks performed by such packages are usually of a low-level nature and include spell-checking, simple punctuation analysis, sentence length and syllable usage, detection of passive voice and split infinitives, and so on. In providing these facilities within the tool, the author is left to attend to the higher-level activities such as idea generation, text translation and document revision.

2. Stages in writing

There are three individual stages usually associated with the process of writing; *pre-writing, writing* and *post-writing* :

- *Pre-writing:* As the name suggests, this is the process the author goes through in creating the initial text. This activity involves generating ideas, developing themes to express, constructing possible arguments, building general section headings, etc.
- *Writing:* This is the process of physically creating the text, more commonly by putting it onto paper, but also perhaps onto a computer via an input keyboard.

- *Post-writing:* This last activity involves evaluating, editing and revising the text to ensure that it 'reads well' and is generally free from 'bad style' errors.

Many computing packages have been developed that assist the author in some or all of these three activities. However, whereas there are tools designed to help the author in the first of these two stages, in general, style analysers are primarily aimed at assisting the author in the two latter stages.

3. Limitations of current style analysers

There are five main limitations associated with current style analysers, as follows:

- Most do not offer any basic text-editing facilities similar to those found on modern word-processors. For example, cut, copy, paste, delete, undo, etc.
- The output generated by current style analysers is usually very basic, perhaps even primitive. At one extreme it is possible to obtain a so-called 'style graph' that draws a bar-chart of how well the author's text fared during analysis. The information derived from such a graph is limited to say the least. At the other extreme there are style analysers which can generate output consisting of volumes of information. Whilst this information is fairly comprehensive in its analysis, it is this very detail which tends to 'bog down' or burden the reader when studying the output.
- Most style analysers do not support any of the various models of writing. However, due to both the complexity and time required to describe these models, no descriptions will be given at this point. The interested reader is recommended to consult the given references (Flower and Hayes 1980a; Cooper and Matsuhashi 1983; Sharples and O'Malley 1988).
- Some style analysers (Ruskin) contain 'style knowledge' in the form of production rules. Therefore, if this information could be accessed, manipulated and used in conjunction with underlying writing models, it would be possible to generate new and novel human-computer dialogues, such as the design and implementation of a suitable discourse analysis module.
- This is the 'catch-all' limitation of most style analysers and can be best described by analogy. Suppose a pupil wanted to learn how to write 'good style' English and presented a teacher with a text. If this teacher represented a current style analyser, the teacher would then take the pupil's document, go away and study the text, compile a separate list of possible style errors and then return both the original text and the comment list. The pupil would then have the rather daunting task of integrating these two sources to eliminate the bad

style detected by the teacher. This process would be repeated until both parties were satisfied with the current state of the text. In addition, it is worth noting that this rather barren dialogue between pupil and teacher does not allow the pupil to understand *why* their text was in error. Neither is this learning reinforced with suitable advice and guidance which would ultimately reduce the pupil's need to depend on the teacher for the detection of bad style in the first instance.

However, a much better approach would be for the pupil to sit down with the teacher and together go through the document stage by stage, and highlight possible instances of bad style. Furthermore, the teacher should also offer explanations as to why the text might be in error, and give solutions that will stop the pupil from making similar mistakes in the future. This interaction should ideally be supported with a complexity of dialogue modelled to the pupil's own abilities and requirements. Thus ensuring that the dialogue is neither too complex, nor too simplistic.

Obviously this analogy description is a gross over-exaggeration of both current style analysers' abilities and of future analysers' requirements, but it does highlight the interaction that subsequent systems must support if they are to be of any practical use.

4. Ruskin

Ruskin (Holt and Williams 1989) consists of two main features; *contextual variables* and *production rules.*

1. *Contextual Variables:* Every time Ruskin is presented with a new document to style analyse, the author must provide several items of information - these are the contextual variables. There are five broad categories of such variables, namely;
    a. **Audience:** their age, educational level, attitude to the author and the author's organisation, how familiar they are with the subject material, etc.
    b. **Purpose:** is the text supposed to teach, amuse, argue, etc.
    c. **Subject:** is the subject material complex, and will it contain a complex vocabulary, etc.
    d. **Use:** will the document have a long life-span, will the audience be pushed for time when reading it, what is its end application, etc.
    e. **Author:** how skilled the author is at writing material of this kind, author's own familiarity with the subject, etc.

In specifying these constraints, Ruskin is able to build up a so-called 'ideal model' of what a document of that type should consist of in terms of 'good' style. And when Ruskin comes to analyse the text, any violations of these constraints can be picked up by the production rules.

2. *Production Rules:* Ruskin's production rules consist of an 'IF' part and a 'THEN' part. The 'IF' part has a condition associated with it which, if found to be true, executes the action associated with the 'THEN' part. The following example production rule is used to detect the presence of long sentences within the author's text.

   IF THE AGE OF THE AUDIENCE IS LOW
   THEN USE FEW LONG SENTENCES.

This is the means by which Ruskin detects bad style within the supplied text.

5. McRuskin

Since one of the primary aims of the McRuskin (McGowan 1989) project was to test the *effectiveness* of the interactive interface and not to design yet another style analyser package, it must be stated that the style analysis performed by McRuskin is somewhat low-level. For example, it can count the number of characters, words and sentences in a document. It can also give a statistical breakdown of these items, such as calculating the average word length, average sentence length, largest word size, etc. However, to ensure that at least one desirable style analysis feature could be assessed, a facility to search for over-long sentences was incorporated into McRuskin. The provision of this mechanism meant that effectiveness of the McRuskin interface could be measured with a style feature found on most style analysers.

6. McRuskin screens

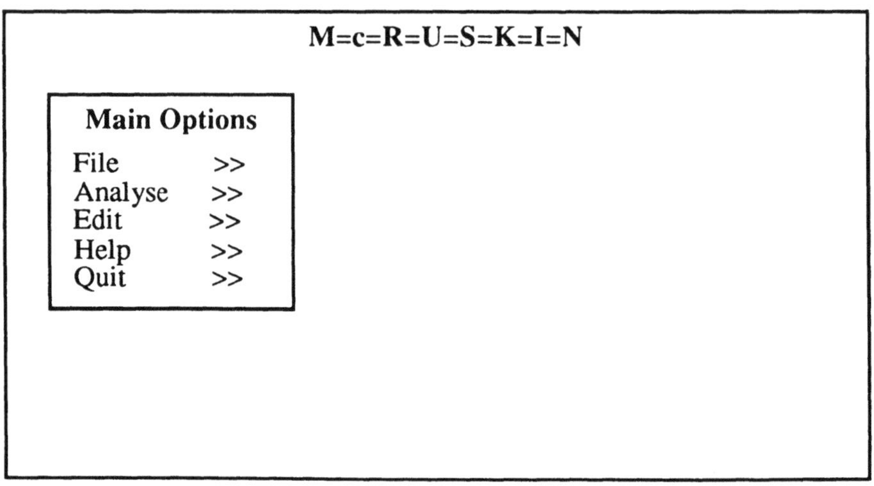

Figure 1. The top-level McRuskin menu. There are four main options available here; File, Analyse, Edit and Help.

Figure 1 shows the top-level McRuskin menu. There are four main options available here; File, Analyse, Edit and Help. These will be explained later as and when required. One of the first tasks to be performed is to load in a text file for analysis and possible revision. Figure 2 shows the display for the 'Load File' option and indicates that the file 'story.txt' has been selected.

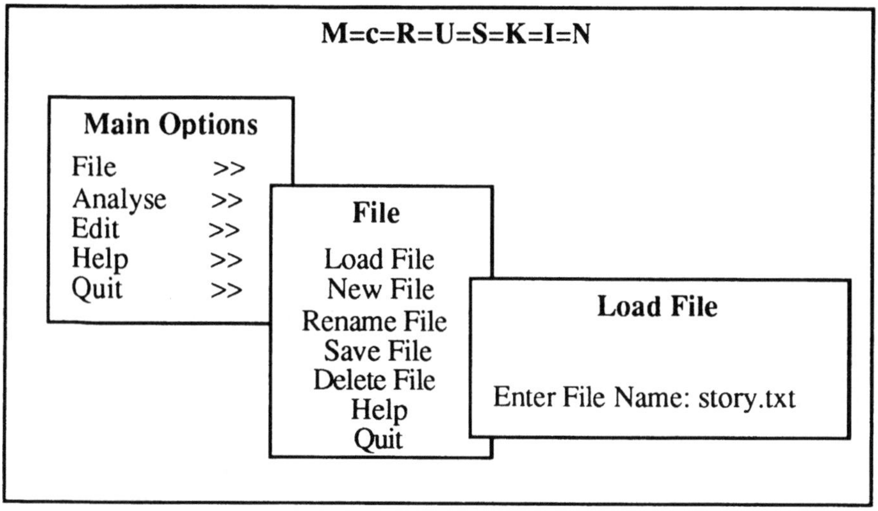

Figure 2. The display for the 'Load File' option and indicates that the file 'story.txt' has been selected.

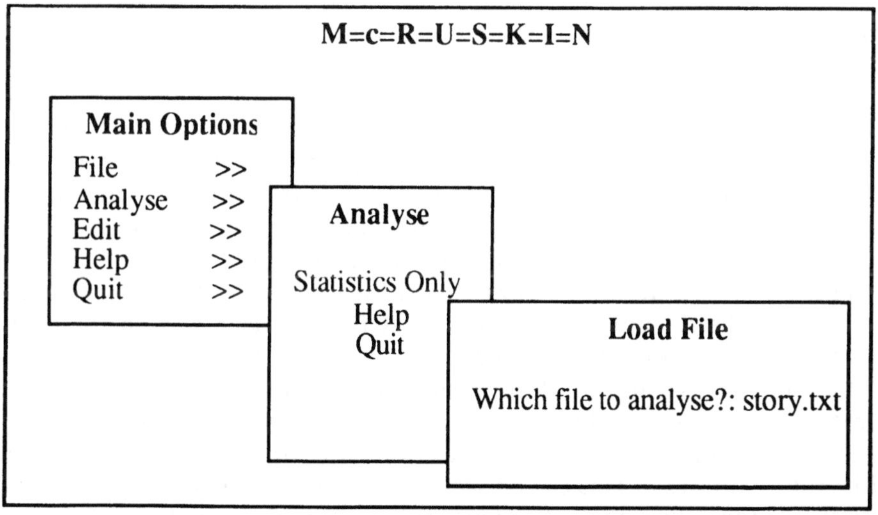

Figure 3. The main screen associated with the Analyse option. This facility allows the user to analyse their text, but not to edit it in any way.

Figure 3 shows the main screen associated with the Analyse option. This facility allows the user to analyse their text, but *not* to edit it in any way. This option could be selected if the user merely wished to do a 'quick check' on their text to ensure it was free from error. Note that the system displays the default file to style analyse.

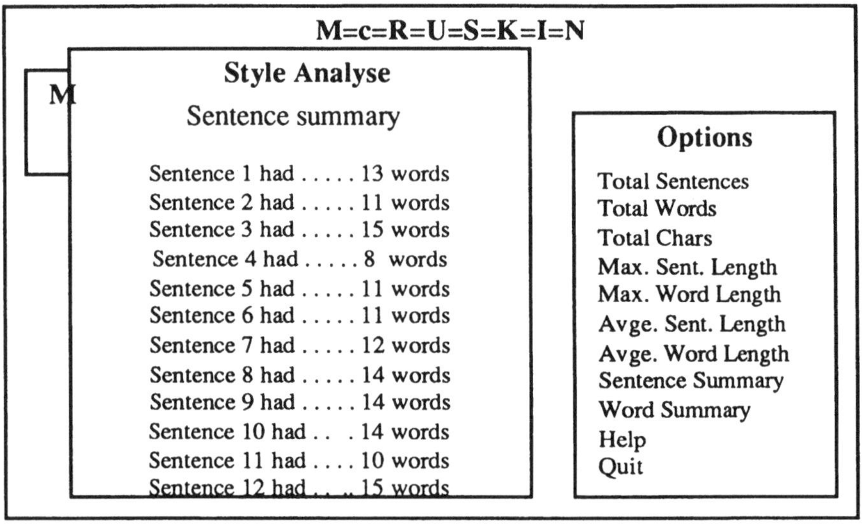

Figure 4. The output generated by selecting the 'Sentence Summary' option.

After performing this style analysis, McRuskin then allows the user to look at various facts and figures associated with the analysed text. Possible options available here include the ability to display word and sentence summaries, statistics on the maximum and average word/sentence length, etc. Figure 4 shows the output generated by selecting the 'Sentence Summary' option.

However, should the user wish to both style analyse *and* edit their text (if required), then the 'Edit' option should be selected from the main menu. Figure 5 shows the McRuskin displays seen at this point. As with the previous option, the default file name is used for loading into the editor.

Figure 6 shows the file 'story.txt' residing in the text editor. In order to style analyse the document, the user must first select a section for analysis. This can be achieved by moving the editor cursor to both the start and end of the block to analyse, and marking these points with appropriate key presses. After doing so the selected block becomes highlighted ready for analysis. The user should then press the CTRL/P keys to bring up the main menu available within the text editor. This can be seen in Figure 7. Of these main options only the first (Sentence Length) will invoke subsequent style analysis. Selection of any of the remaining options will result in a "Sorry. Not yet implemented"message being displayed.

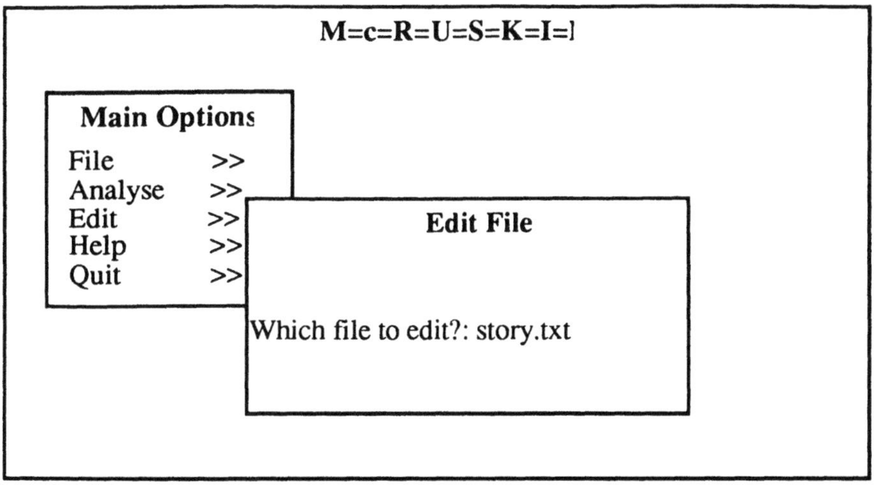

Figure 5. The McRuskin display when Edit has been chosen. As with the previous option, the default file name is used for loading into the editor.

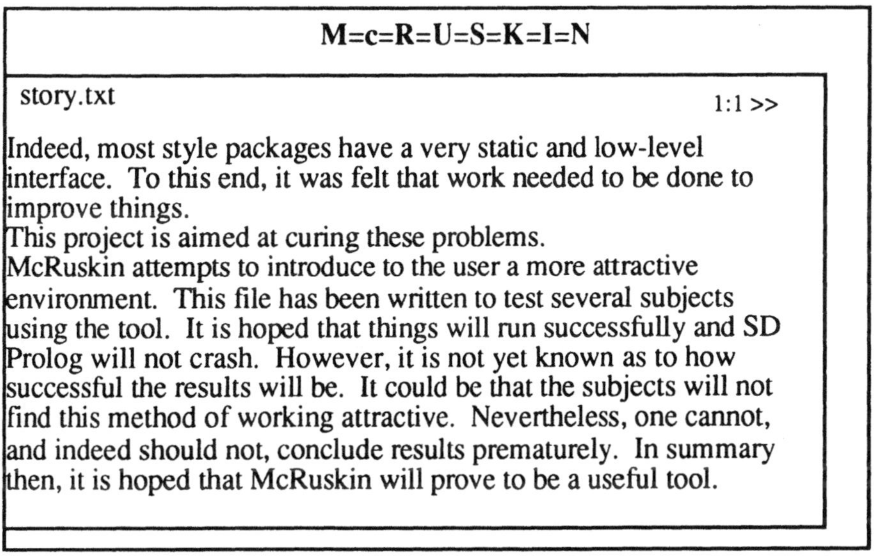

Figure 6. Shows the file 'story.txt' residing in the text editor.

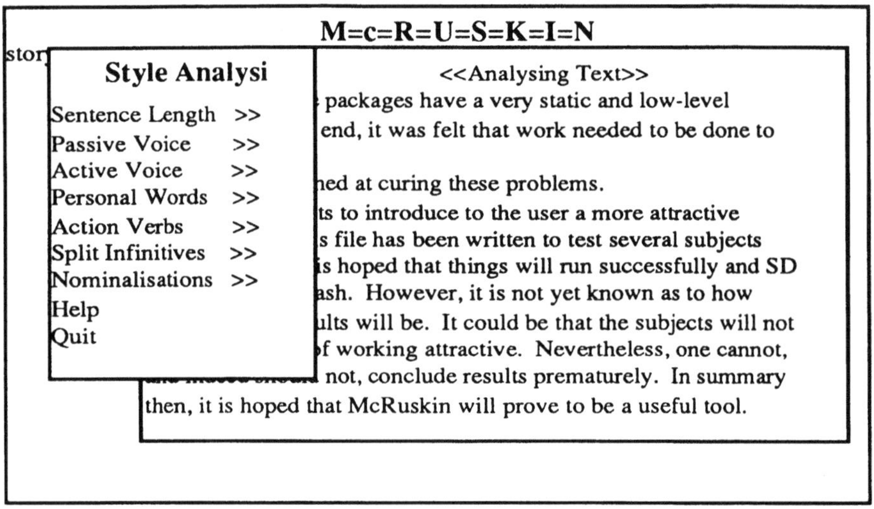

Figure 7. The Style Analysis options available when the user has chosen a block of text for analysis.

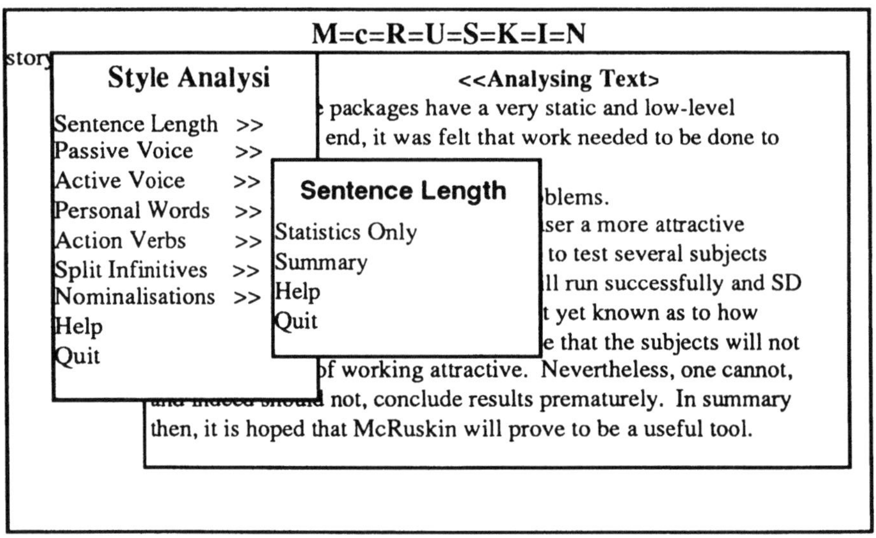

Figure 8. Sub-options available during Style Analysis.

There are a further two sub-options for this Sentence Length option; Statistics Only and Summary. The former of these options allows the user to obtain information very similar in nature to that obtained from the main menu Analysis option (see Figure 4). However, it is the latter option which invokes the main interactive style analysis functions. These two sub-options can be seen in Figure 8. Assuming the system found sentences which it considered too long, the user will be presented with Figure 9. This new screen informs the user that it found occurrences of long sentences within the text. In addition, a menu is displayed here which has two main options; Show Me and Explain (selection of this latter option will enter the user into the discourse module, explained later).

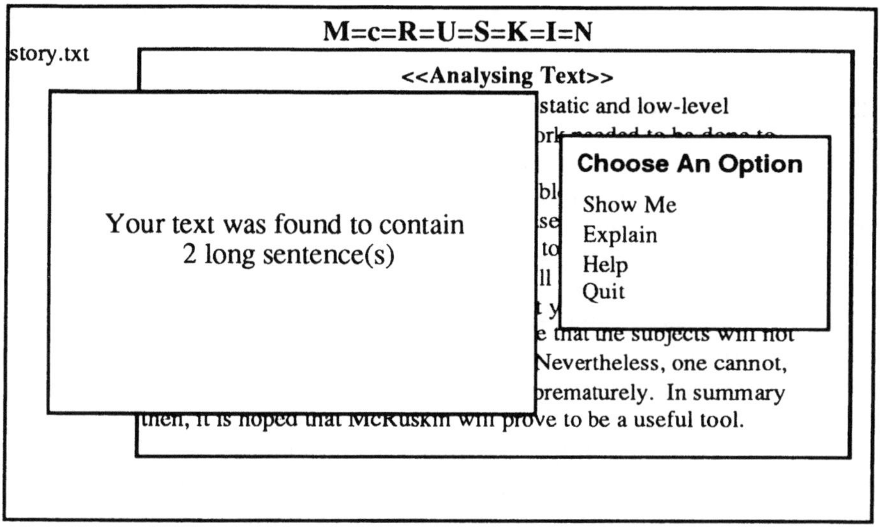

Figure 9. Feedback on Sentence Length.

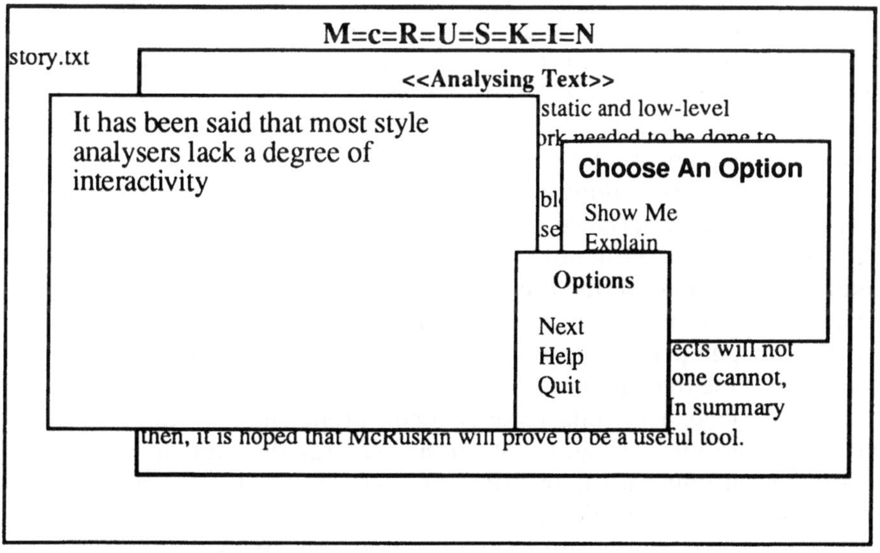

Figure 10. Selection of the Show Me option.

Selection of the Show Me option displays the screen shown in Figure 10. Here the user is able to browse through the collection of over-long sentences detected in the blocked-off text. This can be performed until there are no more sentences to inspect, or the user wishes to return to the editor and edit the relevant sentence(s).

Finally, after editing their text, the user should then leave the editor which will then return them to the top level menu where they can select another option.

7.1. Background to discourse module

McRuskin also embodies a seven-layer discourse module used to help explain style features incorporated into the system. This model has been derived from a number of sources (Moore and Swartout 1988ab, Moore 1988, Cawsey 1988). However, before outlining this model, it would be advantageous to first describe it in terms of basic human-to-human interactions.

Supposing someone (the speaker) had been given the task of describing a specific topic to someone else (the listener) who knew nothing at all about the subject concerned. What approach would the speaker adopt in describing the topic to the listener? In normal circumstances the speaker may first give a brief outline of the topic and hope the listener understood what was said. If, however, the listener did not appreciate fully what had transpired then the speaker may attempt to bring in basic examples of the concept to clarify and reinforce what was said previously.

Assuming the listener did not understand the examples given, the speaker might then try and expand upon the initial brief outline presented earlier. The speaker may also attempt to keep this expansion in general terms, and refrain from introducing new, difficult or complex points that the listener might fail to comprehend. If this detailed description still leaves the listener bewildered or in need of further information, the speaker could then introduce sub-concepts of the parent topic. Inter-relationships which exist between these sub-concepts could also be discussed, along with any other point considered relevant, such as sub-topic function, importance, etc.

If the listener is still not satisfied with what has been said then the speaker could try to describe the concept or topic from a different perspective. For example, in terms of a different person, system, attitude, etc. In adopting this different perspective approach, the listener is presented with multiple views of the same information.

The next stage, assuming listener incomprehension, would perhaps be to describe the various analogies that might exist for the topic in question. This may involve outlining ideas in different systems that have a similarity to the topic currently under consideration.

The last stage would probably involve the speaker interrogating the listener with some general questions. This would ensure that the listener had either understood what had been said previously, or at least had grasped the main points outlined. If the listener's responses to these questions indicated that they had comprehended the current topic then the interaction ceases. If, however, it appears that they had not understood the important issues then the speaker might repeat the entire process. This may involve just re-iterating the same information, or could possibly entail providing new information which still expressed the same thoughts, views and sentiments.

7.2. Seven layer discourse module

Having described briefly the main features of the model, the seven individual stages can now be given:

- Provide a brief description of the topic.
- Give specific examples of the topic.
- Provide a more detailed, but still generalised, description of the topic.
- Describe sub-concepts of the parent topic.
- Describe the topic from different perspectives (views).
- Outline analogies in other areas or systems.
- Confirm understanding by (possibly) interrogating the user.

These seven stages represent a simplified, but realistic, description of the typical procedures person A goes through when describing an unknown concept to person B. How, then, can this model be incorporated into the McRuskin interface, and what features can it accommodate successfully? The best approach here would be to give a typical example session when McRuskin was in the discourse mode. This will help clarify the seven individual stages, the interaction mechanism used, and the features explained to the listener.

7.3. Sentence length discourse

Suppose the user had indicated that they wish to analyse their document for sentence length. That is, search the text for instances of sentences considered too long for a document of that type. After analysing the text, McRuskin might report back that it had found specific occurrences of over-long sentences. The user then has the option of either inspecting and editing the relevant sentence(s), or can request further explanation on the concept of sentence length (see Figure 9; Show Me and Explain options). If the Explain option is selected, McRuskin enters into the discourse mode outlined above.

However, before entering into the full discourse mode, McRuskin asks the user to specify what they consider to be their own understanding, or background knowledge, of sentence lengths. The primary reason for doing so is to shield the user from descriptions which are either too complex, or too simplistic for their own personal abilities. McRuskin asks the user to specify this background knowledge in one of three categories; Low, Average and High. Those users in the Low category will be displayed simplified and low-level text descriptions. Those users in the other two categories will receive increasingly more complex output to reflect their own understanding of sentence length usage.

After specifying their knowledge level, the user is then taken into

McRuskin's discourse mode, described as follows:

Stage 1: Provide brief description
The first stage would involve presenting a brief description of what McRuskin considers is 'good' sentence length for a document of that type. For example;

> "For a document of this type, which you have indicated is for an audience of school children, it is not a good idea to use sentences that contain more than 24 words."

The user then has the option of indicating that they have understood the message, and that they wish to return to inspecting and possibly editing the over-long sentences.

However, if the user wanted more information on what McRuskin had just output then they should select the "Huh?"option from the displayed menu. (For convenience, the following walk through will assume that the user *always* wishes to see more information).

Stage 2: Give examples
The second stage of the model involves presenting examples to clarify what has been said so far. McRuskin, in fact, allows the user to look at examples from three individual sources; (1) their own document, (2) a 'dummy' document aimed at the same audience or (3) a selection of documents of varying type (that is, aimed at different audiences). McRuskin would then display examples of over-long sentences from the source(s) specified by the user. The user is also able to 'travel' back and forth between examples, inspecting the sentences at leisure, until they require further information from McRuskin.

Stage 3: Provide detailed description
The next stage of the model involves displaying detailed information on sentence lengths. This would be aimed at the user's own type of document and not, say, on other types of document such as those outlined in the previous example stage of the model. This further detailed description would, however, still be addressed in a general manner. That is, there would be no reference to other major issues (e.g. alternative style analysis functions) that could confuse the user further. A typical generalised description of sentence length might be:

> "The length of sentences within particular types of document plays a major role in the comprehension of the overall text. If you are writing for an audience that is relatively young, or has very little experience of the subject matter, then you should avoid using over-long sentences. For the type of document you are writing here, you should aim for a maximum sentence length of 24 words. This will ensure that your audience can pay maximum attention to understanding the text, and not on deciphering long or difficult sentences."

This text could, of course, be extended to cover more than just the one paragraph given above. Nevertheless, what is important here is that the mechanism is provided which enables the user to see this detailed, yet still simplified, text.

The system should also provide the facility where the user can travel through the individual screens to re-read specific items of information, if so desired.

Stage 4: Describe sub-concepts

The next stage of the model attempts to describe the sentence length concept by highlighting both its related and sub-concepts. In providing this commentary it is hoped that, by mentioning a sub-concept that the user is familiar with, the user will be able to grasp the relevance of sentence length within documents they create. For instance, typical sub-concepts of sentence length might be 'paragraph length', 'word length' and 'readability'.

Each of these sub-classes will be expanded in turn, in the hope of providing the user with the knowledge necessary to understand the parent concept. A typical example output here might be:

> "Sentence length is very closely tied in with other aspects of the writing process. All of these individual features interact to mould the overall content, readability and style of your document. The readability of a document gives an indication of the age of the audience expected to understand what you have written. It is calculated using several figures such as the average sentence length, average word size, etc. This readability measure, although of no major significance in most circumstances, is useful in some respects. Namely that it gives an indication as to the potential effectiveness of your document in relation to the audience you are writing for."

It is worth repeating here that the level of detail, or 'granularity', of the topics described will depend upon the user's own background knowledge specified earlier. This limited 'user model' allows the user to see only those items of information which they are expected to understand. This facility is used at all stages throughout the discourse model, and is the means by which McRuskin controls system output to the user.

Stage 5: Different perspectives

The next stage of the model involves describing sentence lengths from different perspectives or stances. This could entail discussing the topic from the point of view of the audience, the subject material, the purpose of the document, or its end usage. For example, if describing the importance of sentence length from an audience perspective consisting primarily of school children, a typical view point might be:

> "For your document to have maximum effect, you will need to write text having shorter sentence lengths. You have told me that the audience you are writing for are mainly school children, and that they probably have a neutral attitude to the subject material. You have also hinted at the

possibility of the document having a long life-span. So taking into consideration all of these points, it is vital that your audience appreciates what you have written, and that they can understand the themes, issues and sentiments you describe. School children of this age will soon lose interest in your document if it is difficult to read, lacks a suitable index and frequently uses jargon words with which they are unfamiliar."

Stage 6: Outline analogies

The penultimate stage of the discourse model involves describing various analogies that may exist between the current concept and similar concepts in other systems. For the sentence length analogy this will include outlining the analogy both in terms of actual textual information as well as incorporating statistical information stored as facts within the McRuskin system. For example, a typical output message here could be:

"The maximum acceptable sentence length for a particular document will vary depending on a number of factors, such as the age and educational level of your audience. You have indicated that the document currently under review is aimed at school children. The maximum sentence length for documents of this kind is approximately 18 words. In addition, the maximum acceptable average sentence length for school children is approximately 9.8 words.

The corresponding values in documents aimed at different audience types are as follows:

AUDIENCEMAX. SENT. LENGTHAVERAGE SENT. LENGTH	
College Student	3512.3
School Student	189.8
Business People	3511.2
General Public	2410.2
Audience Unknown	2811.0

It can be seen that in order for you to write clearly it is vital that you take into account the age and ability of your audience. This is true for all ages, but it is more so for people of early years or low educational levels such as those who will be reading your document."

Stage 7: Confirm understanding

The final stage of the discourse model involves asking the user some basic questions to confirm their understanding of the issues and points just described. These questions could range in complexity from trivial posers, right up to severe interrogations. The complexity of questions asked here will depend, as in the previous six levels, on the capability of the user which they specified at the onset of the discourse. A typical question asked at this point could be:

"Which of the following sentences do you consider to be too long for a document such as yours?

(1) It is difficult to say whether Bros. will remain a successful pop group and still attract wide media attention whenever they appear. (2) Similarly, it is also open to question whether they will split up as so many bands do nowadays. (3) What is certain, however, is that they have been thrown onto the pop industry with such speed, and with such hype that their descent will be a hard and painful journey. (4) One can only hope that this will be a long, arduous and devastating nightmare for all concerned."

POSSIBLE RESPONSES

Sentence 1
Sentence 2
Sentence 3
Sentence 4
Sentences 1,3
Sentences 2,4
All Sentences"

The user then enters a dialogue where they are presented with a number of such questions. The responses to these questions are stored and then summated. Users scoring less than a specified internal threshold will be deemed to have failed comprehending the concept, and will be told so. The user will then be asked if they wish to go through all the questions answered incorrectly and inspect the correct responses; an explanation will also be given for each solution to help reinforce the learning process. If, however, the user has answered sufficient correct answers to have 'understood' the concept, they are displayed with a 'congratulations' message.

Regardless of whether or not the user passed the question/answering session, they are then asked if they wish to look at McRuskin's style rules to help clarify why their document may have been in error. After inspection of the style rules, if selected, the user is then returned to the point where they initiated the discourse module. This will be the menu enabling them to inspect and edit those over-long sentences detected by the system.

8. Subject evaluation

The evaluation process relied heavily upon the technique known as 'protocol analysis'(Newell and Simon 1972; Flower and Hayes 1980a). In a verbal, or 'thinking aloud' protocol, subjects are invited to say aloud *everything* they think and *everything* that occurs to them whilst performing the task, irrespective of how trivial it may seem. These protocols are tape recorded during the evaluation process, and can then be analysed later to identify the cognitive processes present during the interaction.

The five subjects were required to analyse and edit a given test file, and to reduce those sentences deemed to be too long. The sample text file had approximately five such sentences, and consisted of approximately 12 sentences in total.

After analysing the subjects' protocols, seven individual features were identified as being present during most interactions. These activities are as follows: (Note: the term 'edited sentence' refers to the current sentence regarded as being too long, and therefore in need of editing.)

- *Reading the edited sentence:* this includes both reading the sentence in part and in full, as well as re-reading the sentence in part and full.
- *Reading sentences adjacent to the edited sentence:* this includes reading those sentences both prior to and after the edited sentence.
- *Deleting unnecessary words in the edited sentence:* this involves searching the sentence for superfluous or trivial words which would not affect sentence meaning if deleted.
- *Paraphrasing the edited sentence:* this includes both paraphrasing the entire sentence as well as smaller, individual sections.
- *Brainwaves:* this involves the subject suddenly realising what they have done wrong, or how they can eliminate the problem, etc.
- *Physically counting the number of words in edited sentence:* this will usually be after the subject has edited the sentence and wishes to verify its overall length. (NB: this activity is mainly sentence length specific, and not usually associated with other style features.)
- *Analysing the text:* this will be to double-check that the edited sentence(s) meet the style analysers approval.

The McRuskin system then entered into the final stage of evaluation. This last stage was primarily to decide if the interface could support all of the seven activities outlined above. The conclusions drawn from this final evaluation revealed that McRuskin could accommodate some, but not all, of these processes.

However, whilst these results uncovered minor drawbacks within the McRuskin interface, they also had the attraction that they enabled a set of 'ideal' interface screens to be developed.

Figure 11 shows the main system menu. Here the user is able to select the required style analysis feature to pass over their blocked-off text. For example, detection of over-long sentences. Other options available here enable the user to check for the presence of passive voice, split infinitives, action verbs, etc.

Assuming the user had selected sentence length, and further assuming the style analyser had found instances of long sentences within the specified text, the user will then be presented with the screen given in Figure 12. This new screen informs the user that the analyser had, indeed, found long sentences in the text, and is awaiting further user input from the new system menu. There are three main options available here; Show Me, Edit and Explain. Selection of the Explain option enters the user into the discourse module described earlier. Selection of the Edit option takes the user onto the screen given in Figure 14, which will be explained later.

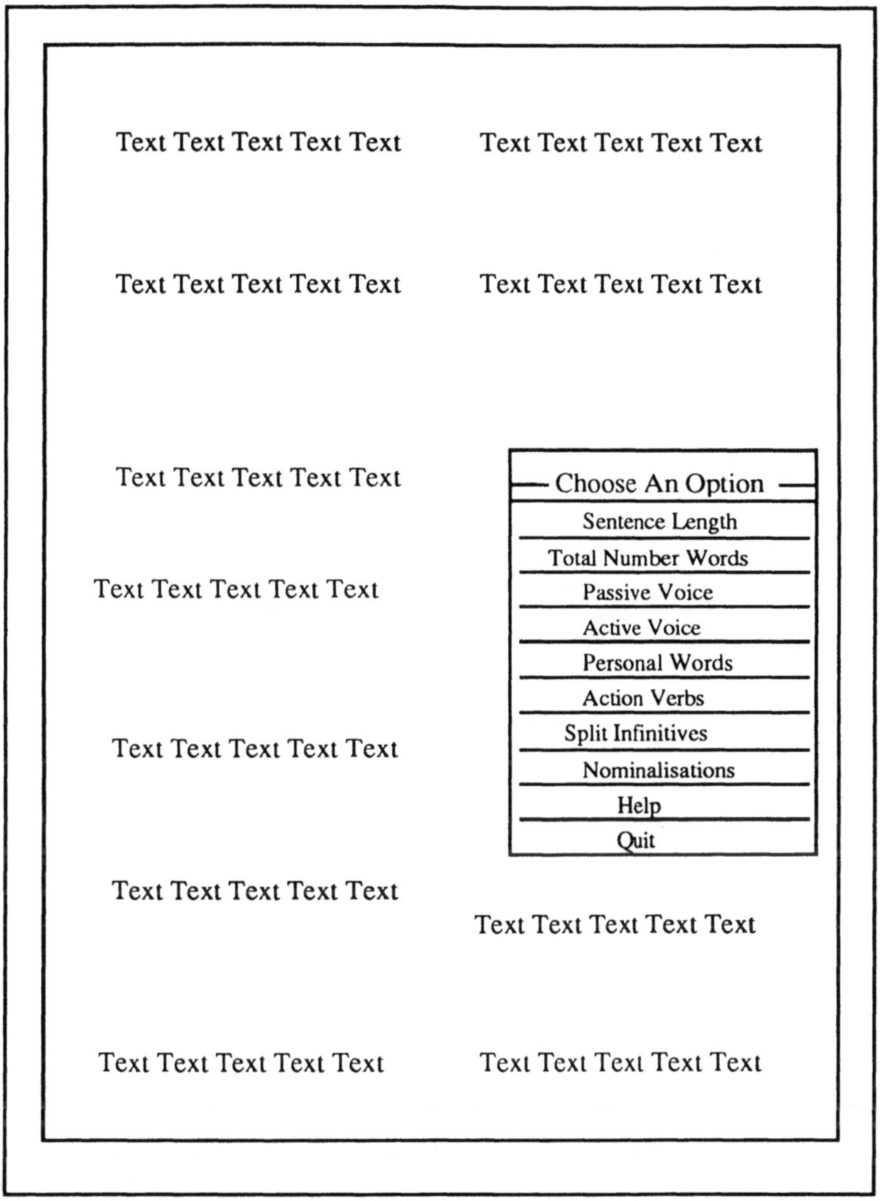

Figure 11 The main menu system.

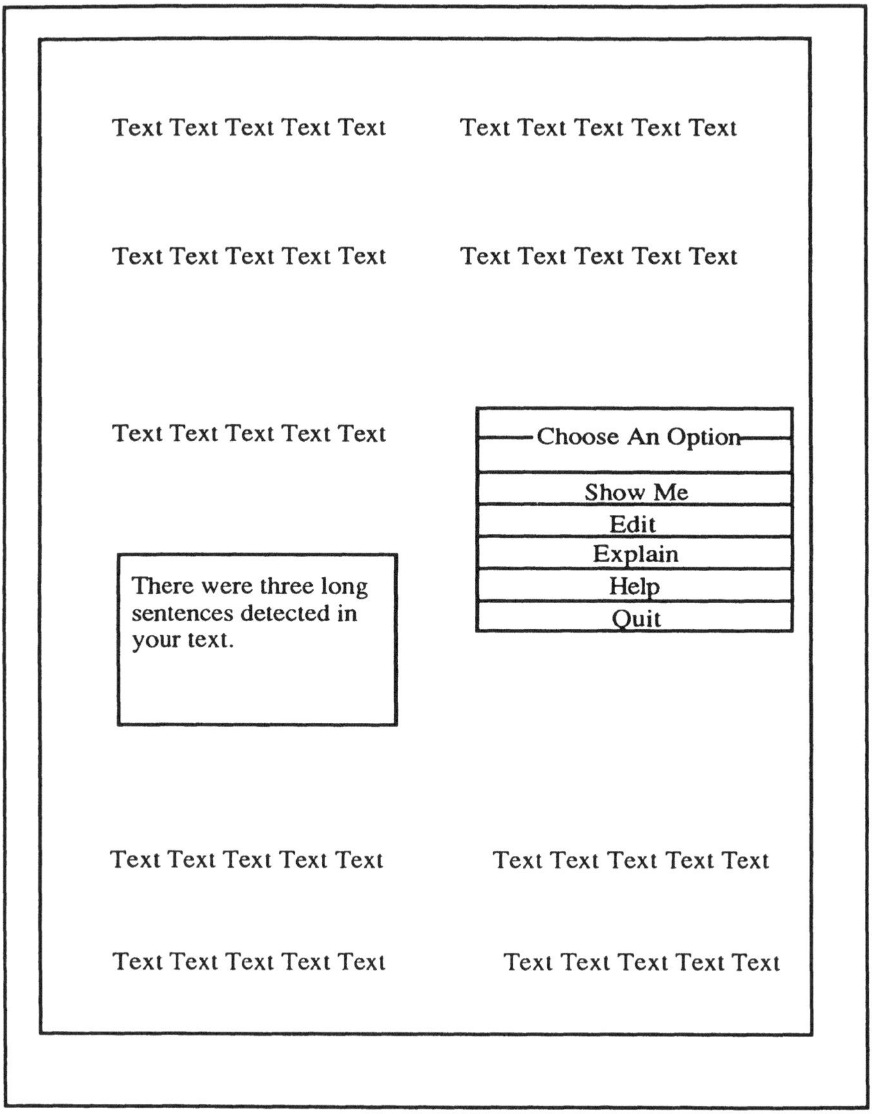

Figure 12. If the 'Explain' option is selected, the user can enter into the discourse module where they can obtain explanations of the selected style feature.

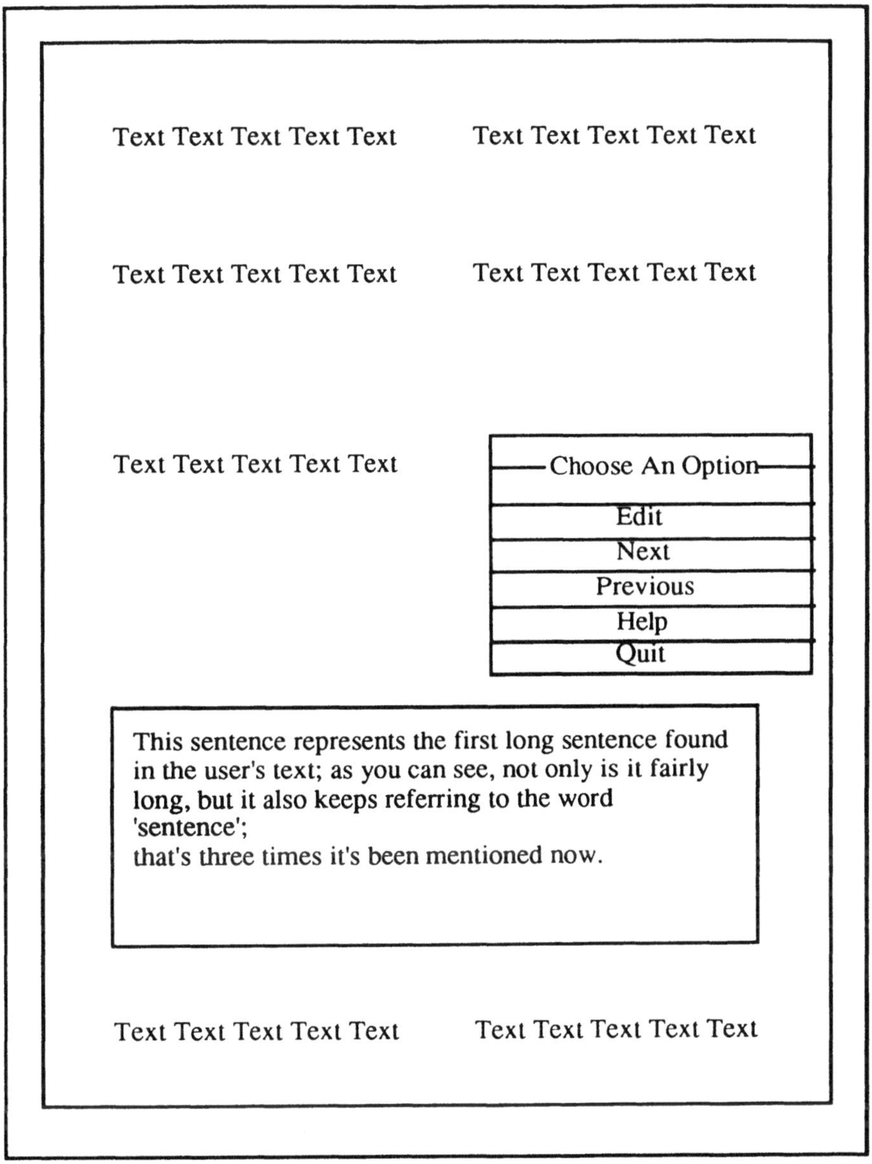

Figure 13. If the 'Next' and 'Previous' options are selected, the user can browse through the collection of over-long sentences detected by the system.

Selection of the Show Me option takes the user onto the screen given in Figure 13. Here the user is shown the first long sentence found in the blocked-off text. Further options at this point allow the user to travel back and forth looking at the collection of over-long sentences found by the system (Next and Previous). The Edit option on this screen takes the user, as with the Edit option found on Figure 12., onto the screen given in Figure 14.

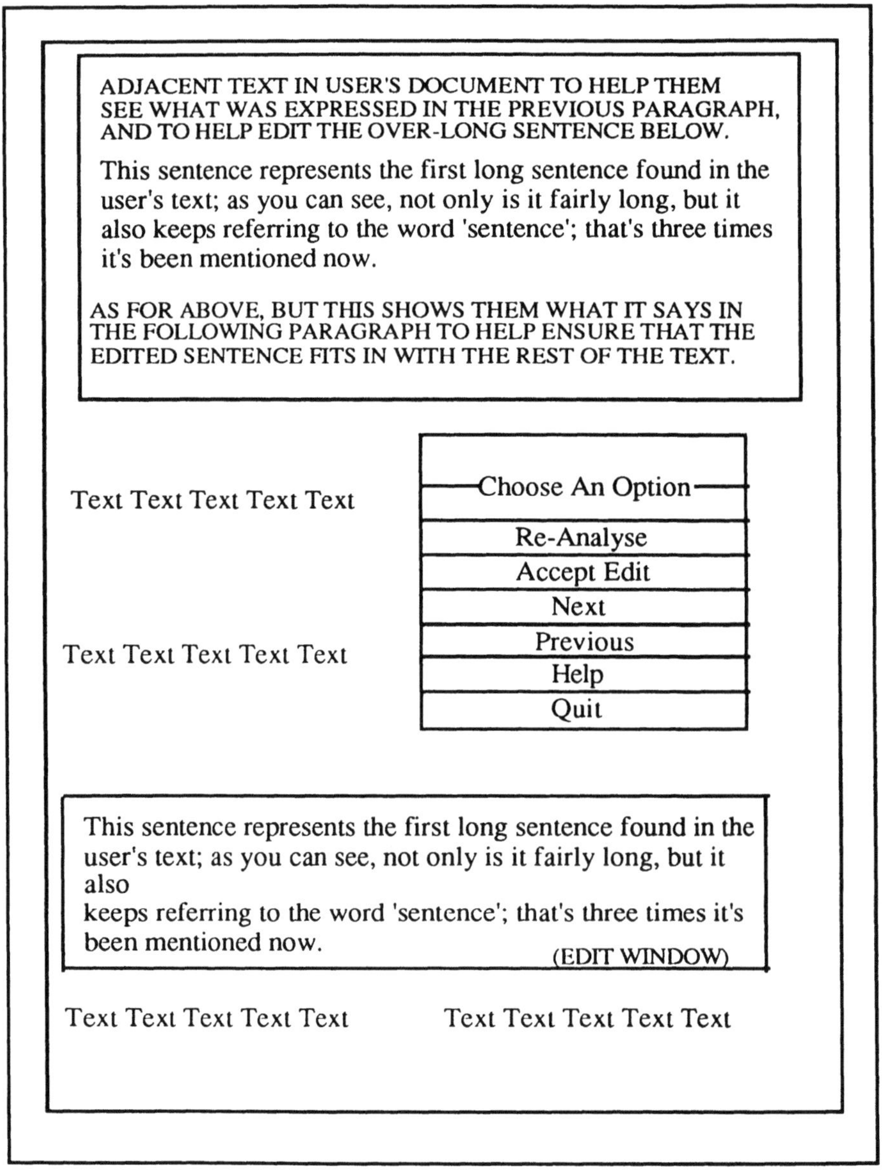

Figure 14. Here, the user is given a copy of the over-long sentence for editing and information regarding surrounding text. Other options allow browsing of other long sentences. One further option enables the user to accept the edited text only after analysis.

This new screen displays a menu consisting of a further four main options; Re-Analyse, Accept Edit, Next and Previous. The Next and Previous options allow the user to browse through the sentences at leisure and decide if updates are necessary or desirable. The Re-Analyse option enables the user to re-check any updates they may have made to particular sentences. Lastly, the Accept Edit option allows the user to replace the edited sentence back into their document at the correct location. This option is required as there would be little point in replacing a sentence with an even larger one which would never pass the style analyser's sentence length checker. This point applies to all the other style analysis features such as passive voice and split infinitives; time and effort could be saved if the edit were accepted if, and only if, it passed subsequent style analysis successfully.

9. Conclusions

A number of comments can be made regarding the information given in this paper. The first concerns the use of protocol analysis during the interface evaluation stage. Although this approach is relatively straight-forward to employ, it does suffer from the drawback that eliciting verbal protocols from subjects can be a difficult process. Subjects may sometimes 'slump' into quiet periods when they are thinking about some activity or process to perform. Worse still, the subjects may even be unaware that they have become quiet, even after the experimenter has stated explicitly that they should think aloud at all times. Nevertheless, if this should occur, the experimenter can easily ask the subject to speak up and describe what they are thinking.

The second point concerns the limited 'user model' incorporated into the discourse module which asked the user to specify their abilities in one of three categories; Low, Average and High. There is one main drawback with this approach; namely, how much weight or credence does one give to the user's judgement of their own abilities? Also, how willing will a user be to show their possible ignorance of a particular style concept? One may find that a given user may not want to admit (even to a machine) that their own understanding of, say, nominalisations, is low, and so will give an inflated estimate of their abilities. If this were the case then it is very likely that the user will be unable to read, let alone comprehend, the consequent output explanations since they have been tailored to a more 'knowledgeable' user.

Thirdly, although the seven layers of the discourse module allow great room for presenting information to the user in new and novel ways, idea generation and manipulation can sometimes be very difficult. This is because it needs a great deal of ingenious thought to formulate ideas that describe a particular style concept which can then be 'inserted' into the appropriate layer of the discourse module. The sentence length example was chosen deliberately since it was apparent that this particular feature had a rich field of ideas to select. However, this may not be true for other style features; greater thought and care may be needed to formulate sub-concepts, different perspective views and possible analogies.

Finally, several of the subjects commented upon the fact that they found it difficult to reduce the lengths of sentences within the given test file. As stated previously, the subjects were required to reduce the lengths of a number of sentences to under 12 words. This, obviously, represents a sentence length well below that expected for school children with low educational ability. The only defence one can put forward here is that the sentences were very simple, and together constituted a simple paragraph which, it is hoped, did not involve a great deal of thought to accomplish the bench-mark task. Another factor which may have compounded this issue centres around the fact that the subjects did not write the test file themselves. Hence, this meant that the text was, in a sense, foreign. However, if the subjects had been allowed to write their own test files then the evaluation process would be encroaching more and more on the pre-writing stages, and there would be no guarantee the sentences would be amenable to reduction below that required for the experiment.

10. References

Cawsey, A. (1988) Generating tutorial explanatory dialogues. Department of Artificial Intelligence, University of Edinburgh, Edinburgh.

Cooper, C. R. and Matsuhashi, A. (1983) A theory of the writing process. .In M. Martlew(Ed). *The Psychology Of Written Language.* John Wiley, Chichester.

Flower, L. S. and Hayes, J. R. (1980a) Identifying the organisation of writing processes. In L. W. Gregg and E. R. Steinberg (Ed) *Cognitive Processes in Writing: An Interdisciplinary Approach.* Lawrence Erlbaum, Hillsdale, NJ.

Flower, L. S. and Hayes, J. R. (1980b) The dynamics of composing: making plans and juggling constraints. In L. W. Gregg and E. R. Steinberg (Ed) *Cognitive Processes in Writing: An Interdisciplinary Approach.* Lawrence Erlbaum, Hillsdale, NJ.

Holt, P. O'B. and Williams, N. (1989) Expert systems for report writing. Technology *Enhanced Training Conference. (tet'89) 18-20 July 1989. Conference Proceedings. Module F: Artificial Intelligence/Expert Systems.* Royal Military College of Science, Shrivenham, Swindon, Wiltshire.

McGowan, S. (1989) Interactive writer's assistants: Updating Ruskin. Unpublished M.Sc. thesis. Department of Computer Science, Heriot-Watt University, Edinburgh.

Moore, J. D. and Swartout, W. R. (1988a) A reactive approach to explanation. UCLA Department of Computer Science.

Moore, J. D. and Swartout, W. R. (1988b) Planning and reacting. UCLA Department of Computer Science.

Moore, J. D. (1988) Responding to 'Huh?': answering vaguely-articulated follow-up questions. UCLA Department of Computer Science.

Newell, A. and Simon, H. A. (1972) *Human Problem Solving.* Prentice-Hall, Englewood Cliffs, NJ.

Sharples, M. and O'Malley, C. (1988) A framework for the design of a writer's assistant. In J. Self, (Ed). *Artificial Intelligence And Human Learning: Intelligent Computer-Aided Instruction.* Chapman and Hall, London.

21

Representing Writing: External Representations and the Writing Process

Mike Sharples
University of Sussex

Lyn Pemberton
Brighton Polytechnic

Abstract

The aim of this paper is, first, to provide a synthesis and critique of contemporary explanations of writing as a cognitive process and, second, to extend these explanations by examining the means by which a writer creates a text through interaction with external resources and media, such as books, notes, pencil and paper, and the ways in which the representational properties of these resources affect the process of idea generation and written composition. We suggest that observed writing strategies can be described as a sequence of transitions between different representational spaces and that the choice of writing medium constrains the process of writing and influences the construction of these representations. We conclude by mentioning the implications of this analysis for the teaching of writing and the design of computer-based writing support tools.

1. Introduction

In recent years the techniques of Cognitive Science, developed to describe human problem solving behaviour, have been applied to the study of writing (Hayes and Flower 1980), with the aim of describing the process of written composition. These cognitive accounts of writing have not unlocked the door to creativity, nor produced infallible guides to good composition, but they have provided an analysis of differences between inexpert and expert writers, a description of writing strategies, and a new approach to the teaching of composition.

Writing is superficially similar to other well studied problem solving activities, such as playing chess, solving cryptarithmetic puzzles, or completing subtraction sums. It is goal directed and decomposable into a sequence of subgoals such as 'plan an outline', 'generate a first draft', and 'revise the text', each of which can be achieved by a sequence of basic actions such as 'generate a plan item', 'swap two sections', 'insert punctuation'. But it cannot be cast in the mould of simple goal directed search. In writing there is no well defined goal state, which means that methods such as means-ends analysis that depend on judging differences between the current state and a goal cannot be used. What is more, unlike chess, where the moves available at any state are independent of the design of the chessboard, the medium imposes its own constraints: the process of writing with a pen and paper is substantially different from that of writing with a typewriter or a word processor.

General problem solving methods are, therefore, inappropriate to the writing task (though the writer may call on them for particular sub-tasks) and an analysis of the process is correspondingly difficult. The usual method has been to study writers in action, producing descriptions of the writer's cognitive structures and processes which can then be generalised by incorporating data from other writers, or the same writer performing different tasks. The limitation of this approach is that it does not directly address the effect of the medium on the writing process, nor does it map out the space of possible writing strategies.

We shall begin by describing a composite model of the writing process derived from other researchers' accounts of writing, and then discuss ways in which this model can be extended and rationalised to account explicitly for a writer's interaction with external media.

2. A composite model of the writing process

In the last decade there have been a number of important studies of the writing process, for tasks ranging from structured expository writing to creative fiction (Cooper and Greenbaum 1986; Frederiksen and Dominic 1981; Gregg and Steinberg 1980; Matsuhashi 1987; Nystrand 1982). The investigative techniques used in these studies have included protocol analysis, structured interviews of writers, analysis of pause information, and analysis of the writer's notes and jottings.

Although there have been differences in emphasis, for instance in the degree to which writing fits into identifiable stages of planning, drafting and revising, there has been unanimity about methodology, in the form of a shared conviction that we can find out more about *how* people write by observing writers in action than by analysing finished texts, and a sense of working towards a single, composite picture of the writing process.

2.1. Writing operations

A writing assignment usually begins long before a writer puts pen to paper. Sometimes there is a clear starting point, as when a student turns over an exam paper and sees the essay title: at other times, the outline of a possible structure for a discussion of some topic begins to form in the writer's mind, or a collection of ideas demands to be written down. At this stage, writing is inseparable from general thinking (Gregg and Steinberg 1980) and there is no clear distinction between ideas and text.

The main goals of the writer are then to plan the text, to generate further ideas appropriate to the task, to turn these into a coherent stream of words, and to ensure that the written product is suited to its audience and purpose. These goals are not normally satisfied in a single sequence of operations. Writing can be iterative (the writer may plan, generate and revise text segment by segment) or recursive (the words may prompt a new stream of ideas). One way to describe the complexities of writing is to list the basic operations and then to show how these can be interleaved to satisfy the writer's multiple goals.

Flower and Hayes (1980) suggest that there are three general classes of writing operation: *planning, translating and reviewing*. *Planning* sets out the framework for a piece of writing. It comprises three types of suboperation: *generating*, in which the writer retrieves information relevant to the writing task from long term memory; *organising*, in which the most useful of the retrieved items are organised into a plan; *goal setting*, whereby the writer creates further goals to guide the writing.

Translating is the action of taking material from memory, under the guidance of the plan and goals, and transforming it into coherent sentences. Cooper and Matsuhashi (1983) decompose translating into further sub-operations needed for generating sentence-level text.

The *reviewing* operation has the aim of improving the quality of the written text and can be decomposed into two sub-operations: *editing*, to alter text, at the time it is produced, to fit the plans and *rereading*, or deliberately going back over the text to look for problems.

A text has embedded levels of structure, from the document as a whole to a single word, and Collins and Gentner (1980) suggest a number of specific editing operations acting at different textual levels. Section-level operations include adding headings, prioritising important points and moving qualifying statements to the start of the section. Operations at paragraph level include forming a series of sentences into a list, adding topic and concluding sentences, and adding connective phrases. Sentence level operations include creating parallel syntactic structures, breaking up a long sentence into several short ones and changing from passive to active voice.

The writing operators do not usually occur in a simple cycle of *plan-translate-review*, but instead form a precedence hierarchy, with the *generate* and *edit* operators normally being of high priority. This means that the translation of ideas into text may be interrupted either when the text needs revision, or when it prompts the generation of new ideas. Britton (1970) describes this latter action as idea generation 'at the point of inscription'. A good writer will make use of ideas that arise during production, either by noting them for later incorporation or by revising the plan to accommodate them. Studies by Sommers (1980) have shown that skilled writers carry out a larger number of major global revisions than do unskilled ones.

Figure 1 shows a model of writing produced by Hayes and Flower (1980), indicating how the main operations might fit together. The picture it conveys is far from complete, and provokes many questions, some of which are addressed in the next section, but it is useful as an attempt to indicate the interrelationships between the internal processes of the writer, and external material, i.e. resources and partly written text.

2.2. Constraints on the writing process

The conditions under which these operations are triggered for a particular text and the range of possible outcomes is restricted by constraints which guide the creation of any piece of writing:

> "The act of writing is best described as the act of juggling a number of simultaneous constraints. This is in contrast to seeing it as a series of discrete stages or steps that add up to a finished product." (Flower and Hayes 1980).

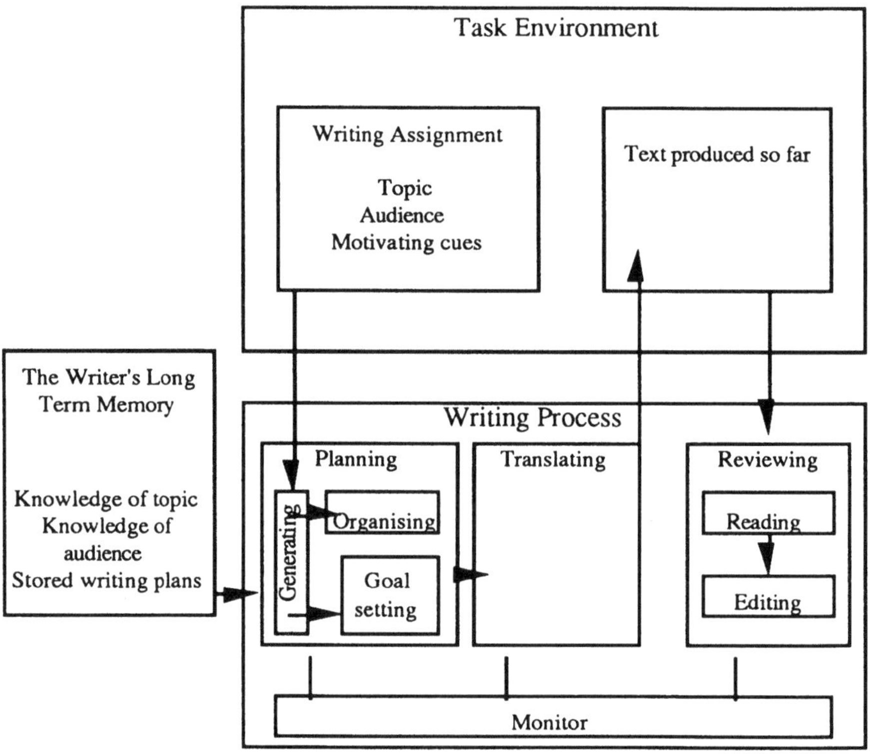

Figure 1. Hayes and Flower model of writing

Some constraints are set by the writer at the start of the task. As the text builds up it will itself impose further restrictions of consistency. Although constraints perform useful functions, restricting the search of memory involved in generating text, ensuring consistency of style and content, and giving a focus to the writing, they also impose cognitive demands:

> "It is no wonder many people find writing difficult. It is the very nature of the beast to impose a large set of converging but potentially contradictory. Furthermore, to be efficient the writer should attend to all these

constraints at once ... Unfortunately, this ideal rarely occurs because of the limited number of items our short term memory or conscious attention can handle." (Flower and Hayes 1980)

Flower and Hayes suggest a number of techniques for reducing the burden of managing multiple constraints. These include: selectively ignoring some constraints (for example by *bracketing*: creating words to set down an idea without worrying about style or meshing them with the rest of the task); partitioning the problem into more manageable sub-problems; setting priorities and *satisfice* ('making do'); drawing on routine procedures.

2.3. Approaches to writing

Each writer will make her own use of the general operators, and the same individual may adopt different approaches for different texts and for different parts of the same text, writing one section in a 'stream of consciousness' style, while painstakingly reworking the wording of another. Bridwell-Bowles *et al.* (1987) indicate two broad approaches to writing, which can be seen as representing the opposite ends of a spectrum.

At one extreme is the *Mozartian,* who produces detailed plans before text. The advantage of this approach is that it allows the writer to create a framework upon which to hang the words, but it demands an ability to produce plans suited to the task, of sufficient detail to guide the translation process. A common trait of poor writers is to develop a pseudo-plan in the form of 'milestones': a string of isolated items to be included at some points in the text. They then face the problem of moving the text from one milestone to the next (Sharples 1985).

At the other end of the scale is the *Beethovian,* who creates text in order to find out what he thinks, interleaving planning and translation. As the text emerges it serves to direct the search of long-term memory and to constrain the selection and organisation of ideas. Although a useful means of pouring out a first draft, a Beethovian approach usually requires that the writer be able to abstract the structure and salient points of the text in order to rework and polish it.

Hartley and Branthwaite (1989) arrived at similar distinction by a different route. Eighty eight productive British psychologists completed a questionnaire on their writing habits, and on their attitudes to and feelings about academic writing. A cluster analysis of the questions concerned with methods of composition found two large groupings. The first group, of 34 people, fit the mould of the Mozartian writer. They reported that they spent time thinking about what they were doing, did not write the sections of an article in a set order, and produced, on average, 3.4 drafts. The other group, of 28 people, spent less time thinking about an article before the structure emerged and were more likely to work in sequence, completing one section at a time. On average they produced 2.0 drafts. The sample were all productive writers and they appear to have overcome the Beethovian's difficulty of creating a well-structured text, presumably by having extensive 'compiled knowledge' (Anderson 1983) of textual structures enabling them to fit material into a framework as they generate it, without the need for extensive pre-planning.

Bereiter and Scardamalia (1987) make a different high-level distinction, distinguishing two approaches to retrieving and using stored knowledge. In the first of these, the naturally acquired process of *knowledge telling*, the writer generates items by probing long-term memory, tests them for appropriateness and writes down those which are suitable. The second method is the more studied *knowledge transforming*, in which knowledge telling is embedded within a process of organising *content problem space*, where problems of belief and knowledge are worked out and *rhetorical problem space*, where problems of achieving goals of composition are dealt with. This process, which roughly corresponds to application of Flower and Hayes' organising and *goal setting* operations, demands deliberate control over the structure of ideas and the process of text production and it is only mastered after considerable learning.

2.4. Writing strategies

In addition to following broad approaches, the writer will choose more specific strategies to meet the task at hand. Research into the writing process has identified the following strategies:

Plan-draft-revise

The writer begins by generating a plan, uses this to form a draft, and then checks over the draft making corrections and alterations.

Outline-draft

The writer creates a list of section headings, in the order they will appear on the page, and then fills them out with text.

Draft-revise

The writer sets down a hurried steam of ideas as words on the page. These form both a first draft and a source of inspiration for further cycles of drafting and redrafting.

Cut and paste

The writer collects together already written material –notes, quotes, extracts from earlier writings –and then organises and alters them to fit the current task.

Within these overall strategies, the writer calls on more specialised techniques including:

Brainstorming

The writer jots down notes without worrying how to organise them. When the ideas dry up the writer organises the notes by, for example, sorting them into conceptual categories.

Following a thread

The writer creates a conceptual network around a topic, spreading outward with subtopics in the form of elaborations, examples, definitions, and also digressions or asides, as in footnotes or notes to ones self. Often the writer does not have much idea of what the eventual structure will look like, since it only emerges when that particular branch of the network has been developed.

Filling a template

The writer recalls a template for a plot, event, or argument from long-term memory and then fills it out. A related technique is *planning by analogy*, where the writer uses the form of an already written text as a guide to planning.

2.5. Implications of the model

The picture of cognition and writing that has emerged from the past ten years of research is of a goal-directed task governed by multiple constraints. There is no simple progression from one stage to another, but instead a cycle of planning, text generation and revision, with the written words acting as triggers for further planning.

The model has clear implications for the teaching of writing and for the provision of tools for writers:

- Writing is more than just presenting words neatly on a page. Much of a writer's time is spent in mustering ideas, forming intentions, collecting resources, and creating plans. A model of writing for use in teaching should be concerned with the entire process, from registering the task to producing a finished manuscript. Students need to learn not only what to write, but also how to write: how to set goals, to organise ideas, to devise and monitor plans, to guide the creation of text, and to make revisions.
- An important aspect of the teaching of writing should be to describe the process of writing, to help a writer uncover his own idiosyncratic ways of working and to develop new ones. This means developing a meta-language to communicate with the student about writing operations, strategies and approaches and to describe the structure of plans and texts.
- Not only do plans guide writing, but the act of writing can give the author new insight, leading him to generate new material, form new intentions and revise plans. Skilled writers are able to keep their text and plans in harmony, monitoring them both and making changes when they drift apart. Teachers of writing should promote these skills, offering the writer ways of capturing ideas as they arise and of making global revisions to the structure of a document.
- There is no single best approach to writing. The teaching of writing should seek to extend a student's existing skills or, where these are

inadequate, to show a range of successful methods and help the student to acquire appropriate ones. Computer systems to support the writing process will be of most help if they fit the writer's perception of the task and assist whichever strategy the writer chooses to adopt.
- A writer defines and manages the task by setting constraints that govern the creation of raw material, plans and text. A writer can be taught well-defined techniques of constraint management, such as outlining, prioritising and bracketing.

2.6. Limitations of the model

The cognitive model of writing that we have described so far (we shall call it the 'consensus model') has broken the stalemate in understanding that prevailed a decade ago and has offered an agenda for future research. It does, however, have some important limitations and these are addressed in this section.

- The consensus model is under-specified with regard to the nature of the representations of the text at each stage of its construction.
- There is no clear distinction between mental structures and analogous ones on an external medium. For example, the phrase 'ideas organising' is commonly used to describe the activity of creating and modifying symbols or words organised as an associative network on some external medium. But physical marks are not ideas; the networks have the nature of an 'intermediate representation', a bridge between mental structures and text, with some of the properties of each.
- The model does not account for the characteristics of different media –paper, computer screen, white board, file card etc. –and the ways that these affect the practice of writing.
- Lastly, the model offers no indication of whether the list of writing approaches and strategies so far described is complete, nor does it provide a framework within which to place them.

3. An extended model of the writing process

We are broadly in agreement with the consensus model, and the account of writing that we shall give here is an attempt to rationalise and extend it, rather than to counter it. We shall lay out a framework within which the strategies identified by other researchers can be set, concentrating on the ways in which a writer realises ideas as symbolic representations. We identify techniques for generating these representations, and present an account of the relationship between such techniques and the media used in writing.

3.1. Representational items

In the previous section we mentioned difficulties in defining the representational properties of the structures a writer creates when setting down ideas, planning and drafting. Typically, a writing plan will contain fragments such as 'introduction' or 'include quote here', and perhaps longer segments of text that have already been completed for inclusion in the draft. Although these all consist of series of words, they differ in function and in the kind of operations that may be performed on them. We suggest that there are three types of text item that a writer produces: *instantiated items, uninstantiated items,* and *annotational items.*

- An *instantiated item* is a series of words with the status of a piece of connected prose. It may need further revision but it serves as a fleshed-out piece of text. We shall call instantiated items notes, but this does not imply any limits to their size, which may range from a single sentence to an entire document.
- An *uninstantiated item* (we shall call it an *idea-label*) acts both as an index to a mental schema and as a place-holder for a piece of text that has still to be created. Given that there is normally a direct correspondence between idea labels in a written plan and the items in the equivalent mental representation, a writer will normally alternate between mental planning and explicit practical operations, such as rearranging items in a list of contents. If the idea label indexes a familiar and well organised schema, for example 'my address', the writer should have little trouble in instantiating it by simple 'knowledge telling'. But if it acts as a label for a broad category of text, such as 'introduction' or 'literature survey', with no precise associated schema, then the writer may need to do a great deal more planning and fleshing out. Since it is typically marked by a phrase or sentence (for example, 'introduction', or 'write more about approaches to writing here') there is no general way to distinguish an uninstantiated item from an instantiated one, except by the role it performs as a temporary structure which will later be replaced by instantiated text.
- An *annotational item* represents a comment on another item of any type, for example to express the writer's intentions ('this paragraph needs to be turned into a list') or assessment ('this is poorly written'). In general, annotational items will not appear in a finished text, except perhaps as footnotes, but they play an important role in guiding revision. The subject of annotational conventions of writers deserves a paper in itself and we shall not pursue it here.

3.2. Representational structures

As well as distinguishing between *instantiated* and *uninstantiated* items, we also need to consider the arrangement of items on a page or screen. We shall call the different types of arrangement views. (There will also be implicit arrangements arising from semantic similarity of items or textual cross-reference, but our concern is with a writer's explicit representational structures.)

There are three general types of view. The items may be unordered, for instance when a writer creates an unsorted set of topics during a brainstorming session. They may be formed into a non-linear structure, such as an associative network or a taxonomic tree. Or they may be arranged linearly, as a series of words. Normally, non-linear views act as intermediate representations between the arrangement of items in the writer's semantic memory and the string of words in a finished text, although the new popularity of hypertext documents has brought texts whose composition is complete at just this stage, and which are not intended to receive a fixed linear form. The two dimensions, of *instantiation* and *view type*, characterise a writer's representation of items on some external medium. This gives the scheme sketched in Figure 2, where each representational structure is shown by a box in the grid.

Type of item

Organisation of items		UNINSTANTIATED	INSTANTIATED
	UNORGANISED	1 *Techniques:* Brainstorming *Representations:* Idea-labels	2 *Techniques:* Note-taking (verbatim) Collecting quotes *Representations:* Notes
	NON-LINEAR ORGANISATION	3 *Techniques:* Following a thread Writing as dialectic *Representations:* Network of idea-labels	4 *Techniques:* Organising notes Filing *Representations:* Network of notes
	LINEAR ORGANISATION	5 *Techniques:* Linear planning *Representations:* List of idea-labels Table of contents	6 *Techniques:* Drafting text Revising text Copying text *Representations:* Linear text

Figure 2. A framework for describing the writing process

3.3. Strategies

For a normal writing task, the aim of the writer is to produce a piece of linear instantiated text, i.e. to reach box 6. However, there are several possible routes to box 6. We suggest that the various writing strategies mentioned above can each be described in terms of a set of transitions from box to box, or from representation to represent. The *plan-draft-revise* strategy, for example, is a progression through boxes 3, 5 and 6, beginning with a plan in the form of a non-linear organisation of idea-labels, which is organised into a linear outline and then fleshed out as a draft. The *draft-revise* strategy is to work entirely within box 6, creating and revising linear text. *Outline-draft* is a movement from box 5 to 6. The writer using the *cut and paste* strategy starts in box 2 with instantiated notes, which are organised and linearised, moving through boxes 4 and 6.

Clearly, not all of these routes will begin at box 1: a writer who has already mentally assembled the material she needs for a document may begin to create a written representation at box 4 or even box 6. Nor will every route necessarily take in all the boxes on its path: a writer might move from initial jottings (box l) to drafting a text (box 6), without feeling the need to construct any explicit intermediate representation.

One advantage of the six box framework is that it allows an explicit distinction to be made between those processes which a writer carries out on some external medium, and those which are performed mentally, or by-passed altogether. A further advantage is that the various strategies already identified by Flower and Hayes and others can be set in a broader context, so that they can be seen as possible choices of route out of a finite set of such choices, rather than as an *ad hoc* listing. Other possible strategies now readily present themselves: *linear outlining*, where a writer moves from an unordered collection of topic words (box 1), to a linearisation of these words (box S), to their translation into full prose (box 6); *fleshing a skeleton*, where the writer constructs a network of "buzz words" (box 3), writes a paragraph of text for each item (box 4), and then forms these pieces into a linear text (box 6). Although it would be unusual for the writer to move from instantiated to uninstantiated text items, this is not excluded. One could imagine, for instance, a writer creating a first linear draft, then labelling each section and using these labels to reorder the text.

The progression through the grid rarely happens just once, with the writer starting at box 1 with a blank sheet of paper and ending at box 6 with a finished product. The network and linear views form organised structures of both nested and sequential items, and the production of each of these items is a writing sub-task. The linear view may consist of chapters, sections, paragraphs, sentences and words, or other embedded textual elements depending on the type of document, and the writer may use different strategies depending on the level and position of the item. In creating this paper, for example, we began with a linear sequence of idea-labels for the major sections and then filled out each in turn. For some of them we created and arranged further labels indicating subsections; for others we instantiated the section as a full draft.

Each sub-task requires a new progression through the grid. Furthermore, as we indicated earlier, a writer captures ideas that arise as she writes and to incorporate them may well involve a further pass through the grid.

3.4. Techniques

Each of the representations described here may be produced by a variety of means according to the task and context. A means of creating all or part of a representational structure, such as a list of ideas-labels or a network of notes, we refer to as a *technique*. Many of these techniques are described in the research literature and are also familiar to any writer: the claim we are making for our model is that it gives a context in which to distinguish these techniques from the more global *strategies*. Each type of representation will lend itself to a variety of creative techniques: for instance, in order to generate idea-labels, a writer might use the technique of *brainstorming*, generating words and phrases related to a starting topic, in no particular order. Alternatively, he might use a form of *note-taking*, jotting down keywords as he reads his source material. Linear organisation might be achieved by the technique of *template fitting*, where the writer organises the sections of her text to correspond to that found in other texts of the same type. Some techniques can be called on to produce several types of representational object: the outcome of a note taking session, for instance, could just as well be a network of verbatim quotations as an unordered set of jottings.

3.5. Core operations

A writing technique can be further decomposed into an ordered sequence of *core operations*. The diversity of writing techniques and strategies arises both from the ordering of these operations and the material to which they are applied. What constitutes core operations will depend on the level of detail to which the analysis is taken. Those we describe apply across types and levels of text. They differ from the operations listed by Flower and Hayes in that they may all be applied to explicit external representations: we do not include operators which apply only to internal mental structures. There are two broad categories of operator: *set constraints, generate, verify* and *transform* are for manipulating material within a representation and *instantiate, organise,* and *linearise* are for making a transition between representations. *Shift focus* is a general purpose operator.

Set constraints

Augment the set of constraints currently in force. (This is a generalisation of the Flower and Hayes *plan* operation). The operation may be carried out explicitly when, for example, the writer collects together resources for a task. It may also be an implicit consequence of the *generate* and *instantiate* operations.

Generate
Set down an item (instantiated or uninstantiated) on some external medium.

Verify
Match one or more items against the current constraints so as to identify possible conflicts.

Transform
Resolve identified conflicts by modifying either the items or the constraints. (*Verify* and *transform* correspond roughly to the Flower and Hayes *review* operation).

Instantiate
Create instantiated text for an uninstantiated item.

Organise
Arrange uninstantiated items into a structural plan.

Linearise
Produce a linearisation of a non-linear representation.

Shift focus
Shift the focus of attention from one item to another.

3.6. Constraints

The operations are governed by constraints which act as filters to restrict the range of possible outcomes. Constraints are not cruel impositions on the writer, they are essential to producing a coherent and organised text. They arise from four sources:

- The *task* set for the writer: its theme, intended audience, purpose, and more specific boundaries such as the maximum number of words or the readability level.
- The *external resources,* such as books, papers, notes, written plans.
- The writer's *linguistic knowledge* and vocabulary, and his internal stock of ideas, schemas and remembered text.
- The *material* that the writer has already created. As a consequence of this, constraints tighten as writing progresses and the writer must either devote more effort to constraint monitoring, or develop techniques of selectively ignoring constraints and suspending the monitoring process.

The constraints can be categorised in terms of the function they perform and their characteristic properties:

Content constraints

These direct a writer's probes of long-term memory. So, for example, a theme of 'confrontation', a setting of a 'a picnic', and an audience of children, will provide constraints that index particular mental associations of facts and schemas. Content constraints ensure that the finished text fulfils the writer's intentions, i.e. that it communicates the author's ideas, beliefs, feelings and arguments to the intended audience.

Resource constraints

These are similar to content constraints, except that they indicate external rather than mental resources: items to be included such as key phrases, passages or quotations, and ones to be avoided, such as jargon words.

Boundary constraints

These define the limits of an item, such as maximum number of words in the document or maximum sentence length.

Structural constraints

These specify the type and ordering of items and provide a framework on which to hang the text. The structure need not specify a strict ordering of items, but can include options and partial orderings, of the form "My research report will have a title, a list of authors (in an order to be determined), an abstract, and possibly acknowledgements... ". It is important for a writer to set them at an appropriate level of generality. Skilled writers are able to create a structural plan that leads smoothly from one main topic to another; without this, the writer must fill the gaps by resorting to general coping techniques such as the 'what next' technique of planning sentence by sentence (Sharples 1985).

Contextual constraints

These ensure consistency between items, for example that abbreviations and spelling are consistent throughout the text.

Constraints can be created piecemeal, but the effort of constructing, storing, and applying appropriate constraints makes severe demands on the human memory and processing ability, and can overwhelm even experienced writers. A more efficient method of constraint management for routine writing tasks is to call on pre-stored *text types*, such as 'research report', or 'newspaper feature'(Pemberton and Sharples 1988). On deciding to produce, say, a *Times* newspaper feature about nuclear energy the writer invokes, by default, a bundle of conventions about structure, topic, function and audience that are known to produce successful results. Learning to write involves acquiring such sets of constraints and developing the ability to mould them to the task.

3.7. Methods

The techniques described above can be carried out using a variety of *methods*, where a method is defined as a technique conducted on a particular medium.

For example, a writer could employ the technique of note taking using a word processor, a series of file cards, a sheet of paper, a Dictaphone, or a white board, to name only a few possibilities. As well as supporting particular representations, the medium also influences subsequent stages in the composition process: the writer who sets down her notes on file cards or sticky notelets would be free to create a spatial representation of her material by, perhaps, spreading them around her desktop, whereas jottings on a single sheet of paper would not lend themselves to this sort of manipulation.

Each medium has properties which make its use more or less appropriate for particular techniques. We can classify these properties in terms of the presence, for a given medium, of certain characteristics:

- Browsable. The medium supports the creation and browsing of large documents, allowing the reader to flick instantaneously between parts of the document.
- Portable. Note taking, in particular, benefits from the use of a medium such as paper, which is easy to carry around.
- Allows reordering. Certain media allow for easy reordering of generated items: blackboards, for instance, allow easy rearrangement of notes, as do word processors. Media such as file cards or sticky notelets, where each item is stored separately, also facilitate reordering. This process is less straightforward with a list written on a sheet of paper, almost impossible with a list stored on a Dictaphone.
- Allows non-linear organisation by means of spatial orderings of items. While it is simple to arrange items in trees, graphs, networks and so on, when each item is on a separate file card, or when the writer is using a white board, this is difficult when items are represented on a word processor.
- Usable in end product. Material stored in a word processor is always available for use in the final version of the document, while that stored on paper, file cards, audio tapes, etc. has to be transcribed at least once before it is presentable as final copy.
- Permanent. Material stored in a word processor or on paper is available for reference and reuse (e.g. for cut-and-pasting), while notes on envelopes or blackboards are not.
- Supports annotations. A medium such as paper lends itself to annotations in the form of arrows, boxes, underlinings, multicolour highlighting and so on. Until the recent introduction of specialised programs, the word processor has not supported such conventions.
- Indexable. Individual file cards, sheets of papers, or files on a word processor can be accessed by means of an index created on the same medium.

Different properties are suited to manipulating material from different representations. For instance, unless all of a writer's source material is either in his head or in his office, he will appreciate portability in the medium when he is gathering raw material. In organising the material, a suitable medium will be one which allows flexible grouping and ordering. The white board, where marks are easy to delete and many different sorts of links can be displayed, scores high here, as do sticky notelets and file cards, which can be formed into groups or even stacks, to represent conceptual or eventual textual structures. A medium allowing annotations is useful throughout the writing process, while for drafting it is the ability to display the whole text at one time which makes a medium particularly suitable. Figure 3 sets out the properties of a number of different media according to their normal usage (white boards, for example, could be made portable, but normally are not).

Property Medium	1	2	3	4	5	6	7	8
Sheet of paper	x	x	-	?	-	x	x	x
Word processor	x	?	x	-	x	x	?	x
File cards	-	x	x	x	-	x	x	x
Sticky notelets	-	x	x	x	-	-	x	?
Black/white board	-	-	x	x	-	-	x	-
Back of hand	-	x	-	-	-	-	-	-
Dictaphone	-	x	-	-	-	x	?	?

Key
1. Supports browsing of large documents.
2. Portable.
3. Supports reordering.
4. Supports non-linear organisation.
5. Reusable end product.
6. Permanent.
7. Supports annotations.
8. Supports indexing.

x :has property.
- :lacks property
? :debatable

Figure 3. Media and their properties

4. Conclusion

In this paper we have drawn upon existing descriptions of the writing process in order to set down a rigorous description of the external representational structures, or *views*, created by a writer during the process of written composition. We have provided an operational definition of *strategies* as movements across views and set down a space of possible writing strategies. We have defined writing *techniques* as implementations of strategies for a particular view, and *methods* as techniques carried out on a given medium.

The model can inform both the teaching of writing and the design of computer-based tools to support the writing process. By learning different approaches and strategies of writing and discovering the effect of different media on the writing process, an inexperienced writer can extend his skills and his ability to deal with new types of writing task.

A writing tool designed on the basis of an explicit model of writing is an embodiment of the assumptions, possibilities, and limitations of that model. By testing the tool with a variety of writers the model can be evaluated and refined. An example of a writing environment based on explicit models of the writing process is the *Writer's Assistant* (Sharples and O'Malley 1987; Sharples *et al.* 1989). As well as offering new facilities for writers, a cognitive-based writing environment can also act as a powerful research tool with which to explore and develop further models of the writing process.

5. References

Anderson, J. R. (1983) *The Architecture of Cognition*. Harvard University Press, Cambridge, MA.

Bereiter, C. and Scardamalia, M. (1987) *The Psychology of Written Composition..* Lawrence Erlbaum, Hillsdale, NJ.

Bridwell-Bowles, L., Johnson, P. Brehe, S. (1987) Composing and computers: case studies of experienced writers. In A. Matsuhashi (Ed) *Writing in Real Time: Modelling Production Processes*. Ablex, Norwood, NJ.

Britton, J. N. (1970) *Language and Learning*. Penguin, Harmondsworth.

Collins, A. and Gentner, D. (1980) A framework for a cognitive theory of writing. In L. W. Gregg and E. R. Steinberg (Ed) *Cognitive Processes in Writing: An Interdisciplinary Approach*. Lawrence Erlbaum, Hillsdale, NJ.

Cooper, C. R. and Greenbaum, S. (1986) *Studying Writing: Linguistic Approaches*. Sage, Beverly Hills.

Cooper, C. R. and Matsuhashi, A. (1983) A theory of the writing process. In M. Martlew (Ed) *The Psychology of Written Language*. John Wiley, Chichester.

Flower, L. S. and Hayes, J. R. (1980) The dynamics of composing: making plans and juggling constraints. In L. W. Gregg and E. R. Steinberg (Ed) *Cognitive Processes in Writing: An Interdisciplinary Approach*. Lawrence Erlbaum, Hillsdale, NJ.

Frederiksen, C. H. and Dominic, J. F. (1981) *Writing: The Nature, Development and Teaching of Written Communication..* Lawrence Erlbaum,

Hillsdale, NJ.

Gregg, L. W. and Steinberg, E. R. (Eds) (1980) *Cognitive Processes in Writing: An Interdisciplinary Approach.* Lawrence Erlbaum, Hillsdale, NJ.

Hartley, J. and Branthwaite, A. (1989) The psychologist as wordsmith: a questionnaire study of the writing strategies of productive British psychologists..*Higher Education,* 18.

Hayes, J. R. and Flower, L. S., (1980) Writing as problem solving. *Visible Language,* XIV (4).

Matsuhashi, A. (Ed) (1987) *Writing in Real Time: Modelling Production Processes.* Ablex, Norwood, NJ.

Nystrand, M. (Ed) (1982) *What Writers Know.* Academic Press, New York.

Pemberton, L. and Sharples, M. (1988) Textual structures in a Writer's Assistant. *Proceedings of the Fifth International Conference on Technology and Education,* 1.

Sharples, M. (1985) *Cognition, Computers and Creative Writing.* Ellis Horwood, Chichester.

Sharples, M. and O'Malley, C. (1987) A framework for the design of a Writer's Assistant. In J. Self (Ed) *Artificial Intelligence and Human Learning: Intelligent Computer-Aided Instruction.* Chapman and Hall, London.

Sharples, M., Goodlet, J. and Pemberton, L. (1989) Developing a Writer's Assistant. In N. Williams and P. Holt (Eds) *Computers and Writing: Models and Tools.* Blackwell, Oxford.

Sommers, N. (1980) Revision strategies of student writers and experienced adult writers, *College Composition and Communication,* 31.

22

The CONST-Project[1]: Computer Instructed Writing Techniques

J. Beeken
G. Geerts
W. Van Belle
University of Leuven

Abstract

The CONST project involves the development of a linguistic and computational framework for text production and analysis in the context of commercial and business communication. Essentially, the framework consists of two central components, an interactive question-answering-procedure and a sophisticated thesaurus containing a compendium of lexical-grammatical collocations, a list of functional items representing different heuristic methods, information about the lay-out of notes, quotations etc., and advice on items related to the chosen text structure.

1. Introduction

Now that the hardware problems for the internal and external communication of reports, memos, letters, offers etc. have been solved but for minor details, the focus of interest is shifting to the content of written communication, which does not always correspond to the minimal standards of intelligibility.

If one wants to come up with texts that have been written correctly and that are text-linguistically and stylistically sound, a large number of requirements must be met. After all, problems of visual presentation, of adaptation to situations and addressees, and of ordering different writing strategies in a logical, and hierarchical, adequate way, are frequent. In order to deal with these problems, different kinds of software need to be used:

- Non-interactive software such as word processors and transmission facilities (e.g. electronic mail).
- Closed interactive software characterised by question-answering-response procedures, answer-dependent feedback, functional help-mechanisms, algorithmic and modular structuring.
- Open interactive software containing instructions and suggestions about formatting, and the choice of phrasing adapted to a specific writing-task.

[1]This project is supported by the 'Fonds voor Kollectief Fundamenteel Onderzoek (FKFO)' no. 2.0088.90.

2. Purpose

A topic on which fundamental research should focus is the analysis of the text-linguistic structuring procedures for use in. commercial and business communication. From the point of cognitive and linguistic research, it seems recommendable to provide a set of interactive modular programs. Consequently, it would be more effective for the individual users to incorporate only those partial programs into their package which are especially useful to them. In particular, a writing package having a gradual and modular structure can lead to an almost perfect writing ability, because of the necessary attention paid to a number of essential parameters such as the formulation of the problem, the intentional structure of the text (i.e. addressees and text purpose), the writing strategy, the text pattern and the text-script.

The main purpose of the CONST-project is to develop educational and business-oriented software for text production, text verification, and eventually automated text production. By means of the educational application students can be taught how to structure, formulate, and write according to a specific text-frame. The business or commercial application will offer employees a wide range of text frames that correspond to the normative examples taken from the organisation's internal communications.

The basic concept of the programs to be developed is to construct a linguistically sound and computationally adequate framework by means of which any type of text can be produced and analysed. Initial applications, however, will be in Dutch.

Moreover, in the field of man-machine communication, the CONST-project can initially be seen as the development of constructive software (see Figure 1.). At this constructive phase, one needs to focus on the writing process or editing process in which the writer is guided. Obviously, on this level the computational component can be considered an extended memory, which contains pre-defined procedures. However, additional data can be stored into this memory at any time. Furthermore, the memory capacity can be extended, hence the description 'productive' memory.

The second and third phases are characterised by the fact that the machine starts to take over – in a reversible way – the human constructing and controlling abilities. These computational abilities can be seen as an expression or application of the principles linked to the construction of expert-systems and the development of artificial intelligence procedures. However, before a suggestive artificial intelligence phase can be reached, the programmer has to concentrate on the diagnostic phase in which attention is paid to the automated flow-charting and the analytical processing. To describe this phase, the term 'productive memory' has been chosen to make clear that the computational component itself has an internal expert-system by means of which it can build a range of new writing procedures. The last phase contains artificial intelligence programs through which the system can rely on its self-constructed productive memory. In addition, it can control and criticise the choices and procedures the human writer has made.

3. General organisation

Essentially, the framework consists of two central components (see Figure 1.), on the one hand, an interactive question-answering-response procedure which is conceptualised as a complex branching package. Through this systematic procedure, information about the specific text-frames and text-scripts is gathered (macro-, meso-, micro-level; writing strategies, formal heuristic methods, ordering principles, etc. ...). The output of this interactive component will be an extended tree-diagram of the chosen general and specific text-structure. As far as the business-oriented programs are concerned, these interactive questioning-programs will be replaced with a set of pre-defined text-frames and texts-scripts, from which the writer can choose a single frame which can be modified to meet the writer's demands.

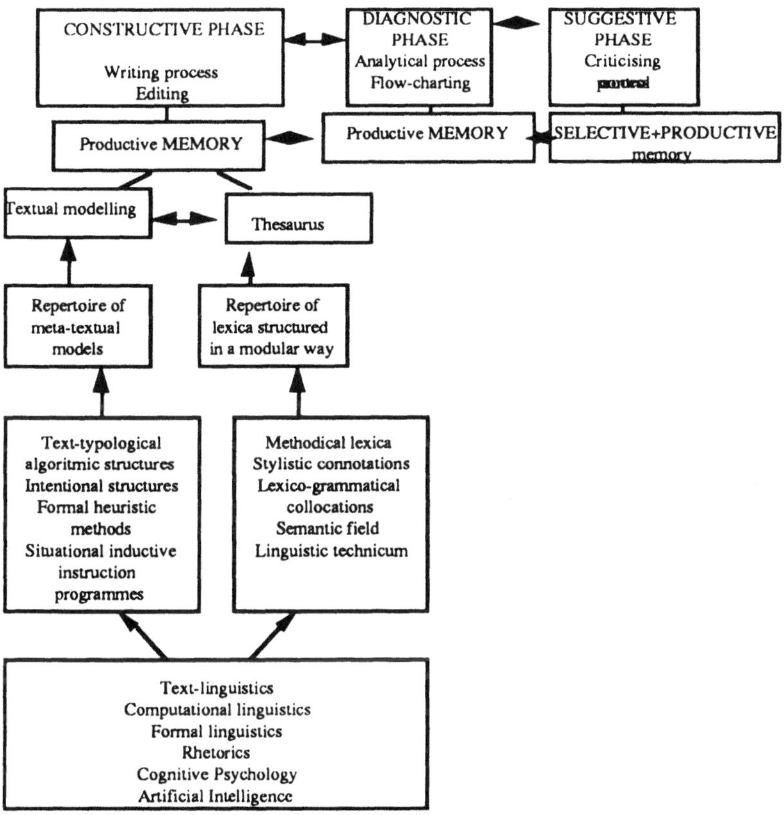

Figure 1. The CONST framework

On the other hand, an elaborated thesaurus will be developed consisting of five sub components:

- A compendium of lexico-grammatical collocations.
- A list of functional and text-cohesive items representing different heuristic methods (methodical lexicon, stylistic connotations).
- Information about the (normative) lay-out of footnotes, quotations, schemes and style sheets (linguistic technicum).
- An elaborated vocabulary of technical terminology (semantic field).
- An advice column suggesting particular items related to the chosen text-structure and the specific level in the text-script.

In order to reach a scientifically valid and usable result, fundamental and applied research must be done in the field of text-linguistics, computational linguistics, formal linguistics, rhetoric, cognitive psychology and AI.

4. The thesaurus

The thesaurus will be organised as a series of lexical data-management programs (LDM), which are components built in a systematic and modular way. These components or lexicons need to be structured in such a way that the user can consult, modify and complete the information stored into the memory.

4.1 Lexico-grammatical collocations

Lexical and grammatical recurrent word combinations are often called collocations. "In English, as in other languages, there are many fixed, identifiable, non-idiomatic phrases and constructions. Such groups of words are called recurrent combinations, fixed combinations, or collocations." (Benson *et al.* 1986).

Lexical Collocations

First, lexical collocations can be nominal lexical collocations (NL) of the form: P+N, P+N+P, A+N, N+N, where P stands for preposition, N for noun and A for adjective. In these cases the noun has the core function (hence nominal lexical collocations). Examples from Dutch and English are:

<u>P+NP</u>
bij voorbaat
in afwachting
in advance
by accident
at anchor

<u>P+N+P(intransitive)</u>
op het kantje af
tot nog toe

<u>P+N+P(transitive)</u>
met het oog op
in antwoord op
in payment of
in search of
in case of

<u>N+N</u>
nijpend gebrek
ernstig bezwaar
rough estimate
crushing defeat
sour grapes.

Second, the class of verbal lexical collocations (VL) can have the form: DO-NP+V, DO-NP+V+P, REFL-N+V, REFL-N+V+P, PP+V, PP+V+P, SU-NP+V, and COMPV+P; where DO stands for direct object, NP for noun phrase, V for verb, REFL for reflexive pronoun, PP for prepositional phrase, SU for subject, COMPV for compound verb. Examples from Dutch and English are:

DO-NP+V	DO-NP+V+P
afspraken maken/annuleren	een beroep doen op
bezwaren uiten/opperen	een aanvraag indienen
muziek componeren	partij kiezen voor
to share an opinion	to make an appeal to
to meet expenses	to attac value to
to reach an agreement	to lose sight of

REFL+V	REFL+V+P
zich vergissen	zich kwijten van
zich verontschuldigen	zich bekwamen in
zich (iets) afvragen	zich beroepen op
	to acquit oneself of
	to imagine oneself in
	to apply oneself to

PP+V	PP+V+P
van de wijs brengen	in de bres springen voor
op de loer liggen	op de hoogte brengen van
voor lief nemen	in discussie treden met
to take for granted	to enter into a discussion with
to put into practice	to step into the breach for
to call into question	to fall in love with

SU-NP+V	COMPV+P
professoren doceren	opwegen tegen
werkwoorden vervoegen	inspelen op
boeken verschijnen	afhangen van
prijzen stijgen	toestemmen in
bombs explode	to break in on
adjectives modify	to catch up to
fires spread	to go through with
governments fall	to feel up to

Grammatical Collocations

Grammatical collocations can be the N-type (NG), the A-type (AG), the V-type (VG) and the P/ADV-type (PG/ADVG) (where A stands for Adjective and ADV for Adverb).

NGs are:	N+P, N+S;
AGs are:	A+P, HET/IT+A+S;

VGs are: V+P, N+V+P, IDV+P, where IDV stands for 'idiomatic complex verb';
PG/ADVGs are: PP+S; P/ADV+S.

A few examples from Dutch and English illustrating these rules are:

N+P
respect voor
keuze tussen
voorkeur voor
the choice between
the thought of

N+S
het feit dat
de vraag of
de eis dat
the fact that
the demand that

A+P
verantwoordelijk voor
behept met
verstoken van
deprived of
averse to
envious of

HET/IT+A+S
het is duidelijk dat
het is ongewoon dat
het is vanzelfsprekend dat
it is obvious that
it is clear that
it is essential that

V+P
vergelijken met
betrouwen op
haperen aan
to correspond to
to rely on
to take after

N+V+P
iemand overtuigen van
iets verkiezen boven
iemand aanzetten tot
to talk someone into
to incite someone to
to compare something with

IDV+P
akkoord gaan met
geloof hechten aan
het gemunt hebben op
to attach credence to
to pin one's hope on
to set great store by

PP+S
onder voorwaarde dat
voor het geval dat
in plaats dat
on the assumption that
in case that
in order that

P/ADV+S
naarmate dat
ondanks dat
zonder dat
except that

The research into the gathering of collocations, is twofold. In the first place, Dutch does not dispose of comparable 'written' lexicons English users can consult, yet. (e.g. Benson, Benson, Ilson: BBI Combinatory Dictionary of English

(1986), and Sinclair *et al.* ii: Collins Cobuild. English Language Dictionary (1987)). Because of this deficiency, the CONST-team is obliged to make its own 'collocational' dictionary. To realise this, one should be able to consult electronically, on CD-ROM for example, the commonly used Van Dale-dictionary (comparable to the 'Oxford English Dictionary' or the 'Petit Robert') to register the lexico-grammatical collocations. Again, the Dutch speaking community has to overcome a technical problem; the Van Dale-dictionary is not (yet) available on CD-ROM. Nevertheless, because our team has been promised that they could check the pack of dictionary files, research can start by the end of the year, and the first outcomes will be expected by the end of 1991.

A second point concerns the research in the domain of database management. The system to be built, must meet several demands, such as flexibility, user-friendliness, adaptability, interactivity.

4.2. Heuristic methods

During the process of writing, the writer can gather information about the so-called 'formal heuristic methods'.

When the writer starts transforming his ideas into words, it is of prime importance that he can dispose of a readable computational module containing answers to questions such as 'How is a comparison, contradiction, definition, cause-result sequence to be formulated?', 'How can I introduce a conclusion or summary at a particular point in the text?' and 'Which linguistic means have the possibility of formulating a hierarchical, gradual and contrastive enumeration?', in brief, 'How can the sub components of the text be related to one another in a logical sequence, by using the correct linguistic expressions (words, constituents, clauses)?'.

Until now, the only lists available in Dutch, contain information about text-cohesive lexical items such as conjunctions and adverbs. However, these lists need to be completed by extended lists of functional abbreviations, prepositional idioms or expressions, and specific clauses having the same text-cohesive function.

Formal heuristic methods playing an important role in notions such as text-cohesion and text-structure are: cause-reason, consequence, purpose, comparison, contrast, concession, condition, limitation-restriction, extent-degree, manner, modality, conclusion, summary, specification, explanation-illustration-clarification, description-definition, enumeration. Some examples from Dutch and English are:

- *Cause-reason:* omwille van, omdat, ter gelegenheid van, als reden aanvoeren; because (of), in view of, in reply to, to give cause to, to give rise to, on the basis of.
- *Consequence:* zodat, dus, ten gevolge van (t.g.v.), dat leidt ertoe dat, een rechtstreeks gevolg hiervan is; so (that), consequently, to result in, to lead to.

- *Purpose:* om, ter attentie van (t.a.v.), met het oog op, zich tot doel stellen, ogen op; as to, in order to, with a view of, to be aimed at, to make something one's aim.
- *Comparison:* (zo)als, analoog aan, vergeleken met, ten aanzien van, volgens wat; een vergelijkbaar geval doet zich voor bij; like, according to, compared to, in proportion to, to equate with, cf., 'quotation', as.
- *Contrast:* maar, terwijl, integendeel, versus (vs.), daartegenover staat, in sterk contrast met het voorafgaande; on the one hand-on the other hand, nevertheless, still, to be in contrast with.
- *Concession:* hoewel, nochtans, weliswaar, laat staan dat, hoe het ook zij, toegegeven dat; in spite of, despite of, even though, although, as it were, be it that.
- *Condition:* zo, in geval dat, in de veronderstelling dat, de condities zijn, stel dat, of het moest zijn dat; if, assumed that, on the assumption that, on condition that, provided that, under the impression that.
- *Restriction-limitation:* uitgezonderd, uitgenomen, in zover (als), beperkt blijven tot; except for, apart from, with the exception of, to be restricted to.
- *Extent-degree:* uitermate, ongeveer, nogal, in die mate, naarmate dat, de mate waarin; as, as much as possible, to a lesser degree, to the extent that.
- *Manner:* via, door middel van (d.m.v.), bij manier van, volgens, zodoende, de manier waarop; like this, by means of, one way or another, the way it is done, the way in which.
- *Modality:* misschien, geenszins, ongetwijfeld, per definitie, in principe, naar mijn mening; probably, maybe, obviously, likely, of course, without doubt, in our opinion, in principle, by no means, not at all.
- *Conclusion:* tenslotte, dus, tot slot, concluderend, dat leidt tot het besluit dat, als besluit; so, then, finally, therefore, to conclude, the final conclusion is, in conclusion I wish to remark, what we can conclude from that.
- *Summary:* kortom, dus, al bij al, samengevat, in ÇÇn woord, kort gezegd; in brief, briefly put, all in all, in a word, in sum, short, in a nutshell, to sum up in a few words, 'to sum up, it may be stated that', 'to sum up, it may be said that.'
- *Specification:* namelijk (nl.), met name (m.n.), in het bijzonder, aangaande, wat betreft, concreet gesteld, duidelijker afgebakend; namely, especially, specifically, stricto sensu, in concreto, particularly, in particular, concerning, regarding, with regard to, with reference to.
- *Explanation-clarification-illustration:* bijvoorbeeld (b.v.), dat wil zeggen (d.w.z.), onder andere (o.a.), ter illustratie, een voorbeeld hiervan is, als daar zijn, zoals, waaronder; for example (e.g.), for instance, that means, that is, id est (i.e.), to illustrate, by way of illustration, among other things.

- *Definition-description:* anders gezegd, met andere woorden (m.a.w.), of beter, anders geformuleerd, in kwestie; in other words, (or) rather, to rephrase, to put things differently.
- *Enumeration:* en ... en, of...of, hetzij...hetzij, respectievlijk, ten eerste, ten tweede, eveneens, daarbij komt nog dat; and...and, or...or, either...either, neither...nor, primo, secundo, in the first place, firstly, secondly, successively, beside, moreover, furthermore, respectively.

The above-mentioned items need to be listed in such a way that they contain information about (1) the contents and (2) the conditions of use on a syntactic, semantic, and text-linguistic level. Because of the extra-sentential value associated with these elements, they provide information about the writing of paragraphs and larger text-components – we are convinced that the construction of this computational component is a matter of major concern.

4.3. Linguistic technicum

To guarantee that the programs can communicate with already existing word processors and grammar checkers [2] , a meta-program or shell has to be constructed. By using such professional writing 'tools', the difficulties concerning spelling, text-formatting, lay-out of footnotes and bibliography need not to be taken into consideration. Furthermore, using these word processors, the writer can benefit from the positive effect automated deleting, copying, overwriting, inserting and moving have on the density of revision, reformulation, and reorganisation of the text.

This CONST-module to be developed will also cover business specific norms and regulations about the lay-out of quotations, examples, schemes, and the pragmatic implications of bold, italic, underlined characters, headers and footers, in brief, the effect of typographical techniques or the impact of 'visual' language.

4.4. Technical lexicons

These systematically organised lexicons will consist of (1) lists of business-oriented terminology, (2) lists of domain-specific synonyms and related lexical items, and (3) a set of frequently used abbreviations. Again, these lexicons are already available in a written version for English (e.g. De Sola 1974) 'The Abbreviation Dictionary' and the range of business-specific dictionaries. Such dictionaries are, however, not available for Dutch. Because of these difficulties, the programs will consist of, at a first stage, a very limited set of actualised data. These data can be elaborated once the computational components function and communicate properly.

---

2 See also D. SCHREURS & G. ADRIAENS: Controlled English (CE): From COGRAM to ALCOGRAM. This volume.

The lexicons comprising the technical, specific terminology and synonyms will be organised in two different ways. On the one hand, the organisation is semasiological, on the other hand, onomasiological. A semasiological organisation stands for a type of organisation dealing with all different meanings a lexical item can have. According to the principles that determine a onomasiological organisation, the lexicon will contain a set of different linguistic items expressing a particular meaning and therefore comparable semantic contents.

4.5. The advice column

This component of the thesaurus can be consulted to gather useful linguistic information about the correct formulation of the specific textual parts situated on all different levels of the writing process. To express, for instance, a specific inter-subsectional relation, the writer will be able to address the advice column to get to know what the right solution or formulation is, taking into account (1) the chosen pre-defined or self-constructed text-structure, (2) the actual branching level or specific branch in the structure and (3) the branching nodes already completed.

In order to attain this, it goes without saying that the computational system should dispose of a high-level artificial intelligent procedure through which this *ad hoc* information can be automatically selected, efficiently stored and correctly 'understood.'

5. Textual modelling

During the writing process the writer can consult (1) the thesaurus (see above) and (2) instruction programs (question-answering-response procedures) by means of which larger text-components are developed in a systematic and structural way. The instruction programs at hand will gather information about and go more thoroughly into (1) the central theme, (2) the formulation or definition of the problem, (3) the text-constructive elements available, (4) the logical structures of organisation, (5) the argumentative order and (6) the different text-typological criteria.

After all, the construction of a particular text implies an interaction between, on the one hand the text pattern and on the other the text purpose and writing strategy.

By text patterns we understand text schemes in which the central theme of the text, the formulation of the problem, and its concretisation are specified.

Frequently occurring text patterns are, for instance, the evaluation pattern, the goal means pattern, the problem solving pattern, the pattern corresponding to the description of an empirical research and, finally, the pattern corresponding to making an appeal or giving a recommendation.

The general purpose of the text can be thought of as 'to inform, to instruct, to evaluate, to recommend, to appeal, to persuade'. Because a specific text is always written for a specific group of addressees, attention has to be paid to their expectations, cultural background, intellectual capacities and relation to the writer.

Once the purpose of the text has been defined, the writer will try to follow a particular writing strategy or discursive strategy to reach the pre-defined goal as quickly and efficiently as possible. Common strategies are: description, explanation or interpretation, argumentation, persuasion, prescription, summary, justification. Obviously, a lot of text purposes require a specific writing strategy. The combinations to be preferred are: to inform/ description or explanation, to convince/ argumentation or persuasion, to recommend/ explanation and argumentation. The writing strategy to be chosen does not only depend on the text purpose, the central theme and the formulation of the problem, it must meet the expectations and the characteristics of the addressees as well.

When these previous components have been determined, the writer can start with a detailed elaboration of the chosen text pattern on the basis of a text purpose and writing strategy. This elaboration is generally known as the text-script.

5.1. Educational applications

The computational-educational application of a particular text-script moves along two phases:

First, an instruction procedure that is intended to help the writer define the following elements as accurately as possible (see Figure 2):

- The central theme+the formulation of the problem.
- The purpose of the text.
- The characteristics of the addressees.
- The writing strategy.

On the basis of this information, the program selects a text pattern containing the general structure of the text. Possibly, more that one pattern is presented. In that case, the final decision is up to the writer.

Second, the instruction program asks the writer questions about the detailed elaboration of the chosen text pattern and text-script. Exhaustive elaboration of a script is absolutely out of the question before the actual writing process takes place. Therefore, one needs to create the possibility of explicitating, adapting, and ameliorating the initial script.

Both programs contain, beside an extensive package of exercise material, an instruction program, based upon the principles of text-linguistic and lexical theories. This program aims at teaching, on an inductive basis, the principles of text-structuring by means of a computer-instructed question-answering procedure (see Figure 3).

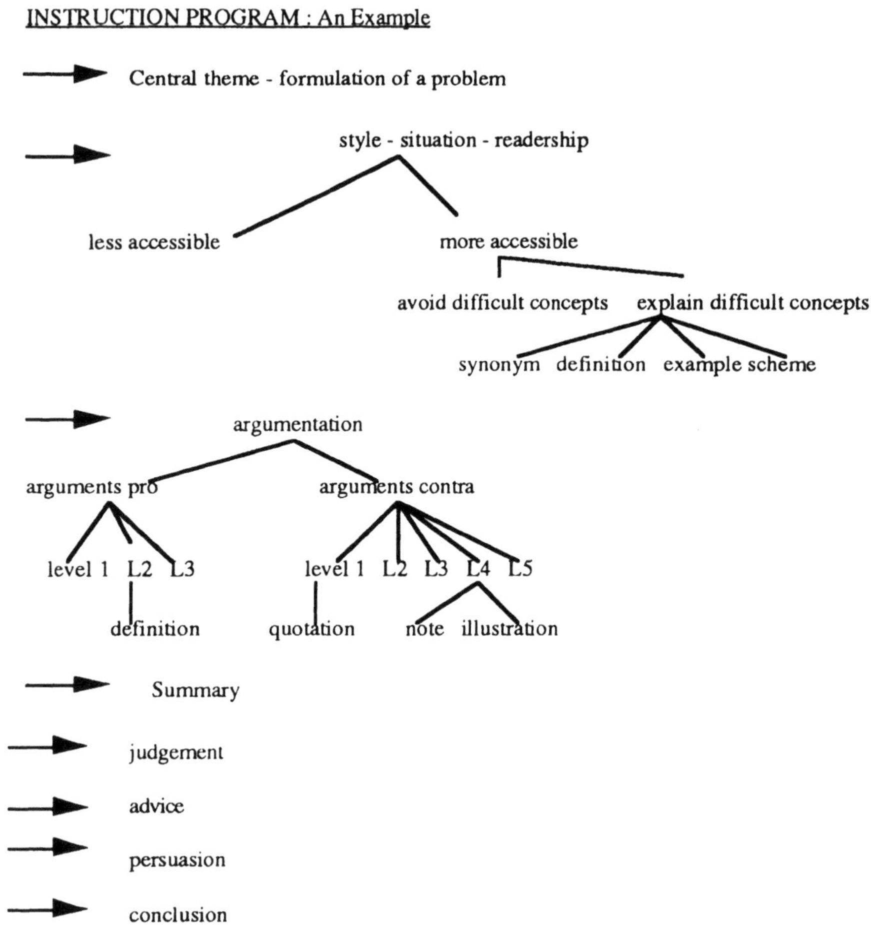

Figure 2. An example instruction programme

In this way, the learners are helped to acquire knowledge, insight and skills in structuring different text-types through a dialogue oriented course.

In searching for the answers to questions asked on a systematic basis, the users learn to distinguish between different text patterns and writing strategies, correct formulations of the problem. They also learn how to make a choice depending on the characteristics of the addressees.

The instruction programs can be outlined as follows. An exercise is selected from the package of learning material by the user. The program itself selects the relevant questions and menus. Beside menus and yes/no questions, some questions need to be answered by means of symbols. When the learner cannot decide on the right answer or the selection of the symbols, help screens are available at any time. Also, the learner has access through help mechanisms to items of information which are a fundamental part of the exercise, but which do not constitute its aim.

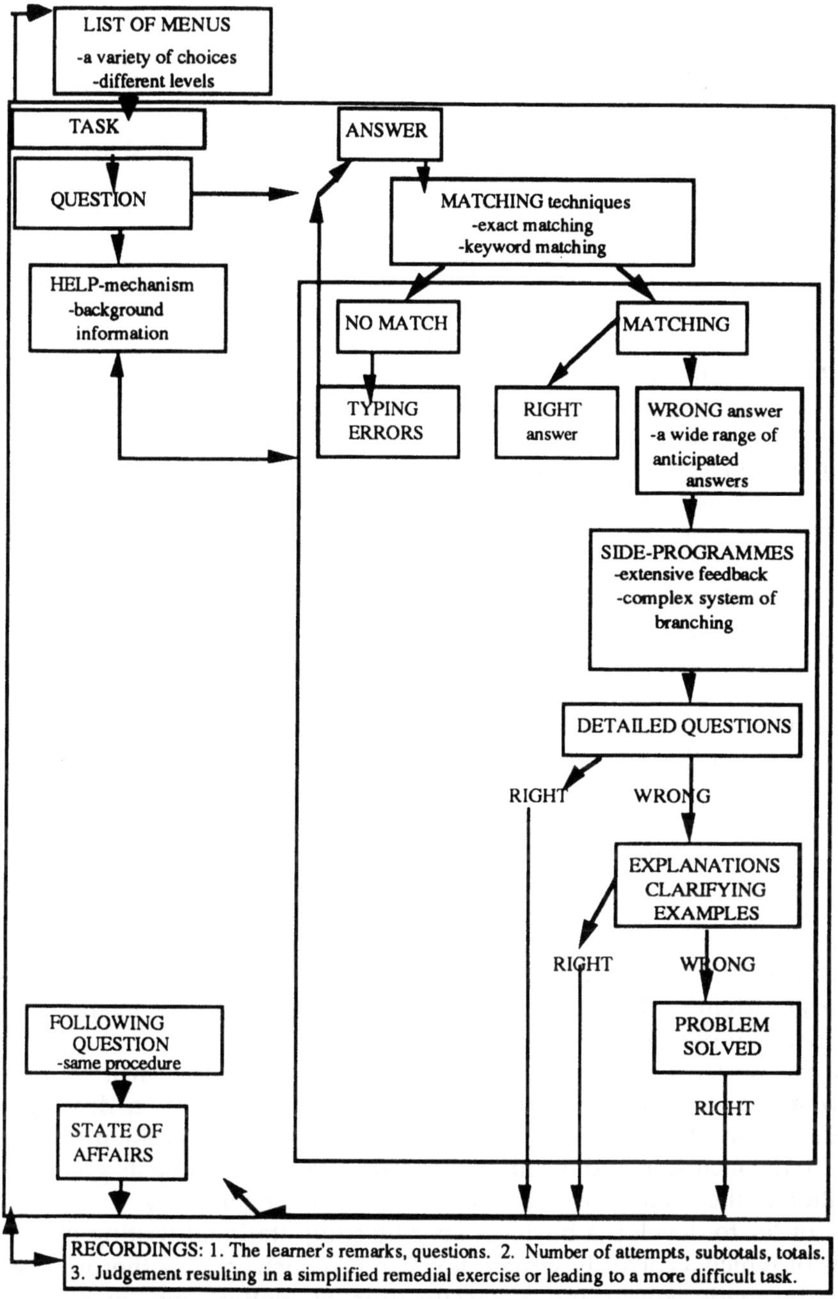

Figure 3. The question-answering procedure

To distinguish between typing errors and, for instance, linguistic or logical errors, a range of matching techniques have to be applied.

Answers to algorithmic questions are subject to keyword matching, whereas symbols need to match exactly one of the anticipated answers.

The feedback and the possibilities of responding are independent of the exercise and questions to reuse (a part of) the program.

A learner can pass through the whole procedure in a short time if the necessary insight can be derived from the answers given. Whenever the insight seems to fail, the learner is guided through a range of additional programs containing explanatory examples and detailed questions. Depending on the questions the learner failed to answer correctly, these additional programs contain one or more stages.

In other words, functional feedback and appropriate flexibility guarantee that the program analyses specific mistakes and reacts in a manner which leads the learner not only to the correction of his mistake, but also to the understanding of the principles beyond the correct solution.

Once the learner has passed through these additional programs, he returns to the main route. Moreover, the learner is continuously informed about his progress in the program (state of affairs) and he can also communicate with the system by entering remarks, findings, and questions.

Finally, the learner is directed to a simplified remedial exercise or to an even more difficult and extended task.

To guarantee an efficient computational support of a top-down analysis concerning a particular script, a thorough analysis of correct and deficient texts that fit into the same text-script is necessary. Moreover, there also needs to be an inventory of the general and specific foundations upon which an evaluation can be based.

5.2. Business-oriented applications

In principle, any text-type (memo, manual, recommendation, report, advice, appeal) can be built according to a finite list of different text patterns. Which pattern is to be classified as the most common in a particular situation, depends to a large extent on factors such as subject or theme, specific business-internal agreements or demands, and addressee-specific expectations.

If the writer, for instance, wants to make an appeal, he will be obliged to follow a sequence that could be outlined as follows: (1) a description or representation of the problem, (2) the explanation of the problem in pros and cons, (3) a conclusion and evaluation based upon the arguments given, or 94) a repetition of the results formulated as a conclusion or summary.

In order to develop a business specific computational writing program by means of which a correctly written text can be constructed, a thorough analysis has to be made concerning a classification of 'better' and 'worse' texts, in addition to the registration of the internal guidelines and regulations.

From this material, a range of specific text patterns is to be generated or deduced. These patterns will be labelled 'immediately usable' in the environment they have to function in. Furthermore, they will meet all the requirements and the readers' demands.

After the writers have generated an adequate and adjusted pattern with the help of the computational system presented, they can start with the detailed elaboration and expression of the text. At this point, it is essential for the writers to dispose of two components. On the one hand, they must be able to consult an enormous systematically organised thesaurus to solve problems about the correct formulation of the different text-parts. On the other hand, the text-structure must be built by means of instruction programs. These programs used in a business environment will be severely limited in comparison to equivalent programs developed for educational purposes. This limitation includes the elimination of instruction program 1. and its substitution by pre-defined text patterns. In that respect, the question-answering procedure will be replaced with a sequence of menu driven instructions.

Whenever a solid and sound text has been produced according to the computational procedure, the system has the possibility of saving the pattern so that it can be used recursively. This pattern saved can also be transmitted to other users via e.g. electronic mail (e-mail). In this way, the company will dispose of a number of text patterns that have been labelled 'correct', and which can be regarded as 'normative'.

5.3. Visual algorithmic branching

Until now, we have been presenting three out of four screen windows: (1) any type of word-processor, (2) the entrance to the thesaurus and (3) the instruction programs. (see Figure 4).

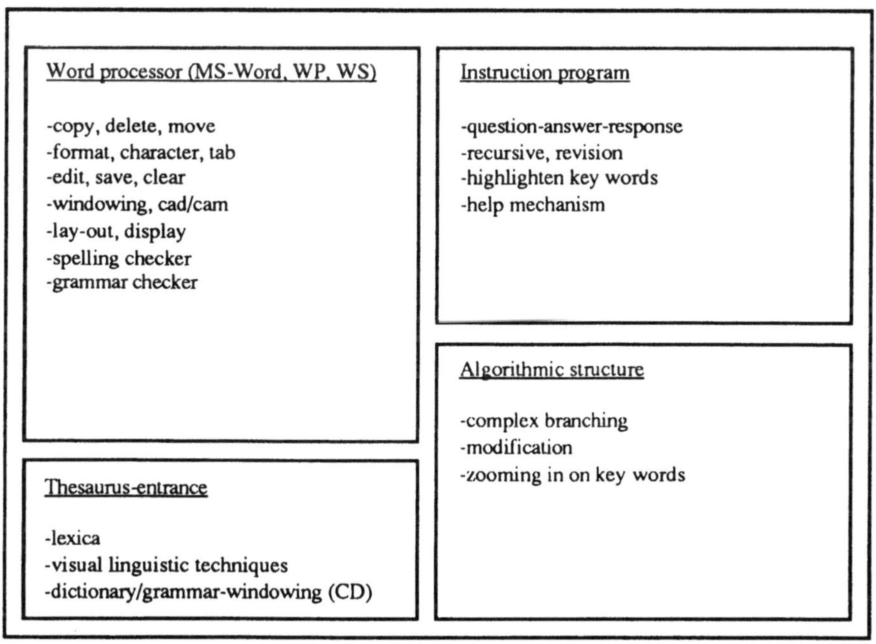

Figure 4. Example screens

A.

Question	Possible answers	Chosen answer
1	a, b, c	b
2	a, b	a
3	a, b, c, d, e	c
31	a, b	a
311	a, b	a+b
3111	a, b	b
3112	a, b , 0	0
. . .		
. . .		
. . .		
6	a, b, c, d	d
. . .		
. . .		
9	a, b, c	c
. . .		
93	a, b, c, d	d
934	a, b	a
9341	a, b, c	c
93413	a	a
. . .		

B.

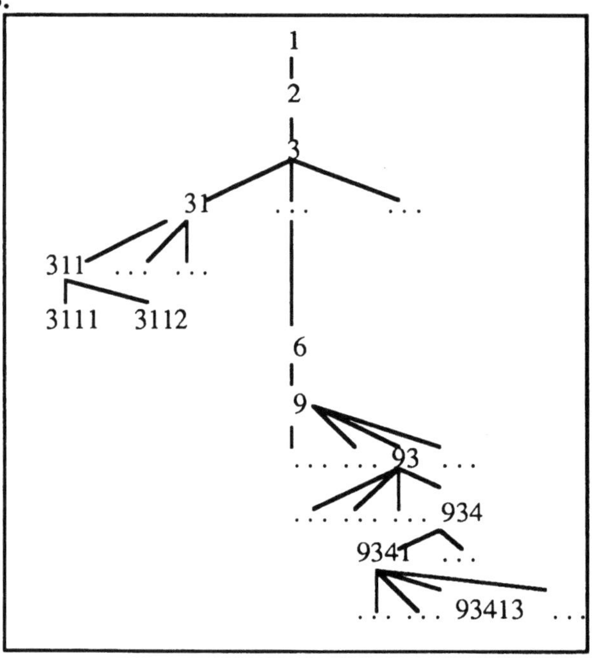

Figure 5. Algorithmic structures

The fourth window represents the 'algorithmic structure' or tree diagram that corresponds to a text-structure. The nodes of such a diagram are labelled by the keywords of the questions or menus that are part of the instruction programs. (see Figure 5, A, B). In that way, the writer disposes of a visual scheme that functions as an exact reproduction of the predetermined choices. The business oriented software, for example, will predominantly consist of pre-defined and pre-printed tree diagrams.

Whenever the writer wants to modify or change a labelled node, and *ipso facto* a specific part of the structure, he can zoom in on that label and *ipso facto* on that part of window (3) he wants to modify.

6. Software

As illustrated by Figure 6, the central program will have the form of what is commonly known as a shell, a meta-program or a sequence of hyper-menus. This shell can be regarded as a 'parasitic' program from which every other program can be evoked.

The other programs to be developed concern (1) the network of instruction programs, 2) the linguistic thesaurus and (3) the graphic algorithmic branching procedures. Each module, however, requires two different programs. The first program gives the author the possibility of entering data. The second program allows the user to consult the data entered.

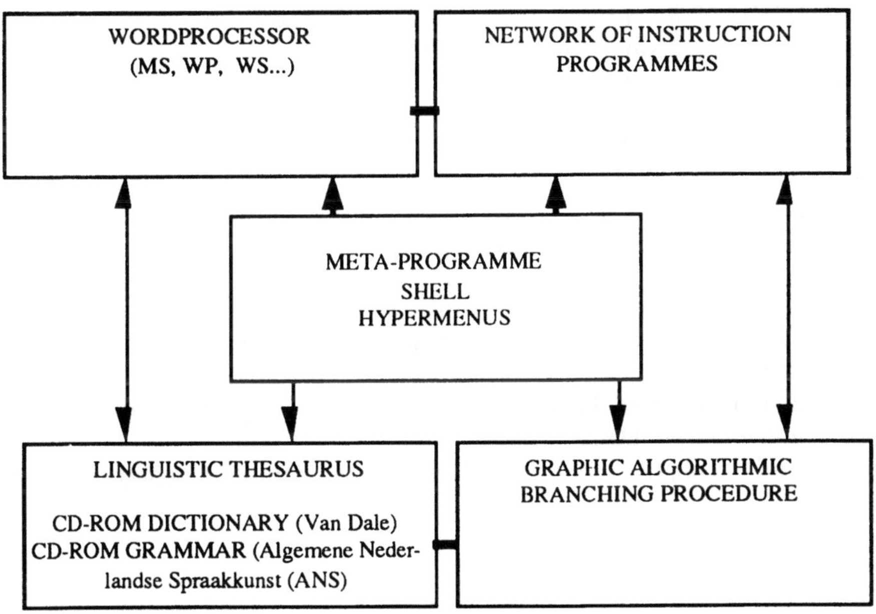

Figure 6. The CONST shell

Because the thesaurus needs to be consulted without the user paying attention to the instruction module or branching module, a communication program will be constructed, linking the word processor to the thesaurus and vice versa. Besides, the instruction programs and the branching schemes must be linked in a flexible way, just as the thesaurus and the branching module.

7. References

Allen, S. (1982) (ed.): *Text Processing, Text Analysis, Text Typology and Attribution.*

Antos, G. and Krings, H. (1989) (eds.) *Textproduktion.Ein Interdisziplinerer Forschungs* Åberblick.

Austin, M (1989). *Effective Writing for Commerce and Industry.*

Biber, D. (1988) *Variation across Speech and Writing.*

Burns, H. (1984) The Challenge for Computer-Assisted Rhetoric, in: *Computers and the Humanities, 18.*

Daiute, C. (1985) *Writing and Computers.*

Hahn, U. (1985) *On Lexically Distributed Text Parsing. A Computational Model for the Analysis of Textuality on the Level of Text Cohesion and Text Coherence.*

Haiman & Thompson (1988) *Clause Combining in Grammar and Discourse.*

Halpern, J.W. and Liggett, S. (1984) *Computers and Composing. How the New Technologies are Changing Writing.*

Jordan, M.P. (1984) *Rhetoric of Everyday English Texts.*

Mann, W.C. and Thompson, S. (1987) Rhetorical Structure Theory. A Framework for the Analysis of Texts. *IPRA Papers in Pragmatics1*, p.79-105, 1987.

McKeown, K.R. (1985): *Text Generation.*

Phillips M. (1985) *Aspects of Text Structure. An Investigation of the Lexical Organization of Text*

Reigeluth, C.M. (1983) *Instructional Design Theories and Models. An Overview of Their Current Status.*

Sharples, M. (1985) *Cognition, Computers and Creative Writing.*

Van Hout-Wolters, B. (1987): *Selecting and Cueing Key Phrases in Instructional Texts.*

Winograd, T. and Flores, F. (1986) *Understanding Computers and Cogntion. A New Foundation for Design.*

Zock, M. and Sabah, G. (1988) (Eds) *Advances in Natural Language Generation.*

23

"IV Storybase": Using Interactive Video to Develop Creative Writing Skills

Rosetta McLeod
Grampian Regional Council

Abstract

Encouraging pupils to develop effective creative writing skills is an important aim for the teacher of English/Language arts. All too often, however, responses from pupils are dull and unimaginative, having been produced to pacify the teacher, rather than as a result of a real desire to write. "IV Storybase", the interactive video version of the original "Storybase"program, was developed as a fun way of stimulating writing skills, by providing pupils with computer-generated ideas for story writing, and linking those to visual stimuli from a videodisk.

1. The background

How do writers get their ideas for a story? Michael Benton discusses the inspiration factor and quotes Henry James who begins his Preface to "The Spoils of Poynton" with an account of a conversation at a Christmas Eve dinner which produced

> "....one of those allusions that I have always found myself recognising as 'germs'. The germ, wherever gathered, has ever been for me the germ of a 'story', and most of the stories straining to shape under my hand have sprung from a single small seed..." (Benton 1982).

A 'germ', though, may equally come from a visual stimulus. John Fowles in "Notes on an Unfinished Novel" says,

> "It started four or five months ago as a visual image. A woman stands at the end of a deserted quay and stares out to sea. That was all ... Those mythopoeic 'stills' (they seem almost always static) float into my mind very often. I ignore them, since it is the best way of finding whether they really are the door into a new world." (Benton 1982)

Inspiration, argues Benton, comes from:

> "the intersection of two complementary recognitions: the one is characterised by the drive to eliminate the inessential, a mental precis through which the writer narrows down his attention on to a single significant focus; the other consists in the recognition that within this focal idea or image lies the latent growth of story; inspiration implies that germination not only can but **must** take place." (Benton 1982).

But what, then, are the implications for the way in which creative writing is being developed in schools? "Foundations of Writing" (Michael and Michael 1987) emphasises the importance of helping children to be aware of how a writer sets about writing a story. In particular they must be familiar with:

- How a writer says WHERE the story happened.
- How a writer tells WHEN the story happened.
- How a writer tells WHAT happened.
- How a writer shows HOW the story was resolved.
- How a writer uses DETAIL to interest the reader.

When children are required to write their own story, however, they are usually required to do so almost instantaneously without sufficient time to reflect and develop their ideas into strands of plot. Teachers want writing to be a highly enjoyable classroom activity and are often disappointed that many pupils see it as a "chore" to be completed as quickly as possible.

Using the computer to create a story is not, of course, a new notion. Andrew Rubin's "Storymaker" (Stonier and Conlin 1985) program, for example, offers children a "tree" of possible stories. It begins by displaying on the screen the first few sentences of a story, and then suggests branches which continue the story. The child can learn about the structure and content of stories by moving along the various paths – each path means a different set of stories with different endings. The whole process involves children in the creation of storylines.

The idea for "Storybase" was conceived some years ago by Colin Fenn from the English Department of Linksfield Academy in Aberdeen. "Lost" had been a title in an examination paper, and teachers marking the responses found that most of the candidates who attempted the rubric wrote about being lost up a mountain; the rest lost themselves on moors. This uniformity of response seemed to be a result of the artificial situation we place pupils in, and the way the whole process of creative writing is taught. Presented with a single word title, a blank piece of paper, and an anxiety to start writing, the pupils clutched at the first straw that came to mind, and that was the most obviously dramatic form of "lostness" that would cover three sides of A4. During the marking of this mass migration to mountains and moors, Fenn remembered Tony Buzan's book "Use Your Head" (Buzan 1984). Buzan, a psychologist specialising in applying perceptual and learning theories to personal and formal education, suggests that an idea used as a stimulus is less likely to generate creative thought than two or more ideas seen together. This is because the brain has a innate ability (need, even) to make connections between disparate ideas: to see order in disorder; to make a sensible interpretation from the seemingly nonsensical. Buzan's startling "proof" of this theory is the Paper Clip exercise.

"How many applications can you think of for paper clips?
Most people (adults and children) will find two or three very quickly and then run out of ideas. Five is a good score.

"Now," says the teacher, "I can think of thousands of ideas. Everyone in the class think of an object, any object."
And as you are told the nouns, connections will be made.
"Book: to mark a place. Shoes: as temporary shoe laces. Lock: pick it."
Note: there was no mention of a restriction on the number of paper clips or how they were used, so:
"Clouds: chop the paper clips and produce rain by 'seeding' the clouds."
Looks impressive but it is really very easy. The pupils are supplying the extra ideas that will spark a creative solution (Fenn 1989).

When Buzan's method was applied to "Lost", the results were startling. The pupils were asked to write down the first few nouns that occurred to them, and then relate those to "Lost" e.g.

> LOST –MONEY –by whom? –OLD LADY –what was it for? –THE RENT –rich or poor? –POOR –eviction???

or

> LOST –HANDKERCHIEF –MONEY –Child has tied money in handkerchief –For what? –Dinner money? –To pay off school bully? ...

Buzan's theories began to change the way creative writing was being taught in the school. The search for a plot no longer seemed a problem to the children. The initial "blank page" hurdle fell when the pupils began to adapt their thinking processes and use the mind's ability to create. Allowing the pupils time, too, for both the thinking and the writing processes led to their beginning to understand that writing is a reflective activity which demands time for reconsideration, for the evaluation of words, and for the re-calling and re-forming of experience. Writing was beginning to become *fun*!

2. Using the computer

Colin Fenn, the designer of "IV Storybase" has written:

> "One of my aims was to encourage children to 'play' with words, not be intimidated or frightened by writing assignments. I also had an uneasy feeling that when I had asked younger children (12-13 year-olds) to examine their own lives for characters and plots, for drama and conflict, I was imposing my own perception of literary values on them – my idea of what was important and worthwhile, which could well be working to dull creativity rather than enhance it. If children could just enjoy writing, without restraints, then 'serious writing' would develop later. With half of my pupils living outwith the usual nuclear definition of family, many did not wish to 'explore' their own lives. Why should they? Why shouldn't writing offer an escape, a chance to create a world with only a tentative connection with reality. Did it matter **what** they wrote as long as they enjoyed the writing and felt that this skill was one worth developing for its own sake. Like art. Like swimming." (Fenn 1989).

And so an experiment began. It was decided that children should be provided with a series of unrelated ideas around which they would construct a storyline. These unrelated ideas would be issued to each child at random by a computer. "Storybase" had been conceived. In essence, the program is a dedicated database, designed to store information for a specific purpose. It carries out the selection of "ideas", and issues a personalised printout for each pupil. To begin with, two files were created: "Gumshoe", which was aimed at first year pupils (aged 12 years), invited the youngsters to write a detective story, while "Europe" for second year pupils, was centred around the development of research and information-gathering skills. The "Europe" file sets the pupil down in a town or city somewhere in Europe, gives him a new persona and a list of bizarre happenings and environments which must be integrated into the story. The file was created in co-operation with the school librarian who ensured that information about all the locations was readily available. She also put together a list of Tourist Information offices to which the pupils could write for brochures.

ASSIGNMENT EUROPE
CHOSEN BY THE COMPUTER FOR JOHN SMITH
Date: 20/5/88 Class: 3A Teacher: Mrs. McLeod

Location:
This is the city or town within which the majority of your story should be set. Try to find information about your location before writing your story.

<u>The computer has selected:</u>
BREMEN

You:
Your storyteller will have a different occupation and personality from your own. You may have to research your occupation before starting your story.

<u>The computer has selected:</u>
DOCTOR

Environments:
These are places within your city or town. Try to spread the environments within the story. You do not need to use them all.

<u>The computer has selected:</u>
POST OFFICE
PHOTOGRAPHER'S STUDIO
CIRCUS
POLICE STATION
RADIO STATION
RECORDING STUDIO

Technology:
There are mainly objects or "things" that have been developed recently. Try to use them naturally within the story. They may give you ideas for your plot.

The computer has selected:
OFFSET PRINTING PRESS
LAMBORGHINI
ROD OF URANIUM
JUKE BOX
FLAGEOLET
SUPERGLUE

General:
There are mainly common-or-garden objects. They will give you ideas and help you with the plot. Try to spread them through the story.

The computer has selected:
MASCARA
FALSE TEETH
BENT COIL
JEMMY
MAUSOLEUM
LANDAU

Incidents:
These are things that happen in the story. Try to blend them naturally into your story.

The computer has selected:
BOAT WITH A HOLE IN IT
ONE DIRTY GLOVE
FOUND: A GLASS EYE
SUGAR IN THE PETROL
WELL-DRESSED WINDOW

"Storybase" is centred around three main principles: writing stories is an exciting and rewarding experience; writing stories should not be limited to a child's personal and social experience: randomly selected ideas help generate plots. The ideas which the computer selects for each child, do not act as a constricting force on the writer, but spur on his/her creativity. Given a number of randomly selected ideas, a child will seek to make sense of them. This produces a plot, and then research into the ideas and thought and discussion about what they might mean, together with encouragement from the teacher, will give creative depth to the story.

These two original "Storybase" files were tested out during one summer term and the resultant pieces of work were quite outstanding. Pupils were given a number of weeks in which to complete their computer-generated assignment, working both at home and during school time. The "fun" element in all of this was one of the main reasons for its success. Pupils were keen to have the computer select their own personalised writing assignment, and the more weird and wonderful the selection of ideas, the better! The children immediately wanted to discuss their assignments, both with the teacher and with other pupils, and so the classroom became a hive of animated discussion on the topic of creative writing. Parents, too, were drawn into the task. One lad, for his "Gumshoe" assignment, was required to construct his plot around "poisoning by deadly nightshade". Library research provided him with pictorial information about the plant and its poisonous qualities, but he needed to know the exact effect that such poison would have on the human body. Could the poison kill? If so, what would the body look like in death? With the help of his father, who took on that specific research task, the necessary information was obtained!

The pupils had tremendous fun with their "Storybase" activities and were encouraged to decorate and illustrate their work to present an attractive end product. They became genuinely interested in effective writing techniques, providing the teacher with an opportunity to discuss techniques such as *in medias res*, flashbacks, cliff-hangers, denouement and so on.

By the end of term, the pupils had completed their "novels". Gone were the days when two sides of A4 was the norm; pupils were writing at great length, enjoying the task, and taking pride in their work. They were also permitted to work with a partner or in a small group, with each child taking responsibility for a particular "chapter". To recognise their achievements, the English department organised a Star Writer Awards Ceremony which was modelled on the Oscar Ceremony. Formal invitations were issued to which pupils had to reply. Many had to research the meaning of RSVP. At the ceremony, nominations were read out in the various categories – best piece of descriptive writing, best characterisation, most original idea, most effective illustrations and so on, and prizes were awarded. Even pupils with learning difficulties stood a chance of winning a category. The two best "novels" were then "published" in the school – senior pupils word processed them and the books were made available in the school library as part of the borrowing stock. In addition, all the pieces of work went on display both in the school library and in the Central Library in Aberdeen. The project was so successful that pupils began to ask for more "Storybase" assignments to work on during the summer holidays!

Pupils were now being stimulated to produce pieces of writing on topics, which, previously, would have been unthinkable. One 13-year-old girl wrote an extremely gripping story entitled "The Great Continental Adventure" which was generated by the "Europe" file. The plot is centred around Baroque Art in Czechoslovakia, and the setting of the story, Prague, has been meticulously researched:

> "The house was in the old town, the historic part of Prague, and I was charmed by the many quaint yet splendid buildings which lined the

streets. They were so full of detail, so interesting, with gargoyles and canopies, balconies and heavy oak doors... Our work began the very next day. Signor Galliano familiarised me with the various styles and artists of the Baroque period, then we went to study some works in the Art Galleries and Museums in Prague... As we were quietly studying one of the major works – the great Rubens masterpiece "The Miracles of St. Francis Xavier" on loan from the Alte Pinakothele in Munich - Signor Galliano suddenly let out a yell which startled the placid art-lovers in the hall."

The story moves through many real locations in Prague, and incorporates, in a very unobtrusive way, all of the seemingly unrelated objects and ideas selected by the computer. Czechoslovakian words and phrases, too, are used!

"Storybase" is now being used extensively in Scottish schools, both primary and secondary. For use with very young children, files can be created which stimulate talk or role-playing activities, but, equally, the program has a place in the curriculum at Standard Grade, (Scottish National examination) level. The following Unit Plan[1] outlines a strategy for its use:

"STORYBASE" **UNIT PLAN**

GENERAL AIMS: to develop skills in story-writing, group discussion, research, reading for information and note-taking.

STIMULUS	METHOD	OBJECTIVE/ OUTCOME
Individual assignment printout (example). Exemplars of finished stories C	Pupils read and discuss in groups	-Discussion - to express reactions, to deploy ideas -Reading - for information -Reading aloud
Teacher explains nature of "Storybase". Identification of storytelling and research techniques C	Class/group discussion of story-telling techniques Listening, note-taking for information on sources, approaches	-Discussion of techniques -Writing - to convey ideas, information
Individual assignments (Pairs/Groups where appropriate) C	Identifying research areas Compiling lists.	-Reading - for information -Writing - to convey ideas, information
Need for information C	Individual research work, may include letters, interview, library work	- Reading - for particular information -Writing - for information, to employ specific literary form -Talk - to create particular effects.
Creating stories C	Writing/redrafting/ discussion, in groups and pairs	- Writing - to employ specific literary form -Reading - to appreciate writer's craft -Talk - to argue, evaluate

[1] "English and the Micro" 1988 (The Scottish Consultative Committee on the Curriculim).

Final product C	Individual choice repackaging, printing, illustration F	- Writing (etc.) - to employ specific literary form
Class collections/ Library C	"Private" reading Review	- Reading - to enjoy and obtain enrichment -Writing - specific literary form
Author "interviews" E	Pairs discussion Role-play Solo Talk(possible video opportunities)	- Talk - to convey information, express feelings, create part effects
Information unearthed in research work E	Selection and compilation of extended information piece (perhaps to form a mini-encyclopaedia) F	- Writing - to convey information
Creating new "Storybase"	Discussion, research (See Group Worksheet)	- Talk - to argue, evaluate, deploy ideas -Reading - for information -Writing - to convey information

NOTES:
C - Core assignment
E - Extension assignment
F - Possible folio piece

Others may include:

- Homework "Storybase" assignment, extending research and writing beyond classroom and school.
- Library "cataloguing"/lending of finished products, establishes "real" audience.
- Class/peer-group assessment of significant features, leading to "awards ceremony".
- Creating a "Storybase" assignment purely as a stimulus for group talk.

Giving children the responsibility of creating a "Storybase" file for others to use, can also produce excellent results and can encourage co-operative learning:

"CREATING A STORYBASE"
GROUP WORKSHEET

1. CHOOSE A CHAIRPERSON AND SECRETARY
   <u>The chairperson will:</u>
   Lead the discussion.
   Ensure that tasks are shared equally.
   <u>The secretary will:</u>
   Collect notes and information which group members produce.

2. WHAT KIND OF STORYBASE DO YOU WANT TO CREATE? WHO IS IT FOR?
   Adventure? Mystery? Crime? Historical? SF? Fantasy? Any others?

3. WHAT POSSIBLE CATEGORIES DO YOU WANT TO HAVE?
   People? Places? Objects? Events? Things people say? Any others?

4. WHAT RESEARCH FACILITIES WILL YOU WANT PEOPLE TO USE?
   Class Library? School Library? Interviews? Information centres?

5. DRAW UP YOUR LISTS FOR EACH CATEGORY
   You must give people reasonable research tasks and targets, but your lists can be as long or as short as you wish. You may do this work individually or in pairs.

6. REPORT BACK TO THE REST OF THE GROUP.

7. THE SECRETARY, HELPED BY THE OTHERS OF THE GROUP, SHOULD DRAW UP A SUMMARY OF THE PROPOSED "STORYBASE"
   You should discuss the result and call in your teacher to comment.

8. WHEN YOU ARE READY, APPOINT SOMEONE TO KEY IN THE INFORMATION TO THE COMPUTER.
   Follow the instructions in the guidebook and REMEMBER TO SAVE YOUR FILE!

9. RUN YOUR NEW PROGRAM
   Take notes and discuss any changes that need to be made. Once you have agreed, make those changes (SAVE YOUR NEW FILE!)

10. WELL DONE! YOU HAVE CREATED A NEW STORYBASE
    You can invite another group to try it out.

3. "IV Storybase"

Interactive video has tremendous potential in education. The ability to harness the power of the computer and the visual stimuli from a videodisk is leading to exciting new computer-related activities in schools. In the UK, the Interactive Video in Schools (IVIS) project, funded by the Department of Trade and Industry, provided eight interactive videodisks with related software. The Domesday project, too, sparked off tremendous interest in this new technology, so that the number of interactive video systems in schools is growing rapidly. A videodisk, which is capable of storing around 54,000 frames (still frames and moving film) offers fast random access when controlled by intelligent computer software. As Leslie Hills has said:

> "The potential uses of interactivity, with enormous fast access, high quality data are obviously many and the applications of disc based IV may

range from use in the primary school as an encyclopaedia with a clever index, encouraging individualised learning, to collections of subject-specific discs in higher education. Library use is also obvious. However there are questions still to be answered about how people can best use visual rather than print sources." (Hills 1986).

The IVIS project had three main aims:

- To investigate the potential of IV as a teaching and learning resource for schools; to identify its strengths and weaknesses; and to examine responses so that future IV packages are created that meet the immediate needs of both teacher and pupils.
- To facilitate the development of IV design skills within the educational sector.
- To explore the practical aspects of implementing technology in schools; to ensure that classroom management expertise exists and is shared, and that there is an awareness of the resources required to introduce teachers to new technology.

In the UK, the National Interactive Video Centre in London, and the Scottish Interactive Technology Centre in Edinburgh are the two main agencies which facilitate the exchange of information, advice and experience between providers and users of interactive video.

Grampian Region was one of the pilot sites for the IVIS project and has continued to explore the potential of interactive technology in all sectors of education. Some of the applications involve pupils and students working at their own pace through pre-structured pathways on a videodisk; others are centred around much more open and flexible learning styles as pupils use utility tools such as Turpin, SIVA or Opensoft for BBC IV systems, to search for information from a videodisk, or even go on to create their own files by selecting, re-ordering and manipulating images (still frames and moving film) from various places on the videodisk. The success of the original text-only "Storybase" program led to consideration of ways in which the program could be adapted for use with an interactive video system, and thus "IV Storybase" was born. The software runs on the BBC IV system.

Like the original "Storybase" program, the IV version enables a teacher to create data-files on appropriate topics from which the computer will choose at random a selection of items (this time, both textual and visual) for each pupil or group of pupils. "IV Storybase" can be used with an active play videodisk, but also comes complete with several ready-made files for use with some of the most popular videodisks in use in schools. The "Gangs" file, for instance, is based on "Challenges", one of the eight IVIS discs. For each pupil, the computer will randomly select images of different members of a gang. Then images of "baddies" are shown, followed by some "neutral" characters such as a newspaper seller or fashion model. Ideas are then selected for the locations in the story, objects and incidents. Another file "Islands", using the "Design" disc

(IVIS) also encourages research skills by including references and clues which must be researched.

Initial responses from pupils seem to show that the images generated by "IV storybase" do help to stimulate imaginative writing. But what exactly do we mean by "imaginative writing"? According to Alan Lynskey:

> "Many teachers take it to mean putting children into an imaginary situation, usually of a highly coloured nature, and asking them to write about it. 'Imagine you are a cabin boy on a pirate ship. Tell what it is like.' This might well produce a good result but only if the background is explored, discussed, animated, and, better still, if it is part of a theme 'Pirates' which would provide a full involvement in the relevant situations and experiences." (Linskey 1984).

Files produced using "IV Storybase" can be integrated into thematic project work already being undertaken in the classroom, or, equally, the program itself might act as the motivational stimulus for other related activities, such as research and information gathering, or the study of a particular literary genre.

When the image is on the screen, the pupil must take careful notes of the elements which he/she has particularly noticed. The visual stimulus is not intended to be adhered to faithfully, but is meant only as a prompt to trigger the imagination. One lad, for instance, looked at a still of a man with a long pole sitting on a window-ledge and, rather than thinking of why the man was there and what he was doing, began instead to focus on the building which seemed rather an impressive one, reminiscent of a museum or art gallery. This train of thought then became one of the strands in the plot of the story. The ability to look "into" rather than "at" a visual image is constantly encouraged by the teacher.

"Cars in a car park" seems a very straightforward clue, but when accompanied by an image displaying hundreds of cars parked close together in a field, then thoughts might turn towards a race-meeting, a pop-concert, or even a football match.

At the moment, the main constraint on the production of files for "IV Storybase" is the limited number of suitable videodisks which have immediate use in education. Ideally, listening skills could be developed too, if a piece of moving film with an appropriate sound track was selected. This, of course, is very difficult to incorporate using existing videodisks. The intention is, however, to produce a dedicated "IV Storybase" videodisk which would contain a large range of visual and auditory "clues".

Obviously, the creator of data-files (whether teacher or pupil) must have a highly developed imagination. The Swedish videodisk "Gamla Stan", containing an historical overview of the old part of Stockholm, might seem to have little relevance for Scottish children. The videodisk begins with a very attractive piece of moving film showing planets revolving round the sun. This in itself provided the idea for a science-fiction theme, and so the file "Time Bandits" was created.

ASSIGNMENT BANDITS
CHOSEN BY THE COMPUTER FOR MICHELLE
Date: 25/1/90 Class: 2D Teacher: Miss Bowman

The Crime:
You are about to enter the murky world of the TIME BANDITS! From another galaxy, able to adopt any form, they will kidnap...

The computer has selected:
THE TIME BANDITS HAVE ARRIVED...
THE TIME BANDITS ARE COMING...

Your Task:
You are the only person who can foil the TIME BANDITS. But it will not be easy for they can transport themselves from the present to the past and back again.

The computer has selected:
THE VICTIM –THE QUEEN

Characters:
These people are involved in your story. They might help you. On the other hand they may be TIME BANDITS. Use each character carefully.

The computer has selected:
PORTRAIT OF A YOUNG MAN
A STURDY LOOKING CHAP. FRIEND OR FOE?
WHO IS THIS MYSTERIOUS DARK FIGURE? WHAT IS HE CARRYING?
MAN IN OFFICE. TRY TO THINK OF THE PART HE WILL PLAY IN YOUR STORY
WHO IS THIS MAN IN THE CROWD? HE IS LOOKING STRAIGHT AT YOU...

Locations:
These are the places that will feature in our story. They will help you devise the plot.

The computer has selected:
A SNOWY COUNTRY SCENE
AN ANCIENT ENTRANCE. WHO GOES HERE:
A FISH MARKET. A PLACE TO HEAR THE GOSSIP
A VERY NARROW ALLEY. DARK AT NIGHT.....
A MARKET. WHAT CAN YOU SEE? WHAT CAN YOU BUY?

Objects:
These objects will play a part in your story. Exactly how they are used is up to you.

The computer has selected:
AN ENVELOPE WITH STAMPS
A STATUE IN A SHOP WINDOW, OR IS IT?
A FAMILY TREE. A CLUE?
A DRAWING OF A CASTLE KEEP

Incidents:
No pictures. You will have to use your imagination to see how these strange events will fit into your story.

The computer has selected:
A BLOOD-STAINED RAG
BEING FOLLOWED...
A CROWD AT A DOORWAY. WHAT HAS HAPPENED?

Marshall McLuhan, writing about the importance of the visual image, argues:

> "If we open a 1938 copy of *Life*, the pictures or postures then seen as normal, now give a sharper sense of remote time than do objects of real antiquity". (McLuhan 1974).

In a similar way, the visual images of old Stockholm from "Gamla Stan", particularly the old moving film, provide an atmospheric setting for the pupils' stories, and the still frames of artistic masterpieces are used to develop ideas for plot and characterisation, Michelle, aged 12, begins her Time Bandits story:

> "Marie sat in an old flower-patterned armchair in front of the living room window of the tiny flat which her family rented. Marie's father worked in an iron-ore mine one hundred miles north of Stockholm, where they lived. Outside the streets were dark, the only light coming from the pale orange streetlights. Even the moon was misted over with a thick sheet of factory smoke, making it almost invisible. It had been like that for as long as she could remember, and she supposed it would always be.

Then, suddenly a light so strong it almost blinded Marie settled over Stockholm. It was getting brighter and brighter until Marie couldn't stand it any longer. She rushed over to the settee and hid her face in a cushion. Her attempts to block out the white light were no use. The light flooded the room almost as if it were penetrating the walls. "News flash"" blared the TV. "A UFO has been sighted over Stockholm..." The Time Bandits file can be easily integrated into a literature-based science fiction unit of work.

"IV Storybase" has been introduced to teachers and pupils in the Grampian area as part of an in-service programme. A teacher from each of the schools (primary and secondary) which have an interactive video system was invited to attend an in-service day, accompanied by a pupil. The thinking behind this was two-fold: firstly, the notion that, as far as technology is concerned, pupils tend to learn faster than adults; secondly, the hope that, when back in school, the pupils would be able to pass on their expertise to others, both pupils and staff. Tom Stonier and Cathy Conlin rightly comment that:

> "the main problem is not with the hardware or the software, but with the liveware ... many teachers are so frightened of computers that they never find out how easy it is to run one." (Stonier and Conlin 1985).

Certainly during the "IV Storybase" in-service days, it was noted that it was the pupils (and the youngest was nine years of age) who were assuming the dominant role in the pupil-teacher partnership. They were quick to appreciate the thinking behind the software, and when it came to the creation of their own files, the ideas they suggested were particularly inventive. Alexis Beedie, aged 9, from Mosstodloch School, describes the day:

> "IV Storybase at Oldmachar.
>
> On Wednesday the 24th of January, my Mum and I set off for Mrs. Rennie's house. When we got there my Mum dropped me off and then she went to school. Mrs. Rennie and I set off from her house at approximately 8.20 a.m. and got to the academy at approximately 10.05 a.m. We were shown to the library and had some refreshments before starting the work with IV computers.
>
> The first thing we did was get a piece of paper and a pen or pencil and played the paper clip game. We had to write down as many things as we could think of which could be done with paper clips. After that we were shown by Mr. Fenn why the "Storybase" for IV was created. I found this extremely interesting and a great idea.
>
> Next we were shown by Mr. Paton how to use it, which looked quite complicated but wasn't really! Next we were told to go to one of the IV systems. There were five, but we only used four and Mr. Paton used the fifth one.
>
> First Mrs. Rennie and I got the disc called "Gangs". We loaded the computer and then typed in all the information, like my name, my teacher's name, what class I was in etc. Next the computer came up with who was going to be in my gang, who were the baddies, what objects came into my story, some people who might turn up in my story, the incidents that might happen during my story and where my story or adventure would take place. Once I had finished, the computer printed out all the writing that would be of some help to me. If I had been a pupil wanting to write a story on Gangs, my print out would give me heaps of ideas. After that we went for lunch.
>
> Everything seemed bigger than my primary school, even the choice of lunch. Once we got back to the library we were told how to select pictures from the big videodisk and store information onto our work disc. Then we went back to our IV system and tried it for ourselves. First we browsed through the disc, picking up pictures of people, places and objects, etc. which we might want to use.

After we had done that, Mr. Paton came over to us and gave us a blank floppy disc. We told the computer to take the information and pictures we had chosen and put them on the blank disc. This didn't take very long and soon we had our own copy of the information and pictures. We also got a copy of the questions which were asked on the disc.

At about 3.00 p.m. it was time to go and Mrs. Rennie and I set off for Mosstodloch. It was quite a long journey and eventually I got home at about 4.35 p.m. I felt very tired but I had really enjoyed myself."

4. Creating files for "IV Storybase"

While the "IV Storybase" program contains several sample files for immediate use, teachers and pupils are encouraged to create their own files using any active play videodisk which is appropriate. The program can be used with video images or with text only, and an initial Menu offers:

- Test only mode.
- Video simulation mode.
- Video mode.

Video Simulation Mode is an option that allows the user to input picture selections and captions without having to have a videodisk player connected. This, of course, assumes that there is an index of frame numbers available and that the user has already selected the images he/she wishes to use.

In Storybase Edit Mode, the user can create or amend files of images and ideas. A Browse facility allows any active play videodisk to be examined, so that selections of still frames or pieces of moving film can be made. Inviting a group of pupils to browse through a videodisk as the first step towards a creating file, is, in itself a useful exercise as the youngsters, through discussion, accept or reject images, make notes, and generate ideas. When agreement has been reached on the structure of the file and the visual and textual stimuli to be used, the file can then be created. Group activities of this type promote the development of interpersonal skills, oral communication skills, problem-solving skills, decision-making skills, critical thinking skills and so on.

First of all, the various Categories (up to a maximum of six) must be defined. These usually cover areas such as Setting, Characters, Events and Objects. For each Category, a brief explanation must be given, and the number of items which the computer must select must also be defined e.g.

Category 2: Setting.

Information on category 1:
This is the town or city where most of the story is to take place. You may need to do some research first.
Number (in range 0 to 6) to be selected from category 1: (1).

Category 2: People.

Information on category 2:
These are the characters who will appear in your story.
Number (in range 0 to 6) to be selected from category 2: (4).

After all of the categories have been defined in this way, the information is saved to a temporary file and the user is asked to input file items under each category e.g.

PEOPLE Entry 1. Create Y/N?

The functions keys are then used to toggle sound, vision, and the window option on and off. The required frame number can be typed in after TAB has been pressed, and, when the image is shown, parts of it can be "blacked-out" with the Window option. The user must also decide if the image is to be a still frame, or a piece of moving film, in which case the start and finish numbers must be defined. A caption for each image must also be created e.g.

This young lad is one of the characters in your story. Look at his scruffy clothes and hairstyle. What sort of boy is he?

Good captions should provide some sort of prompt, without being too definitive or prescriptive. If the computer is to select, for example, four different characters for each pupil, then a large number of file items must be defined in the PEOPLE category. This can be a time-consuming task, but, again, many imaginative files have been created by pupils themselves. Their level of involvement is extremely high as they reach a consensus regarding the choice of images, and work together to formulate appropriate captions. Older pupils, creating files for younger children to use, must give consideration to the sorts of theme, visual stimuli and language which are suitable for the audience.

5. The role of the teacher

Using new technology in the classroom requires that teachers examine their role, and also to consider effective classroom management techniques. With the development of individual and group learning, the importance of discussion has become recognised and the onus is very much on the teacher to provide opportunities for pupils to exchange ideas. Tom Stonier and Cathy Conlin claim that "no other educational tool encourages conversation as much as does a computer". (Stonier and Conlin 1985).

When an interactive video system is taken into the classroom for an activity like "IV Storybase", then the focus of attention is centred on the system rather than on the teacher. The latter is no longer the primary conveyor of information, but must adopt a much more supportive advisory and tutorial role, organising and working with groups of pupils, or helping an individual child. Children nowadays are brought up in an environment of electronic mass media, gaining much of their early education through the visual medium.

Teachers nowadays need to spend time helping children to respond to visual stimuli, both still pictures and moving images. Pupils seem to react to images both imaginatively and emotionally, and the teacher must decide whether the difficulty or complexity of an image is appropriate for the target audience.

"IV Storybase" is very effective as a group activity, but problems can be created for the teacher in arranging access for each group to the IV system while keeping other groups fully occupied. Pupils must be given every chance to discuss the task amongst themselves, to listen to each other's views, to criticise and evaluate each other's achievements. Access to resource information must also be arranged.

6. "IV Storybase" in action

Danestone Primary School on the outskirts of Aberdeen has built up tremendous expertise in the use of interactive video. The school was involved in trialling materials for both the IVIS and the Domesday project, and has recently been trying out "IV Storybase" with a class of eleven year-old pupils. The teacher decided to devote two weeks before the Easter holidays to the project, and arranged that each group of pupils would have five sessions devoted to this task. In the first of these, pupils, in pairs, would be called to the system to obtain an assignment. A file entitled "Isles" had been produced using the Design (IVIS) videodisk. This file required pupils to produce an adventure story, set on a Scottish island, about the search for a stolen treasure.

ASSIGNMENT ISLES
CHOSEN BY THE COMPUTER FOR LAURA
Date: 19/3/90 Class: 7 Teacher: Mrs. Kerr

Characters:
You will meet a number of people on your search for a stolen treasure. Study these people clearly and note down your observations

<u>The computer has selected:</u>
MAN AND WOMAN ON A MOTORBIKE. THIS PAIR MAY BE UP TO NO GOOD ...
MAN PULLING CAR FROM GARAGE. WHY? WHERE IS HE GOING? WHO IS THE MYSTERIOUS PERSON IN THE BACKGROUND
GIRL DRINKING COKE. A LIVELY PERSON BUT WHAT IS SHE REALLY LIKE?
GIRL WITH SUNGLASSES. WHY DOES SHE HIDE HER EYES? WHERE IS SHE GOING? WHAT DOES SHE KNOW?

Locations:
These are places that can be used in your story. They will help you create the plot. Try to use at least two of them.

The computer has selected:
A LANE. WHAT LURKS BEHIND THE RAILINGS?
HOUSE AT THE BACK OF A LARGE CHURCH. WHO LIVES HERE? WHAT GOES ON BEHIND THIS SMART FACADE?
A MUSEUM. CONTAINS A GREAT MANY SECRETS
A ROAD IN A PARK
A RESIDENTIAL BARGE. VERY USEFUL FOR MOVING SILENTLY AND UNNOTICED THROUGH THE COUNTRYSIDE

Objects:
These are some of the objects that may play a part in your story. They will give you ideas that will help with plotting the story.

The computer has selected:
A CAMERA
A RADIO-CASSETTE RECORDER. OR IS IT?
A MOTORBIKE WITH TWO MYSTERIOUS RIDERS
A BOOK OF MAPS

Incidents:
These are things which might happen in your story. Try to include at least two of them.

The computer has selected:
YOU FIND A FILM
A RIDE IN A BUS TO NOWHERE
A MESSAGE IN THE PERSONAL COLUMNS
YOU FIND A BUNDLE

Island:
This is the island where you find the treasure. It is a real place and you will need to do research before you start the story.

The computer has selected:
SHETLAND ISLANDS

Isle Incident:
These are some of the things you might find or might happen to you on the island. Try to use at least two of them.

The computer has selected:
MYSTERIOUS PLANT. CAN IT BE USED FOR ANYTHING?
TWO BOATS UNDER CONSTRUCTION. WHO IS BUILDING THEM AND WHAT ARE THEY GOING TO BE USED FOR?
JELLYFISH. LARGE AND DANGEROUS.

Talking was encouraged as a sifting/sorting process and, by the end of this session, the pupils had a clearer idea of the structure of their storyline and of ways in which they could integrate into the plot the various items chosen by the computer. They also had a number of areas which they needed to research.

Research tasks were undertaken during the third session. A tray had been stocked by the teacher and this contained maps, tourist brochures on Scottish Islands, pictorial information, train and ferry timetables, and various suitable magazines. The children were also encouraged to acquire other appropriate research materials themselves, perhaps by visiting a travel agency or library.

In the remaining sessions, the pupils were given time to begin the writing task and were encouraged to work with a partner to review and redraft the work produced, paying attention to areas which caused them problems - spelling, punctuation and paragraphing. The teacher's role was very much that of consultant, taking the opportunity to join in the discussions and give advice on the development of character, descriptive writing, creating suspense, and other techniques which the children were keen to use. What became immediately apparent was that the visual images had been particularly useful in encouraging the children to describe landscape and character, and the resultant stories had a strong feeling of atmosphere. The pupils were by now enthusiastically engaged in the craft of writing, and felt a real sense of "ownership" or "authorship". Those who wished, and most did, were encouraged to complete their work during the holiday period, and to illustrate their "novels" in any appropriate way.

7. Conclusions

Impressions so far suggest that "IV Storybase" is an extremely effective resource for stimulating imaginative writing. The motivational element of assignments being issued as if by magic from the computer and personalised for each child ("Chosen by the computer for ... ") cannot be ignored.

This, together with the effect of the visual images, means that pupils are approaching the writing task with new enthusiasm, and are not overawed by the idea of writing at length. Initial fears that the visual images might restrict rather than stimulate the imagination seem to have been unfounded, as pupils are, sensibly, using the videodisk images as triggers to spark off their ideas.

Making sense of visual images is a skill that must be nurtured, and the simple cognitive task of describing in detail what appears on the screen is one which needs to be encouraged.

Much more time, too, is being spent in the planning process, as the young writers, advised by the teacher, think about the structure of the story, the development of character, and the influence of setting and atmosphere.

"IV Storybase" can be easily integrated into the curriculum for English/Language arts. The new National Curriculum for English (in England and Wales) demands that in the area of Speaking and Listening (Attainment Target 1), "Pupils should be able to participate as speakers and listeners in a group engaged in an active task" and that they "should be able to contribute to and respond constructively in discussion". In Writing (Attainment Target 3), they ought to have practice in writing stories which show "an understanding of the rudiments of story structure by establishing an opening, characters, and one or more events". While there are many ways for a teacher to ensure that these goals are achieved, "IV Storybase" is another tool to expand the teacher's normally available resources, a tool which is effective, motivational, and above all, fun.

8. Acknowledgements

I should like to thank Colin Fenn, the designer of "Storybase" and "IV Storybase", and Donald Paton who wrote the programs.

The pupils and staff of schools in Grampian Region, have, as usual, been invaluable, giving of their time, often at very short notice, to try out the software.

9. References

Benton, M. (1982) How authors write - how children write: towards a rationale for creative writing. In A. Adams (Ed.) *New Directions in English Teaching.* Farmer Press.

Buzan, T. (1984) *Use Your Head.* Ariel.

Fenn, C. (1989) Storybase. *ETC Journal*, 3.

Hills, L. (1986) *Interactive Video in Education.* Scottish Council for Educational Technology.

Lynskey, A. (1984) *Children and Themes.* Oxford University Press, Oxford.

McLuhan, M. (1974) *The Selection and Use of Instructional Media.* Kogan Page.

Michael, B. and Michael, M. (1987), *Teacher's Guide for Foundations of Writing.* Jordanhill College

Stonier, T. and Conlin, C. (1985). *The Three Cs - Children, Computers and Communication.* Wiley, Chichester.

24

Story-Building with Computers: Effects on Reading Comprehension, Vocabulary, Attitude and Writing

Deborah Little
University of Illinois at Urbana-Champaign

Abstract

The study investigated effects of writing-related software on reading comprehension, vocabulary, attitude, and writing. The researcher used the Non-equivalent Control Group Design with sixth grade students in two rural schools.

Three goals were to discover whether gains were achieved in students' comprehension and vocabulary as a result of supplemental reading activities with computer-presented writing software; to determine whether attitudes towards reading changed as a result of story-building; and to observe whether writing skills developed as a result of writing interactive stories.

Participants were pre- and post-tested in comprehension, vocabulary, attitudes and writing. For each variable, group differences were analysed. Differences between males and females who received the treatment were also investigated. Results were obtained from an analysis of covariance. Results indicated that including computer-presented writing software in the reading curriculum can be a helpful activity.

Implications for reading/writing instruction include the need to plan structured sharing of stories; to use mapping techniques for reading and writing across genres; to pursue story-building for group instruction in reading/writing; and to relate story-building to traditional reading activities.

1. Introduction

Most teachers, regardless of their area of expertise, will probably agree with Russell Hunt's (1985) statement, "Common sense dictates that reading and writing are related". The nature of that relationship has been a frequent question for educational investigations since the early 1900s.

Some well known educational researchers have suggested that reading and writing are different phases of similar processes (Pearson and Tierney 1984, Smith 1984, Squire 1984). These and other researchers agree that writing in the reading curriculum is a natural, possibly necessary, activity to be included in the array of experiences required to help students become competent readers.

Until recently, stories for classroom reading were limited to selections from traditional basal readers, paperbacks, or library books. Observing active participation in reading was limited to watching the turning of pages during silent reading periods, listening to students' oral reading, and leading group discussions after reading a story. None of these observations was an accurate measure of active participation in reading.

The growth of microcomputers in schools, and the demand for quality software, has created a new resource for story selections. A type of software that is gaining popularity is story-building software, or interactive stories. Readers are given choices that enable them to control the story's outcome. Reading in groups, or alone at a computer, provides a means for teachers to observe active readers – students making choices about the directions a story takes.

One software distributor has a story-building program that includes a text editing feature (word processor). Readers write original interactive stories, building a story for others to read or reread themselves. This particular software, *Story Tree*, (Brackett 1984) may provide teachers with an efficient method of observing active readers. Additionally, story-building software may help students make a connection between reading and writing and produce gains in reading and writing, the focus of the study.

At this time there is mainly anecdotal information from teachers, parents, students and software distributors regarding the positive effects of story-building software (Balajthy and Reinking 1985). Conducting this study was an attempt to validate positive effects that computer-presented story-building may have on students' reading, vocabulary, attitudes towards reading and writing skill.

2. Review of related literature

A review of research on reading and computers indicates that supplementing the reading program with computer assisted reading materials has a positive effect on reading achievement for many students. The type of software used for comparative studies reviewed was drill and practice which emphasised decoding skills. However, many reading specialists hold that after the third grade, emphasis on meaning in reading should replace the emphasis on decoding skills (Chall 1967). Though some activities to increase meaning, i.e. new words, may be accomplished through drill and practice activities, there are more appropriate ways of emphasising meaning, particularly if the end goal is for readers to understand an entire selection, rather than isolated words. Further, reading specialists have suggested that using what the learner already knows may help build reading comprehension, especially when writing is integrated into the reading curriculum (Anderson *et al.* 1985).

Until recently, reading and language arts software emphasised decoding skill and was primarily of the workbook-drill or practice-format. Earlier attempts to enhance reading programs by integrating the curriculum with reading software had little variety to choose from. Still, on standardised post-tests, students using supplementary computer-assisted instruction (CAI) reading materials often out-score students using other supplementary materials. Though the differences between groups' are not always statistically significant, there is evidence to indicate that reading software is at least as good as other supplementary materials used for improving reading achievement (Anelli 1977,

Litman 1977, Ortmann 1983, Sedlacek 1984). In addition, of the studies reviewed that included measures of student attitude, all reported positive results (Anelli 1977, Caldwell 1973, Diamond 1969. Results of computer assisted instruction at Bath Elementary School 1979, Sedlacek 1984).

3. Methodology and design

The uniqueness of the present study is that it analyses the effects of integrating writing-related software with the processes involved in comprehension. The study involved students and teachers in regularly assigned reading classes. This approach permitted the exploration of the implications of including this type of software in the array of materials currently used in the reading curriculum.

Campbell and Stanley (1963) describe one of the most frequently used experimental designs in educational research – the Non-equivalent Control Group Design. This design consists of an experimental and control group, each of which are given pre- and post-tests. The groups are non-equivalent because they are made up of subjects in naturally assigned classrooms, as similar as possible in the given situation, yet not similar enough that a pre-test can be eliminated. This particular quasi-experimental design is well-suited to the investigator who conducts research using a sample selected from a given population. Though there were certain limitations to using the described research design, i.e. threats to internal and external validity, the advantages outweighed those possible threats.

Sixth graders from two rural public elementary schools were the subjects of the study during the fall of 1986. The entire sixth grade from one school was the experimental (computer) group; the entire sixth grade from the other school was the control (non-computer) group. The reading curriculum in each school included reading selections from textbooks; building vocabulary, spelling and comprehension through post-reading exercises; and encouraging independent selection and reading of library and trade books.

After all data were gathered and scores obtained, teachers in both settings were given the results. Data shared with teachers were presented for individuals as well as groups, though the focus of the study itself was on group, not individual, differences.

Extensive teacher training for using the selected software was not necessary. The reading teacher for the experimental group was already familiar with the selected software. Approximately three hours were devoted to reviewing the tutorial, emphasising the importance of "mapping", and discussing ways to integrate the software into the reading program. The teacher was provided with a timetable for student sessions; sign-in sheets for laboratory time; copies of the written tutorial; master disks for the software; two Apple II+ computers for the classroom; and the accompanying manuals.

The control group students and teachers continued with their regularly scheduled reading curriculum. No special emphasis on writing was added to the reading activities in the control school. Students in the experimental group were involved in activities relating to the selected software in addition to their regularly assigned reading work. Three days each week were reserved for work relating to story-building, two days for using the computer and one day for off-line planning and editing.

The computer laboratory included six Apple IIe computers and one dot-matrix printer. Another Apple IIe was available in the school office, and two additional Apple II+ computers were in the reading classroom. To make efficient use of the nine computers available, each student was assigned a partner. One class period was devoted to an introduction to the software. Students worked with partners reading a pre-programmed selection included on the story disk. A discussion time after reading the sample was used to introduce the concept of "mapping"as a way of pre-writing. A second class period was devoted to how to create their own story "maps".

Included in the software is a written tutorial that guides the user through the creation of a mystery using a partially completed "map". The tutorial instructs the novice on various features of the text editor and encourages the completion of the mystery. One class period was devoted to using the written tutorial. Students next began to plan original stories using "mapping".

In addition to completing story maps, all pairs of students were required to write out each frame for original stories. Students were encouraged to take turns at the keyboard as they typed. The remainder of the story-building activities included printing early drafts, editing off-line, entering corrections at the computer, and printing final drafts.

Pre- and post-tests were administered to experimental and control groups in reading comprehension, vocabulary, reading attitude and writing. Descriptions of each test and the results of an analysis of covariance are presented below.

The standardised test selected to measure reading was the Metropolitan Achievement Test: Reading Instructional Test, Intermediate, Forms JI and KI 1978 Edition using two sub-tests: reading comprehension and vocabulary in context. Form JI was the pre-test; Form KI was the post-test.

The reading comprehension test –designed to assess the use of context clues, literal comprehension, and inferential comprehension – includes a total of 60 items from 11 graded passages, ranging from third to tenth grade. Each passage is followed by multiple choice questions. Students may refer to passages when answering.

4. Results

Both groups made gains in reading comprehension from pre- to post-test. No significant differences ($p < .0648$) were found between groups. Students in the control group gained 4.83 points from pre- to post-tests, and students in the experimental group gained an average of 3.25 points from pre- to post-test. Students who used computer-presented story-building in their reading curriculum did not score significantly higher than students who had not used writing-related software in their reading curriculum.

An analysis of the main effects also showed no significant differences on the basis of sex. Females increased an average of 3.84 points from pre- to post-test; males, an average of 4.70. An analysis of group by sex revealed no significant differences between males and females in the experimental group. Females gained an average of 1.40 points; males gained 4.65 points. Regardless of gender, students' scores in reading comprehension increased during the time frame of the study.

The vocabulary test –designed to provide a closer look at students' understanding of words –is composed of 24 items. Both semantic and syntactic clues are included to test knowledge of vocabulary in context.

Results from the vocabulary test revealed some changes from pre-to post-test for both groups. Based on the analysis of group means, a significant difference between groups was observed. The control group scored significantly higher ($p < .0310$) than the experimental group on the vocabulary post-test. Students in the control group demonstrated an average gain of +47 from pre- to post-test. Experimental group students did not show positive changes, indicating an average difference of –44 from pre- to post-test.

Further examination of the main effects indicated no significant differences on the basis of sex. Male subjects' growth in vocabulary tended to be higher than females. On the average, males scored .34 points higher from pre- to post-test, and females scored .04 lower. The analysis comparing group by sex indicated that there were no significant differences between males and females in the experimental group. Females' scores decreased an average of 1.35 points and males' scores increased an average of .20 points.

To measure attitudes towards reading, the Dulin-Chester Reading Attitude Scale (Dulin and Chester 1975) was given. Only one form of the attitude scale is available; thus, the same form was used to determine pre- and post-test scores. The scale consists of 20 forced-choice items, each of which has a reading and non-reading choice, with a 5-step response scale. Summed scores range from a low of 20 to a high of 100. Scores above 65 represent a high attitude towards reading; scores below 45 represent a low attitude; and scores between 45 and 65 represent an average attitude.

Neither control nor experimental subjects made positive changes in attitudes towards reading during the time frame of the research. Both groups remained in the average range between 45 and 65 points. The control group pre-test mean was 52.71; the post-test mean was 51.77, a negative change. Likewise, the experimental group made a negative change from pre- to post-test in attitudes towards reading. Their pre-test mean was 54.39; the post-test mean was 53.92.

The main effects also indicated a lack of significant differences in attitudes towards reading on the basis of sex. Scores for females decreased an average of 1.45 points; scores for males decreased 0.13 points. An examination of average gains demonstrated that treatment males made positive changes in attitudes. Males receiving the treatment demonstrated an average increase of 1.33 points from pre- to post-test. Scores for treatment females decreased an average of -

0.51. Though treatment males increased in attitudes and females decreased, the difference was not statistically significant.

Finally, to measure writing skills, student writing samples were rated by two trained raters using the Illinois Functional Writing Scale. The rating scale combines two approaches to evaluating writing–holistic and analytic judgements. The holistic feature provides an integrated evaluation based on a global judgement of how effectively the essay addresses the assignment. Analytic judgements examine a writer's ability to focus on the topic, provide support and elaboration, organise ideas, and use standard English. Scores range from a low of 1 (absent) to a high of 6 (well-developed). A move from a score of 3 (developing) to 4 (developed) is reported to represent significant growth in writing development ("Write On Illinois!" *A Users Guide to Scoring Student Essays* 1984).

For the study described, two different narrative writing prompts were administered to obtain pre- and post-test data. All writing samples were scored by each rater using the original papers rather than photocopies of student samples. Raters requested originals noting that reading and evaluating from originals was more reliable than using photocopies. Names were deleted to eliminate any possibility of sex bias; pre- and post-writing samples were rated at the same time to control for any bias based on testing date. The score used in calculating change is the integrated holistic score, which gives a total picture of writing development. Scores of participants in the study ranged from a low of 1 to a high of 5.

No significant group differences were reported for writing development. Control participants' scores decreased an average of 0.18 points, and experimental participants increased an average of 0.26 points. Furthermore, a larger percentage of students in the experimental group moved from ratings of 3 or lower on the pre-test to 4 or higher on the post-test than in the control group. Though this growth did not result in statistical differences, according to the guidelines of the scale, a movement from 3 or lower –undeveloped writing –to a score of 4 or above –developed writing –represents significant development.

A significant difference ($p < 0.0002$) was reported on the basis of sex. Females made significantly greater gains than males from pre- to post-writing samples. On the average, females scored 0.10 points higher on the post-test; males scored 0.15 points lower on the post-test. The statistical analysis of group by sex indicated a significant differences ($p < 0.003$) between males and females in the experimental group. Females in the treatment group scored higher than males, demonstrating an average gain of 0.57 points, while males demonstrated an average increase of 0.05 points.

In addition to the measures previously described, three other pieces of data were gathered – time spent using the computer, student responses to an informal post-treatment questionnaire, and teacher comments. The information was only obtained from the treatment site. No analysis was performed to correlate time spent on the computer with individual or group gains on any of the four dependent variables. The descriptive information was obtained to enrich the statistical analysis, providing a broader context for the findings.

Students signed in to use the computers and software for a total of 75.5 hours. Most of the computer time occurred during assigned lab periods –a total of 13 45-minute sessions. Not all students used the computer during every reserved session. Six additional sessions were recorded during lunch, study hall and after school. Students who used the computer on their own time, did so on their own initiative.

An average computer session for students was 29 minutes long. The time included only the periods spent using the software to write, edit and read stories, not time spent revising and editing off-line. Information collected regarding time spent at the computer was shared with the teacher. This information provided the teacher with some insights about individuals regarding time-on-task and academic gains.

Students completed a post-treatment questionnaire. They did not identify themselves by name, but did indicate their sex. Thirty-nine students completed the questionnaire – 15 females and 24 males. A request for student comments was included to get a learner's point of view regarding the software and the writing-related activities.

Students were asked to give one word that they felt best described the software. Most descriptive words reflected positive feelings about the software. Some positive words used to describe the software were *amusing, fun, neat, fantastic, exciting, outrageous* and *awesome.* Negative words included stupid, odd, poor, boring and hard. When asked if they would like to use the software again, three females and four males gave negative responses. There were 32 positive responses from 12 females and 20 males.

Overall, students appeared to enter the activity with enthusiasm for computers in the reading class. Some students indicated that they were bored in reading and hoped that the computers would make reading more interesting and fun. A few students, who were eager to use the computer because they thought reading would be easier, were surprised to learn that using the software required thinking, planning, writing and reading – all the hard work they usually did in reading. Several students indicated that they originally thought computers were for playing games. After using the software, they said they realised computers were also for learning.

The teacher's post-treatment comments were made in response to three statements. The first concerned the teacher's expectations of the software. She reported that she expected the mapping activities to help students write better, more fully developed narratives. Since using computers in her classes usually met with student approval, she also anticipated active and enthusiastic participation of most students. A final expectation concerned proof-reading and editing. She hoped this project would encourage students in self- and group-editing, a task dreaded by her students.

A second set of observations dealt with what seemed to be happening while students were using the story-building software. The teacher noted that some students "caught-on" to the software quickly, while others did not. Some students were still struggling to understand the connection between mapping and writing at the end of the project. She indicated that there was a mixture of good and bad feelings about writing with the software, but no noticeable type of student who seemed to be meeting with success. Overall, she said using the software seemed to have a positive effect.

The final query asked what the teacher would change if she used the software on a regular basis. Her suggestions were:

- Don't pair children–it causes management problems.
- Have a trained aide or volunteer to help during lab times.
- Begin with some keyboarding practice.
- Include more computer lab time.
- Obtain more computers–one for each student.
- Develop a different tutorial than the one provided.
- Spend four or five class periods introducing the concept of "mapping", relating it more specifically to writing "choose your own adventures"–the students saw this reading and writing activity as similar to "choose your own adventure books".
- Use the software for small group writing experiences in conjunction with reading instruction, using "choose your own adventure"literature.
- Integrate the software better with the present curriculum.

Generally, the teacher's comments and suggestions were positive. She reported that she plans to use the software in the future.

5. Recommendations

Significant differences reported in some earlier studies, in contrast to a lack of significant differences in the present study, suggest that further investigation of the relationship between computer-related writing and reading comprehension is warranted, especially as computers become commonplace in reading classrooms.

First, *it is recommended that the present study be replicated over a longer period of time, preferably an entire school year.* Both the experimental and control groups demonstrated positive growth incomprehension during the 7-week time-frame of the study. Noting whether the treatment or control group demonstrates greater gains after a longer exposure to the treatment is recommended to give a clearer picture of possible effects of using computer-presented story-building. In addition, testing students following a year, with no specific treatment, is suggested to give an indication of the long-range effects of computer-presented story-building.

Second, *it is recommended that future research concerned with vocabulary growth make use of tests that better reflect the reading curriculum.* The basis for recommending further research on the relationships among reading, computer use, writing and vocabulary development concerns the test instrument. Students in the present study scored lower on the vocabulary post-test than the pre-test, an unanticipated result. The decrease may have been a result of a test that contains too few items, or a test that does not measure reading in a manner reflecting the instructional program. Two states, Illinois and Michigan, are developing tests that reflect reading practices better (Valencia 1987). Using one of those tests (or a similar test) in future studies examining the relationship between computer-related writing and vocabulary is suggested.

Third, *it is recommended that case study or ethnographic research be conducted to better determine changes in student attitudes towards reading resulting from the use of story-building with computers.* The intensive nature of case studies and ethnographic research permits more detailed and sensitive analysis of attitudes than is possible on a rating scale. In the present study, scores obtained from an attitude scale did not reflect positive changes indicated in a post-treatment questionnaire. The need for continued research on attitudes towards reading is further indicated by inconsistent results in previous studies. Based on scores obtained from the Estes Reading Scale, one study reported no relation between attitudes and reading achievement when computers were used to supplement the reading curriculum (Sedlacek 1984). However, a study that used a study-specific scale, revealed that students using computers in reading instruction had significantly higher attitudes towards reading than students not using the computer (Caldwell 1973).

Fourth, *it is recommended that further research be conducted to better understand male-female differences connected with using computer-presented story-building.* There were no statistical differences in comprehension gains between groups. Yet, within the experimental group, males scored higher –though not statistically different–than females. This trend for greater growth in comprehension for males indicates that continued research on computer-related writing and reading relationships, with particular attention on gender effects, might prove revealing.

Writing improvement also seemed to be related to gender. Treatment females scored significantly higher than males on writing samples that assessed writing. Continued investigation of gender effects resulting from computer interaction is further indicated by differences between males and females reported in the present study.

Fifth, *it is recommended that future studies be designed to correlate student growth in various areas with the amount of time spent interacting with the software.* Though student time at the computer was logged, the present study was not designed to examine relationships which may exist between time on task and individual change. Anelli's (1977) research on the effects of time on reading improvement reported that neither time nor frequency of CAI affected achievement. A review of related literature revealed no other studies on the relationship between time on the computer and reading achievement. Future studies in this area are indicated to fill this gap. In addition, investigating the relationship between time on the computer and reading achievement may indicate a particular type of learner who can best benefit from computer-related writing.

6. Implications for instruction

The results of this study, observations of the teacher, and comments from students reveal that the questions involved in the use of computer-presented story-building are complex, touching on many aspects of reading instruction. Some implications drawn from the study are presented below.

The first implication for instruction is that more class time needs to be devoted to teaching the concept of mapping as a way of organising ideas. Though most students learned to use the features of the software quickly and with relative ease, the concept of mapping presented more difficulty. Some students were still confused with mapping as a way of pre- writing after 7 weeks. Simpler forms of mapping, such as those suggested by Heimlich and Pittelman (1986), can be used to prepare students who have difficulties.

For all students, a longer time frame of working with all the story-building activities –mapping, writing, editing, reading and sharing – was indicated. Students at all levels need time to become comfortable with the special style of organising, writing, editing and reading required by mapping and story-building.

A second implication is that more structured sharing of original stories is necessary to help students get a sense of writing for real audiences. It is important that class time be organised in a manner that includes more opportunities for sharing of ideas. As with other kinds of writing, (Britton *et al.* 1975, Applebee 1981) sharing original stories at various stages of development may give students a sense of responsibility to the intended audience –other students. Too often, a teacher is the only audience for student generated writing.

Sharing stories at different stages can be accomplished during weekly or bi-weekly sessions in which students critique stories. In these sessions students should be encouraged to read critically for supporting details, logical choices and correct usage.

A third implication for instruction is that mapping and story-building activities can be used to teach students to read and write across genres. Genres other than the narrative form are studied in reading instruction. They lend themselves to activities associated with story-building. The reading of expository selections could be enhanced by the use of mapping as a means of noting main ideas and supporting details. Furthermore, science materials, i.e. reports of experiments, could be organised through mapping. In this sense the teacher can use the software and related activities to facilitate reading and writing in the content areas.

A fourth implication is that story-building and the related activities are well-suited to group work. Small group work is not anew approach to the teaching of reading and writing or other school subjects. As Diparo and Freedman (1987) indicate, group techniques have been documented in American education since the early 1900s. Recent research (Johnson *et al.* 1984) has confirmed that students learn from each other, give each other constructive feedback, and begin to get a sense of learning through co-operation.

Story-building with computers is especially suited to group work. Students tend to congregate at the computer and discuss stories of classmates that peak their interest. They seem to enjoy sharing maps, especially the complex ones. Also, students help others, sharing their experiences and knowledge freely.

A fifth implication for reading instruction is that story-building and the related activities need to be more closely related to the traditional curriculum. Due to the short instructional component of the study –7 weeks – some regularly scheduled reading activities were temporarily suspended. Over a year long study story-building activities could be more closely related to on-going reading activities.

Several ways of achieving this integration are possible. For example, teachers can have students create an agreed-upon class map for a story read from a basal reader. They can assign groups to suggest and write "what if" situations to add branches to a particular story map. Teachers might have students share responsibilities for typing, editing and printing an original class story created with mapping. Teachers can assign groups to discuss ideas for original writing to share with students from other classes. Finally, teachers can have students use maps as pre-reading to predict the outcome of a reading selection.

In summary, statistical findings led to the conclusion that including computer-presented story-building in the reading curriculum is at least as good as other supplementary reading materials for improving reading achievement. Positive results of this study also provide teachers and parents with more evidence that computers are a vital resource in support of the "three R's".

7. References

Anderson, R. C., Hiebert, E. H., Scott, J. A., and Wilkinson, I. A. G. (1985). *Becoming a nation of readers: the report of the commission on reading.* National Institute of Education, Washington, DC.

Anelli, C. M. (1977). Computer-assisted instruction and reading achievement of urban third and fourth graders. *Dissertation Abstracts International,* 38, 6662A. (Microfilms No. 78-04582)

Applebee, A. N. (1981). *Writing in the secondary school: English and the content areas* NCTE (Report No. 21). Urbana, Ill.

Balajhty, E. and Reinking, D. (1985). Micros and the first R. *Electronic Learning.*

Brackett, G. (1984). *Story tree [Software].* Scholastic, New York.

Britton, J., Burgess, T., Martin, N. McLeod, A., and Rosen, H. (1975). *The Development of Writing Abilities.* Macmillan, London.

Caldwell, R. M. (1973). A comparison of a programmed text and a computer based display unit to teach reading skills to semi- literate adolescents. *Dissertation Abstracts International,* 35, 1491A-1492A. (Microfilms No. 74-20,910)

Campbell, D. T., and Stanley, J. C. (1963). Experimental and quasi-experimental designs for research on teaching. In N. L. Gage (Ed), *Handbook* *of Research on Teaching* : Rand McNally, Chicago, Ill.

Chall, J. S. (1967). *Learning to Read: the Great Debate.* McGraw-Hill, New York.

Diamond, J. J. (1969). *A report on project GROW: Philadelphia's experimental program in computer assisted instruction.* Philadelphia School District, Philadelphia, PA. (ERIC Document Reproduction Service No. ED 035 272).

Diparo, A., and Freedman, S. W. (1987). Historical overview: groups in the writing classroom (Tech. Rep. No. 4). University of California, Center for the Study of Writing, Berkeley, CA.

Dulin, K., and Chester, B. (1975). *The Dulin-Chester reading attitude inventory.* The University of Wisconsin at Madison, Madison, WI.

Heimlich, J. E., and Pittleman, S. E. (1986). *Semantic mapping: classroom applications.* International Reading Association, Newark, DE.

Hunt, R. A. (1985). Reading as writing: meaning-making and sentence combining. In D. A. Daiker, A Kerek, and M. Morenberg (Eds), *Sentence Combining.* Southern Illinois University Press, Carbondale, Ill.

Johnson, D. W ., Johnson, R. T., Holubec, E. J., and Roy, P. (1984). *Circles of learning: Cooperation in the classroom.* Association for Supervision and Curriculum Development, Alexandria, VA .

Litman, G. (1977). Relation between computer-presented instruction and reading achievement among fourth, fifth and sixth grade students. (Doctoral dissertation, Northern Illinois University). *Dissertation Abstracts International,* 38, 2003A.

Metropolitan achievement tests: Reading instructional tests, Intermediate (Forms JI and KI). (1978).The Psychological Corporation, Chicago, Ill.

Ortmann, L. N. (1983). The effectiveness of supplementary computer-assisted instruction at the 4-6 grade level. *Dissertation Abstracts International, 45 140A.* (University Microfilms No. 84-08204)

Pearson, P. D., and Tierney, R. J. (1984). On becoming a thoughtful reader: learning to read like a writer. In A. C. Purves and N. Niles (Eds), *Becoming readers in a Complex Society: Eighty-Third Yearbook of The National Society for the Study of Education: Part I .* University. of Chicago, Chicago, Ill.

Results of computer assisted instruction at Bath Elementary School. (1979). Martha Holden Jennings Foundation, Cleveland, Oh. (ERIC Document Reproduction Service No. ED 195 245).

Sedlacek, C. J. (1984). A study comparing achievement and attitude differences in fifth-grade remedial reading students taught using computer-assisted instruction and conventional management programs. *Dissertation Abstracts International, 45 1980A.* (Microfilms No. 84-23514)

Smith, F. (1984). Reading like a writer. In J. M Jensen (Ed), *Composing and comprehending* ERIC/RCS. Urbana, Ill.

Squire, J. R. (1984). Composing and comprehending: two sides of the same basic process. In J. M Jensen (Ed), *Composing and Comprehending* . ERIC Clearinghouse on Reading and Communication Skills, Urbana, Ill.

Valencia, S. (1987). The Illinois effort. Paper presented at the National Council of Teachers of English, Louisville, KY.
"Write on Illinois!"A users guide to scoring student essays. (1984). Illinois State Board of Education Program Assessment. Springfield, Ill.

MIX
Papier aus verantwortungsvollen Quellen
Paper from responsible sources
FSC® C105338

If you have any concerns about our products,
you can contact us on
ProductSafety@springernature.com

In case Publisher is established outside the EU,
the EU authorized representative is:
Springer Nature Customer Service Center GmbH
Europaplatz 3, 69115 Heidelberg, Germany

Printed by Libri Plureos GmbH
in Hamburg, Germany